The Morality of Knowledge in (

Each time we take a turn in conversation we indicate what we know and what we think others know. However, knowledge is neither static nor absolute. It is shaped by those we interact with and governed by social norms – we monitor one another for whether we are satisfying our rights and fulfilling our responsibilities with respect to knowledge, and for who has relatively more rights to assert knowledge over some state of affairs. This book brings together an international team of leading linguists, sociologists and anthropologists working across a range of European and Asian languages to document some of the ways in which speakers manage the moral domain of knowledge in conversation. The volume demonstrates that if we are to understand how speakers manage issues of agreement, affiliation and alignment – something clearly at the heart of human sociality – we must understand the social norms surrounding epistemic access, primacy and responsibilities.

TANYA STIVERS is an associate professor of sociology at the University of California, Los Angeles.

LORENZA MONDADA is a professor in the Department of Linguistics at the University of Lyon II, and Director of the ICAR Research Laboratory (CNRS, University of Lyon).

JAKOB STEENSIG is an associate professor in the Department of Linguistics, Institute of Anthropology, Archaeology and Linguistics, Aarhus University, Denmark.

Studies in Interactional Sociolinguistics

EDITORS
Paul Drew, Marjorie Harness Goodwin, John J. Gumperz,
Deborah Schiffrin

The Morality of Knowledge in Conversation

Edited by

Tanya Stivers
University of California, Los Angeles

Lorenza Mondada
University of Lyon II

Jakob Steensig
Aarhus University, Denmark

CAMBRIDGE
UNIVERSITY PRESS

CAMBRIDGE
UNIVERSITY PRESS

University Printing House, Cambridge CB2 8BS, United Kingdom

Cambridge University Press is part of the University of Cambridge.

It furthers the University's mission by disseminating knowledge in the pursuit of
education, learning and research at the highest international levels of excellence.

www.cambridge.org
Information on this title: www.cambridge.org/9781107671546

© Cambridge University Press 2011

First published 2011
First paperback edition 2014

A catalogue record for this publication is available from the British Library

ISBN 978-0-521-19454-9 Hardback
ISBN 978-1-107-67154-6 Paperback

We dedicate this book to Gail Jefferson and her legacy
(1938–2008)

Contents

Contributors

BIRTE ASMUß, Centre for Corporate Communication, Aarhus School of Business, Aarhus University, Denmark

N. J. ENFIELD, Language & Cognition Group, Max Planck Institute for Psycholinguistics, Nijmegen, and Centre for Language Studies, Radboud University, The Netherlands

AULI HAKULINEN, Department of Finnish, Finno-Ugrian and Scandinavian Studies, University of Helsinki, Finland

KAORU HAYANO, Language & Cognition Group, Max Planck Institute for Psycholinguistics, Nijmegen, The Netherlands

TRINE HEINEMANN, SPIRE, MCI, University of Southern Denmark, Denmark

JOHN HERITAGE, Department of Sociology, University of California at Los Angeles, USA

LEELO KEEVALLIK, Department of Modern Languages, Uppsala University, Sweden

MARDI KIDWELL, Department of Communication, University of New Hampshire, USA

ANNA LINDSTRÖM, School of Humanities, Education and Social Sciences, Örebro University, Sweden

LORENZA MONDADA, ICAR Research Laboratory, CNRS, University of Lyon, France

JACK SIDNELL, Department of Anthropology, University of Toronto, Canada

MARJA-LEENA SORJONEN, Department of Finnish, Finno-Ugrian and Scandinavian Studies, University of Helsinki, Finland

JAKOB STEENSIG, Department of Linguistics, Institute of Anthropology, Archaeology and Linguistics, Aarhus University, Denmark

TANYA STIVERS, Department of Sociology, University of California at Los Angeles, USA

Preface

This book arises from a series of collaborative efforts that began in 2003 as an international project on affiliation in social interaction led by Anna Lindström: "Language and social action: a comparative study of affiliation and disaffiliation across national communities and institutional contexts." That project resulted in, among other things, the creation of a research network of conversation analysts focusing on what has been emerging as a new and particularly significant dimension of talk-in-interaction – namely the displays of and negotiations concerning participants' epistemic status relative to one another. The turn to epistemics was a natural extension of the prior interest in affiliation. We will argue in this book that to understand affiliation – and indeed cooperation more generally – we must understand how interactants manage the domain of knowledge. The process leading to this volume included four workshops: two in Aarhus, Denmark; one in Lyon, France; and one in Nijmegen, the Netherlands – each of which substantively shaped not only the individual contributions but also our collective thinking about the domain as a whole. For this reason we express gratitude to our fellow contributors who inspired and intensively discussed each chapter of this book over the course of its development. It is for this reason too that, although the introduction was formally written by the editors, it represents a thought process that all contributors were part of.

We dedicate this book to Gail Jefferson and her legacy. Gail was an inspiration to all of us, and this publication represents our chance to acknowledge our individual and collective debt to her. Although Gail did not hold an academic appointment for much of her career, her intense interest in how conversation worked never flagged. Her first contribution to the field is represented in every conversation analysis (CA) paper that has been published – her transcription system revolutionized what and how people study conversation. With it, a revised understanding of how people take turns in interaction was made possible in the Sacks, Schegloff and Jefferson 1974 paper. Her early intuitive recognition of, for instance, the relevance of the precise onsets and offsets of overlapping speech and of who laughs and when will continue to bear fruit in years to come.

Gail was well known for her vivacity but also for her uncompromising character as a scholar and an individual. Both of these qualities were apparent in her approach to data. On the one hand she was uninhibited in the creativity she brought to working with data, actively encouraging others to use intuitions and explore unexpected analyses. She was intolerant of those who retreated to received wisdom (especially "the literature") for support – even her own – or who relied on established analytic constructs in their approach to data. On the other, Gail was equally uncompromising in her subsequent requirement that intuitions and the like be grounded in the data. Agreement among the group was never sufficient: "Analysis is not a matter of consensus" she would say, challenging us all to demonstrate the correctness of our analysis.

Gail relished argument. For those who would tussle with her, there were rewards to be had, for in these arguments we learned not only about the data over which we argued but often about the interaction in which we were involved.

Whether we learned from Gail in data sessions, on workshops, or only from the extraordinary inciveness of her intellect that she showed in her papers, all of us share her unbridled enthusiasm for working collaboratively to understand the underpinnings of social interaction. Gail's writing and her approach to data more generally also reflect the fact that her finger never left the pulse of the interactants themselves – who they were to each other, what they were trying to accomplish and what they were trying "to get away with," as she used to put it. From her earliest papers, how and when interactants affiliate with one another and how and when they push the boundaries of normativity were at the heart of her analyses. We see this across much of her work, but particularly that on overlap, story telling and laughter. This interest in normativity and cooperation is fundamental to the endeavor of this project with its interest in how epistemic practices influence, and are influenced by, affiliation and alignment. The CA community has lost not only one of its founders but also one of its most ardent scholars and teachers. However, her legacy is strong and we hope to strengthen it further here.

THE CONTRIBUTORS

Acknowledgements

We would like to thank Paul Drew and Helen Barton for their support of this project. Paul was one of the original members of the Affiliation Project out of which this project emerged, and as series editor encouraged this volume's preparation. Helen, as the Cambridge University Press linguistics editor, was equally supportive and encouraging and helped shape the book in its early stages. For assistance in preparing the book, we thank Annelies van Wijngaarden and Menno Jonker for diligent and careful work. This project was carried out on a shoestring budget. For making our larger group meetings possible, we are grateful to the Department of Language and Business Communication and the Aarhus School of Business at arhus University; the ICAR Research Laboratory in Lyon, the CNRS and the University of Lyon; and the Max Planck Institute for Psycholinguistics in Nijmegen. Thanks are especially due to Stephen Levinson. Both smaller and larger collaborative meetings were possible due to his support.

The cover art represents Elaine Badgley Arnoux's *See Saw Margery Daw*, 2004, oil on canvas. The painting's focus on imbalance in an interactive setting is a nice way of capturing one of the primary preoccupations of this volume. This piece comes from a collection of eight large canvases known as *Once Upon a Time* in which Badgley Arnoux depicts allegorical nursery rhymes. They are political and societal statements concerning the eight epochs of her life. This oeuvre also includes sculpture, giving more emphasis and strength to the stories within the paintings. Badgley Arnoux lives and works in San Francisco, California, and continues to embrace the complexities of life, taking the human element of light and shadow into figurative landscapes, sculpture and conceptual art. She strives to integrate her technical skills, soaring fantasy and spiritual underpinnings to plumb the depth of creativity. We are grateful for Elaine's generosity in allowing us to use this piece for the book cover.

Transcription and glossing symbols

Transcription

1 Temporal and sequential relationships

A

Overlapping or simultaneous talk is indicated in a variety of ways:

[Separate left square brackets, one above the other on two successive lines with utterances by different speakers, indicate a point of overlap onset, whether at the start of an utterance or later.

]   Separate right square brackets, one above the other on two successive lines with utterances by different speakers, indicate a point at which two overlapping utterances both end, where one ends while the other continues, or simultaneous moments in overlaps which continue.

B

=   Equal signs ordinarily come in pairs – one at the end of a line and another at the start of the next line or one shortly thereafter. They are used to indicate three things:

1) If the two lines connected by the equal signs are by the same speaker, then there was a single, continuous utterance with no break or pause, which was broken up in order to accommodate the placement of overlapping talk.

2) If the lines connected by two equal signs are by different speakers, then the second followed the first with no discernable silence between them, or was "latched" to it.

3) If two words are connected by equal signs then the two words sound "latched" or run together.

C

//   A double slash marks the onset of an embodied action in the talk.

/   A single slash indicates embodied action that coincides with talk.

D
(0.5)   Numbers in parentheses indicate silence, represented in seconds; what is given here in the left margin indicates second of silence. Silences may be marked either within an utterance or between utterances.

E
(.)   A dot in parentheses indicates a "micropause," usually less than 200 milliseconds.

2 Aspects of speech delivery, including aspects of intonation

A
.   The punctuation marks are not used grammatically, but to indicate intonation.

?   The period indicates a falling, or final, intonation contour, not necessarily the end of a sentence. Similarly, a question mark indicates rising intonation, not necessarily a question,

,   and a comma indicates slightly rising intonation, not necessarily a clause boundary.

?,   A combined question mark and comma indicates a rise stronger than a comma but weaker than a question mark.

_   An underscore following a unit of talk indicates level intonation.

;   The semicolon indicates that the intonation is equivocal between final and slightly rising

\   The backslash indicates that intonation is mid-falling.

B
: :   Colons are used to indicate the prolongation or stretching of the sound just preceding them. The more colons, the longer the stretching.

C
-        A hyphen after a word or part of a word indicates a cut-off or self-interruption.

D
word   Underlining is used to indicate some form of stress or emphasis, either by increased loudness or higher pitch. The more underlining, the greater the emphasis.

E
°   The degree sign indicates that the talk following it was markedly quiet or soft.

°°   When there are two degree signs, the talk between them is markedly softer than the talk around it.

F
^   The circumflex symbol indicates a rise in pitch.

G
| The pipe symbol indicates a fall in pitch.

H
> <   The combination of "more than" and "less than" symbols indicates that the talk between them is compressed or rushed.

<>   Used in the reverse order, they indicate that a stretch of talk is markedly slowed or drawn out.

<   The "less than" symbol by itself indicates that the immediately following talk is "jump-started," i.e., sounds like it starts with a rush.

I
hhh   Hearable aspiration is shown where it occurs in the talk by the letter "h" – the more h's, the more aspiration. The aspiration may represent breathing, laughter, etc.

(hh)   If it occurs inside the boundaries of a word, it may be enclosed in parentheses in order to set it apart from the sounds of the word.

.hh   If the aspiration is an inhalation, it is shown with a period before it.

J
A number sign, or hash sign, indicates gravelly voice quality on the sound(s) that follow or that are between two number/hash signs.

K
£   The British pound sign indicates "smile voice."

L
%   The percent sign indicates crying voice.

M

" "   Quotation marks indicate that the talk within is produced as
           reported speech.

3 Other markings

A

(( ))   Double parentheses are used to mark transcriber's descriptions
           of events, rather than representations of them. Thus ((cough)),
           ((sniff)), ((telephone rings)), ((footsteps)), ((whispered)), ((pause))
           and the like.

B

(word)   When all or part of an utterance is in parentheses, or the speaker
           identification is, this indicates uncertainty on the transcriber's
           part, but represents a likely possibility.

C

( )   Empty parentheses indicate that something is being said, but no
           hearing (or, in some cases, speaker identification) can be achieved.

D

Italics   Italics, boldface and caps are used for different sorts of emphasis
BOLD   in different chapters. They may indicate an embodied action or
           the focal phenomenon, and in chapters relying on languages other
           than English, they may indicate the original language.

Glossing

_	The parts to each side of the underscore are one word in the original language
-	A hyphen indicates that a morpheme is separable in the original language
(parentheses)	In the translation line this indicates that the item was not present in the original language
0/1/2/3	Zero/First/Second/Third Person
ADE/ADS	Adessive
ADV	Adverb
ALL	Allative
ASP	Neutral aspect
ATP	Antipassive

AUX	Auxiliary
CAUS	Causative derivation
CL	Classifier
CLI	Word-final clitic
CMP	Completive
COM	Comitative
COMP	Complementizer
CON	Connective
COND	Conditional
CP	Copula *be*
DAT	Dative
DEICT	Deictic
DET	Definite determiner
DIM	Diminutive
DIR	Directional
DIST	Distributive
ELT	Elative
EMP	Emphasis marker
ESS	Essive
EXIST	Existential predicate
FP	Final particle
GEN	Genitive
GI	Emphasis clitic
ILL	Illative
IMF	Imperfective
IMP	Imperative
IMS	Impersonal
INE	Inessive
INF	Infinitive
INS	Inessive case
INST	Instrumentalis
ITJ	Interjection
L	Nominal linking particle
N	Nominalizer particle
NAME	Proper name
NEG	Negative auxiliary or particle
NP	Noun phrase
PAR	Partitive
PAS	Passive
PERF	Perfective
PL	Plural
POS	Possessive suffix

PPT	Past participle
PREP	Generic preposition
PRO	Pronoun
PRT	Particle
PST	Past tense
Q	Question clitic/particle
QT	Quotative particle
RED	Reduplication
REFL	Reflexive pronoun
REL	Relational noun suffix
RES	Resultative derivation
SG	Singular
SP	Subject particle
SPN	Supinum
SUBJ	Subjunctive
TAG	Tag question marker
TP	Topic particle
TRA	Translative
VOL	Volitionality marker
OTHER CAPITALS	Untranslated particle

Part I

Introduction

1   Knowledge, morality and affiliation in social interaction

Tanya Stivers, Lorenza Mondada and Jakob Steensig

Introduction

In everyday social interaction, knowledge displays and negotiations are ubiquitous. At issue is whether we have epistemic *access* to some state of affairs, but also how *certain* we are about what we know, our relative *authority* and our differential *rights and responsibilities* with respect to this knowledge. Implicit in this conceptualization is that knowledge is dynamic, graded and multi-dimensional and that our deployment of and reliance on epistemic resources are normatively organized. As Drew puts it, there is a "conventional ascription of warrantable rights or entitlements over the possession and use of certain kinds of knowledge" (1991: 45). As in any normatively organized system, we can and do hold one another accountable for justifiably asserting our rights and fulfilling our obligations with respect to knowledge. It is in this way that we see the epistemic domain as morally ordered.

This orientation to and monitoring of the moral order might seem completely different from the moral reasoning used in tasks requiring judgements of whether a given scenario (e.g., about sharing resources or unintentionally killing someone) is morally acceptable or not (e.g., Hauser 2006; Henrich *et al.* 2004). However, the micro-level moral order can be understood as cut from the same cloth as other forms of moral reasoning. And these micro-interactional moral calibrations have critical consequences for our social relations, most directly through our moment-by-moment alignments and affiliations with others.

Although there is a longstanding interest in knowledge asymmetries in social interaction, since the turn of this century there has been a rapid escalation in work on epistemic primacy in conversation. One reason is that it has become clear that if we are to understand how interactants manage

Thank you to all the contributors who helped to shape this introduction through the workshops we participated in together, our conversations about these topics and comments on earlier versions of this chapter. Thanks especially to Nick Enfield, Kaoru Hayano and John Heritage for coming into the intellectual trenches with us in the final stages of writing.

3

issues of agreement/disagreement and affiliation/disaffiliation, something critical to cooperation and pro-sociality in human behavior, we need a better understanding of the contribution of epistemic stance. This book gathers work by several of the scholars who pushed this domain of inquiry forward early on and adds to it work by scholars new to the domain. We consider asymmetries of knowledge at the micro-interactional level, examining a variety of different conversational practices for managing these epistemic dimensions with an eye toward the moment-by-moment moral and affiliational implications of these practices.

The volume is organized into two main sections with a final section that works toward a theory of the domain. The first set of chapters takes epistemic resources as a point of departure and studies the consequences of their use for affiliation and alignment in the ongoing social interaction. The second set of chapters starts with affiliation processes or problems and studies how epistemic resources are used in dealing with them. This introduction has three main sections. In the first section, we review relevant strands of research on knowledge. In the second section we discuss key notions in the study of knowledge in social interaction. In the third section we outline how knowledge is moral and exemplify our conceptualization of alignment and affiliation.

Background

A concern with the nature of knowledge goes back to at least Plato in his dialogue *Theaetetus* and spans the fields of philosophy, psychology, history, anthropology, sociology, communication and linguistics. This introduction attempts to situate our interest in the intersection between knowledge and morality in social interaction rather than provide a comprehensive overview.

In the cognitive sciences, an interest in knowledge is dominated by a concern with the individual mind. Shannon and Weaver's (1949) well-known communication theory, for instance, takes as its point of departure the "communication model," according to which an "information source" sends a message that is ultimately received by a "destination." The theory looks at how information can be transmitted (typically in a technical system) with as little loss of information as possible and has been expanded to cover human–human interaction. In this light, knowledge can be seen as information that comes from one mind, is encoded into a message in a language and sent via a channel to be decoded by another mind, which is then trying to recover the original message, or intention (see also Levelt 1989).

Cognitive scientists have been pushed to acknowledge the social context of knowledge through the rise of concepts such as social cognition (e.g.,

Fiske and Taylor 1984; Forgas 1981; Showers and Cantor 1985; Wyer and Srull 1984) and distributed cognition (e.g., Hutchins 1995; Lave 1988). Lave's term "situated cognition" emphasizes that knowledge should be conceptualized as "stretched across mind, body, activity and setting" (1988: 18). For instance, math skills that are readily deployed in everyday contexts of shopping or weight management are not necessarily replicable in a classroom setting (Lave 1988). Similarly, Hutchins speaks of "cognition in the wild" (1995) referring to the native habitat of cognition, which is naturally occurring culturally constituted human activity – contrasting with the experimental laboratory where cognition is studied "in captivity" (see also Goodwin 2000). While from these perspectives what one individual knows is shaped by the social context, such a focus on cognition still does not address the processes through which knowledge is managed socially.

Sociologists' interest in knowledge has been with how knowledge is constructed and represented, on the one hand, and how it can be "owned," on the other. The sociology of knowledge tradition has argued that "society's influence extends into the structures of human experience in the form of ideas, concepts and systems of thought" (McCarthy 1996: 1). Although knowledge in this tradition was initially viewed, following Marx, as determined by social conditions (Mannheim 1936, and, for overviews, see McCarthy 1996; Stark 1991[1958]), Schütz argued that knowledge is socially constructed, derived from people's life experiences and must be communicated in order to become a reality (1962). Although this latter view was somewhat suppressed by behaviorist orthodoxy, the notion bloomed in the 1960s in the social constructionism of Berger and Luckmann (1966). Relatedly, Moscovici's introduction of "social representations" argues for the idea of a reality by consensus (1981, 1990, 2000). Currently, there is debate over whether knowledge can or should be separated from culture or whether it should be subsumed under it (Barth 2002; McCarthy 1996; Sidnell 2005).

This move away from social determinism was taken still farther by Garfinkel. In his move toward understanding everyday social behavior, he viewed such behavior as a matter of "accountable moral choice" (Heritage 1984b: 76). Thus, whereas classical views of society saw social norms as a behavioral constraint (Durkheim 1997 [1893]) or as a form of regulation (Parsons 1937), Garfinkel (1967) joined elements of Schütz's phenomenological, social constructionist view with elements of Parsons's voluntaristic theory of action and showed that everyday knowledge is sustained through the joint use of a variety of ad hoc practices (such as letting various discrepancies pass) (p. 21). Through these ad hoc practices, both normative and epistemic departures from the fabric of social constructs were waved through, becoming insignificant from the point of view of the maintenance of the fabric itself (Heritage 1984b).

Garfinkel's ethnomethodological methods have since been brought to bear in scientific and work settings where knowledge is explicitly constructed and debated (Garfinkel, Lynch and Livingston 1981; Luff, Hindmarsh and Heath 2000; Lynch 1985; Middleton and Engeström 1996; Mondada 2005; Roth 2005). For instance, Lynch (1985) studied the way in which agreements and disagreements are ordinarily achieved within shop work and shop talk in a neurosciences laboratory. And, Garfinkel *et al.* (1981) describe the progressive discovery of a pulsar on the basis of the tape recordings of a night of observation within an astronomy team, and its transformation from an unknown object to a "Galilean" epistemic construct.

Finally, as noted by Heritage, this volume, sociologists have been concerned with territories of knowledge and their maintenance since Durkheim's (1915: 415–447) identification of the limits of society with the limits of its collective representations. Thus, knowledge has been viewed as a domain that groups or even individuals can have primary rights over. For instance, Holzner's (1968) notion of "epistemic communities" (see also Holzner and Marx 1979) separates groups of individuals who share privileged epistemic authority over some domain (see also Sharrock 1974). On a more individual level, Goffman's work on territorial preserves asserts that individuals have territories over which they have primary rights, including "information preserves" (1971a: 38). Included in this preserve are "facts about himself to which an individual expects to control access while in the presence of others" (pp. 38–39). He goes on to include, in a list, "biographical facts about the individual over the divulgence of which he expects to maintain control" (p. 39). Goffman thus implies that one's knowledge, particularly personal knowledge, falls within one's own information preserve, and that "territorial offenses" can thus occur with respect to knowledge just as they can with respect to possessed objects.

While sociologists have primarily attended to the social construction of knowledge and to knowledge as a norm-governed domain, outside of the conversation analytic tradition there has been little sociological attention paid to knowledge in communication. In contrast, within the language sciences there has been a broad concern with how knowledge is shaped by language and managed by the speaker vis-à-vis his/her interlocutors, but relatively little concern with the domain as norm-governed.

Studies of information structure, for instance (Halliday 1967; Krifka 2007; Lambrecht 1994; Schwabe and Winkler 2007), are concerned with how speakers take into account the communicative needs of their interlocutors (Chafe 1976). The field has largely focused on distinctions in topic

(Jacobs 2001; Li and Thompson 1976; Reinhart 1981), focus (Jackendoff 1972; Rooth 1985) and givenness of information (Schwarzschild 1999). In all of these cases, though, the concern is with how information is packaged differently depending on the status of the information relative to the interlocutor.

Linguists have also paid considerable attention to epistemic stance (Biber *et al.* 1999; Chafe 1986; Lyons 1977). This work focuses on issues of certainty (Givón 1982, 1989), reliability (Chafe 1986) and particularly evidentiality. Evidentiality is grammaticalized with moderate frequency across languages. According to *The World Atlas of Language Structures* (de Haan 2008), 57 percent of the 418 languages surveyed exhibit grammaticalized evidentials for at least indirect evidentials – marking the relevant knowledge as indirect or inferred rather than observed first-hand (see also Aikenvald 2004; Johanson and Utas 2000; Willett 1988). According to Fox "all languages – including 'nonexotic' languages like English – make use of evidential marking" (2001: 168).

Although, as mentioned, there is relatively little work in the language sciences that addresses knowledge as a moral domain, there were some notable front-runners in this respect. First, Hill and Irvine's edited collection discussed what role giving evidence might play in epistemic authority, responsibility and entitlement in discourse (1993). Second, some of the most comprehensive work on epistemic stance is Akio Kamio's on "territories of information" (1994, 1995, 1997). Although he did not rely on spontaneous naturally occurring talk, his work advanced our conceptualization of knowledge by considering it in relative terms such that information can belong to one individual either exclusively or to a greater extent, relative to his/her interlocutor. The model not only deals with the relationship between what the speaker believes about her/his own information state and that of the hearer, it also includes consideration of social/cultural norms about who should properly know what.

Knowledge in social interaction

Two main strands of research have addressed how knowledge is managed in and through social interaction (see Sidnell 2005: 19–51, for an overview). The first strand of research has primarily been carried out by discursive psychologists who have examined how knowledge, cognition, the mind and other psychological constructs are dealt with as topics by participants in interaction (Edwards 1997; Edwards and Potter 1992; Potter and Wetherell 1987; te Molder and Potter 2005; van Dijk 2006).

The second strand of research is located primarily within conversation analysis and has focused not on the content of what is said but on epistemic positions taken through language and embodied action. This strand attempts to join sociology's interest in knowledge as a norm-governed domain and the intricate practices of language usage. This strand also represents the intellectual heritage of this volume. Some conversation analytic studies have involved institutional settings where epistemic asymmetries can be expected to color the interaction (in various ways and to varying degrees). These conversation analytic studies focus on interaction practices rather than the setting, though they do so in a social context where epistemic asymmetries are salient due to the fact that lay people seek professional services precisely because they lack epistemic access to the relevant domain (e.g., legal knowledge, medical knowledge, tax knowledge, psychological knowledge) (Drew 1991).

Two institutional sites in particular serve as illustrations of how these confrontations between different epistemic cultures and practices are achieved within social interaction: courtroom interactions and medical interactions. Courtrooms are places where "what has really happened" is constructed through various versions, often incongruent and disjunctive (Pollner 1987), often relating to different kinds of evidence and authority: direct versus indirect access, first-hand versus second-hand knowledge (Drew 1992; Komter 1995, 1998). Similarly, in medical consultations, although patients have superior knowledge of their illness experience, physicians have superior medical knowledge to diagnose and the authority to prescribe (Heritage 2006; Heritage and Robinson 2006; Peräkylä 1998, 2002). Highlighting one or the other type of knowledge and authority can be a resource to negotiate diagnoses and treatments. For instance, physicians routinely articulate their findings from the physical examination, to which patients otherwise have no epistemic access, using "online comments" (Heritage and Stivers 1999; Mangione-Smith *et al.* 2003). These online comments serve as a resource for securing patient agreement to subsequent diagnosis and treatment. Conversely, parents may highlight their knowledge of their children in order to negotiate for prescription treatment (Stivers 2002).

Key notions in the study of knowledge in social interaction

Epistemic asymmetries in such lay–professional contexts are transparent in comparison with asymmetries in everyday interaction. However, as Linell and Luckman (1991) warn, the lack of epistemic asymmetry that is so characteristic of institutional interaction does not in any way suggest that ordinary conversation is epistemically symmetrical. Moreover, in contrast to institutional contexts, in the mundane context evaluative and epistemic stances are more tightly intertwined (Ochs 1996). This volume takes

Table 1.1 *Dimensions of knowledge in conversation*

Dimension	Description
Epistemic access	Knowing vs. not knowing Degree of certainty Knowledge source Directness of knowledge
Epistemic primacy	Relative rights to know Relative rights to claim Relative authority of knowledge
Epistemic responsibility	Type of knowable (Type 1 vs. Type 2) Recipient design of actions Recipient design of turns

epistemic asymmetry in conversation as its focus and examines a range of interactional practices that are involved across a variety of languages. As summarized in Table 1.1, there are three primary dimensions of knowledge that interactants treat as salient in and for conversation, particularly with respect to asymmetries: (1) epistemic access, (2) epistemic primacy and (3) epistemic responsibility.

As indicated early on in this chapter, epistemic access, primacy and responsibility are governed by social norms which influence, and are influenced by, social alignment and affiliation. In conversation, interactants show themselves to be accountable for what they know, their level of certainty, their relative authority, and the degree to which they exercise their rights and fulfill their responsibilities. As Drew put it, "When speakers orient to their asymmetrical position as regards some knowledge, they orient to the normatively organized social distributions of authoritative access to bodies or types of knowledge" (1991: 45). Thus, interactants treat knowledge as a moral domain with clear implications for their relationships with co-interactants. In this section we discuss each of the three epistemic dimensions and then go on to discuss the morality of the domain in the following section.

Epistemic access

Epistemic access has long been of interest in studies of social interaction. In contrast with the approach taken in research on information structure which takes for granted that speakers know which information another has access to and which s/he does not, conversation analytic studies of interaction explore the practices for establishing another's access as well as interactional resources used to manage presuppositions of access, elicit access, claim access and qualify claims of access. This section discusses each of these areas in turn.

With respect to epistemic access, at least two related social norms exist: speakers should not inform already knowing recipients about some state of affairs (Goodwin 1979; Sacks 1992: 441); and, relatedly, speakers should avoid making claims for which they have an insufficient degree of access (Heritage and Raymond 2005). The latter claim is similar to Grice's second sub-maxim of quality which asserts "Do not say that for which you lack adequate evidence" (Grice 1975: 41).

It follows that interactants generally have good command over who in their social world has, or could be expected to have, prior access to particular news or events, even very young children (Kidwell and Zimmerman 2006). A speaker's assessment of his/her recipient's access is typically reflected in the presuppositions of the relevant turn: by offering a news announcement, the speaker treats his/her recipient as unknowing (e.g., "I got a raise today"); conversely, by requesting information, the speaker treats the recipient as knowing (e.g., "What did you buy?").

Moreover, conversationalists adeptly juggle knowing and unknowing interlocutors as Goodwin (1979) has famously shown in the course of a single turn constructional unit (TCU). In the utterance on which Goodwin focuses, "I gave up smoking cigarettes one week ago today actually", although the speaker's wife, a knowing recipient, is not the original target of the speaker's news announcement, when the speaker finds himself gazing at his wife during this turn's production, he transforms his utterance from an announcement that he has quit smoking into the remembering of an anniversary of his quitting smoking. Thus the epistemic access of the various participants – knowing and unknowing – is taken into account.

A vast majority of the time, interactants' presuppositions about their interlocutors' access are on target – recipients of news announcements typically do *not* have prior epistemic access, and recipients of requests for information typically *do*. This can be conceptualized as one form of epistemic congruence, "epistemic access congruence" – specifically, interactants agree on who has, and who does not have, access. However, speakers do not always achieve epistemic access congruence. In Extract 1, Tara begins to tell Kristina about an event that happened the night before. As a news announcement, a relevant and aligned response would treat the announcement as news (e.g., with a newsmark such as *Oh really?* or a change of state token such as *Oh* in English [Heritage 1984a], *A* in Japanese [Saft 2001] or *Ou* in Mandarin [Wu 2004]). By contrast, at possible completion of the first TCU, Kristina claims prior access (also citing that she was in fact with Tara when this event happened).

(1) (see transcription conventions at the beginning of this volume)
1 TARA: My mom left me this who:le long message on my cell
2   phone last night about thuh directions,
3 KRIS: → Yea(h)h I kn(h)ow, I was there.
4   (1.0)
5 TARA: #huh# ((cough))
6 TARA: #heh heh# ((laughter))

Subsequently, Tara does not pursue any other sort of uptake. There is a full second of silence during which Tara gazes at Kristina (line 4). Then there is a bit of laughter, and another participant initiates a new sequence about a different matter (data not shown).

Similar issues of presuppositions inhabit question–response sequences. In posing a question to a particular recipient, the questioner presupposes recipient access as well as willingness to answer the question. While answer responses align with a presupposition of access, claims of an inability to answer disalign (Beach and Metzger 1997; Heritage 1984b; Stivers and Robinson 2006). Hence, a presupposition of epistemic access fails – or appears to fail: Goodwin observes that claims not to remember can actually be a resource for encouraging participation (1987).

Although speakers make presumptions about access much of the time in social interaction, there are a variety of interactional practices to ascertain others' access. The most overt of resources are the various forms of interrogative syntax, morphology and prosody to request information (e.g., "What would you like for your birthday"). More covertly, Pomerantz observes that people commonly tell what they know about some state of affairs as a way of "fishing" for information (e.g., "Your line's been busy") (Pomerantz 1980). Such remarks are commonly responded to with disclosures (though evading such a remark is clearly less accountable than with other more overt practices [Stivers and Rossano 2010]).

Pre-announcements and story prefaces are social actions that are virtually dedicated to this function (e.g., "Did you hear X"; "Have I told you X"; "Guess what") (Jefferson 1978; Sacks 1974, 1978; Schegloff 2007a; Terasaki 2004 [1976]). An illustration is shown below. At line 1 the would-be story teller begins with a story preface. Progress to the telling proper hinges on whether he mentioned this already to Gio. The go-ahead in line 4 denies prior knowledge and facilitates the teller's progress to the telling.

(2)
1 LAN: → Did I mention to you that I got yelled at by
2   one of our neighbors today?
3   (0.2)
4 GIO: No,
5   (0.8)
6 LAN: Yeah I was ... ((continues))

Such practices are important prerequisites to actions in conversation, not only for announcements and tellings but also for such actions as assessments. Even when interactants have mutual access, there are still a variety of ways in which they may perform agreement. Pomerantz (1984a) proposes that assessments about referents/events to which both interlocutors have access set up a fundamentally different response relevance from those to which only one speaker has access. Specifically, Pomerantz shows that when both interactants have access to the referent, there is a preference for agreement about the assessment, accomplished through upgrading the first assessment (1984a). For instance, in the extract below, J and L both have access to the weather being assessed. In response to J's initial assessment of the day as "beautiful", L agrees and then offers an upgraded assessment "it's jus' gorgeous".

(3) (Heritage 2002a: Example 2)
1 J: T's- tsuh beautiful day out isn't it?
2 L: → Yeh it's jus' gorgeous ...

As mentioned above, the second norm related to access suggests that speakers should not assert claims without sufficient access. We see this in the way speakers are generally cautious about making claims that imply access. For instance, in German, speakers have separate receipt tokens for indicating a shift from "not knowing to knowing" (*Achso*) and for receipting information without claiming that the repair now allows them epistemic access (*Ach*) (Golato and Betz 2008: 16). Speakers of Danish make a similar distinction with *Nå* as a change-of-state token and *Nåja* as a "realization token" (Emmertsen and Heinemann 2010).

More pervasive are the variety of ways in which speakers downgrade the *degree* of access that they claim. Although epistemic access is typically conceptualized as binary – K+ or K– (Goodwin 1981; Heritage and Raymond 2005) – people can show varying levels of certainty and can differentiate between direct and indirect access. For instance, Kärkkäinen shows that such lexical certainty markers as "I think," "maybe," "probably" are pervasive in ordinary conversation (2003). Heritage and Raymond (2005) show that other forms of epistemic downgrading include the use of tag questions. Relatedly, Clift shows how something as seemingly unrelated to evidentiality as reported speech can function as an "interactional evidential" (i.e., a device that is dependent on its occurrence in a specific sequential position, after assessments, to claim epistemic authority) (Clift 2006). And Fox (2001) shows that even without grammaticalized evidentials in English, evidential marking indexes authority, responsibility and entitlement.

An illustration of epistemic stance marking in English is shown in Extract 4. It is February in Southern California, and Mom has served slices of watermelon with the evening meal. In this case we see two instances of epistemic stance marking coming to the foreground of this interaction. First, Dad does not know how much Mom spent on the watermelon and thus his assertion that it was expensive ("#cost uh pretty penny,#" [lines 4/6]) is downgraded with his selection of the epistemic verb "bet" (line 4). He marks his assertion as an inference about the price based on the season. Second, Mom's "looks" epistemically downgrades the certainty of her assessment of the out-of-season watermelon as "good". She has not yet tasted it but has sliced it up for the meal and can therefore assess it at least on the basis of its appearance.

(4)
```
1 MOM:      .h >Alright.< Now we have ro:lls, an' butter Ci:n?, an'
2           you have watermelo:n?
3           (0.5)
4 DAD:   →  .hh [Boy an out of season watermelon. I bet that #cost=
5 MOM:          [And-
6 DAD:      =uh pretty penny, #
7 MOM:   →  ^No: it wasn't ba:d but it: looks good_=I mean it's: r:e:d;
8           (0.5)
9 MOM:      Better th'n- some °of 'em_°
```

Thus, we can conceptualize access as K+/K- but also as graded depending on the sort of access the interlocutors have – direct versus indirect; substantial versus minimal. However, access remains largely concerned with the individual's knowledge state in absolute terms. By contrast, epistemic primacy, to which we now turn, is not only graded but inherently relative.

Epistemic primacy

In social interaction people orient to asymmetries in their relative rights to know about some state of affairs (access) as well as their relative rights to tell, inform, assert or assess something, and asymmetries in the depth, specificity or completeness of their knowledge. This asymmetry can be termed *epistemic primacy*. Just as speakers are concerned about whether their interlocutors already know about what they wish to tell, or are able to answer their questions, and just as recipients are concerned to indicate when they already knew something they weren't expected to know or didn't know something they were expected to, so too are conversationalists concerned to indicate *relative rights to knowledge* and *relative knowledge*, particularly if their authority or rights are not being attended to (e.g., Drew 1991; Heritage 2002a; Heritage and Raymond 2005; Schegloff 1996a; Stivers 2005a).

Sacks suggests that there is a norm such that new knowledge, particularly "big news," should be given out in order of relational closeness indicating a sense of who has superior rights to know (Sacks 1992 [1967]: I, 561). It is easy to recognize the norm in the sense that breaches in this ordering can cause major relational fissures. For instance, hearing that your best friend is having a baby or is getting married from an unrelated and less intimately connected colleague can strain or even break the friendship. There also appears to be a norm that speakers should make assertions only when they have sufficient knowledge and rights to do so, and that speakers with more detailed and in-depth knowledge have primary rights to make assertions and assessments regarding this domain (see Heritage and Raymond 2005; Stivers 2005a). Consider the difference between the kind of knowledge two people might have about life in Tokyo: one person has lived there for ten years and another has only visited. Although both have epistemic *access* to the place's merits and deficits, there is a qualitative difference in the depth of that knowledge – a difference in epistemic authority.

These three norms – that one should give access in order of relational closeness, one should make assertions only with sufficient access and rights, and those with more authority have greater rights to make assertions in the domain – are visible in the range of resources interactants rely on to claim or combat claims of epistemic primacy. A first resource is sequential position. Asserting something in first-position (whether a description or an assessment) carries an implied claim that the speaker has epistemic primacy over the claim (Heritage 2002a). In order to mitigate against this implied claim speakers may downgrade their assertion. This can be done, for instance, by using epistemic mitigation such as "I think" or "maybe" (Kärkkäinen 2003; Stivers 2005a) or through the use of a tag question (Heritage and Raymond 2005).

Speakers can also convey an inferior epistemic position implicitly through the differentiation between what Labov and Fanshel call "A event knowledge" – knowledge possessed primarily by the speaker – and "B event knowledge" – knowledge possessed primarily by the recipient (Labov and Fanshel 1977). Assertions about states of affairs in the world are understood as requests for confirmation when they are said by a person with less epistemic authority over the domain to a person with greater epistemic authority – even when produced with declarative intonation. Consequently, when speakers make "B-event statements," they are *not* heard to be asserting epistemic primacy but as soliciting confirmation (see also Heritage and Roth 1995). An illustration is shown in Extract 5 below. John has been talking about how he came to quit smoking and has described a film he saw during a course on kicking the habit. He observes that a person wouldn't be taking a course to stop smoking if s/he wasn't determined to stop (lines 1–3).

```
(5)
1 DON:       The point is you wouldn't take that course
2            if you weren't determined in the
3            first [place.
4 TER:             [(I'm nna [go mo:  [my)
5 JOH:                    [Mm hm, [
6 DON:  →                         [They ju[st- just give you that=
7 ANN:                                    [Well,
8 DON:  →    =bit of support.
9 JOH:  ⇒   Th't's right.
```

When Don asserts "They just- just give you that bit of support." (lines 6/8), although this is done declaratively, as an assertion, this is not, in fact, an experience or sentiment that he has epistemic authority over. Rather, it is John who has authority over this sentiment and indeed the turn is confirmed. With "Th't's right.", John also claims greater authority to say whether or not the sentiment expressed by Don was accurate for him.

Just as offering an assertion or assessment in first position implies a claim of epistemic primacy, 'going second' is vulnerable to being heard as acquiescing to an inferior epistemic position. This is particularly true with "mere" agreements such as "Yeah" (Heritage 2002a). Thus, just as speakers can work to combat implied claims of epistemic primacy inherent in initial sequential position, so too can they combat implied claims of epistemic inferiority in second position. Heritage and Raymond have shown that whereas tag questions in first position *downgrade* a claim of epistemic primacy, in second position, the use of a tag question or negative interrogative challenges the prior speaker's claim of epistemic primacy by resetting the sequential position of the utterance (Heritage and Raymond 2005). Both tag questions and negative interrogatives make a second position agreement again relevant.

Heritage has also shown that, in responsive position, speakers may assert independent access as a way to combat a first position claim of epistemic primacy (2002a). In contesting claims of primacy, recipients suggest that a more symmetrical orientation should be (or should have been) taken, or they may even suggest that they have epistemic primacy (Heritage 2002a: 204–205). For instance, two dog breeders are discussing when Norman might breed a young dog of his.

```
(6) (Heritage 2002a: 204–205)
1  Ile:      No well she's still a bit young though isn't
2            [she<ah me]an:=
3  Nor:      [S h e : :]
```

```
4   Ile:        =uh[:
5   Nor:          [She wz a year: la:st wee:k.
6   Ile:        Ah yes. Oh well any time no:w [then.]
7   Nor:                                      [Uh:::]:[m
8   Ile:                                             [Ye:s.=
9   Nor:        =But she[:'s (            )]
10  Ile:   →            [Cuz Trixie started] so early [didn't sh[e,
11  Nor:   →                                          [°O h : :  [ye:s.°=
12  Ile:        =°Ye:h°=
```

As Heritage discusses, "Here Norman's *oh*-prefaced agreement (line 11), in conveying the independence of his assessments from Ilene's, also alludes to his epistemic priority with respect to the information in question" (p. 8).

Epistemic congruence can be conceptualized not only with respect to agreement on access, as discussed earlier, but also with respect to agreement on epistemic primacy – if we agree that you have greater authority and/or more rights than I do, then we have achieved epistemic primacy congruence (see Hayano this volume; and Heinemann, Lindström and Steensig this volume). Conversely, if we disagree over who has greater authority and/or more rights then we are in an epistemically incongruent situation. If we return to Extract 6 above, we see that in overlap Ilene works (line 10) to downgrade her claim to epistemic primacy as Norman contests her (thus far) implied claim. Thus, in overlap they achieve epistemic primacy congruence.

One reason we may insist on our epistemic position is because this is so intertwined with how we relate to one another and indeed who we are to one another. Epistemic primacy is sometimes derivable from social categories (e.g., teacher, mother, grandmother) (Raymond and Heritage 2006; Sacks 1972a, b; Schegloff 2007b). However, epistemic primacy can also be derived more locally from interactional roles (e.g., teller, producer of the trouble source, producer of the first position assessment) (Heritage and Raymond 2005; Lerner 2003; Schegloff 1996a; Stivers 2005a). For instance, in his description of the practice "confirming an allusion," Schegloff (1996a) documents how speakers sometimes allude to some state of affairs without articulating them explicitly. In such situations, if their interlocutor then articulates the state of affairs (e.g., Speaker A has indicated but not stated that she's been drinking; Speaker B actually articulates this: *You've had something to drink*), the alluding speakers will typically use repetition to assert primacy over the point (e.g., by then stating *I had something to drink*).

Similarly, in Extract 7 (Stivers 2005a: 147) epistemic primacy is derived from Lance's interactional role. Lance, Gio and Judy are housemates cooking dinner together. Judy has proposed having red wine. Although

Lance has agreed to the proposal, he teasingly adds a condition in lines 3–4/6. In overlap, Gio asserts an additional issue "It's uh school night." (line 7). Critically, Lance has already taken a position that Judy should restrict her drinking due to what happened "las'=time."

```
(7)
1   LAN:  Great_
2         (0.2)
3   LAN:  .h As long as you don't have too much.= "cuz
4         you remember what happen'=las'=time."
5   GIO:  h [h(h)
6   LAN:    [(Got chel got °drunk didn' sh-)
7   GIO:    [An' it's uh school night.
8         (1.0)
9   LAN:  It is a school night.
10        (0.4)
11  LAN:  Mister- <two jacks already>,
```

Gio's assertion is hearable as treading into Lance's domain by asserting why Judy should be careful with her drinking. In response, Lance does a "modified repeat" (line 9) which orients to his own primary rights to assert that it is a school night (Stivers 2005a). His rights here are certainly not rooted in more nuanced knowledge of which days constitute school nights and thus this is not a matter of epistemic authority. Rather, his claim of primary rights is rooted in the fact that he had already adopted the carer role in this situation. Moreover, Lance, who has not been drinking, is in a morally superior position to take a stance toward restricted drinking, a position that he points out Gio is not in (line 11) due to his having already had two Jack Daniels's that evening.

Epistemic responsibilities

In the last section we discussed some of the asymmetries that exist with respect to a person's *rights* to know. Persons also have particular *responsibilities* with respect to knowledge. For instance, Pomerantz (1980) distinguishes between two types of knowledge. She observes that "Type 1 knowables are those that subject-actors *as* subject-actors have rights and obligations to know" whereas "Type 2 knowables are those that subject-actors are assumed to have access to by virtue of the knowings being occasioned" (1980: 187; see also Sacks 1975). Accordingly, one has a right as well as an obligation to know such things as one's name, what one is doing or has done, how one is feeling, etc. By contrast, one is not held accountable to the same degree for what one knows about, for instance, the comings and goings of other people.

Although interactants may, as Pomerantz suggests, orient to being more accountable for Type 1 knowables than Type 2 knowables, in interaction, question recipients still routinely treat themselves as responsible for being able to answer a question addressed to them, whether regarding a Type 1 or a Type 2 knowable, and generally provide accounts for not knowing (Clayman 2002; Heritage 1984b; Stivers and Robinson 2006). Thus epistemic responsibility clearly extends beyond highly personal information.

Relatedly, just as interactants orient to a social norm against telling others what is already known, so too do interactants treat each other as responsible for knowing what is "in the common ground" (Clark 1996; Enfield 2006), and for retaining what they have come to know, the principle of recipient design (Sacks and Schegloff 2007 [1979]). This is true both with respect to action design and turn design. Thus, one has a responsibility not to perform particular actions (e.g., requesting information), if one knows the answer. Emmertsen and Heinemann (2010) show that interactants monitor one another for whether or not their social actions observably take into account knowledge to which they have known access. In Danish, speakers have particular resources to retroactively indicate that they had access to something but initially failed to indicate that access. Relatedly, Wu (2004) shows that final *a* in Mandarin, with a flat or slightly high pitch, may be used to contest a displayed lack of knowledge and thus imply a responsibility for knowing (see also Haviland [1987: 349] on Tzotzil).

Finally, recipients have a responsibility to make use of what they know about their interlocutors in designing their turns. For instance, interactants have a responsibility to take into account how their recipients will recognize a particular person or place and refer accordingly (Sacks and Schegloff 2007 [1979]; Schegloff 1972; Stivers, Enfield and Levinson 2007). Evidence for this is offered both by the fact that speakers will repair their turns in order to adjust the design of the reference (e.g., from a descriptive recognitional to a name) and by the fact that recipients will offer alternative referring expressions (e.g., a name to replace a descriptive recognitional) (Schegloff 1996b).

In social interaction conversationalists attend not only to who knows what, but also to who has a *right* to know what, who knows *more* about what, and who is *responsible* for knowing what. We have observed that speakers monitor themselves as well as others with respect to these issues, and both can and do hold each other accountable for failing to exercise their epistemic rights and fulfill their obligations. Sidnell discusses this under the rubric of "policing knowledge" (2005: 171–186). Relatedly, return to Extract 1, where Kristina could have let pass that Tara was re-telling a story about her mother's phone call. Instead, she asserts "Yea(h)h I kn(h) ow, I was there." With this claim, as we discussed earlier, she treats Tara as violating the norm against telling a recipient what she already knows, but note also that in her second TCU, Kristina mildly chastises Tara for not remembering that her access to this information was quite direct – she was *with* Tara when this event transpired. Tara thus failed doubly since she failed also in her responsibility to keep track of her prior interactions with Kristina.

Similarly, in Extracts 6–7 we see that Norman and Lance are monitoring Ilene's and Gio's relative rights to assert or assess states of affairs. In both cases the other speaker is treated as having committed a form of "epistemic trespassing." Lance treats Gio as relatively less entitled to instruct Judy about drinking; and Norman treats Ilene as less entitled to make claims about his dog.

We have discussed a range of social norms in the domain of knowledge. With respect to access, for instance, we should not tell others what they already have access to. Relatedly, we should take what we know into account in our own actions. We have also discussed norms regarding the order in which people should come to have access to some state of affairs. As a final illustration, with respect to epistemic primacy, existing work suggests that there may be a norm that speakers should have epistemic primacy if they assert or assess some state of affairs first in a conversation. As with other social norms in conversation, here too we expect evidence to be partially distributional in that speakers can be expected to abide by the norms most of the time, but there should be other forms of evidence in speaker behavior as well. In the work reviewed here, as well as in contributions to this volume, we see ample orientations in the ways speakers' actions are designed (e.g., with the use of pre-tellings when access is unclear; and *oh*-prefaces to agreements or modified repeats of assertions in cases of primacy violations).

The morality of knowledge and its implications for interactional cooperation

Insofar as interactants hold each other accountable for the rights and responsibilities associated with epistemic access, primacy and responsibility, knowledge is a moral domain with important implications for managing social relationships. In this section we sketch these connections and discuss how this volume documents the morality of knowledge in interaction.

In abiding by or violating each of the norms discussed above (and other related ones), we make morally accountable choices that have not only informational consequences but also relational ones. A substantial amount of research suggests that human behavior is prosocial and highly cooperative (Axelrod 1984; Henrich *et al.* 2004). In the structures of social interaction we see a variety of evidence for this, from a turn-taking system that provides equal access to the floor (de Ruiter, Milterer and Enfield 2006; Sacks *et al.* 1974; Stivers *et al.* 2009), to a preference for responses that are bias-matched relative to the preceding action (Heritage 1984b; Pomerantz 1984a), to a preference for agreement / matched stance (Heinemann 2005; Heritage 1984b; Pomerantz 1984a; Sacks 1987a). Enfield observes that "The pursuit and exploitation of mutual knowledge, shared expectations and other types of common ground ... not only serves the mutual management of referential information, but has important consequences in the realm of social, interpersonal affiliation" (Enfield 2006: 399). Thus, he introduces the idea that there is both an "informational imperative" and a "social imperative" that compels cooperation in conversation.

Although conversation analytic studies discuss a wide range of cooperative behaviors, each has been considered in isolation. Although the characterization of any of these behaviors is precise within the relevant study, *across* the conversation analytic literature how these different sorts of cooperative behaviors are discussed varies considerably. Here we propose a distinction between two main levels of cooperation: alignment and affiliation. We argue that the preference for both is normative and moral.

Cooperation in conversation: alignment and affiliation

In interaction we position ourselves vis-à-vis our interlocutors in a variety of ways, moment by moment, TCU by TCU. Actions as seemingly innocuous as news announcements, offers of help and requests for help, both through being done at all and through their design, convey something about the social relationship between the speaker and recipient. For instance, in announcing personal news the speaker treats the recipient as a friend. In how recipients respond to actions, they also position themselves relationally vis-à-vis speakers. Whether we agree with each other about an evaluation (e.g., that a restaurant was good), whether we share the same perspective on some state of affairs (e.g., that an event was funny) and whether we are willing to give or receive help from another (e.g., granting a request or accepting an offer) are all forms of cooperation.

In this book our concern is with the link between knowledge and cooperation. We have suggested that there are a variety of social norms governing knowledge. However, our adherence to, violation of and enforcement of these social norms affect our social relationships moment by moment. We conceptualize the mechanisms through which this occurs as broadly situated in two main forms of cooperation: alignment and affiliation.

Broadly, we conceptualize *alignment* as the structural level of cooperation and *affiliation* as the affective level of cooperation (Stivers 2008).

Thus, aligning responses cooperate by facilitating the proposed activity or sequence; accepting the presuppositions and terms of the proposed action or activity; and matching the formal design preference of the turn. By contrast, affiliative responses cooperate at the level of action and affective stance. Thus, affiliative responses are maximally pro-social when they match the prior speaker's evaluative stance, display empathy and/or cooperate with the preference of the prior action. Whereas we can speak about alignment for any responsive action, affiliation is not necessarily always relevant. For instance, it may be difficult to affiliate with a request for information from a stranger such as "Where is the elevator?"

Although the extent to which affiliation is possible may vary, many actions do make relevant both alignment and affiliation in the response. For instance, consider requests. The affiliative response to most requests, regardless of format, is to grant them (Heritage 1984b). However, whether that granting is also aligning is contingent on the design of the request. For instance, in Extract 8 the request turn prefers a negative response at a formal level but an affirmative response on an action level, thus setting up cross-cutting preferences for a cooperative response (Sacks and Schegloff 2007 [1979]; Schegloff 2007a). To affiliate with this request the recipient must disalign.[1]

(8) (Levinson 1983: 363)
C: You don't have his number I don't suppose

In story telling, Stivers (2008) shows that aligning behavior includes the use of continuers which pass on an opportunity to take a full turn of talk (Schegloff 1982). Disaligning behavior can include more interruptive behavior, such as requesting clarification or assessments. However, these disaligning behaviors can be disaffiliative (e.g., challenges to the telling or to components of it [Stivers 2008]), or affiliative (e.g., assessments which endorse the teller's stance [Bavelas, Coates and Johnson 2000; Goodwin 1986; Goodwin and Goodwin 1987; Goodwin 1980]).

Lastly, consider the assessment context. Return to Extract 3:

(3) (Heritage 2002a: Example 2)
1 J: T's- tsuh beautiful day out isn't it?
2 L: →   Yeh it's jus' gorgeous ...

Here, a maximally aligning response is congruent with J's position that L has epistemic access to the state of affairs being assessed, the weather in this case, and is congruent with J's position that they have equal rights to

---

[1] Curl and Drew (2008) suggest that a negatively formulated request such as this one adopts a stance that the speaker is less entitled to make the request than would be the case with a positive formulation.

assess the day. An aligning response is thus contingent on this presupposition of access. This upgraded agreement is thus affiliative and aligning. However, the two concepts are separable insofar as a disaffiliative response such as a disagreement could nonetheless be aligning, moving the sequence forward and accepting the terms and presuppositions of the first assessment. Conversely, an agreeing response could nonetheless challenge the presupposition of, for instance, equivalent epistemic access (e.g., Heritage 2002a; Heritage and Raymond 2005).

This sketch might be understood to imply that maximal alignment and affiliation, because they are cooperative, are thus optimal in interaction. However, this is not necessarily the case. Consider Heritage's point that one reason speakers assert epistemic independence is to push against the interpretation that they are "merely" going along with the opinion of their interlocutor (2002a). Indeed, asserting independent epistemic access or equivalent epistemic rights, although less aligning than the acquiescent *yeah*, is a resource with which recipients can, in some situations, assert *stronger* affiliation precisely by asserting more agency over their response (see Heritage and Raymond in press; Stivers and Hayashi 2010). In this way, what may lack in cooperation can be seen as a sacrifice in the service of what is ultimately a more pro-social stance.

Finally, conversation analytic work has long documented that delay has communicative significance such that, with respect to adjacency pairs, for instance, fitted responses tend to be faster; delay indicates trouble, or at least possible trouble (Heritage 1984b; Jefferson 1989; Pomerantz 1984a; Sacks 1987a; Sacks *et al.* 1974; Stivers *et al.* 2009; Stivers and Robinson 2006). A delay may indicate that there is trouble with respect to sequential progress (e.g., Stivers and Robinson 2006), or it may indicate that there is trouble with agreeing with the evaluative position indicated by the speaker's action or turn design (e.g., Pomerantz 1984a). Delay thus commonly precedes disaligned as well as disaffiliative responses. When delay precedes aligned or affiliative responses it may suggests hesitancy, whereas no delay in producing a disaligned or disaffiliative response suggests a lack of consideration in producing something uncooperative (Brown and Levinson 1987; Heritage 1984b; Pomerantz 1984a).

Cooperation at the micro-level in social interaction has at least the facets we have discussed here. When we consider knowledge with respect to cooperation, we see that knowledge is intricately woven into cooperation at different levels, and we see that different forms of cooperation may be optimal in different situations. The chapters in this volume examine this complex intersection of knowledge, morality, affiliation and alignment.

About this volume

As noted at the beginning of this chapter, social interactionists have become increasingly interested in issues of knowledge asymmetries. Studies in this area represent one of the, if not the, largest growth areas in conversation analysis in recent years. However, there has not yet been any effort to synthesize or take stock of this work. This volume represents the first such effort, bringing together a set of scholars who have worked together systematically in an attempt to achieve terminological and conceptual coherence across the domain. The chapters rely entirely on video and audio tapes of spontaneous naturally occurring conversation from a variety of settings and languages.

Each chapter addresses the issue of how participants in social interaction juggle informational and affiliational imperatives (Enfield 2006: 399) but do so in varied ways.The first set of chapters, by Mondada, Hayano, Stivers, Heinemann *et al.* and Sidnell, focus on situations where there is an epistemic asymmetry and then examine the consequences of this with respect to alignment and affiliation in the interaction. In these chapters authors begin with an observation of some sort of epistemic disparity, whether in terms of access (Mondada), primacy (Hayano), or responsibility (Stivers and Heinemenn *et al.*). In these chapters we follow the ramifications that such epistemic disparities have in terms of the social relationships among the participants.

The second set of chapters, by Heritage, Keevallik, Asmuß, Hakulinen and Sorjonen, and Kidwell, focus on alignment and affiliation problems and examine how and when epistemic resources are mobilized to manage these relational issues. Thus, virtually the inversion of the approach taken by the first set of chapters, these authors begin with an issue of social relations – typically a problem for affiliation or agreement – and examine the varied ways in which epistemic resources exacerbate or ameliorate this problem. These chapters also cut across the epistemic domains looking at affiliation with respect to access (Heritage, Keevallik, and Hakulinen and Sorjonen), authority (Kidwell) and a combination of the two (Asmuß and Sidnell).

Finally, in the last section, Enfield takes stock of the state of our understanding in this domain and offers a framework for how the range of issues connected with the asymmetries of knowledge, including sequential position, authority and agency, can be integrated. Throughout the volume we show how knowing is not simply a matter of having information. It is a source of disagreement and a resource for reaching agreement, and this relies on a mutual accountability for and orientation to the norms governing the domain.

Conclusion

Knowledge is a topic that has been on the radar screen of intellectual thought for over 2,000 years. However, in this long and winding history, it has only relatively recently been thought to ask how it is that in conversation we treat "knowing" as moral. And it has only been in conversation analytic studies of epistemics that the tight relationship between agreement, affiliation and alignment, on the one hand, and norms of knowing, on the other, has been acknowledged. One goal of this volume is to demonstrate that if we are to understand how speakers manage issues of agreement, affiliation and alignment, something clearly at the heart of human sociality, we must understand the social norms surrounding epistemic access, primacy and responsibility.

It is a hallmark of conversation analytic studies that the discipline moves forward one practice at a time. The discovery of interactional practices is likened to the charge of a biologist describing a new find. However, as the discipline moves into its fifth decade, we should begin to see how these findings relate to one another. A second goal of this volume is therefore to bring together a set of studies in one domain of inquiry in order to synthesize concepts and terminology. Thus, we hope to have made advances in our understanding of the various dimensions of knowledge as well as in our understanding of alignment and affiliation.

The study of knowledge as a moral domain could be viewed as a mountain to climb simply because it's there. However, we believe that this enterprise is not only that. One of the most fundamental goals across the social sciences is to understand human sociality. And one of the basic questions with respect to our sociality is the extent to which our behavior is pro-social and cooperative. Evolutionary theories pit social imperatives against informational imperatives in trying to explain how we came to have language (e.g., Nettle and Dunbar 1997). What, the reader might ask, does this have to do with the morality of knowledge? We suggest quite a lot. If we want to understand pro-sociality, we must understand how, when and to what extent people cooperate in social interaction at the micro-level. But understanding such cooperative behaviors as agreement is, this book shows, fundamentally impossible without considering epistemic access, primacy and responsibility. The interconnectedness of these domains reveals just how little we understand about our social behavior and about how it is that we relate to one another. This book therefore represents a collective effort toward solving this puzzle.

Part II

Affiliational consequences of managing
epistemic asymmetries

2 The management of knowledge discrepancies and of epistemic changes in institutional interactions

Lorenza Mondada

Introduction

This chapter offers a detailed analysis of social practices in which participants orient to the knowledge of their partners as a condition for engaging in the activity, for ensuring the progressivity of talk and action, and for attributing blame and responsibility. In these contexts, participants routinely orient toward the relevance of who knows, what s/he knows, and what s/he is expected to know, and to possible incongruities between the epistemic expectations of prior turn and the format of next actions.

These aspects play an important role in ordinary conversation but also in institutional interactions, where normative and moral expectations coupled with epistemic perspectives are strongly associated with membership categories and category-bound activities, and where the relevant distribution of knowledge and expertise is consequential for the achievement of tasks and practical purposes, as well as for social affiliation. This chapter deals with a professional setting – a call center – where epistemic discrepancies are closely related to issues of professional trust, competence and authority.

This chapter deals with displays of epistemic positions as they can be observed in a context of "reality disjunctures" (Pollner 1975, 1987), in which divergent and contradictory versions of the world are expressed. It focuses on discrepant epistemic perspectives on a situation in which a knowledgeable speaker claims *not to know*. It also focuses on changes of epistemic positions within the unfolding activity, in which a participant initially supposed not to know acquires a new epistemic position. Far from being static features attributed to participants, epistemic positions are dynamically negotiated in the activity, being displayed, claimed, attributed, revised and also being newly acquired. Thus, this chapter

I would like to thank Tanya Stivers, Jakob Steensig, Auli Hakulinen and Marja-Leena Sorjonen for comments and reactions to earlier versions of this paper.

analyzes an interwoven series of practices dealing with epistemic discrepancies, which recognize, minimize or dissolve them.

This chapter also deals with the resources sequentially mobilized by participants in order to display their knowledge. More precisely, it describes occurrences of epistemic verbs in their negative form – such as *je ne sais pas, je ne connais pas, je ne vois pas* in French, glossable as "I don't know," "I am not aware of," "I don't grasp" – in a particular sequential environment: in second position, after a first action which has projected a positive response and an action presupposing that the recipient does know.

After a first example of the way in which the progressivity of the interaction relies on or is blocked by the aligned or disaligned expression of epistemic positions, based on recordings of itinerary descriptions, this paper analyzes a single case of a video-recorded conference call in a call center dealing with the problematic locating of a caller searching for help. Within this call, the locally dispatched garage mechanic, who is supposed to find the caller's car, manifests discrepant spatial knowledge in repeated turns claiming that he does not know where it is. These turns perform different actions – treating the terms of the previous action as problematic, and even rejecting them and refusing to collaborate, or manifesting the recognition of a more knowledgeable speaker, after a change in relative epistemic authorities has been displayed. The detailed analysis of multiple displays of non-knowing, of their distribution in changing sequential environments and their transformation within the course of the call, contribute to the study of epistemic statuses as practical accomplishments in time and action. We will discuss each in turn.

Knowledge and progressivity of talk and action: the example of itinerary descriptions

Participants orient to the progressivity of talk (Stivers and Robinson 2006: 386), treating congruent knowledge displays and knowledge expectations as a crucial condition for the activity to be carried out.

Itinerary requests in public space (discussed in this section) and the locating of problems for help dispatch (discussed in the next section) are social practices in which this orientation concerns the spatial competence of the participants. Co-participants can either display spatial competences congruent with the request, the question, or the action of the previous turn and realize an aligned next action (Extract 1) or they can express their inability to do so (Extract 2). This paper develops the latter case, dealing with the management of diverging knowledge claims and responses of speakers who are expected to know but who claim that they don't know. Whereas in the literature positive claims of knowledge have been investigated in the

form either of epistemic markers or of epistemic stances in interaction
(cf. Heritage 1984a, 1998, 2002a; Heritage and Raymond 2005 – see also
Asmuß this volume), negative epistemic claims have been much less studied
(but see Keevallik this volume; Heinemann *et al.* this volume). When they
have been analyzed, they have been treated as (positive) resources for the
pursuit of the interaction, such as a "fishing device" (Pomerantz 1980) or
as a practice for increasing participation and co-tellership (Goodwin 1987).
This chapter aims to explore negative and discrepant epistemic claims as
a threat to the progressivity of the interaction, which generates changes in
the attributions of responsibilities and moral authority to the participants.

Itinerary requests addressed by a person in the public space to a passer-
by (Mondada 2009) are centrally based on expectations relative to the kind
of knowledge conditioning the delivery of the itinerary description. In this
kind of practice, it is common that either the requester or the producer of
the description mentions their knowledge, as in the following excerpt (for
an explanation of the conventions for gesture, see the end of this chapter):

(1)
```
1 F:   l'église     saint-roch, vous savez pas    où    elle est?
       the church  saint-roch, you   know  NEG  where  it    is?
       the church of saint-roch, don't you know where it is?

2 C:   l'église saint-roch, *je sais.*      [ah oui,        [(je fais l'  ef  [fort)
       the church of saint-roch, I know.  [oh yes,        [(I  do my be  [st)
                          *big nod*

3 F:                                        [vous savez, (.)  [ah:::         [enfin,
                                            [you know, (.)   [oh:::         [at last,

4      (0.*5)
  c        *hand on her chin, thinking posture, reorients her body–>

5 C:   euh::
       ehm::

6      (1.*1)
  c    -->*raises head and looks in the right direction–>

7 C:   pour* aller au plus cou:rt,   ((delivers itinerary))
       in order to make it brief,
       --> *
```

In this opening, F and another woman walk toward a passer-by, C, and
ask her for directions to a tourist landmark, the saint-Roch church. C's
knowledge is treated as a condition for engaging and progressing the
activity both by F's request (line 1) (also oriented toward the possibility
that C may not know – through the negative question design) and by C's
actual response (line 2): C first confirms her knowledge and then engages
in the itinerary description. Her alignment is shown by her use of the same
left-dislocated referent as in the request and of the verb *je sais*, which is

prosodically focused and also bodily highlighted, by a big nod. Her answer is acknowledged by F (line 3), who seems to refer to other previous unsuccessful attempts to obtain the itinerary. This answer projects the coming description, both in the form of a *euh* projecting more talk to come (line 5) and a body posture exhibiting an ongoing reflection and a reorientation of C's body toward the relevant starting point for the description.

Itinerary requests treat the addressed participant as possessing adequate knowledge, making relevant membership categories such as "local," "native" or "expert" (or taxi drivers or policemen). This categorization of the passer-by and the possession of knowledge are two associated issues, visible in the following interaction, where E and F make the same request of a couple, A and B:

(2)
```
1 E:  euh.::: pardon l'é- euh l'église saint-roch s'il vous plaît?
      ehm::: sorry the ch- ehm the church of saint-roch please?

2     (3.2)

3 A:  euh.:+.:: alors,
      ehm::: so,
          +turns back-->

4     (1.0)

5 B:  ah moi je suis pas     d'ici,      *alors °j' sais     pas    *[du  t[out°*
      oh me  I   am  NEG from here,  so    °I know    NEG   [at   all°
      oh  myself, I'm not from here,  so °I don't know at all°
                                           *shrugs his shoulders      *turns away*
6 E:                                                           [ah a [h
7 F:                                                           [ah
8     *(0.5)              *+(0.5)
   b  * walks behind his wife* stays behind her==>
   a                          -->+turns towards E and F==>
9 A:  i me semble qu'i faut que vous repart++iez par là ((continues))
      I think you have to start from there
                                       ++points in front of her==>
```

In this case, the task of giving directions is assumed by one participant, A, who engages immediately in the planning of her explanation (line 3), and is rejected by another participant, B, who explicitly denies knowledge (*j'sais pas* line 5) and accounts for it in terms of membership categorization, as a "non-local" (*ah moi je suis pas d'ici* line 5). His inability to carry out the requested task is further displayed by his walking behind his wife, who responds alone to the itinerary requesters.

These excerpts show how knowing can be a pre-condition for engaging in a social activity. Sequentially, the requester orients in first position to the other as possibly knowing; in second position, the other responds, either assuming or denying his/her knowledge. On this basis, either talk continues or the conversation is closed.

A single case: a knowledgeable speaker who does not know

In this chapter, I focus on a single instance of talk, a ten-minute telephone conversation to a call center which works as a "perspicuous setting" (Garfinkel and Wieder 1992) for the exploration of the articulation between discrepant knowledge attributions, place formulations, and normative and moral expectations, as well as membership categories.

In this conference call, three people are talking together: the call-taker (C-T), working in a French call center dealing with calls for help from Spanish citizens experiencing problems while traveling in France; the caller, Jordi (JOR), a Spanish driver traveling with his wife (WIF), whose car is stuck in a small village not far from Bordeaux; and a car mechanic (MEC), who has been dispatched by the call-taker to tow away his car. Jordi is waiting for the mechanic. Although the latter has driven to the place where Jordi is supposed to be, he cannot find Jordi. The conversation unfolds as they try to identify the right location where they are supposed to meet, a village called *Cadillac*: both agree on certain spatial information but disagree on, and do not share, other indications. At the end of the call, the call-taker discovers that they are in fact in two very different places: the car mechanic is in Cadillac, and Jordi is in Cadillac-en-Fronsadais, 60 km away. Both places have a similar name, are in the same department, are about 20 km from Bordeaux and are located off the highway.

The call is a good example of what Pollner (1987) calls "reality disjunctures," where different participants hold different versions of reality that are contradictory, even if they try to preserve the supposition of a common perspective on a common world (Schütz 1962). These disjunctures can be resolved in different ways (1987: 77): they can be maintained, if they don't have pragmatic consequences for the activity going on; they can be dissolved, by proposing accounts for their discrepancies; or they can be precluded, when one version prevails over the other. These various solutions show that epistemic discrepancies are not static, but evolve over time. This chapter explores these different practices, as well as the resources that manifest the changing epistemic positions – paying particular attention to the high frequency of use of knowledge verbs such as *savoir, connaître* and *voir* in French. In this sense, the single case analysis allows for an analysis of the systematic distribution of these linguistic resources within the talk and how they change over time.

The manifestation of the problem

The problem emerges as Jordi, the Spanish driver, who has previously called the call-taker asking for help, rings back, complaining that he is still waiting for the garage mechanic (Extract 3). A few seconds after Jordi's call, the French mechanic calls back too, inquiring about the Spanish driver whom he has not yet found (Extract 4).

(3) (Jordi's second call to the call center)

1 C-T: *cuenteme.*
        tell me.

2 JOR: *todavia no ha llegao aqui:: eh: la grua,*
        yet it has not arrived here:: uh: the crane

3 C-T: *ah no puede ser, el me dijo que:: en media hora y h*
        oh that's not possible, he said to me that:: in half hour and h

4   *ya ha pasado: cuanto tiempo?*
        how much time has already passed?

5 JOR: *pues una hora si,*
        well one hour yes,

6 C-T: *no puede ser. bueno (.) permitame un segundo voy a mirar.*
        that's not possible. alright (.) give me a second I will look.

(4) (Mechanic's second call to the call center)

((MEC has just given the reference number of the case and C-T discovers that it concerns Jordi, who is waiting on line))

1 C-T: *j'ai j'ai j'ai l- j'ai le clien::t e::n ligne en fait*
        I have I have I have th- I have the customer:: on: line actually

2 MEC: *et oui, je ne le trouve pa:s, ça fait longtemps que je le cherche.*
        oh yes, I don't find him, it's a long time that I search for him.

3   (0.5)

4 MEC: *hah ha ha* ((laughs))

5 C-T: *a:ttendez, on va faire une chose, je vais essayer de nous*
        wait, we'll do something, I'll try to connect us

6   *mettre en: conféren:ce,*
        in a telephone conference,

In both cases, the turn stating the reason for calling (Extract 3, line 2; Extract 4, line 2) is formatted with a negative expression, presenting the problem and displaying the expectations of the speaker. In Extract 3, Jordi proposes a negative description which focuses on the (long) time elapsed from his last call; the call-taker's response is both normatively oriented (*no puede ser* repeated twice, lines 3 and 6) and refers to the mechanic's commitment (*el me dijo* line 3): both speakers blame the mechanic, manifesting the common expectation that he should have arrived within a shorter time.

In Extract 4, the car mechanic manifests his problem in finding the driver, although showing his commitment in having searched for him for 'a long time' (2). This both manifests a complaint about the time spent searching and exhibits his willingness to solve the case; it lets transpire a different possibility for blame concerning the absence of an exact location for the client.

These calls manifest the expectations related to the management of the case, and to the previous commitment (calling for help, promising to dispatch help, agreeing to help). They also exhibit the identities of the participants implied by them. Jordi is not only a "help seeker" but a "to be helped," as well as a "client" who is entitled to receive help; the car mechanic has agreed to supply help, and is not only a "helper," but also a professional contracted to bring help and paid for that – thus morally and contractually obliged to do so; the call-taker is responsible for the client's case and is also the "dispatcher" of help. Thus, a series of membership categories are made relevant here (Sacks 1972a,b), not only "helper"/ "helped" but also "client"/ "service provider," "dispatcher"/ "dispatched." Spatial categories are made relevant too, the dispatched mechanic being a "local," whereas Jordi is categorized as a "foreigner" and the call-taker operates at a "distance." All of these categories are consequential for the kind of knowledge expected from each of the participants – some categories being seen as "owning" knowledge (Sharrock 1974).

These membership categories are related to rights and obligations which produce moral, normative and even contractual expectations – occasioning blame and accounts, issues of mutual trust as well as negotiations about who is responsible for the case, who "owns the case." Categories are also related to competences: to be in charge of coordinating help presupposes that the call-taker knows the exact address and that the local garage mechanic knows the location to which help must be delivered. Attributions of knowledge are based on local assumptions, expectations, category-bound rights and obligations; moreover, attributions of knowledge, as well as participants' displays of knowledge, can change as the interaction unfolds.

The conjunction of the participants: the opening of the three-way call

Having both the client and the car mechanic on line, the call-taker connects the participants in a single conference call. This decision constitutes a first step in solving the problem; it exhibits the call-taker's positioning of the other participants and of herself, in a way which considers that the solution has to be found in a distributed way – that the problem is "owned" by all of the participants – heading off the potential attribution of blame to her.

(5)

1 C-T: *allô?*
          hello?

2 MEC: [*ouIh,*
          [yeah,

3 JOR: [*si,*
          [yes,

4 C-T: *oui bah on est en conférence, eh:: señor, yo estoy*
          yes well we are connected, eh:: sir, I am

5 F: *con el señor de la <u>grua</u>.*
          with the mechanic of the <u>crane</u>.

6   (0.5)

7 JOR: *si:h,*
          yes:h,

8   (0.3)

9 C-T: *eh: necessi- (.) que el lo esta buscando hace   tiempos °me::m°*
          eh: need-   (.) who he you is   searching makes time   °CON°
          eh: need- (.) who has been searching for you for a while °but°

10   *no- y no lo encuentra*
          no- and doesn't find you

11   (1.2)

12 JOR: *pues (.) aquí estoy en la- en la   plaza   del   pueblo estoy,*
          PRT (.) here am   en the- in the square of_the village am,
          well (.) here I am in the- in the square of the village I am,

13   (1.0)

14 JOR: *en la plaza se llama carl de gaulle*
          in the square called carl de gaulle

15   (0.4)

16 C-T: *(y-;i-) allô monsieur?*
          (and-;he-) hello sir?

17 MEC: *oui,*
          yes,

18 C-T: *i me dit qu'il est dans la place charles de gaulle.*
          he tells me that he's in the square charles de gaulle.

19   (0.6)

20 MEC: >°*ah oui mais je sais pas où elle est moi,*°<
          >°oh yes but I don't know where it is myself°<

21   (0.2)

22 MEC: *j'ai   fait   plusieurs places,*
            I've done various   squares,
            I went to various squares,

23   (0.4)

24 MEC: *je me suis déplacé à pied parce que- et en fait,*
            I walked because- actually,

25   *de quelle couleur elle est la voiture?*
            what color is the car?

26   (0.6)

27 JOR: *ner-, noir.*
            bla-, black.

28   (0.5)

29 MEC: *NOIR?*
            BLACK?

30   (0.4)

31 JOR: *noir. [oui,*
            black. [yes,
32 MEC: *[el- (0.3) elle est noi:re.*
               [it- (0.3) it is black.

33   (0.2)

34 MEC: *ouais mai::s la place   du général de gaulle,*
            yeah bu::t the square of general de gaulle,

35   *j'sais   pas   où   elle est moi.*
            I know NEG where it   is   me.
            yeah but:: I don't know where the square general de gaulle is.

36   *(0.7)*
  c-t   *sticks out her tongue*

37 MEC: *je connais pa:s la::: cette ville   là,*
            I   know   NEG the::: that town there,
            I don't know the::: that town there,

38   (0.5)

39 C-T: *att [endez*
            wai [t a minute
40 MEC: *[vous m'ave- (.) vous m'aviez dit pla:ce du général de gaulleh?*
              [you told- (.) you told me square general de gaulle h?

41   (1.0)

42 JOR: *oui,*
            yes,

This opening shows a variety of ways to refer to the client's location as well as the epistemic claims associated with them. On the one hand, Jordi is engaged in formulating his position, translated by the call-taker for the car mechanic; on the other hand, the mechanic displays that the terms of his description are problematic for him.

The summons (line 1) (Schegloff 1968) opens a new participation framework (Goodwin and Goodwin 2004) for the triangular call, to which both the car mechanic (line 2) and Jordi (line 3) answer, each one in his language. The call-taker presents the reason for the call in a bilingual turn, orienting to the languages of the addressees, first in French, addressing the mechanic, then in Spanish, to Jordi (Auer 1995). She presents the problem through a translation of what the mechanic just said in the previous call (lines 9–10; cf. Extract 4, line 2), in a way that makes Jordi's response relevant as a next action – the announcement working as a "fishing device" (Pomerantz 1980).

Jordi's response occasions a series of referential formulations which offer various versions of the location (Schegloff 1972). The location he gives (*aquí estoy en la- en la plaza del pueblo estoy* line 12) begins with a deictic (*aquí*), which is then transformed into a spatial description (*en la plaza del pueblo*), treating the village as known (as shown by the use of the definite article before *pueblo*) and taking for granted that it has only one square (as shown by the use of the singular definite article before *plaza*). When the description is not responded to (line 13), Jordi orients to a possible trouble and offers a new elaboration of the spatial reference, specifying the name of the square (line 14). After a summons addressed to the mechanic (line 16), this information is translated by the call-taker: her translation merges the two formulations produced by Jordi (lines 12 and 14), and refers directly to Charles de Gaulle Square, treating it as known but without supposing that it is the only square of the village (*la place Charles de Gaulle* line 18 contrasts with *la plaza del pueblo* line 12). The call-taker, like Jordi, treats the village as taken for granted: participants single out as relevant a level of spatial reference which is *inside* the village.

This announcement of Jordi's location projects a response from the mechanic: the expected aligned response would express his recognition of the place and consecutive actions taken to reach it; instead, after a delay, a disaligned response is produced.

The mechanic's disaligned response states that he does not know where that particular square is (line 20), in a lower voice and with a fast pace. Claiming not to know is a way of questioning the epistemic congruency between the previous and the next action and of dealing with the terms of Jordi's description as inadequate: the announcement cannot be responded to.

The mechanic then adds information about his own movements, which produce the accountability of the search actions he has already initiated. This occasions another version of the environment in which he is moving, which refers to the village having various squares (line 22) (using the plural rather than the singular used by Jordi). He then inserts a sequence questioning Jordi about the color of his car (lines 25–32). These details – exhibiting the active and serious engagement of the mechanic in the field in a way that is sensitive to the blame attribution which is in the air – presuppose his and Jordi's co-presence in the same place (Schegloff 1972: 83–84) – since the car's color supposes its visibility, recognizable either retrospectively or prospectively to someone actively searching for Jordi's car, walking and looking around.

After the completion of a side sequence (Jefferson 1972), the mechanic concludes with a double denial of knowledge: first by resuming the previous denial about the location of the square (*j'sais pas où elle est* line 35, resuming line 20); second by stating *je connais pa:s* (line 37), referring to the town with a stretched definite article (*la:::*), self-repaired into a demonstrative (*cette*, reinforced by a deictic, *là*). The latter manifests his trouble expressing the spatial reference and points to a place that has no existence other than in the discourse that has previously mentioned it.

In this institutional setting, the mechanic is supposed to know and he is treated as knowing by both the call-taker and the client. Epistemic incongruence is raised when the knowledgeable speaker states that he does not know, and when he disaligns with actions projecting recognition of the location. In the unfolding of the call, these positions are first maintained, the expertise of the mechanic not being overtly questioned. Nevertheless, they represent a threat to the progressivity of the call and they are ultimately transformed and curtailed.

Resources for expressing epistemic positions: knowledge verbs

During the conference call, the car mechanic repeatedly states that he does not know where Jordi is. These repeated claims allow us to study the use of "I don't know," the specific turn formats in which it figures, and the actions it performs in interaction as well as the actions it responds to and the ones it prompts next. The negative epistemic expressions by which the mechanic refers to his spatial knowledge are observable in the entire call, although having a specific and systematic distribution: whereas at the beginning of the call he uses two French verbs, *savoir* and *connaître*, which can both be translated in English as "to know," in the second part of the call he uses the evidential verb *voir* ("to see") in a metaphorical way. Confronted with these repeated claims not to know, by a participant who is supposed to be the native geographical expert, the other participants revise their knowledge assumptions and attributions, and alter their epistemic positions by using alternative sources of knowledge. Thus, the analysis of this particular call permits an investigation of some systematic practices by which participants assume, deny, attribute, revise and acquire epistemic positions within the interaction.

Among the resources used to formulate states of knowledge explicitly, French offers two verbs – *savoir* and *connaître* – corresponding to "to know" in English (cf. other romance languages, e.g. Italian *sapere* vs. *conoscere*, Spanish *saber* vs. *conocer*, Portuguese *saber* vs. *conhecer*, but also Germanic languages, e.g. German *wissen* vs. *kennen*, Dutch *weten* vs. *kennen*, etc.). These two verbs have been described in the grammatical tradition referring both to their syntactic constraints (in our case, *savoir* is followed by a completive clause, whereas *connaître* is followed by a NP) and to their semantic values. For Picoche (1986: 127–131), *connaître*, followed by nominal arguments, refers to concrete objects, whereas *savoir*, followed by propositions, has a more abstract and analytic reference. For Remi (1986), *connaître* refers to a general representation of the object, constructed through experience, while *savoir* refers to detailed knowledge, constructed through discursive acts (propositional knowledge). For Franckel and Lebaud (1990), *ne pas connaître* implies that the referent does not exist within the perspective of the speaker, who questions the very existence of the object; *ne pas savoir* refers more to the properties of the object, seen from the perspective of the speaker (this accounts for the fact that I can say *je connais X* and at the same time say *je ne sais pas X*).

These descriptions rely on the syntax and the semantics of these forms, but do not take into consideration the sequential position in which these resources are being selected and mobilized. Our analysis aims to highlight the different implications of the two verbs in a specific sequential environment, in second position after an announcement projecting a positive response.

Claiming not to know and questioning the terms of the previous action (*je ne sais pas*)

At the beginning of the call, the car mechanic repeatedly states that he does not know where Jordi is. These disclaimers of knowledge occur in a particular sequential environment and select a particular resource, the verb *savoir*, as in the excerpts below:

(6) (cf. Extract 5)
18 C-T: *i me dit qu'il est dans la place charles de gaulle.*
          he tells me that he's in the square charles de gaulle.
19   (0.6)
20 MEC: >°*ah oui mais je sais   pas   où   elle est moi,*°<
          oh yes but I know NEG where it is   me,
          >°oh yes but I don't know where it is myself °<
          ((13 lines omitted))
33   (0.2)

34 MEC: *ouais mai::s la   place   du général de gaulle,*
           yeah bu::t   the square   of general de gaulle,

35   *j'sais   pas   où   elle est moi.*
           I know   NEG where it   is   me.
           yeah but:: I don't know where the square general de gaulle is.

36   (0.7)

(7)

1 C-T: *voilà: e- à peu près à vingt kilomètres de bordeaux i me dit,*
          there it is: eh- about 20 km from Bordeaux he tells me,

2   (1.5)

3 MEC: *alors là::   je sais   pas. j' sais   pas   où   i   sont hein.*
          PRT DEICT:: I   know   NEG. I   know   NEG where they are PRT.
          well then I don't know. I don't know where they are right.

4   *là   je suis incapable de:*
          DEICT I   am unable   to:
          then I am unable to:

In first position, the call-taker offers a description of Jordi's location, based on his tellings (*i me dit* either at the beginning of the turn, Extract 6, line 18, or at the end of the turn, Extract 7, line 1). In this way, she attributes the terms of the location to Jordi and does not take any responsibility for the details of the location – acting as a mediator, a translator, but not as the source of the description.

This description works as an announcement and is addressed to the mechanic: the expected response is a display of recognition – as a necessary preliminary to the subsequent action, undertaking Jordi's rescue. But the next action is *not* a claim of recognition by the car mechanic, who disaligns with the previous turn. After each announcement, there is a gap (Extract 6, line 19; Extract 7, line 2), followed by a disclaimer of knowledge.

The mechanic's turn is formatted as a dispreferred second (Pomerantz 1984a; Heritage 1984b): in Extract 6, there is a change-of-state token (*ah oui*) (Heritage 1984a) which registers the announcement, followed by the conjunction *mais* and the negative epistemic expression; in Extract 7, there is another conjunction and a deictic, which is stretched (*alors là::*) followed by the negative expression. In the latter case, lines 3–4, the absence of knowledge is formulated thrice: the first time without any verb argument (*je sais pas*), the second with a relative sentence referring to the unknown location (*j'sais pas où i sont*), the third by using an adjective in an incomplete expression (*là je suis incapable de:*) (the end of the latter construction is easily projectable and thus can be considered pragmatically complete; on the other hand, the fact that it is left syntactically incomplete can display that the issue is delicate – cf. Chevalier [2008] on unfinished sentences in French).

In this way, the mechanic is resisting the projected action and its terms (cf. Keevallik this volume), implicitly casting doubt on the version offered and questioning the responsibility of its sources.

Later on, another occurrence of *je ne sais pas* is observable in a longer excerpt, where it responds, as in the previous cases, to an announcement concerning Jordi's location. In this case, the location is offered in response to a question initiated by the car mechanic himself, asking Jordi, thanks to the call-taker's mediation, if he can provide a relevant visible landmark – launching a new search concerning the immediate space around him:

(8)

```
1  MEC:   et qu'est qu'y a autour de lui. (.) autour de lui y a
           and what is there around him. (.) around him there is

2          ( ) il faudrait qu'il me dise ce [qu'il y a autour de lui.
           ( ) he should tell me what       [is there around him.
3  C-T:                                      [que- que mas
                                             [wha- what more do you

4          ve- ve algun hote:l, algun resta:urante: algo asi?
           se- see any hote:l, any resta:urant: something like that?

5          (1.2)

6  JOR:   e::l restaurante::
           the:: restaurant::

7  WIF:   <((beside JOR)) la table gourmande>

8  JOR:   la table (.) gourmande

9          (1.1)

10 C-T:   voilà.    le restaurant la table gourmande
           that's it. the restaurant "the greedy table"

11         (0.1)

12 C-T:   non? ça vous dit rien?=
           no? it doesn't tell you anything?=

13 JOR:   =gourmande ( )

14         (0.9)

15 MEC:   qu'est-ce que c'est la table gourmande. c'est quoi?
           what's the table gourmande. what is it?

16 C-T:   c'est un restaurant,
           that's a restaurant,

17         (1.2)

18 MEC:   c'est^un re- c'est^un: c'est^un restauran:t, c'[est:?
           that's a re- that's a: that's a restauran:t, that's?
19 C-T:                                                   [°ouais::°
                                                          [°yeah::°
```

20 JOR: *c'est un restaurant, (.) °oui°.*
         that's a restaurant, (.) °yes°.

21   (0.4)

22 MEC: *c'est un restaurant?*
         that's a restaurant?

23   (0.2)

24 JOR: [*ouih,*
         [yeah,

25 C-T: [*°oui°*
         [°yes°

26   (1.0)

27 MEC: *ah ah ah ah ah ah ah alors là   je- je sais   pas   où*
         ((vocalizations))   PRT DEICT I- I   know NEG   where
         ah ah ah ah ah ah ah so then I- I don't know where

28   *c'est là h [ein?*
         it is there [isn't it?

The question asked by the mechanic works as a pre-sequence (Terasaki 2004 [1976]; Schegloff 2007a), similar to the pre-sequences preparing the delivery of advice (Heritage and Sefi 1992) or of bad news (Maynard 1991). These pre-sequences aim at establishing a common ground on which all the participants can align, prior to the achievement of the next action. In this case, however, the completion of the pre-sequence is not followed by the mechanic's advice.

The pre-sequence is initiated by the mechanic, asking a question of Jordi (lines 1–2). This is mediated by the call-taker, who immediately translates it (lines 3–4). The translation is more specific than the original (cf. *qu'est-ce qu'y a* line 1, *ce qu'il y a autour de lui* line 2, vs. *que mas* expanded into *algun hote:l, algun resta:urante:, algo asi?* lines 3–4), and indeed Jordi and his wife answer by giving the name of a restaurant (lines 6–8).

The next action is *not* a display or claim of recognition of the proposed landmark, but a series of delays (cf. the pauses in lines 9, 11, 14, 17, 21, 26), and a series of alternative actions, such as a request for clarification (line 15), requests for confirmation (lines 18, 22). Jordi and the call-taker align across these sequences (lines 19–20, 24–25). After a last gap (line 26), the mechanic's disaligned response takes the form of a delayed (by the turn-initial expressive vocalizations) *je sais pas où c'est là* (lines 27–28), claiming it is impossible to respond, given the terms of the problem proposed by the call-taker and the help-seeker.

This excerpt shows the problem produced by the absence of recognition after an announcement giving spatial information on the basis of which an action is expected from the mechanic. The next expected and projected action is the recognition of the place; an alternative next action is a request for confirmation or clarification. The latter retrospectively manifests the problematic character of the description for its recipient: the landmarks given are repeated and anaphorically referred to but never autonomously reformulated, displaying that they do not fit with his local geography and are thus irrelevant to it; prospectively, this suspends the progressivity of the ongoing activity.

Dealing with reality disjunctures (*je ne connais pas*)

Denials of knowledge from the car mechanic use not only *je ne sais pas* but also another knowledge verb, *je ne connais pas*. The first occurrences of this verb are in the opening:

(9) (cf. Extract 5, lines 34–37)
34 MEC: *ouais mai::s la place du général de gaulle,*
          yeah bu::t the square of general de gaulle,

35   *j'sais   pas   où   elle est moi.*
          I know NEG where it   is me.
          yeah but:: I don't know where the square general de gaulle is

36   (0.7)

37 MEC: *je connais pa:s   la:::   cette ville   là,*
          I know   NEG the::: that town there,
          I don't know the::: that town there,

In lines 34–35, the mechanic repeats, in a dislocated way, the referential expression used by the call-taker and then adds *j'sais pas*: in this way he exhibits resistance to the terms she used. Moreover, the redoing of the subject of the verb (*moi*) is right dislocated, highlighting his agency. In line 37, after a pause, the mechanic states his absence of knowledge with another verb, *je connais pa:s*, followed by the verb's argument which concerns another, more general, spatial entity, the "town" – first introduced hesitantly by a definite article (*la:::*) and then self-repaired into a deictic form (*cette ville là*), referring to the town as it has been referred to in the previous talk.

On the one hand, with *j'sais pas* the speaker points to the problematicity of the terms of the announcement, although continuing to engage actively in the activity; in merely repeating the referential expression used by the call-taker, left-dislocated and thus positioned in an initial and syntactically autonomous position, he rejects the relevance of the spatial description provided by Jordi and the call-taker, refusing to align or affiliate with the terms of the previous action. Similar resistance has been identified by Lynch and Bogen (1996) relative to the use of *I don't remember* in a trial as a resource for refusing to align with the terms of the question, and by Metzger and Beach (1996) relative to the use of *I don't know* as a method for preserving alternative discrepant versions of past events by witnesses and lawyers. Moreover, verbatim repetition of the question before answering has been described by Bolden (2009) as treating the question as problematic by contesting and resisting its agenda and presuppositions.

On the other hand, with *je connais pa:s* the mechanic displays that he has no idea about the spatial entity being referred to: the stretched hesitating article, repaired with a demonstrative, points to an entity which is unknown and which has been discursively introduced: the participant not only resists the *terms* of the description, but also the *object* of the description itself. If the former is a threat to progressivity, the latter is clearly a closing implicative, since by stating *je connais pa:s* the mechanic closes the sequence and refuses to engage further in the activity and to collaborate.

The verb *je ne connais pas* occurs in two other contexts, which explicitly address the issue of the name of the village. The village is referred to in two different ways, with the simple name *Cadillac* and the compound name, *Cadillac-en-Fronsadais*. Although during nearly the entire call the participants try to maintain the identity between these two places, this is one of the points at which the reality disjuncture is most difficult to preserve. More particularly, the mechanic exhibits non-recognition and even ignorance of *Cadillac-en-Fronsadais* as a village, first displaying it in the next turn, as in Extract 10, and then expressing it with *je ne connais pas*, as in Extracts 11–12:

(10) (first occurrence of the compound name)
1   C-T: *et, le village c'est cadillac. c'est ça?*
             and, the village is cadillac. isn't it?

2   (0.4)

3   MEC: *ca[dillac*

4   JOR: [*oui,*
             [yes,

5   (0.5)

6   JOR: *cadigliac, (0.4) en, (0.2) fra:n- (0.4) fran:sa::fran, (1.8)*

7   F: *frei[nsavail,*

8   MEC: [°°*qu'est-ce qu'il a-*°°
             [°°what does he-°°

9   (0.6)

10 MEC: °*qu'est-ce qu'il a dit?*°
             °what does he say?°

(11)

1   MEC: *mais il n'y en a- mais il est pa:s il n'est-*
             but there aren't- but he's no:t he's n-

2   *il n'est pas à cadillac là.*
      he's not in cadillac there.

3   (2.0)

4 C-T: *ba::h apparemment c'est cadillac de fransaté:euh::*
      PRT apparently it's cadillac en fransaté:eh::

5 MEC: *mais il   ne:-   moi je connais pas:,*
      but   he NEG me I   know   NEG

6   *je connais pas ce   ce   nom là*
      I   know   NEG that that name there
      but there is no- I don't know, I don't know that that name

7 F: *donc c'est pas le- c'est pas la: la bonne ville en fait.*
      so it's not the- it's not the: the right town actually.

(12)

1 C-T: *cadillac en fronsadais, c'est pas ça, c'est pas votre: euh:::*
      cadillac en fronsadais, that's not that, that's not your ehm:::

2   (0.8)

3 C-T: *c'est pas près de v- d' où   vou- d' où   vous êtes monsieur?*
      it is not near to y- to where you- to where you are sir?
      it's not near where y- where you- where you are sir?

4   (0.7)

5 MEC: *ah non, > je connais pas ce nom là.<*
      oh no,   > I don't know that name there.<

6   (0.2)

7 MEC: *comme- comment vous m'aviez dit,   france?*
      ho-   how   you me had   said, france?
      ho-how did you tell me, france?

In Extract 10, the call-taker checks the name of the village. The mechanic responds first, with the simple name (line 3); Jordi responds in overlap (line 4) with a positive *oui* but then adds (lines 6–7) a repair, transforming the toponym into a compound name. The pronunciation of the name is difficult and the mechanic exhibits no recognition of it, asking the call-taker to "translate" what Jordi says.

In Extract 11, the mechanic denies that Jordi is in *Cadillac* (line 1); after a silence, the call-taker neither agrees nor disagrees, but specifies that he is in *Cadillac-en-Fronsadais*. Again, in a *mais*-prefaced turn, the mechanic produces a self-repaired negative fragment (*il ne:-*) a first negative verb without argument (*moi je connais pas:*), and a second negative verb with the argument *ce nom là* (line 6). The closing implicative relevance of this statement is explicitly expressed by the call-taker in the following turn (line 7).

In Extracts 11 and 12, the negative verb with the argument *ce nom là* is produced in response to a negative question projecting non-recognition of the place (see the section on contrasting epistemic positions below for more details). Moreover, in Extract 12, it is followed by a display of non-recognition, in a request for confirmation in which the place name is misspelled and truncated.

Je ne connais pas asserts the mechanic's non-recognition of the *name* more than of the *place*; attributes the problem to a discursive realm (more than to reality); and associates it with (and even attributes it to) Jordi's opaque pronunciation, reading or spelling of the name. In this way, Jordi's version of the facts is dismissed. In these turns, the mechanic seems to focus more on the attributions of blame and on the accountability for his failure – that is, on the moral issues of who is to blame and who is responsible for the "wrong" place formulation – than on the pursuit and progressivity of the action of finding the location.

In this first half of the call, the mechanic's recognition of place descriptions is expected by the call-taker and by Jordi and systematically disclaimed by using the verbs *je ne sais pas* and *je ne connais pas*. On the one hand, *je ne sais pas* refers to the location with a spatial completive clause (*je ne sais pas où CMP*) or with a repeat of the previous referential expressions used by the call-taker and Jordi – without any other characterization of the substantial features of this place, since the mechanic never adds a characterization of the place which would be his own. On the other hand, *je ne connais pas* mostly refers to the name of the place, more than to the place itself. The first verb resists the terms of the description; the second denies the very existence of the place. Whereas the former does not question the existence of the place but questions the terms of its description, opposing other descriptions and alternative search procedures, the latter questions the very existence for him of the place's name and reference in discourse, denying not only Jordi's competence but also his capability of making the name recognizable. Thus, *connaître* focuses even more strongly than *savoir* on the moral issues related to the epistemics: in this sequential environment, *je ne connais pas* refuses not only to align with the terms in which the location has been formulated but also to collaborate with a search that is based on these terms, as shown by its closing implicative feature. With *je ne connais pas*, the reality disjuncture is maximal and cannot be resolved, since the very existence of the place is questioned.

Evolving epistemic positions

In this context of increasing problematicity in the epistemic position of the car mechanic, the epistemic position of the call-taker evolves dynamically, gradually emerging as the voice of authority and a primary source of knowledge.

Various practices and resources contribute to the achievement of the call-taker's new epistemic primacy: first, she progressively orients to the mechanic as possibly not knowing; second, she assumes a more active role, by turning to a resource in her environment, the computer. This allows her to produce more detailed and authorized contributions, expressed by a positive epistemic stance, *je vois*, concurrent with the mechanic's negative expression *je ne vois pas*. I'll discuss each of these in turn.

Realizing that the knowledgeable speaker possibly does not know: negative questions

After the opening, in which the call-taker addresses the garage mechanic as a native and an expert expected to know the local geography, she progressively displays another orientation, anticipating more and more the possibility that he does not know. Most often, this orientation is displayed in questions projecting a negative response (the first occurrence is visible in Extract 8, line 12, in the turn *non? ça vous dit rien?*[1]). They manifest her realization that he does not or cannot know, and they are confirmed by displays of non-knowing, which occur just after this particular turn format, as in the following extracts:

(13) (cf. Extract 12 above)

1 C-T: *cadillac en fronsadais, c'est pas ça, c'est pas votre: euh:::*
          cadillac en fronsadais, that's not that, that's not your ehm:::

2   (0.8)

3 C-T: *c'est pas près de v- d'où vou- d'où vous êtes monsieur?*
          it's not near where y- where you- where you are sir?

4   (0.7)

5 MEC: *ah non, >je connais pas ce nom là.<*
          oh no, >I don't know that name there.<

(14) (cf. Extract 17 below, lines 9–15)

1 C-T: *c'est pas du tout le ca- c'est pas près de chez vous?*
          it's not at all the ca- it's not near your place?

2   (0.7)

3 MEC: *mai:s c'est dans le   trente <u>trois</u> hein cadillac,=*
          but: it's   in   the hirty <u>three</u> PRT cadillac,=
          but: cadillac is in the ((department number)) thirty <u>three</u> right=

4 C-T: =*ou<u>i</u>, (.) [oui oui,]*
          =y<u>es</u>, (.) [yes yes,

---

[1] In French, interrogatives can be realized either in a syntactically marked form, with *est-ce que* or with a verb–pronoun inversion, or in a prosodically marked form, as here.

5 MEC: [*mais::*]::[: (   )]
                     [but::]:: [: (   )]

6 C-T: [*et ici c'est marqu*]é,
                     [and here it's written,

7 MEC: *mai::s là je- je vois pas où i sont.*
        but there I- I don't see where they are.

In these two extracts, the questions are asked using a negative format and are responded to with denials of knowledge. Interestingly in both cases the place formulation is the product of multiple tries, transforming the initial formulation: in the first case (Extract 13) four subsequent versions are tried and suspended: *c'est pas ça* ("that's not that" line 1), *c'est pas votre: euh:::* ("that's not your ehm:::" line 1), *c'est pas près de v-* ("it's not near y-" line 3), *d'où vous êtes* ("where you are" line 4). The first is syntactically complete, but is transformed into another one, introducing a reference to the second person (*votre:*). Although incomplete, this form projects a noun which is strongly recipient-oriented and expected to be recognizable, referring to a recipient's "possessable." But the mechanic does not respond, and after a long pause (line 2), the call-taker reformulates the personal reference, explicitly referring to a place which is supposed to be "close" to the mechanic's place (not only a place which belongs to the mechanic but also a place to which the mechanic belongs – cf. Schegloff [1972]). The series of formulations both orients to the non-response and to the contrast between the place formulations referring to *vous* and the denial of knowledge, as well as the denial of responsibility. In the second case (Extract 14), the call-taker again changes the initial generic third person reference (*c'est pas du tout le ca-* line 1) into a second person reference (*c'est pas près de chez vous?* line 1). After an insertion sequence (lines 3–4) which delays the answer, the mechanic again expresses his lack of knowledge (lines 5, 7).

These formulations manifest a change in the orientation of the call-taker toward the mechanic: the latter is more and more considered as "possibly not-knowing" and thus as not "owning" the case; the consequence is that the call-taker re-orients to herself as responsible for it.

Alternative sources of knowledge: turning to the computer

In the middle of the call, the call-taker not only redefines the mechanic's epistemic position, she also actively undertakes other actions that can provide alternative sources of knowledge and, ultimately, a solution to the puzzle. These actions imply a change in her activity and her body position within her workspace: whereas at the beginning of the call she is mainly bodily oriented toward the phone, and exclusively engaged in talk, when the first contradictions emerge she turns to her computer and engages in multi-tasking.

The first time she turns to her computer is tightly coordinated with the emerging strong denial of knowledge by the mechanic – in order to make observable the coordination between talk and computer-related actions, the following transcript integrates details of what appears on the computer screen ("scr" in the transcript):

(15) (cf. Extract 7)

```
 1   C-T:   voilà: e- à peu près à vingt kilomètres de bordeaux i me dit,
             there it is: eh- about 20 km from Bordeaux he tells me,
 2          (1.5)
 3   MEC:   alors là::   je sais   pas. j'sais   pas où   i      sont* hein. là
             PRT DEICT::  I  Know  NEG. I know NEG where they   are    PRT DEICT
             at this point I don't know. I don't know where they are. over there
     c-t                                     >>was leaning on the phone* sits up–>
 4          je suis in*capable de:
             I am unable to:
     c-t            -->*scratches head–>
 5          (0.5)
 6   MEC:   e[*h:::* mais ils sont-] mais ils sont à cadillac même? (.)*
             e[h:::    but  they are-] but they are in cadillac itself? (.)
     c-t    –>*,,,, *looks at and manipulates her papers--------------*
 7   JOR:   [(                      )]
 8   MEC:   *dans* dans la ville?
             in in town?
     c-t    *...  *hand toward keyboard–>
 9          (0.2) * (0.6)
     c-t         –>*goes with her mouse on Internet Explorer–>
10   C-T:   OUI, i me dit qu'il e:st en plei::n dans
             YES, he tells me that he's in the middle of
11          la place en *fait.
             the square actually.
                          –>*selects the page www.mappy.com/BtoB/mappy/v2/–>
12          (0.9)*
     c-t         –>*
13   MEC:   oui mai:s quelle place?
             yes bu:t which square?
14          (.) y a       *y a      [y    en   a:  y    en    a]
             (.) there's   there's [there PRO is: there PRO is]
             (.) there're  they're there are some there are some
     scr                  *the mappy web page appears–>
15   C-T:                 [°e  :  :  :  :  :  :  :  :  :]
```

```
16          dix, (.)  de*  places
            ten, (.)  of   squares
            (there are) ten squares
     scr             -> *
17 C-T:     la pla*ce:: charles de gaul*le,
            the square:: charles de gaulle,
                    *turns slightly towards phone*
18          *(0.5)
     c-t     *writes www.mappy.com/--->
```

A significant change of bodily posture is observable, while the mechanic repeatedly claims that he doesn't know (line 3). At the end of the second formulation, the call-taker, who was turned to the phone until then, sits up (line 3) and begins to scratch her head (line 4). After this negative formulation, the mechanic adds a question (line 6), which is expanded (line 8): during this time, the call-taker inspects her desk covered with diverse documents and manipulates them (line 6); then she turns her hand and her body toward the computer.

Her embodied conduct is sensitive to the sequentiality of talk: she scratches her head when the mechanic denies knowing and she begins to actively explore her work environment in a sequential position in which the question "what's next?" (Schegloff and Sacks 1973) is particularly relevant – in the absence of any indication that the mechanic will be able to help. This exploration ends by focusing on one among the available tools, the computer. From that moment on (line 9), the call-taker engages in a parallel activity, consisting of activating the program Internet Explorer (line 9), in selecting a website which provides maps and itineraries (www.mappy.com), and finally in typing the search for a location. Thus, here the call-taker engages in multiple simultaneous activities (Mondada 2008), talking on the phone and searching the internet: both are strongly coordinated, the latter being sensitive to the emergent and dynamic sequential unfolding of the former.

This extract shows two peculiar aspects of knowledge in interaction: first, knowledge in interaction is emergent and dynamic, being achieved by the participants' actions and thus locally defined by them in an occasioned way; second, knowledge in interaction is variably distributed not only among the participants, but also within the material environment, as it is both shaping action and shaped by the action – as the call-taker's embodied searches show.

More particularly, her initiation of internet searches is highly sensitive to the reality disjunctures and the negative epistemic claims being expressed in the phone interaction; internet activities are both autonomous from the call and very precisely coordinated with it (cf. Mondada

2008). The results of these searches allow the call-taker to produce a new geographical description of Jordi's location, and eventually to solve the puzzle.

Call-taker announces results: *je vois*

Not only the initiation of internet searches, but also the public announcement of their result is timely coordinated with the ongoing call, and is oriented to its specific sequential unfolding.

The announcement of the first result occurs just after another disclaimer of knowledge by the mechanic. The call-taker progressively adopts a new and contrasting epistemic stance within which she actively provides the knowledge the car mechanic is unable to produce:

```
(16)
1 MEC:  ah ah ah ah ah ah ah  alors  là        je- je sais  pas    où
        ((vocalizations))     PRT DEICT I-  I   know  NEG  where
        ah ah ah ah ah ah ah so there I- I don't know where
2       c'est  là    h[ein?
        it is DEICT [PRT?
        it's that place right?
3 C-T:                [a- attendez je v- je vois ici
                      [w- wait I s- I see here
4       sur euh::::: sur le logiciel, y a:      [(.) cadillac en frRONSADAIS
        on ehm::::: on the screen, there is: [(.) cadillac en frONSADAIS
```

As the mechanic states that he does not know (lines 1–2), the call-taker reads what she sees on her screen (lines 3–4); she indicates the source of her knowledge, using the perception verb *je vois* and the deictic *ici* (line 3), which is made explicit by the reference to the computer screen (line 4). This reference to the computer allows her to produce a substantial contribution – here the toponym, which is pronounced without any hesitation and by highlighting the compound form (contrasting with the very hesitant first pronunciations of it – not shown here).

So, as the call goes on, the source on which the call-taker relies changes: she relies first only on Jordi's place formulations, which are translated as they are produced and later recycled in the conversation; she then increasingly relies on another source of knowledge, her computer and the internet website Mappy. Her contribution to the interaction changes, as well as her membership category: at the beginning she merely translates Jordi's information, addressing it to the mechanic who is treated as in charge of resolving the case; in the second part of the call, she actively produces the relevant information, taking responsibility for the case.

Contrasting epistemic positions (*je ne vois pas* vs. *je vois*)

The announcements of the outcomes of the call-taker's searches are expressed in turns which refer to the source of her knowledge – mentioning the internet – and which formulate her activity, making it public – using the verb *je vois*, "I see". This verb is used literally, referring to what she sees on the screen. Interestingly, in this new context, in which the call-taker is emerging as the competent provider of spatial information, the car mechanic expresses his own epistemic stance by using the same verb, in a negative form, and in a more abstract sense (*je ne vois pas*, "I don't grasp (it)").

Voir in the literature has been dealt with not only as a perception verb but also as an epistemic verb. Franckel and Lebaud (1990: 59–62) describe its semantic features as characterized by the "localization" of the referent, addressing its "visibility" for the speaker. Whereas *je ne connais pas* negates the referent from the perspective of the speaker, *je ne vois pas* questions not its existence but its (visual) intelligibility. Moreover, *voir* is an inchoative verb, related to the fact that the visibility of its referent can be progressive for the speaker, in the process of its discovery, unveiling and apparition – reminiscent of the "internal time" of Vendler's classification (in which *to see* is an achievement type of verb [1967]). From a pragmatic perspective, Lambrecht (1994) refers to *voir* as a device for introducing new topics within the discourse, grounded in perception, even when it is used in a metaphorical way.

These descriptions of the verb's semantics are based on aspectual properties of the referred-to events or cognitive processes; they ignore the sequential environments and the actual practices in which these verbs can be selected by the speakers.

In our data, the distribution of *je ne vois pas* occurs in a different context from *je ne sais pas* or *je ne connais pas*: it is used after a change in the epistemic positions of the participants has occurred, one participant not claiming to be or not being recognized as knowledgeable any more and the other assuming a knowledgeable position. In this new context, *je ne vois pas* is used by the mechanic after spatial information has been given by the call-taker, in a turn which is voiced and assumed by her and which delivers substantial details. This contrasts with the first spatial formulations, which were more general and fragmented and which were voiced by Jordi. While Jordi's localizations were resisted and dismissed, the call-taker's descriptions are respected but still not recognized. The negative epistemic verb *je vois pas* is used by the mechanic when he is confronted with a *competent* version of the location – whereas he was treating Jordi's as incompetent. This competent version is introduced with the verb *je vois* in a perceptive sense and the mechanic's selection of the same form as an epistemic verb displays his orientation toward the contrast and the inversion of epistemic positions. Thus, the selection of the verbs is situated and sensitive to their relative epistemic stances as they are redistributed in the sequential organization of the talk.

Here are two occurrences of both the affirmative and the negative forms of *voir*, both characterized by the fact that they close a sequence initiated by a very general question asked by the mechanic, to which the call-taker provides very specific answers:

(17)
```
1  MEC:  et (.) et c'est quoi ça? °au juste°. c'est le nom du:: (0.2)
         and (.) and what's that? °actually°. is that the name of:: (0.2)

2        c'est le- c'est le nom de quoi ça. de la vi:lle::? d'une:=
         it's the- it's the name of what this thing. of the to:wn? of a:=

3  C-T:  = oui, c'est le nom du village où mon client se trouve, il es:t
         = yes, it's the name of the village where my client is, it's:

4        c'est le département- c'est tren- le code postal
         that's the department- that's thirt- the postal code

5        c'est trente trois deux cent quarante.
         is thirty three two hundred and forty.

6        (1.8)

7  MEC:  °ah ouais, mais je voi- je vois pas,°
         °oh yeah, but  I  s-   I  see  NEG
         °oh yeah, but I (don't) s- I don't see,°

8        (0.7)

9  C-T:  c'est pas du tout le ca- c'est pas près de chez vous?
         it's not at all the ca- it's not near your place?

10       (0.7)

11 MEC:  mai:s c'est dans le trente trois hein cadillac,=
         but it's in the thirty-three PRT cadillac,=

12 C-T:  = oui, (.) [oui oui, ]
         = yes, (.) [yes yes  ]

13 F:              [mais : : ]::   [: (              )]
                   [but : :  ]::   [: (              )]

14 C-T:                            [et ici c'est marqu]é,
                                   [and here it's written

15 F:    mai::s là je- je vois pas où i sont.
         but there I- I don't see where they are.
```

(18)
```
1  MEC:  oui mais c'est- c'est quoi ça au juste c'est un restauran:t?
         yes but it's- what's this actually it is a restaurant?
```

```
 2  F:      c'[est uneuh villeuh? c'est quoi?]
            it [is a: town:? what's that?    ]
 3  C-T:      [non non non, ça          ] c'est la ville,
              [no no no, that           ] it's the town,
 4          (0.5)
 5  C-T:   ça c'est le nom de la ville
           that is the name of the town
 6  MEC:   ah: mais là là: là je là je vois pas.
           oh: but there there: there I there I don't see.
 7          (1.0)
 8  MEC:   al*ors là je vois pas du tout hein,*
           well now I don't see at all do I,
     c-t        *scrolls page and centers again on the itinerary*
 9  MEC:   j [e vois] pas du tout he[in,
           I   don't see at all do I,
10  C-T:      [je v-  ]              [ici je vois, c'e:st à trente
              [I s-   ]              [here I see, it's: thirty
11         kilomètres de bordeaux, exactement.
           kilometers from bordeaux, exactly.
```

Extracts 17 and 18 begin with very vague questions initiated by the car mechanic: in the former, the object is very fuzzy (c'est quoi ça? line 1, where the pronoun ça has both a wide and vague reference), and in the latter the question deals with a topic that has already been clearly established. In second position, an answer is given by the call-taker, no longer translating Jordi's position but directly voicing her own visual experience, offering various evidences (Extract 17, lines 3–5; Extract 18, lines 3–5). In third position, the mechanic produces a negative epistemic expression, using the verb je ne vois pas either without an argument (Extract 17, line 7; Extract 18, line 6) or with a locative (où i sont Extract 17, line 15), possibly intensified (pas du tout Extract 18, line 8) and repeated, prefaced as dispreferred (ah ouais, mais Extract 17, line 7; mai::s là line 15; ah: mais là là: là Extract 18, line 6; alors là, line 8).

The resolution of the case

The verb voir is also used to announce the final result, bringing the call to a close:

```
(19)
1          (0.6)
2   C-T:   .h mire, no. yo estoy viendo aqui- monsieur, je pense
           .h look, no. I see here- sir, I think
3          qu' [on va lai- on va laisser tomber en tout cas bah:
           we' [ll giv- we'll give up in any case well:
```

```
 4  MEC:    [°oui°
            [°yes°
 5  C-T:    je: on va vous payer le déplacement bien sûr,
            I: we'll pay you for the trip of course,
 6  JOR:    [°(                                          ] )°
 7  MEC:    [oui mais ils sont où, ils sont où là.       ]
            [yes but where are they, where are they there. ]
 8  C-T:    eh- je vois ici, ils v- ils sont à soixante kilomètres
            eh- I see here, they v- they are 60 km
 9          de cadillac en fait h.
            from cadillac actually h.
10          (0.4)
11  MEC:    ils sont à comBIEN?
            are they at how many (kilometers)?
12  C-T:    soixante kilomètres, d'après le logiciel.
            sixty kilometers, as indicated by the software.
13          (0.4)
14  MEC:    <AH:::::, (0.7) > voilà.
            <OH:::::, (0.7)> here it is.

            ((eleven lines omitted, about the difference between the toponyms))

26  C-T:    c'est pour ça que vous connaissiez pas. hhh
            that's why you didn't know. hhh
27  MEC:    d'accord non je connaissais pas le: le nom là
            okay no I didn't know the: the name there
28  C-T:    en tout cas merci beaucou:p,  [et: bah::  (.) et
            in any case thanks a lot,     [and: PRT (.) and
29  MEC:                                  [bah de rien
                                          [PRT no problem
```

The last announcement of the result of the call-taker's internet search gives the solution to the geographical puzzle: looking at her screen she first announces in Spanish that she sees something (line 2), promptly switching into French before completing the announcement which she addresses to the car mechanic (lines 2–3), not revealing what she found but anticipating its consequences – inviting him to abandon his mission (line 3) but assuring him of his salary (line 5). The suspended announcement is pursued by the mechanic's question (line 7): the call-taker's answer begins again with the verb *je vois*, locates the source of knowledge with the deictic *ici* and then delivers the news that Jordi and the mechanic are 60 kilometers apart, in two different villages (lines 8–9). A request for clarification is produced by the garage mechanic with a surprised voice (line 11) and the news is delivered again by making the source of authoritative knowledge explicit (line 12). This news is receipted with a change-of-state token (Heritage 1984a) by the mechanic (line 14).

A few seconds later, the call-taker produces an account, making acceptable his reasons for not knowing (line 26), re-establishing social affiliation at the end of the case. He confirms again his absence of knowledge of the village – again referring to the name and not the named object, maintaining his refusal to collaborate on that village. After this account, the call is brought to a close.

Conclusion: reversing knowledge asymmetries

This chapter has focused on various practices for dealing with a reality disjuncture and on different ways of expressing a negative epistemic stance in talk-in-interaction. The analysis has described a range of lexical resources used (*je ne connais pas, je ne sais pas, je ne vois pas*), their sequential environment – after a question or an announcement concerning a spatial location projecting a positive response – and their distribution within a call.

As the call unfolds, a series of transformations of the epistemic postures is achieved by the participants. At the beginning, the source of location information is Jordi, and the call-taker acts mainly as a translator, making his information available for the mechanic, recognized as being in charge of the case. Toward the end of the call, Jordi's contributions are fewer and when he speaks he is not listened to. The call-taker asserts an independent epistemic stance and action, assuming responsibility for the case. Moreover, whereas in the first part of the call the call-taker deals with the mechanic as owning the relevant geographical knowledge, in the second half of the call she gradually displays that she considers him to be less and less knowledgeable. The mechanic too changes his way of contributing to the resolution of the case: whereas at the beginning his disclaimers of knowledge are immediately followed by an alternative action he initiates, asking precise location questions and actively attempting to find other ways of solving the problem, in the second part of the call, he initiates fewer sequences and does not contribute relevantly to the search. More precisely, at the beginning, he responds to Jordi's spatial descriptions with disclaimers of knowledge expressed either by *je ne connais pas* or *je ne sais pas*. In the second part of the call, he is confronted with the call-taker's information, responding with *je ne vois pas*.

A consistent distribution of the epistemic verbs is observable. They are all used in second position in response to a first turn either asserting spatial information or asking a question about a location. *Je ne connais pas* is followed by a NP which is very tentatively expressed, with a lot of hesitations, referring to an obscure toponym; *je ne sais pas* is followed by either a repeated locative clause or a clause referring anaphorically to a previous description. The former refuses to engage with the object of the description, the latter resists the terms of the description, treating them as inadequate; the former refuses to collaborate to a request treating it as illegitimate, whereas the latter displays the incapacity of collaborating given the terms of the previous action, and recognizes a false attribution of knowledge.

In the second part of the call, *je ne vois pas* admits not recognizing the terms of the previous description, which is expressed by a stance claiming *je vois*: the former admits a contrast with an alternative authoritative version expressed by the latter. Whereas *je ne vois pas* is most frequently free standing, *je vois* introduces detailed and substantial information. Both features achieve the epistemic position of the car mechanic as useless.

These changes show that states of knowledge and epistemic positions are not immutable but are dynamically achieved over time by participants.

Claiming not to know is a practice that addresses both epistemic and moral issues. Saying *I don't know* is a way by which a participant who is expected to know both disclaims his knowledge and refuses the terms of what he should know, thus not only disaligning with the previous speaker and his version of the world, but more radically casting suspicion on his knowledge and legitimacy. This epistemic and moral stance blocks the progressivity of talk and action.

One of the consequences of this position – an uncollaborative stance of somebody supposed to bring help and to collaborate with the help dispatcher – is that the other participants revise their knowledge assumptions and knowledge attributions and change their own epistemic positions by using alternative sources of knowledge. The study of the entire call permits us to document the call-taker's change of posture, becoming more and more actively in charge of the search for the location and progressively acquiring the relevant spatial knowledge.

Thus, this chapter shows the outcome of a detailed analysis of a unique telephone call combining single case analysis and analysis of collections. The numerous occurrences of epistemic verbs within the call permit a systematic analysis of their sequential positioning and of the composition of the turns in which they occur; the analysis of their distribution and attribution within the entire call permits a longitudinal study of change as the action unfolds. Knowledge does not have a fixed and immutable status but is a dynamic process which both is negotiated within the interaction and changes over time. Analysis of *je ne sais pas*, *je ne connais pas*, *je ne vois pas* across the telephone call documents the change in the distribution of knowledge within the participation framework of the call. While one participant, initially considered an expert, is recategorized as unknowing, another participant, initially considered unknowing, actively changes her position – from merely translating to actively questioning and finally mobilizing other sources of knowledge, eventually solving the case.

Thus, a detailed analysis of a single telephone call can cast some light on the interactional use of epistemic verbs, on the adoption, negotiation and management of epistemic and moral issues in a context of discrepant knowledge, and on the epistemic changes undergone by participants over time.

Additional transcript conventions

Multimodal details have been transcribed according to the following conventions (see Mondada 2007 for discussion):

* *	delimit descriptions of one speaker's gestures and actions
+ +	delimit descriptions of another speaker's gestures and actions
*--->	gesture or action described continues across subsequent lines
*--->>	gesture or action described continues until and after excerpt's end
---->*	gesture or action described continues until the same symbol is reached
>>--	gesture or action described begins before the excerpt's beginning
....	gesture's preparation
----	gesture's apex is reached and maintained
,,,,,	gesture's retraction
c-t	participant making gesture is identified in small characters when s/he is not the speaker or when the gesture is made during a pause
scr	description of what appears on the computer screen

3   Claiming epistemic primacy: *yo*-marked assessments in Japanese

Kaoru Hayano

Introduction

In everyday conversation, when a speaker adopts an evaluative stance toward a referent that is accessible to his/her recipient (a first assessment), this invites the recipient to convey his/her evaluative stance about the same referent in the next turn (a second assessment). Second assessments can be formulated as agreements or disagreements in multiple ways, and their design manifests a systematic preference for agreements over disagreements in interaction (Pomerantz 1984a).[1] For instance, Pomerantz (1984a) observes that for English conversation a speaker who is agreeing with a prior assessment often proffers an upgraded evaluation (e.g., "It's just gorgeous," to agree with "It's a beautiful day") while a disagreement tends to be prefaced with a same-degree, or formulated via a downgraded, evaluation. This bias toward agreement can be seen as a way in which speakers orient to the maintenance and maximization of social solidarity in interaction (Heritage 1984b: 265).

However, agreement or disagreement on evaluative stances is not the only issue that matters when interactants assess a referent in conversation. Interactants also display their concern with their and their interlocutor's epistemic stances vis-à-vis the referent (Goodwin and Goodwin 1987; Hayano 2007a, b; Heritage 2002a; Heritage and Raymond 2005; Kanai 2004; Morita 2005; Raymond and Heritage 2006; Schegloff 1996a; Sorjonen 2001). When speakers produce a first assessment, they adopt not only an evaluative stance but also an epistemic stance. Employing

I would like to thank all the contributors to this volume for the inspiring input that I received in the course of the development of this work. I am especially indebted to John Heritage, Lorenza Mondada, Tanya Stivers and Leelo Keevallik for their invaluable comments. I am also grateful to Paul Drew and Harrie Mazeland for their comments on early versions of the chapter and to members of the Language and Cognition group at the Max Planck Institute for Psychology (Nijmegen) for sharing their insights.
[1] There are exceptions to this principle. For instance, when a first assessment is self-deprecating, disagreement is preferred to agreement (Pomerantz 1984a).

linguistic resources, they embody how they see information or knowledge to be distributed between them and the recipients. In the following turn, the recipients of the first assessment, in addition to an evaluative stance that agrees or disagrees with the first speaker's, takes an epistemic stance, which is either compatible or incompatible with the first speaker's. This chapter investigates how interactants' orientations to epistemic stances are manifested in assessment sequences in Japanese conversation. In particular, I demonstrate that the intensity of evaluation is not only indicative of its status as an agreement or a disagreement, but is also strongly contingent on the speaker's epistemic stance. In order to make clear the distinction between these two dimensions, I refer to the (in)compatibility of interactants' epistemic stances as "(in)congruence" and the (in)compatibility of their evaluative stances as "(dis)agreement."

The focus of my analysis is on the use of a Japanese final particle *yo* in assessment sequences, which I argue claims "epistemic primacy" (Raymond and Heritage 2006). In some sequential and interactional contexts, to claim epistemic primacy with *yo* is appropriate and congruent with the interlocutor's epistemic stance. However, *yo* is also used when a claim of epistemic primacy is not evidently appropriate or the interlocutor is claiming to have equivalent knowledge, in which case s/he has to provide some support for the claim of epistemic primacy. Through a detailed analysis of such cases, I demonstrate that a speaker of a *yo*-marked assessment recurrently manipulates the intensity of the evaluation in order to provide support or a basis for the claim of epistemic primacy.

The data used for this chapter consist of fourteen hours of face-to-face conversations and fifteen hours of telephone conversations between native speakers of Japanese. All the face-to-face conversations are video-recorded, except for Extract 11, which comes from an audio-recorded conversation. The telephone conversations are drawn from the CallFriend corpus of the TalkBank database. Excerpts from CallFriend are re-transcribed by the author. Names of the speakers may be changed from the original transcript distributed by TalkBank. For a detailed description of TalkBank, see MacWhinney (2007).

Japanese particle *yo*

The final particle *yo* is often studied in contrast with the particles *ne* and *yone*, which occupy the same syntactic slot as *yo* and are often argued to have complementary functions to it. They are used frequently in informal conversations but not in formal speech or written text. *Yo* and *yone* generally occur at the end of a sentential turn constructional unit (TCU)

(Sacks *et al.* 1974), after the predicate of the sentence.[2] On the other hand, *ne* occurs in various syntactic positions and even as an independent response token (Tanaka 2000). None of these particles is attached to interjection responses.[3]

Many researchers treat these particles as markers of the speaker's stance regarding the state of knowledge or information (Kamio 1990; Kanai 2004; Katagiri 2007; Katoh 2001; Kinsui 1993; Koyama 1997; Morita 2002). *Yo* is described as a marker of information that is not shared by a recipient (Cheng 1987; Katoh 2001; Koyama 1997), or as an epistemic marker of "authority on the part of the speaker that is not open to negotiation on the part of the hearer" (Morita 2002: 227), while *ne* is often described as marking shared information (Kamio 1990; Katoh 2001).

As will be shown in the following sections, *yo* is typically used when the speaker knows the referent better, has first-hand experience with it or has prior knowledge of it, while the addressee does not have any access to the referent or has only second-hand experience, or knowledge that is based on the ongoing here-and-now occasion. Based on this, and along the line of previous studies, especially Morita (2002) and Katoh (2001), I argue that the particle *yo* is used to claim "epistemic primacy" (Raymond and Heritage 2006): a speaker claims to be in a "one-up" position on the addressee in terms of knowledge about or epistemic access to the referent. It should be emphasized that it is the *relative* epistemic stance between interactants that is the issue here; a *yo*-marked utterance may be hedged or epistemically downgraded, as long as the speaker is ready to claim to know better than his/her interlocutor.[4]

Some researchers criticize a characterization of the particles based on the distribution of information with counter examples (e.g., Kinsui 1993). Such criticisms are valid only under the assumption that the use of particles is rule-governed and should be predictable based on an objectively discernible distribution of knowledge or information. However, the

[2] *Yo* can occur at the end of a phrasal TCU within a sentential TCU (see Lee [2007] for an example). However, the use of *yo* in this environment sounds coarse and has sociolinguistic constraints. In fact, my data do not have any instance of *yo* in the intra-sentential position.

[3] The exception is *hai yo*. *Hai* is an affirmative interjection response and *hai yo* can be used to offer something, roughly corresponding to 'Here you go' in English, to respond to a summons or a request. However, its use has sociolinguistic peculiarity and does not occur in these data.

[4] The particle *yo* is also used in actions in which the issue of epistemic stance plays little role, such as requests or suggestions. Investigating the function of *yo* in such contexts is a topic for another study.

distribution of information is often equivocal or negotiable. The particles are used reflexively to index a certain epistemic state (Kanai 2004; Katoh 2001: 43; Morita 2002, 2005: 121).

Particles *ne* and *yone* are often used reciprocally in an assessment sequence, as will be exemplified later in Extracts 2 and 3 (Morita 2005).[5] Through the reciprocal use of *ne* or *yone*, interactants establish that they share equivalent access to the referent. On the other hand, in order to claim and establish epistemic primacy, the speaker must have a reasonable basis for the claim. Indeed, a speaker of a *yo*-marked assessment often formulates the turn so that it includes some support for the claim of epistemic primacy. For instance, Morita (2005) illustrates two resources that a *yo*-marked assessment speaker employs to give support to his claim of epistemic primacy. In her example, which is shown below as (1), S(higeo) and his sister T(aeko) are talking about Shigeo's three-year-old grandchild. After Taeko has learned that the grandchild walked quite a long distance that day, she makes an assessment, remarking how well he walked (line 3). The assessment is marked with *ne*, inviting agreement (Morita 2005; Tanaka 2000). In response, Shigeo produces a *yo*-marked agreement.

(1) (Morita 2005: 130)
3 T: *yoku ano ko aruita* **ne!**
      well that boy walk_PST FP
      How <u>well</u> that boy walked **ne**!

4 S: → *aruku* **yo**. *arukasenakya.*
      walk FP walk_CAUS_must
      He <u>does</u> **yo**. We must make him walk.

As Morita (2005) argues, drawing on an observation by Goodwin and Goodwin (1987), Shigeo's use of the present tense, in contrast with Taeko's use of the past tense, suggests that it is not an unusual event to him, though it is to Taeko (see also Heritage [2002a] and Heritage [2002b] for discussions on the tense as a resource to index different types of epistemic access). That is, Shigeo is evoking his prior knowledge independent of this occasion and indexing his epistemic primacy, to which a parent

---

[5] Some researchers who study the particles *yo* and *ne* treat *yone* as a compound of *yo* and *ne,* in which each of the two particles maintains its respective semantics (e.g., Kinsui 1993; Morita 2002, 2005; Takubo and Kinsui 1997). However, I argue that *yone* has its own semantics as an independent particle that cannot simply be described as the sum of the semantics of *yo* and *ne*.

or grandparent is generally entitled (Raymond and Heritage 2006). Morita also points out that by adding *arukasenakya* ('we must make him walk'), Shigeo indexes his responsibility as a grandparent, which also contributes to differentiating his position from Taeko's.[6]

In this example, tense and the reference to the speaker's social responsibility are shown to be resources to give a basis to the speaker's epistemic primacy embodied with *yo*. In this chapter, I illustrate another resource that is recurrently employed to give a basis for a claim of epistemic primacy in *yo*-marked assessments: the intensity of the evaluation.

Evaluation intensity in interaction

A second assessment is understood as an agreement or disagreement with the first assessment that precedes it (Pomerantz 1984a). Whether a second assessment is heard as an agreement or disagreement is most fundamentally determined by the valence of the evaluation and its compatibility with the first assessment, but the intensity of the evaluation also plays a crucial role (Pomerantz 1984a). Pomerantz (1984a) observes that, in English conversation, a fully affiliating agreement is often upgraded; downgraded second assessments tend to be heard as disagreements; and same-degree evaluations are often found to preface disagreement.[7]

In contrast, in my Japanese data, agreements with same-degree evaluations are about twice as common as those with upgraded evaluations and their recipients do not treat them as insufficient or as prefaces to disagreement, as exemplified by Extracts 2 and 3.[8] Extract 2 is an exchange between a beautician (BT) and a customer (CT). Prior to line 1, they heard the

---

[6] Taeko's first assessment includes a descriptive term *yoku*, which Morita translates as 'how well' and which is missing in Shigeo's second assessment. Thus, a reader may wonder if a change in the degree of evaluation is observed in this case. However, the use of *yoku* in this case seems to contribute to making the utterance exclamatory rather than expressing the literal meaning of *yoku* ('well'). In addition, because of the difference in the constructions of Taeko's and Shigeo's assessments (i.e., Taeko's is an exclamatory utterance while Shigeo's is a declarative sentence), it does not seem to simply compare the intensity of their assessments.

[7] Mondada (2009b) reports context-specific contingencies that provide intricacy to this general pattern.

[8] "Weak" agreement that can preface disagreeing components (Pomerantz 1984a) is reported to be done through "anaphorical agreements" in Japanese interaction (Hayano 2007b). Anaphorical agreements are those agreements that include an anaphor *soo* ('that'), such as *soo da ne* ('that is (true)-*ne*'). They are argued to indicate that the view was formed subsequent to the production of the first assessment, while repetitional agreements, i.e., agreements that repeat the key descriptor used in the first assessment, claim epistemic independence. How this distinction between anaphorical and repetitional agreements interacts with the different epistemic stances marked with the final particles is beyond the scope of this chapter.

beautician's assistant sneeze loudly from the back of the beauty salon, and the beautician remarked on it in a somewhat teasing tone. The customer's assessment about the weather of the day (line 1) is hearable as a defense of the assistant.

(2)

```
1 CT:  →  kyoo    datte    sa^mui desu  mon.
          today   because  cold   CP    FP
          (Well) (it's) ^cold today.

2          (.)

3 CT:      [( )

4 BT:  ⇒  [samui desu YONE:,= kyoo  wa  ne [:,
          cold  CP   FP  :     today TP  FP
          (It's) cold yone:,=today (it) is ne:,

5 CT:                              [(so:-) [nn:,
                                           ITJ
                                   (tha:-) Yeah:,

6 BT:  →                           [kion:
                                    temperature
                                    The temperature:

7      →   hai, [hikui desu yone,
           ITJ   low   CP   FP
           Yes, (it's) low yone,

8 CT:  ⇒     [kion         wa- hikui desu yo[ne:,
              temperature  TP  low   CP   FP
              The temperature is- low yone:,

9 BT:                            [ha:i,
                                 ITJ
                                 Yeah:,
```

Here, agreements are formulated with evaluations of the same intensity as the first assessments (lines 4 and 8). Note also that all the assessments are marked with the particle *yone* (lines 4, 7, 8) except for the customer's first assessment at line 1, which is marked with the final particle *mon*, marking the turn as an excuse for the assistant's sneeze. Thus, in this sequence, the interactants are agreeing with each other without either one claiming to know better than the other, and same evaluations are not treated as insufficient or as prefacing disagreement.

Similarly in Extract 3, the second assessment proffers a same-degree evaluation, which is not followed by disagreement or treated as problematic. Here, a pottery instructor (INST) is commenting on a teapot that her student (STUD) made and receives agreement from the student.

(3)
1 INST: → *de-*   *(0.2)* *a^tsui* **ne**.
                  and   thick FP
                  And- (0.2) (it's) ^thick ne.
2 STUD: ⇒ *Atsui desu* [***ne***:.
                  thick CP   FP
                  (It's) thick **ne**:.
3 INST: [*Un*:.
                                ITJ
                                Yeah:.

Both first and second assessments are marked with *ne*, and the same evaluation (line 2) is treated as an unproblematic agreement.

As these examples show, same-degree evaluation is commonly found in a second assessment that is treated as a full agreement, and proffering an upgraded evaluation is rather marked in Japanese. Another recurrent feature of assessment sequences in Japanese exemplified here is the use of *ne* and *yone* in reciprocal first and second assessments; interactants establish congruent epistemic views that they share equivalent access through these particles.

Interestingly, however, the tendency reverses if we look at sequences with *yo*-marked agreements; a claim of epistemic primacy accompanies upgraded evaluation more often than it does same-degree evaluation. I argue that, by proffering an upgraded, stronger and more specific evaluation, which is, in principle, more accessible to the party who knows better than to the novice, the speakers are giving support to the claim of epistemic primacy that they are putting forward. In what follows, we first look at *yo*-marked first assessments, where *yo* is observably used to claim epistemic primacy. We then examine *yo*-marked second assessments.

Yo-marked first assessments

While the use of *ne* and *yone* is more common in first assessments, first assessments about referents that are presented as inaccessible to the recipient are typically marked with *yo*. For example, in Extract 4, an assessment that is part of an offer is marked with *yo*. Here, Eiko, Nami and Yumi are having a lunch break from a pottery lesson at Yumi's home. Each of them brought food for herself. Nami has told the others that she has just started to prepare a lunch box for her husband to take to work and is studying what food would be good to put in it. Eiko has pieces of salmon in her lunch box, and at lines 1–2, Eiko offers them to Nami to try as a suggestion of them as good food for a lunch box.

(4)

            [((Eiko pushes her lunch box to Nami))

1 EIKO: → [<u>ko</u>no shake   oishii **yo**. chotto tabete goran.

             this   salmon good FP a_little eat   try

             <u>Thi</u>s salmon is good **yo**. Try (it).

2   → <u>ko</u>suko no shake.

             Costco L   salmon

             (It's) salmon from <u>Co</u>stco.

             [((Nami reaches toward the lunch box))

3   [(0.2)

4 NAMI: *hn::::.*

             ITJ

             I see.

             [((Nami eats the salmon))

5   [(3.3)

6 EIKO: *nanka shio:mi mo choodoii   tte iu   ka,*

             like   saltiness also temperate QT say or

             (It's) like, the salti:ness is right (or something),

7 NAMI: ⇒ *aa:: honto da,*

             ITJ true CP

             Oh:: (you are) right,

8   (0.2)

9 NAMI: ⇒ *oihii   oihii.*

             delicious delicious

             (It's) good (it's) good.

At lines 1–2, Eiko produces three TCUs, all of which contribute to offering the salmon as something that Nami has not had and should try and to getting Nami to accept the offer. In the first TCU, she informs Nami with a positive assessment marked with *yo* (*<u>ko</u>no shake oishii yo* 'This salmon is good *yo*'); in the second TCU, she explicitly offers it (*tabete goran* 'Try (it)'); in the third TCU, she specifies that the salmon comes not from an ordinary supermarket but from Costco. The particle *yo* is used in an assessment whose objective is to present the referent as something that the speaker has experienced but the recipient has not, which supports the characterization of the particle *yo* as a marker of epistemic primacy. In response to this, Nami accepts the offer by taking a bite (line 5), acknowledges Eiko's turn as informative and newsworthy by providing an agreement prefaced with *aa* (line 7), the interjection that is often treated as the equivalent of the English "change-of-state" token *oh* (Heritage 1984a), and further agrees with Eiko by proffering a second assessment (line 9).

In Extract 5, *yo* is used in the turn that is observably devoted to showing that the speaker knows the referent better than the recipient. Two sisters-in-law, Kazu and Yoko, are having tea in the late afternoon in a room at Kazu's home, which looks down to her balcony, and are appreciating the flowers there. Prior to the extract, Yoko asked a question about a particular kind of flower on the balcony. Kazu's response concludes with the assessment in line 1.

(5)
```
1   KAZU:       °kore ga mata kawai[i:_
                this SP also   pretty:
                °These are also pretty:_

2   YOKO:                             [kawaii yone. [au   mon.=
                                      pretty  FP    suit FP
                                      They are) pretty yone, (They) suit
                                      (other flowers).=

3   KAZU:                                           [nn,
                                                     ITJ
                                                     Yeah.

4   YOKO:       =choodo  [ne:.
                perfectly [FP
                =perfectly ne:.

5   KAZU: →                [asa      ga ka  [waii no   yo,
                           morning SP pretty     PRT FP
                           (they are) pretty in the Morning yo.

6   YOKO:                                   [n::
                                             ITJ
                                             Yeah::

7           (0.5)

8   KAZU: →   Really,
             hontoni moo,
             really   EMP

9           (0.7)

10  KAZU: →   >ano< (.) <asa      wa> moo me ga sameru hodo   kawaii.
             well       morning TP EMP eye SP wake   degree pretty
             >Like< (.) <in the morning,> (they are) so pretty (they) wake (me) up.

11  YOKO: ⇒   aa  soo,=
             ITJ that
             Oh are they,=

12  KAZU:     =nn!
             ITJ
             =Yeah!
```

In response to Kazu's assessment, Yoko produces a *yone*-marked agreement (lines 2 and 4).[9] By producing a second assessment, Yoko claims to have independent access to the flowers (Pomerantz 1984a), and the particle *yone* is used to claim equivalent knowledge.

However, at line 5, Kazu reformulates her assessment, marking it with *yo*. Here, she narrows the referent of the assessment from the flowers to how they look in the morning (*asa ga kawaii no yo* '(they are) pretty in the morning *yo*'). In other words, Kazu redefines the referent such that it is exclusively accessible to her – the one who lives and spends mornings in the house – not to Yoko.[10] The use of *yo* in this turn in contrast with the use of *yone* and *ne* in Yoko's turn indicates that it claims epistemic primacy over Yoko.

Yoko does not immediately respond to Kazu's reformulated assessment (line 7), which can be seen as possible resistance of Kazu's claim of epistemic primacy. Kazu then pursues a response (Pomerantz 1984b) at line 8 and again at line 10. In these turns, she upgrades the evaluation (*hontoni moo* 'Really', line 8; *me ga sameru hodo kawaii* '(they are) so pretty (they), wake (me) up', line 10). By so doing, she implies that the flowers that she is talking about are qualitatively different from those that Yoko is now looking at, thus providing a basis for her claim of epistemic primacy. Yoko finally produces a news receipt response at line 11, acknowledging Kazu's epistemic primacy and thus taking a stance that is epistemically congruent with Kazu's.

Extract 6 is a particularly interesting case because we can observe participants' orientations to the incongruence of their epistemic stances. Here, Mari and Ami are chatting at a café a week after Michael Jackson's death. Mari says she has only glanced at the news, whereas Ami has been following the news closely. Prior to the extract, Ami asked Mari if she liked Michael Jackson, and Mari responded that she liked him when he was younger, and brought up a song that he sang with Paul McCartney as her favorite song of his. However, it turned out that she was thinking of the song "Ebony and Ivory," a song that addressed racial issues, which in fact was not sung by Paul McCartney and Michael Jackson but by Paul McCartney and Stevie Wonder. The song Michael Jackson and Paul McCartney sang is "Say Say Say." The fact that Michael Jackson sang a

---

[9] Though the right dislocated adverb phrase choodo ('perfectly' line 4) is marked with ne, the entire ulterance is heard as yone-marked, since it is the particle that makes the main predicate that conveys the speaker's epistemic stance.

[10] This shift in the scope of referent may have been triggered by Yoko's second assessment (lines 2, 4) that could be heard as somewhat qualified; by saying that they suit other flowers perfectly, she might be undermining the beauty of the flowers in question on their own right, and Kazu might have felt motivated to defend it.

song that also addressed racial issues contributed to Mari's confusion.[11]
Ami explained all of this to Mari, saying that she too had been confusing
these songs and had looked them up on the internet. After this confusion
is clarified, Mari makes an assessment about the song "Ebony and Ivory"
(line 10): *ebonii and o(r)aiborii ii yo are* ("'Ebony and Ivory" is good **yo**,
that [is]').

(6)
1 AMI: <u>YA</u>*:ppari s(g)a:, are machigae yasui* **yone::**_
            after_all PRT   that mistake   easily FP
            That's easy to mistake **yone::**_

2   *ebonii ando aiborii ne:,=*
            ebony and ivory   FP:
            "Ebony and Ivory" ne,=

3 MARI: =*sono atashi sono s-ebonii ando aiborii* ^ *to*
            well   I   well ebony and   ivory   and

4   [*say*] *say say ga go(h)ccha* [*ni(h) .hh* >*nante*] *yu   no*<=
            say   say say SP mixed.up   how   say PRT
            Well, I, well, 'S-Ebony and Ivory' ^and 'Say Say Say'
            were mixed up(h) .hh how do (I) say,=

5 AMI: [*un*]   [*hh*   *soo,*   ]
            ITJ   right
            Yeah   hh Right,

6 MARI: =[*hito*] *tsu no-* [(*.hh*) *nanka* <u>*kategori*</u>(*h*)*i̥*] *ni* *hai*]*tteta*=
            one   L   like   category   to enter
            =(They were) in like a single- .hh <u>category</u>(h)=

7 AMI: [( )]   [*bhe hhe hhe he h hhe*]

8 MARI: =*kedo* [∶,]
            but
            =bu:t,

9 AMI: [*poo*]*ru ga dete   kuru ka(h)ra(h)* **ne,**=
                      Paul SP appear come so   FP
                      (That's) be(h)cau(h)se Paul appears (in those songs) ne,=

10 MARI: → =*u:n.* [>*are demo*<] *ebonii ando (r)aiborii ii   yo are.*
            ITJ   that but   ebony and   ivory   good FP that
            =Yeah:. >But   that < 'Ebony and (r)Ivory's is good **yo**, that (is).

11 AMI: [*u:n,*]
            ITJ
            Yeah,

12 AMI: ⇒ ^*are wa* ^*ii   yo*[*ne:,*] [*a: ∶ ∶ ∶ ∶   are*]*wa*=
            that TP good FP   that TP
            ^That is ^good **yone:**, tha::::that is=

────────────────────────

13 MARI: →   [are ii] [yo, sugoi ii   yo,]
                              that good FP very good FP
                              That's good yo, very good yo,

14 AMI: ⇒ = i [i   n da kedo mai] keru kanke(h)e na(h)i n da(h) yo=
                  good N CP but Michael concern   not   N CP   FP
            =good but Michael is no(h)t i(h)nvo(h)lved yo=

15 MARI: [u : : n,   ]
              ITJ
              Yeah::,

16 AMI: ⇒ =[a(h)re(h)H] H H [hh   h   h   h   ]
             that
             =(not) in tha(h)t (song).H H H hh h h h

17 MARI: [h h h]   [.h u:n, burakku an] do wh-whito=
                                 ITJ black   and   white
              h h h   .h Yeah:, "Black and wh-White"=

18   =wa ne,
              TP   FP
              =is ne,

19 AMI: u:[n,]
              ITJ
              Yeah:,

20 MARI: [u]:n,
              ITJ
              Yeah:,

As she produces an assessment about "Ebony and Ivory" (line 10), she claims epistemic primacy with yo. However, she is not in an advantageous position to do so given that she mistakenly thought it to be a song by Michael Jackson.[12] Not surprisingly, Ami does not accept this claim. She proffers a second assessment, marking it yone, a particle recurrently used when interactants have equivalent access to the issue (line 12). Here incongruence emerges between their epistemic stances; Mari claims to know better, while Ami claims to know as much.

In the next turn, Mari reasserts her initial assessment again marking it with yo and produces yet another yo-marked assertion, this time upgrading the assessment from ii 'good' to sugoi ii ('very good' line 13). Pomerantz (1984a) calls a sequence with such a reassertion in the third position a "disagreement sequence": when a speaker of a first assessment is disagreed with by its recipient, s/he often reasserts the position s/he has taken in the third position, upgrading the intensity of the evaluation (Pomerantz

<hr>

[12] Mari's seemingly "reckless" claim of epistemic primacy here may be understood as her attempt to compensate for the face loss due to her earlier mistake about the singer of the song.

1984a: 68). That is precisely what Mari is doing here, even though Ami has clearly agreed with Mari as far as the evaluation of the song is concerned. What is motivating Mari's reassertion in third position seems to be the incongruence of their epistemic stances. Just as disagreement regarding evaluative stances often engenders the first speaker's reassertion of his/her evaluative stance, incongruence regarding epistemic stances leads to sequence expansion in the same way. The implication is that epistemic incongruence is dispreferred and bears consequences for the development of the course of interaction.[13]

This sequence does not end here: overlapping with Mari's *yo*-marked reassertion (line 13), Ami reasserts her position yet again (*are wa ii n da kedo* 'that is good but' lines 12, 14). However, this is not simply another reassertion of her evaluative stance. This prefaces the second half of her turn (*…maikeru kanke(h)e na(h)i n da(h) yo a(h)re(h)* 'Michael is no(h)t i(h)nvo(h)lved – *yo,* (not) in tha(h)t (song)'), in which she reminds Mari of the information that Mari should have known if she is to claim epistemic primacy over the song but did not (lines 14, 16). Ami's use of *yo* here and the claim of epistemic primacy embodied through it contests Mari's claim of epistemic primacy, though it is mitigated by Ami's laughter that is produced with and after the turn (Haakana 2001). Mari does not insist further; she laughs along with Ami, and shifts the focus of the topic to the other song that was sung by Michael Jackson (line 17).

In this section, we have examined cases in which first assessments are marked with *yo*. The sequential context and how the *yo*-marked assessments are responded to offer evidence that the particle marks a claim of epistemic primacy, which can be accepted, resisted or rejected by recipients. I argued that the sequence organization found in a sequence with epistemic incongruence suggests that there is preference for epistemic congruence over epistemic incongruence. It should also be noticed that claiming epistemic primacy does not necessarily undermine social solidarity, though it inherently suggests asymmetry in interactants' epistemic stances, which often works against social solidarity (Heritage 2002a: 211). Extract 4 was one such case, where salmon was presented as inaccessible to Nami with *yo*, not to make an egocentric epistemic claim but to make an offer and promote the chance of acceptance.

---

[13] Previous studies also discuss the possible preference organization that involves participants' knowledge states. For instance, an announcement prefers a response that accepts it as news (instead of "already known") as well as affiliates with the assessment of the news (Terasaki 2004 [1976]; Schegloff 2007b: 60–61). While the status of a piece of information as news or as "already known" is constitutive of the action of announcement, whether one has epistemic primacy or not, which is the issue in Extract 6, does not seem to change the fact that they are talking about a referent that is accessible to both Mari and Ami and therefore a second assessment is the relevant next action (Pomerantz 1984a).

Yo-marked second assessments

When speakers make an assessment in first position, they claim and exhibit independent access to the referent (Pomerantz 1984a) and, unless it is epistemically downgraded, imply a claim of primary rights to assess the referent (Raymond and Heritage 2006: 684). Consequently, a claim of epistemic primacy in second assessments is commonly incongruent with the first speaker's epistemic stance and thus speakers working to assert epistemic primacy in this sequential position are under additional pressure to establish credentials for their epistemic primacy. Not surprisingly, most agreements in my corpus are *not* marked with *yo*; the use of *ne* and *yone* are far more common than *yo* in agreements. By contrast, *yo* is frequently used to mark disagreements. In this section, we first focus on those rather marked cases where agreements are marked with *yo* and illustrate how the speaker manipulates the intensity of the evaluation in order to provide a basis for their claim of epistemic primacy. Then in the following section, *yo*-marked disagreements are examined.

Yo-*marked agreements*

First, see Extract 7, an excerpt drawn from a conversation among four university students. They are having a plate of sushi they took out from a sushi restaurant. Yumi has had sushi from this restaurant before, and she is the one who suggested they have a sushi plate from there. After they unwrap the sushi plate and are getting ready to eat it, Kumi, looking at the plate, remarks that there are no "throw away" pieces such as *kappa* (cucumber rolls), meaning that the plate is filled with good pieces. In response to this, Yumi makes a *yo*-marked second assessment (line 4).

(7)
```
1 KUMI:  →  nanka kappa          toka sute    ga nai jan.
            like  cucumber_rolls etc. discard  SP not TAG
            (It's) like there is no discard like cucumber rolls.

2        →  sute  [goma    [ga.
            discard_piece  SP
            No piece to discard.

3 MAKI:     [n n    [:. honto.
            ITJ         right
            Yeah:. (You're) right.

4 YUMI:  ⇒         [zenzen nai yo.
                   at_all  not FP
                   There aren't at all yo.
```

5   (1.0)
6 YUMI: *(sooyuu no de-) (.) a   demo sooyuu menyuu m̲[o aru.*
               such   N   with   ITJ but   such   menu   also be
               (With such pieces-) (.) Oh but there are a̲lso such menus (in the
               restaurant).
7 HIRO: [*he: a-*=
                                                         ITJ ITJ
                                                         Hmm: oh-

8   =^*soo   na   n   da:,*
               that CP N   CP
               =there ^are:,

While Maki agrees with Kumi, acknowledging it as a view that she has not
had (*nn:. honto.* 'yeah. (You're) right' line 3), Yumi's second assessment at
line 4 involves more than agreeing: she claims epistemic primacy through
the particle *yo*. Additionally, she upgrades the evaluation by adding the
intensifier *zenzen* ('(not) at all'). This can be seen as a way to indicate that
she, without having to look at every piece on the plate, already knows it
thoroughly, which is distinct from the epistemic access that Kumi and the
others are gaining by looking at it here and now. Thus, Yumi is claiming
epistemic primacy over the referent and employs the degree of her evaluation to provide a basis for her claim. In addition, Yumi's reference to
another menu that does have "pieces to discard" (line 6) after one second
of silence (line 5) supports this analysis. In this turn, Yumi exhibits her
knowledge about other menus in the restaurant, knowledge which is not
shared by the others. Thus, this can be seen as her attempt to pursue a
response that acknowledges her epistemic primacy and probably gives her
credit for having recommended the restaurant and the plate. Although
Kumi does not give either of these possibly relevant responses, Hiro
acknowledges the newsworthiness of Yumi's turn, thereby at least accepting her claim of epistemic primacy (lines 7–8).

   In contrast, in the exchange that shortly follows Extract 7, Maki
acknowledges that Yumi has a level of access that she does not have when
she makes an assessment of the taste of the sushi (line 14).

(8)
14 MAKI: → *honto da: oi^shii **ne**.*
              really CP good   FP
              (You are) right, (it's) ^good **ne**.
15 YUMI: ⇒ *nn::.*
              ITJ
              Yeah::.

16   (1.0)
17 YUMI: *shinsen.=koko.*
              fresh   here
              (Sushi is) fresh.=In this (restaurant).

Though Maki is the first to eat the sushi on this occasion, she nonetheless formulates her assessment as if it were responsive to an initial assessment by Yumi (*honto da:* '(You are) right'). Through this formulation, she acknowledges that Yumi is the one who knew the sushi resturant and recommended it. Yumi responds with an interjection *nn::.* 'yeah::.', through which she simply accepts Maki's assessment without taking issue. That is to say, she does not object to the epistemic stance that Maki has taken. Compared with this exchange, we can see that Yumi's *yo*-marked second assessment in (7) is concerned with claiming and establishing her epistemic primacy, which has not been acknowledged.

In the next example, a speaker who has first-hand knowledge of a referent claims epistemic primacy over an interlocutor who only has second-hand knowledge through the use of *yo*, and gives support to the claim by an upgraded assessment. Extract 9 is a telephone conversation between Hiro and Taro. Hiro recently moved to Boston, and Taro lives in San Diego and has never been to Boston. Prior to the excerpt, Hiro has told Taro that he and his wife decided to move to Boston not only because it is suited to his business but also because it is a fun place to live in. Following this, Taro brings up his friend who recently visited Boston (lines 4–5) and quotes his/her positive assessment about it (line 7). Hiro responds to this with a *yo*-marked second assessment at line 8.

(9)
1 HIRO: *ma   jaa,   (1.0) koko ni shi yoo   ka tsutte.*
             well then   here to do   VOL   Q   say
             (We were like) "well, then, (1.0) shall (we) decide on this (town)."

2 TARO: *aa   soo.*
             ITJ that
             Oh I see.

3 HIRO: *hai.*
             ITJ
             Yes.

4 TARO: *n::?, .hh nanka ore no tomodachi de ne:, yappa ano::*
             ITJ   like   I   L   friend   as FP   also   uhm
             Mm::. .hh Well, my friend ne:, uh::m

5   *saikin   bosuton ni (itteta)   hito   ga ita   n da kedo:,*
              recently Boston to going_PST person SP was N CP but
              (s/he) recently (went) to Boston as well, bu:t,

6 HIRO: *hai,*=
              ITJ
              Mm-hm,=

7 TARO: → =.*hh yappa   sugo:- ii   machi da tte itteta   ne,*
                 expectedly ver- good town CP QT saying_PST FP
              =.hh (as one would expect,) (s/he) was saying that (it) was a ver-
              good town ne.

8 HIRO: ⇒ *su[ngoi] ii   desu yo.*=
              very   good CP FP
              (It's) very good yo.=

9 TARO: [egh]((cough))

10 TARO: = *machi ga koo- chotto- (0.2) >nante no<*
               town SP this a_little   what PRT
              =The town is like- a little- (0.2) >how do (I) say<

11   *renga zukuri no ie   ga ookute:?,*
              block made L house SP many
              there are many houses of brick?,

12   (.)

13 HIRO: *nn,*
              ITJ
              Mm-hm,

14 TARO: *nde:: maa- rekishi mo kanjirushi sa:,*
              and well history also feel   PRT
              A::nd well- (one) can feel the history as well,

15   (0.4)

16 TARO: .hh

17 HIRO: *Amerika de ichiban furui machi janai desu ka koko,*
              America in most   old   town TAG CP Q here
              (It) is the oldest town in America, right?

18 TARO: *aa soo,*
              ITJ that
              Oh is it,

19 HIRO: *nn.*
              ITJ
              Yeah.

20 TARO: *hnn:_*
              ITJ
              Mm:_

By providing a quoted assessment, Taro is referring to a source of information that he has about Boston, besides Hiro. When Hiro agrees with this at line 8, he marks his second assessment with *yo* and claims epistemic primacy. Here again, the intensity of the evaluation is modified as a resource to provide support for his claim.

In Taro's quoted assessment, he cuts off his talk right before the last vowel of the intensifier *sugoi* ('very') is articulated (*sugo:-* 'ver-') and puts the stress on the adjective *ii* ('good'). The natural stress for the phrase *sugoi ii* ('very good') would be on *sugoi* ('very'). However, the stress is put on *ii* here, because of which the intensifier is heard to be abandoned. Hiro, in contrast, puts emphasis on the intensifier (*sungoi*) in his second assessment. By differentiating his evaluation from Taro's quoted evaluation in terms of the intensity, Hiro invokes a basis for claiming that he knows Boston better than Taro, and better than Taro's friend, who merely visited Boston, while Hiro lives there.

Taro does not acknowledge or overtly attend to Hiro's epistemic claim but continues to report what he heard about Boston from the friend (lines 10–11 and 14), which can be understood as resistance to Hiro's claim of epistemic primacy. Probably because of this, Hiro backs down at line 17; as he says that Boston is the oldest town in the United States, he conveys that he assumes Taro knows this as well through the use of an agreement-eliciting sentence-final form (*janai desu ka* 'right?'). However, Taro did not know this and responds with a news receipt (line 18) and then with an interjection *hnn:*, with which he registers the preceding turn as informative (line 20). With these responses that display the lack of knowledge, Taro takes an epistemic stance that is congruent with Hiro's earlier claim of epistemic primacy. Consequently, Hiro establishes his epistemic primacy and subsequently starts to describe Boston, treating Taro as an uninformed recipient.

In Extract 9, we observed a case in which a speaker claims epistemic primacy over an object of which he has first-hand knowledge. In Extract 10, the interactional motivation for claiming epistemic primacy seems to come from an ongoing interactional contingency. Here, male friends Shin and Toshi are talking on the phone. Shin, who could graduate from college soon but was planning to transfer to another school, has told Toshi that he is thinking of investing some time to build up his body before he transfers. Toshi first laughed at this idea and then said that Shin should transfer now if he wants to do so at all. The extract starts when Shin is defending his idea, arguing that it would be too late if he does not work on his physical strength now, implying that this has to be done before transferring to and starting with another school.

(10)

1 SHIN: *o- osoku natte   kara hitoride ganba roo   toka*
              l- late   become after alone   try   AUX etc.
              If (I/we) l-later think like

2   *omotte mo   ganbare nai yo.*
              think   though try_can not FP
              "I'll work (to get physical strength) on my own," (I/we) won't be
              able to work hard **yo.**

3   (1.0)

4 TOSHI: → *-maa na, =moo   [soro]soro kudarizaka da=*
              well FP already almost   downhill   CP
              (You)-may be right,=

5 SHIN: [*nn,*]
                                 ITJ
                                 Yeah,

6 TOSHI: → *=kara [(na),]*
              so   FP
              =cuz (it's) almost downhill.

7 SHIN: ⇒   [*kuda*]*rizaka mo ii   toko da **yo** moo.*
                     downhill TP good place CP FP already
                     (It's) far into downhill **yo**, already.

8   (0.3)

9 SHIN: *onaka   hekomashito kanaito moo   natsu   madeni.*
              stomach flatten   must   EMP summer till
              (I) have to flatten (my) stomach before summer.

10   (0.5)

11 TOSHI: *.hhh ho- majide: honto:*
                   rea seriously really
              .hhh Rea- seriously really

12 SHIN: *n::n,*
              ITJ
              Yeah,

13   (0.2)

14 TOSHI: *hajimari soo   da mon.*
              start   seem CP FP
              (It) looks like (it's) starting (in my body).

After Shin's claim, Toshi concedes, hesitantly agreeing with Shin (*maa na*
'(you) may be right' line 4). He then makes an assessment *moo sorosoro*

kudarizaka da kara (na) ('cuz (it's) almost downhill'), apparently referring
to the physical condition of people their age (lines 4–6).

Shin responds to this assessment produced as a part of a concession with
a *yo*-marked agreement. Shin, being the one who has been arguing that he
should work on his physical strength now, not later, has a reasonable basis
to claim that he does not need Toshi to tell him that it is downhill and that
he knows this better than Toshi. In addition, in this context, it is in his
interest to establish this view as a basis for justifying his plan to invest time
to build up his physical strength before starting at a new school. To that
end, Toshi's formulation, which is downgraded with *sorosoro* ('almost'),
is not sufficient. Thereby, while agreeing with Toshi on the basic valence
of the evaluative stance, Shin claims epistemic primacy over the view and
upgrades the intensity of the evaluation to *kudarizaka mo ii toko* ('far into
downhill').

After a short delay of Toshi's response (line 8), Shin adds that he has
to flatten his stomach before summer (line 9), referring to a manifesta-
tion that his body is already going downhill. Toshi, on the other hand,
says that it is almost starting, indicating that downhill has not yet started
for him (lines 11 and 14). By focusing on his own body instead of Shin's,
Toshi may be avoiding agreeing with Shin's self-deprecating comment
(Pomerantz 1984a).

In this section, we have seen that the intensity of the evaluation is recurrently upgraded in *yo*-marked agreements. By differentiating their evaluative stance from the interlocutor's in this way, speakers not only claim to
know better but *show* this through their stronger or more precise evaluation. This is a method for the speaker to legitimize or provide support to
his/her claim of epistemic primacy while agreeing with the basic valence
of the evaluation proffered by the first speaker. In the next section, I focus
on *yo*-marked disagreements, in which a speaker takes the opposite valence
of the evaluation from the first assessment speaker's. It will be shown that
the intensity of the evaluation is manipulated differently depending on the
speaker's orientation to the dispreferredness of the disagreement.

Yo-*marked disagreements*

While the use of *yo* in an agreement is uncommon, forthright disagreements are frequently marked with *yo*. This has been remarked by
researchers: Masuoka (1991) says that *yo* is used when interactants are
disagreeing with each other or there is a gap in their respective knowledgeability; Katoh (2001) suggests that, while better knowledge is crucial
to the use of *yo* in cases when interactants are in agreement, that is
not the case when they are in disagreement. Alternatively, I argue that the

issue of knowledgeability and the issue of agreement or disagreement are not mutually exclusive. That is to say, proffering a forthright disagreement often implies that the second speaker has the "better" or "more legitimate" view because s/he knows the issue better. Indeed, in many of the cases with *yo*-marked disagreements, the speakers invoke epistemic primacy as a basis for their disagreement.[14]

See Extract 11. Rika and her aunt Kayo are talking about cats. Kayo owns a cat while Rika has never owned one. At line 1, Rika makes an assessment about how often cats meow. By marking the assessment with *yone*, Rika indicates that she expects Kayo to share the knowledge and invites an agreement. However, Kayo disagrees, marking her assessment with *yo* (line 3).

(11)
```
1 RIKA:   → neko  tte- kekkoo- yoo  nakutemo- naku  yone:,
             cat   TP  fairly    need without   meow  FP
             Cats meow fairly- often without reasons- yone:,

2             inu    tte  saa,
              dogs  TP   PRT
              (Whereas) dogs,

3 KAYO:   ⇒ naka    nai  yo:,  = sonnani.
             meow   not  FP       that.much
             (They) don't meow yo:,=(not)that often.

4 RIKA:      a ^soo na no?
             ITJ that CP PRT
             Oh (they) ^don't?

5 KAYO:      nn.
             ITJ
             No.

6            (0.8)

7 KAYO:   ⇒ hon:tto:ni shizuka yo.
             really     Quiet   FP
             (A cat / My cat) is rea:lly: quiet yo.

8 RIKA:      hee.
             ITJ
             I see.
```

<hr/>

[14] The frequent deployment of *yo* in second assessments that straightforwardly disagree with first assessments is contrastive with the use of *oh* in the context of disagreement in English interaction reported by Heritage (2002a). Heritage shows that *oh* is hardly found in a disagreeing second assessment but is reserved for the third position, where the first assessment speaker holds his/her position following the interlocutor's disagreement, and that *oh* escalates ongoing disagreement. In Japanese, even mitigated disagreements (see Extract 11, for example) are marked with *yo* and the sense of escalated disagreement is not indexed by *yo*.

Kayo straightforwardly disagrees with Rika by negating Rika's assessment with the negation particle *nai* ('not'), and marking it with *yo*. In this case, because of the asymmetry in their experience with cats, which surfaced earlier in the conversation, Kayo can reasonably claim to know them better than Rika does. This *yo*-marked disagreement is mitigated with the post-positioned qualifier, *sonnani* ('(not) that much'). With this qualifier, the difference between their views is minimized. It is after Rika immediately backs down, treating Kayo's view as new information (line 4), that Kayo upgrades her evaluation (line 7), marking it with *yo*.

Minimization or mitigation is a recurrently observed feature of a dispreferred response (Pomerantz 1984a; Heritage 1984b). Forthright disagreements take the opposite valence from first assessments, and, thus, incompatibility of the two evaluative stances is transparent. In such cases, speakers' orientation to minimizing disagreement may manifest itself in the form of qualifying the intensity. This is an interesting contrast with *yo*-marked agreements, where a second assessment takes the same valence as the first but is slightly differentiated from it by adjusting the intensity.

Extract 12 is another example of a *yo*-marked disagreement, in which the claim of epistemic primacy is made as a vehicle for a pro-social action, namely disagreeing with a self-deprecation. Kazu and her husband, Ken, are hosting Kazu's female friends Masa and Yuki for dinner. Masa brought a bottle of wine, and when she gave the bottle to the hosts, she specifically said it was Japanese wine. The following exchange occurs after they have tasted the wine. At line 1, Masa says to Ken that it does taste like Japanese wine, inviting agreement with *ne*. Ken explicitly disagrees with Masa marking it with *yo* (lines 2–3); he takes the opposite valence of the evaluation from Masa's.

(12)
```
1 MASA:    nanka nihon  no aj [i  ga suru n[e?,]
           like   Japan L   taste SP do  FP
           (It's) like, (it) has a Japanese taste ne?,

2 KEN:  ⇒
                            [.shh          [iya] nihon  no aji
                                           ITJ  japan L   taste
                            .shh No (it) doesn't have

3       ⇒ shi nai yo,  f-nanka d- [do- (   )]
          do not FP     like
          a Japanese taste yo, (it's) like

4 MASA:                     [nanka sa,]
                            like   PRT
                            Like,
```

5 YUKI: *n*[*n*]
            ITJ
            Mm hm,

6 MASA: [*ya*]*ppari ho- gaikoku no to   chigau_*
            after_all   foreign L with different
            (It's) different from foreign (wine)_

7 YUKI: °*hn*[*n :,*]
            ITJ
            °I see:,

8 MASA: [*nanka*] [*kuu-*
            like   ai-
            (It's) like, the ai-

9 KEN: [*maa furansu* [*no wain-*]
                            well France L   wine
                            Well, French wine-

10 MASA: [*k<u>uu</u>ki ga*] *shittori shiteru.*
                                      air   SP wet   being
                                      The <u>air</u> is moisturized.

By assessing the wine in categorical terms – "Japanese" or "not Japanese," rather than evaluative or descriptive terms (e.g., "good" or "sweet") – Masa and Ken display their knowledge of wine in general, for they need to be experienced with wine in order to be able to tell what other wine this particular wine is similar to or dissimilar from. When Ken disagrees with Masa, he claims to know wine better than her, and the subsequent exchange shows their orientations to such an epistemic issue. Following Ken's disagreement, Masa refers to "foreign wine" from which, according to her, this particular wine is different (line 6). At line 9, Ken begins to contrast it with French wine, though this gets interrupted by Masa's second description of the wine that sounds as if she is mocking a *sommelier* (line 10). The use of *yo* in Ken's disagreement contributes to making the epistemic issue explicit between the interactants.

It should also be remarked that Ken's disagreement does not have features of a dispreferred response: it is not delayed or mitigated in any way. This may be due to a possible implication of Masa's assessment as a self-deprecation. Given that the wine was Masa's gift, the description that it has a Japanese taste can be heard as unauthentic or negative and thus self-deprecating, after which a disagreement is preferred (Pomerantz 1975, 1984a). In fact, later in this occasion, it turns out that Ken believes Japanese wine is generally too sweet, while this particular wine is dry, which he appreciates. Therefore, in this case, disagreement is done as an affiliative move, which is likely to be providing him with extra motivation for claiming epistemic primacy and strongly insisting on his position.

Conclusion

In this chapter, I have examined assessments in Japanese conversation that are marked with the final particle *yo*, a marker of epistemic primacy. It was demonstrated that the intensity of the evaluation is recurrently differentiated from the co-participant's in order to give support for the claim of epistemic primacy that the speaker is putting forward. The implication is that the intensity of evaluation is not only contingent on a second assessment's status as an agreement or disagreement as is pointed out by Pomerantz (1984a), but is also contingent on epistemic stance. When interactants' epistemic stances are incongruent, the sequence may exhibit similar features to a sequence with a disagreement: expansion of the sequence in which a speaker reasserts his/her original stance, be it evaluative stance (in the case of a disagreement sequence) or epistemic stance (in the case of a sequence with epistemic incongruence). This finding suggests that congruence in interactants' epistemic stances is preferred to epistemic incongruence in a similar way to agreement being preferred to disagreement. It was also suggested that though a claim of epistemic primacy inherently suggests asymmetry between interactants, which may not be pro-social in itself, there are cases in which the claim is made for such pro-social interactional goals as promoting an offer (Extract 4) or rejecting a self-deprecation (Extract 12).

In general, agreement promotes or maintains social solidarity while disagreement impairs it (Heritage 1984b), and the preference for agreement over disagreement is robust in interactional organization. However, interactants also have a social want for detachment, a want to claim and prove their uniqueness and distinctiveness from others (Heritage and Raymond 2005: 36). A claim of epistemic primacy inherently suggests asymmetrical, differentiated epistemic stances between interactants. What a Japanese speaker may try to achieve by marking an assessment with *yo* is to establish uniqueness from his/her interlocutor, while also attending to the maintenance of solidarity by agreeing with the basic view of the assessment.

4   Morality and question design: "of course" as contesting a presupposition of askability

Tanya Stivers

Introduction

When speakers ask polar (i.e., *yes/no*) questions they generally make relevant confirmation or disconfirmation. Yet even a brief look at everyday social interaction reveals that there is a myriad of ways to do so. The conventional varieties (i.e., "yeah"/ "no", "mm hm"/ "mm mm", "uh huh"/ "uh uh" and head nods/shakes) are common (Heritage 1998; Raymond 2003). For instance, in Extract 1, taken from a phone call, Joyce tells her brother Stan what she has bought a mutual friend for his birthday. In response Stan's partial repeat requests confirmation (Schegloff, Jefferson and Sacks 1977). Joyce confirms with "Yeah." (line 4).

(1)
```
1 J:    =Well don't tell Bernie but I got him a hat
2          fer his birthday.
3 S:    Oh you got Bernie a hat?
4 J: →  Yeah.
5          (.)
6 J:    Cuz you took his.
```

In Extract 2 Mark and Kim are eating dinner together when Mark tells Kim that he did not talk much with two of his work partners. This implies that they were both around at work. She requests confirmation of this in line 6. Mark confirms with "Mm hm," in line 8.

(2)
```
1  MARK:    So_ (1.0) ya know. (3.8) Didn't really have too much
2               conversation with Jack or Mike today,
3               (2.5)
4  MARK:    Little bit but_°
```

This chapter was equally informed by the development of this joint project and the questions project within the Multimodal Interaction Project at the Max Planck Institute. Thank you to John Heritage, Jakob Steensig and particularly Nick Enfield for improving the clarity of the argument along the way and for commenting on earlier versions of the chapter.

```
5                  (2.5)
6   KIM:           Did they work?,
7                  (0.8)
8   MARK:    →    Mm hm,
9                  (0.8)
10  KIM:           Both of 'em worked?
```

In a recent cross-lingusitic study of question–response sequences 77 percent of answers to polar questions in English were done with one of these varieties of *yes* or *no* interjections (Stivers 2010).[1]

At times, however, speakers confirm in other ways. The most common alternative is to do a partial or full repetition of the question. In Extract 3 Mike has just commented that he's "uh committed kinda guy." Jessie acknowledges this claim with "Uh huh:," a head nod, a smile (beginning in line 3) and then a teasing request for confirmation done as an appendor question (Sacks 1992: 660–663; Schegloff 1997: 510–511, 2000b: 239) to his prior comment from line 1. Mike confirms not with an interjection but with the more agentive "E:verything." (line 6) (Heritage and Raymond in press).

```
(3)
1   MIKE:          I'm uh committed kinda guy.
2                  (0.5)
3   JESS:          Uh huh:, ((nodding))
4                  (0.5)
5   JESS:          £Tuh e(h)verythi(h)ng?,
6   MIKE:    →    E:verything. ((slight nod))
7   JESS:          Mm hm:,
```

Raymond has shown that repetitional answers such as this, through their departure from the terms set by the question (that made relevant "yes" or "no" as an answer), treat the question's design as problematic (Raymond 2003). Heritage and Raymond (in press) and Stivers and Hayashi (2010) argue that repetitional answers primarily focus on a rejection of the reduced agency over the question's terms that is otherwise implied by an unmarked interjection such as "yeah".

Stivers and Hayashi have shown that question recipients also do confirmation with "transformative answers" which take issue with the terms of the question by, for instance, qualifying or replacing them (2010). An illustration of this is shown in Extract 4. Here Tara confirms that she "cried to him on the pho:ne" but qualifies this claim by retroactively adjusting the terms of the question in her answer "Not on purpose;" (line 2).

---

[1] And in fact this was true in most other languages in the study as well (Stivers, Enfield and Levinson 2010).

(4)
1 KRIS: You cried to him on the pho:ne?
2 TARA: Not on p<u>ur</u>pose;
3   (0.4)
4 KRIS: Oh::, ([that's cu^:te.)

Yet another way that question recipients can address a problem with the question is through a preface. A preface may be to either an interjection or a repetitional answer. One well-studied example of this is *oh*-prefaced responses to inquiry (Heritage 1998). Two examples are shown in Extracts 5–6. Extract 5 is taken from a news interview. The interviewee (Acton) has just mentioned (lines 1–3) that he and his students translated some work by Eliot into Chinese for the first time. Immediately following this disclosure is the question "Did you learn to speak (.) Chine:se." (line 5). The interjection takes the form of "Oh yes." Heritage argues that, with it, the interviewee "treats it as obvious that he would have learned the language, and thereby implies that the inquiry questions something that might have been presupposed in virtue of the prior talk" (1998: 294). In this sense, the question is inapposite (see also Heinemann 2009).

(5) (Heritage 1998: 294)
1   Act: .... hhhh and some of thuh– (0.3) some of
2   my students translated Eliot into Chine::se.
3   I think thuh very first.
4   (0.2)
5   Har: Did you learn to speak (.) Chine [:se.
6   Act: →   [.hh Oh yes.
7   (0.7)
8   Act: .hhhh You ca::n't live in thuh country
9   without speaking thuh lang [uage it's=
10 Har: [Not no: course
11 Act: =impossible .hhhhh

Similarly, in Extract 6 taken from a telephone call between friends, in response to a question that is heavily tilted toward confirmation with the declarative + tag "aren't=you," the recipient confirms not with a "mere" confirmation "Yeah" but with an *oh*-prefaced confirmation.

(6) (Heritage 1998: 303)
1 Sus: You guys er gonna dr<u>i</u>ve up aren't=you,
2 Mar: → <u>Oh</u> yea:h.
3 Sus: That's what I <u>figu</u> [red.
4 Mar: [Yeh.

With the *oh*-prefaced response the speaker indicates that the question was problematic in terms of its relevance, presuppositions or context (Heritage 1998) and indicates that it was inapposite.

Still other forms of answering rely on "marked" interjections. These forms of confirmation are "marked" in the sense that, although they are affirmative interjections, they are not varieties of *yes* or *no* (Heritage and Sefi 1992). These interjections are relatively uncommon. In the previously cited study of question–response sequences, marked interjections comprised only 1 percent of answers (Stivers 2010). Little research has been done on marked interjections, but it is likely that each functions somewhat differently from the others. Still, there is some coherence across them in that, even though speakers are confirming, they are not *only* confirming (Heritage and Raymond 2005; Raymond and Heritage 2006).

Consider "Absolutely", for instance.[2] Although it is relatively uncommon, it does occur on occasion as the sole confirmation, as in Extract 7. Here, in an interview between talk-show host Phil Donahue and a psychologist regarding a parent–child relationship, Donahue asks his interviewee a declaratively formatted request for confirmation. In response she confirms with "Absolutely." (line 3).

```
(7) (Phil Donahue)
1  PD:        So it is possible then for a parent to be too
2             much of a buddy with the child:.
3  KH:  →     Absolutely.
4  PD:        .hhhh Ah- ih is it (0.2) so uhh- (0.5) doctor
5             [hhh    uh-    Harrison  ]=
6  KH:        =[AH AND ITS NOT just be]ing a buddy either Phil.
7             Its yahh- ah you will provi [de me with se ] lf
8  PD:                                    [I understand ]
9  KH:        esteem by virtue of your accomplishments . . .
```

In Example 8 Skip has called Jim to enquire about a ride. In response to the pre- "You coming past the doo:r," Jim confirms with "Certainly?". In contrast to "Absolutely.", this marked agreement seems to have an obliging quality to it, treating the pre- as recognizably a pre-request (Schegloff 1988c, 2007a; on presequences, see Terasaki 2004 [1976]).

```
(8)
1  JIM:       J. P. Blenkinsop good morning,
2             (.)
3  SKIP:      Good morning Ji:m,
4             (0.5)
5  SKIP:      Uh it's Skip.
6  JIM:       ^Hiyuh,
7  SKIP:      You coming past the doo:r,
8  JIM:  →    Certainly?
```

---

[2] The ways a speaker can confirm are many but, to provide a few more examples, consider "Definitely", "You betcha", "That's right" and "Bingo".

```
9                (0.8)
10 JIM:          What time wouldju like the car Sah.=
11 SKIP:         =Uh well ehhh hhehh hhhehh hhehh .hh Oh that's m:ost
12               unexpected of you hhh::: n(h)o it's v(h)ery nice'v you to
13               offer huhh uh-^heh heh-u-hu-.ehhh £Thanks very much.£
14               .h[hh
15 JIM:             [Eh:m I wz planning tih lea:ve: here at just about twenty
16               to: so you know I'll be with you . . .
```

This chapter's focus is on another marked interjection, "Of course", as
it occurs in responses to inquiries, typically requests for confirmation or
requests for information. An initial example is shown in Extract 9. Here,
Nancy is asking Hyla a series of questions about Hyla's boyfriend who
has just moved away. In line 2 the first question is answered with "Yea:h,".
The next questions are content questions (lines 5 and 12). The target question at line 16 treats the last name "Freedland" as a Jewish name and both
requests confirmation that this is in fact the case and teases Hyla about
toeing the line in dating Jewish boys.

```
(9)
1  NAN:    =.hhh Dz he av iz own apa:rt [mint?]
2  HYL:                            [.hhhh] Yea:h,=
3  NAN:    =Oh:,
4          (1.0)
5  NAN:    How didju git iz number,
6          (.)
7  HYL:    I(h) (.) c(h)alled infermation'n San Fr'ncissc(h)[uh!
8  NAN:                                            [Oh:::.
9          (.)
10 NAN:    Very cleve:r, hh=
11 HYL:    =Thank you [: I-.hh-.hhhhhhhh]hh=
12 NAN:              [W'ts iz last name, ]
13 HYL:    =Uh:: Freedla:nd. .hh [hh
14 NAN:                      [Oh[:,
15 HYL:                         [('r) Freedlind.=
16 NAN:    =Nice Jewish bo:y?
17 HYL: →  O:f cou:rse,=
```

Hyla's answer "O:f cou:rse," confirms that the boy is Jewish. However, it
does more than that. "Of course" also challenges one of the most fundamental presuppositions of a polar question – that both *yes* and *no* are possible answers. A challenge to this presupposition is, I argue, tantamount
to challenging the question's "askability" (Sacks 1987b: 217). Thus, when
Hyla confirms with "Of course", she addresses Nancy's tease as well as
her question by conveying that not only is this boy Jewish but a question

about his Jewish identity is not really askable. The askability of the question hinges on its insinuation that Hyla might be the sort of Jewish girl who would be willing to date non-Jewish boys. By confirming with "Of course", Hyla takes the moral high ground, asserting that such a possibility is unthinkable.

A similar example is shown in Extract 10. Here, during a phone call, Shirley is telling her friend Geri about what happened the night before. In particular, in line 1 Shirley announces that Geri's mother met Michael (Shirley's boyfriend). This is delivered as a story preface (Sacks 1974), and, following the newsmark in line 2, acting as a go-ahead, Shirley goes on to detail what happened. At the point where Shirley describes how Geri's mother's dog tried to jump in Shirley's car, Geri asks "So didju interdu:ce 'er?" (line 28).

```
(10)
 1  SHI:       Uh:m yer mother met Michael las' night.
 2  GER:       Oh rilly?=
 3  SHI:       =Ye:ah.
 4  ( ):       .hh-.hh
 5  GER:       ^Oh:::.=
 6  SHI:       =Yeah.She wz taking Shiloh out just ez we w'r coming back
 7             fr'm dinner.

             ((15 lines omitted – story telling))

23  SHI:       [.hh So 'e tried tih jump in the car.
24  ( ):       .hh
25                     (.)
26  GER:       Oh: boy,h=
27  SHI:       =cuz I wz js' getting ou:t.=
28  GER:       =S[o didju]interdu:ce 'er?
29  SHI:         [(    )]
30  SHI:   →   Of COU:rse.
31  GER:       e-Ye::h,
32  SHI:       .hh- So: yihknow she said hi: ez- ez he tried tih yank'er
33             up'n down the block .hhhh y'know ioh wz kind'v a funny way
34             t'say hello.
35  GER:       Ye::h,=
```

In response to the question Shirley answers "Of COU:rse." (line 30). This response offers a confirmation. However, it also treats the alternative (that, with Michael there at the car and Geri's mother's dog trying to jump into their car, Shirley failed to introduce the two) as inconceivable. When speakers respond with "Of course" they contest the presupposition of the question that both confirmation and disconfirmation are possible and thus treat the question as unaskable. Unaskable questions are frequently questions that insinuate something that, based on existing epistemic access, should not be insinuated. With "Of course" question recipients commonly take the moral high ground, asserting that what was insinuated is inconceivable. This claim is grounded in: (1) the contexts in which "Of course" is offered as an answer, and (2) subsequent orientations to unquestionability. I go through these in turn in what follows.

Data

This chapter draws on approximately twenty-five instances of "Of course" in American and British spontaneous naturally occurring conversation. The number of instances is small primarily because marked interjections occur only rarely in response to inquiries (Stivers 2010). However, the practice I discuss is very consistent across all examples in the collection. In addition, I make use of instances of similar tokens in data in other languages, in particular *natuurlijk* in Dutch,[3] *mochiron* in Japanese[4] and *certo* in Italian,[5] all of which seem to function in the same way that "Of course" does in English, though there may be subtle differences that could (and should) be explored. For these reasons, I believe the evidence is clear enough to sustain the analysis presented here.

Analysis

Contexts of use

"Of course" is used primarily when questioners suggest, through their question, that something morally problematic may be the case and when questioners have epistemic access to the answer either from interactional history or from general knowledge.[6] For example, return to Extract 10. In this case the target question – "So didju interdu:ce 'er?" (line 28) – suggests that Shirley might not have introduced her boyfriend to Geri's mother. Such a position is morally problematic since what sort of person would Shirley be to have failed to introduce her boyfriend to her friend's mother with the two there together at the car? Moreover, even if Geri had doubts about Shirley's character, the answer is inferentially available in the prior stretch of talk. At line 1, Shirley asserted that "yer mother met Michael las' night." If the two "met" last night and the telling has ended with Geri's

---

[3] Thank you to Jan Peter de Ruiter for allowing me access to his corpus.
[4] Thank you to Kaoru Hayano for supplying Japanese cases from her corpus.
[5] Thank you to Federico Rossano for providing several Italian instances.
[6] Although negating "Of course" answers exist, they are rare. It is for this reason that I talk about affirmatively designed questions.

mother's dog trying to get into Shirley's car and the three individuals standing together, she could infer that Shirley introduced them. Shirley's "Of course" directly contests the insinuation that she might have failed to introduce them.

A similar case is shown in Extract 11. Here in response to Joyce's implicit accusation that Stan "took" Bernie's hat, Stan denies this ("^I didn't take his.") and goes on to assert that he actually bought Bernie's hat. Joyce responds with a request for confirmation: "Oh you paid him for it." (line 8). This turn insinuates that Stan might have taken the hat without paying for it. Although Joyce's declarative turn format treats confirmation as expected, the action still treats disconfirmation as possible. Stan, by contrast, treats disconfirmation as inconceivable. Similarly to Extract 10, here too the answer is also inferentially available in Stan's just-prior turn (line 6).[7]

```
(11)
1  J:    =Well don't tell Bernie but I got him a hat fer his birthday.
2  S:    Oh you got Bernie a hat?
3  J:    Yeah.
4        (.)
5  J:    Cuz you took his. It's sort of like
6  S:    ^I [didn't take his.<I paid him for it. what he paid for it.
7  J:       [m
8  J:    Oh you paid him for it.
9  S: →  Of ^course!
10 J:    Oh:. So I got him one sortuvv li:ke that.
```

In Extract 12 several Japanese friends are having dinner together at Kazu's house. Yoshi's husband Masao has not yet arrived and prior to this day there had been some question as to whether he would be able to come at all. At line 1, Yoshi asks Kazu whether there is enough sushi (most likely to know whether she should save some from her own plate for her husband). Kazu confirms that there is enough with a repetitional answer in line 3 followed by the final particle *yo*. This particle is typically analyzed as an index of epistemic authority (Morita 2002) or epistemic primacy (Hayano this volume). Here Kazu is the hostess and the *yo* indexes her access to whether there is enough sushi. After a micropause Kazu continues by making explicit that she has sushi set aside for Masao (line 5).

```
(12)
1  YOSH:    anta osushi wa tariru no.
            you  sushi  TP suffice FP
            Hey, (is there) enough sushi.
```

---

[7] Heritage (1998) notes that participant orientations to self-evident answers also do not block question recipients from prefacing responses to inquiry with "Oh".

```
2              (0.2)
3   KAZU:      -tariru yo?,
               suffice FP
               (There is) enough.
4              (.) ((Yoshi gazing at Kazu))
5   KAZU:      masao san no mada:- [aru,
               Masao Mr. L   still    be
               (There) still is Mister Masao's,
6   YOSH:                          [na-kuru yotee shiteta no?=
                                    come   plan  doing FP
                                    Were (you) planning to have (him) come?
7   KAZU:  →   =mochiron.  ((with head nod))
               Of course.
8              (0.8)
9   KAZU:  →   m:ochiron. ((with small head nod))
               Of course.
10             (0.6)
11  YOSH:      osewa    kakema [su.
               trouble  cause ((formulaic))
               (I'm) giving (you) trouble.
               ((=Thank you / Sorry for the trouble.))
12  KAZU:                     [m:ochiron.
                               Of course.
13  MAKI:      itadakimasu.
               Bon Appetit.
```

Despite Kazu's explicit assertion that sushi is set aside for Masao, Yoshi asks whether Kazu had planned on Masao coming (line 6). This question implies that Kazu might not have planned on this and insinuates that Kazu might be a hostess who would run short of food for her guests. Kazu refutes this with *mochiron* ('Of course'; line 7 and again in line 9). Here again, as in Extracts 10–11, "Of course" is offered in a context where the questioner suggests that something morally problematic may be the case and where the questioner had epistemic access to the answer. Once again "Of course" treats as untenable the presupposition that Kazu might not have planned for Masao to come to dinner.

Extracts 10–12 show cases where the answer to the question is inferentially available in the just-prior stretch of interaction. Another context where "Of course" is offered is when the questioner has epistemic access to the answer via interactional history (relatedly, see Clark [1996] on common ground). These questions too typically suggest something morally problematic. Extract 9 was that sort of case. From Nancy's history with Hyla, she should know that a boyfriend of Hyla's would be Jewish (indeed, this is why it works as a tease as well). Extract 13 is taken from a pediatric medical visit. Here the doctor is wrapping up the treatment recommendation in lines 1–8 and in line 11 indicates that he will get something for the patient and mother and then leaves the room (line 12). After approximately 10 seconds the girl, playfully swinging her legs while still seated on the examination table, asks "Okay. Do I get uh lollipop?". There has been no mention of a lollipop in the encounter with the physician prior to this. It is likely that this is a standard reward for the girl following a visit to the doctor. However, the girl's question treats *no* as a possible response, thus suggesting that the mother may be the sort of person who might not give the girl a lollipop (despite previous occurrences or promises).[8]

(13) (Girl is around seven years old)
```
1   DOC:      An' that makes uh pretty good (.) mixture.
2             You're giving 'er uh teaspoon
3             (>uh thuh<) Triaminic,
4   DOC:      .hh
5   MOM:      °°Okay.°°#
6   DOC:      An' you could mix in with that theh:=uh
7             (.) about three quarters of uh teaspoon
8             uh Robitussin DM,
9             (.)
10  MOM:      Okay, (  )
11  DOC:      Uh: s:o (0.2) (lemme get th'm:,)
12            ((door closes))
13            (10.0)
14  PAT:      Okay. Do I get uh lollipop?
15            (0.8)
16  MOM:  →   Of course_ when we're (.) done.
17            (1.0)
18  PAT:      Are we all done?
19            (1.0)
20  MOM:      I don't think so. ((shaking head))
```

In response, the mother's "Of course_" confirms that the girl can in fact have a lollipop. It also counters the insinuation that the mother might have denied the girl. In this case, epistemic access comes not from the just-prior interaction. Rather, this knowledge is rooted in previous trips to the doctor after which the girl has likely received a lollipop.

---

[8] We do not know whether the lollipops are normally in the mother's bag, in which case this may be hearable to the mother as a request for one, though this does not change the analysis here.

A question's unaskability can also be rooted in more basic cultural or general understanding. For instance, in Extract 14 taken from a field note, TS is just back from Southern Spain and has been telling a work colleague, MB, about the trip. MB mentioned having visited the area some years before. In line 2 TS asks MB whether she visited the Alhambra – probably the most culturally significant and most visited site in the area and commonly the primary reason people visit Granada. The question though suggests that both *yes* and *no* are possible answers and implies that MB might be the sort of person who might not have visited the place.

(14) (Field note TS 2/2008)
1 MB: We went to Granada too.
2 TS: Oh didju, Didju visit the Alhambra,
3 MB: → Of course.

In response, MB answers "Of course.", thereby contesting the possibility of *no* as an answer. Here it is not that MB had already stated that she had visited the Alhambra, but if she visited Granada as a tourist she almost certainly would have visited this palace. Thus, her contestation of the pre-supposition of TS's question is rooted not in its unaskability relative to prior interactions but in general world knowledge and in who TS should know her to be – the kind of person who would certainly want to visit such a significant site.

Another case of this type is shown in Extract 15. This exchange is in Italian, between two friends sitting together. A has been joking about an Italian actress who has a huge amount of hair – Moira Orfei. At line 1, A asks B whether B thinks that the actress has a wig. With the question, A presupposes that *no* is a possible answer, suggesting that either she or her interlocutor might think such hair was real (either way is problematic).

(15)
1 A: *Ma secondo te   c'   ha la   parrucca? hu hu hu*
            But in your opinion CLI has the wig
            But in your opinion does she have a wig? Hu hu hu

2 (0.2)

3 B: *Certo.   Scherzi.   No no son   tutti   suoi*
            Of course Joke.2SG No no be.3PL all   hers
            Of course. Are you kidding me. No no they are all hers

4   (0.2)/((Nodding))

5 A: *Secondo   s- (0.4) Anche secondo me*
            According t-   also   in my opinion
            According t- (0.4) Also in my opinion

In response, B answers *Certo.* ("Of course"). The use is the same as in previous examples – here B counters A's presupposition that B could suppose the actress does *not* have a wig as untenable, and treats the question as unaskable. As was the case with Extract 14, here the appeal is to general knowledge rather than a previous part of the interaction. The grounding appears to be simply how much hair a person can naturally possess. Finally, see Extract 16. Here two Dutch friends are talking. They are copresent but lack visual access to each other. They are discussing Papuan people who, B says in line 1, have bones in their noses which cause them to talk in a very nasal manner (line 4).

(16)
```
1  B:   =Die  hebben  toch     ook   ( )  van die     botten
        They  have    actually also  ( )  of   these  bones
        They  actually also have like these bones

2       in  hun   neus – volgens mij        [is het heel   raar    als
        in their nose  according=to me   is it  really  strange  if
        in their noses – which to me is really strange if

3  R:                                       [Ja in'daad.
                                            Yeah indeed.

4  B:   die   dan  praten. 'n   *praten die   een beetje zo:.*/((nasal))
        they then talk.  And talk     they a    little   so
        they then talk. *An' they talk a bit like this.*/((nasal))

5  R:   [Ja  in'daad ja.
        Yeah indeed  yeah.

6  J:   [.hh-  Ja::(h) huh huh huh huh?,
               Yeah

7  R:   Maar mis-  e-=volg' mij          praat die   ook   met
        But  mayb- u- according=to me talk   they also  with
        But  mayb- u- according to me they also talk with

8       vlaggen of=zo of  met  symbo:len.
        flags    or so or  with symbols
        flags or something or with symbols.⁹

9       (0.2)

10 B:   Ja:
        Yeah

11 R:   (Maar eeh) Praten die   ook   g'woon echt?,
        But   uh  Talk   they also  normal really
        But uh Do they also talk normally really?,
```

⁹ Native Dutch speakers also report this to be an unusual expression and not idiomatic. They suggest that this could come from the idea of using symbols in the written language though clearly here the speaker is discussing spoken language.

12 B: → *M # ja#   'tuurlij:k.*
             mm yeah of cou:rse.
13 R: *Ja?*
             Yeah?
14 B: → *'tuur' we::l,*
             'course.

In line 7 R identifies some of the ways in which their speech is unusual
(though what exactly he means is unclear). He then asks the target question
Praten die ook g'woon echt?, ('Do they also talk normally really?,'). This
question suggests the morally problematic possibility that Papuan people
might be incapable of talking normally. This is treated as inconceivable by
B with *M ja 'tuurlij:k* ('Mm Yeah of cou:rse.') (line 12), and "Of course" is
offered as a response again (line 14), in a more reduced form, when R challenges B's confirmation (line 12) (on post-response pursuit of response,
see Jefferson [1981]). Here again the issue is that by general knowledge it
should be obvious to R that Papuan people, like all people, can "talk normally." B's response treat's R's question as suggesting the untenable position that Papuan people would be unable to do so.

These cases illustrate that "Of course" is consistently used in contexts where the questioner suggests that something morally problematic
may be the case, through a question design that treats both confirmation
and disconfirmation as possible or has epistemic access to the answer.
In this data set, both factors appear consistently. Epistemic access may
be through just prior interaction (Extracts 10–12), through interactional
history (Extracts 9 and 13) or through general knowledge (Extracts
14–16). Asking a question that insinuates something morally problematic
in a context where the speaker can, at the very least, infer the answer is
doubly problematic.

Orientations to unaskability

The other form of evidence that "Of course" contests the presupposition
of question askability comes from cases where this reaches the surface of
the interaction. Example 17 was shown earlier as Extract 9. Reproduced
here we can also see how Hyla's "O:f cou:rse," is treated by Nancy. In third
position Nancy receipts the "Of course" with a repetition of it. This treats
the response as remarkable and thus teases Hyla again. "Of course" here
suggests both that Hyla would not consider a boy who was not Jewish *and*
that his being Jewish, in the context of these Jewish girls, seems also to
underscore his good qualities.

(17)
```
1   NAN:    =.hhh Dz he av iz own apa:rt[mint?]
2   HYL:                            [.hhhh] Yea:h,=
3   NAN:    =Oh:,
4            (1.0)
5   NAN:    How didju git iz number,
6            (.)
7   HYL:    I(h) (.) c(h)alled infermation'n San Fr'ncissc(h)[uh!
8   NAN:                                                    [Oh::::.
9            (.)
10  NAN:    Very cleve:r,hh=
11  HYL:    =Thank you[: I- .hh-.hhhhhhhh]hh=
12  NAN:             [W'ts iz last name,]
13  HYL:    =Uh:: Freedla:nd. .hh [hh
14  NAN:                          [Oh[:,
15  HYL:                             [('r) Freedlind.=
16  NAN:    =Nice Jewish bo:y?
17  HYL: →  O:f cou:rse,=
18  NAN:    ='v [cou:rse,]
19  HYL:        [hh-hh-hh] hnh .hhhhh=
20  NAN:    =Nice Jewish boy who doesn' like tih
21           write letters?
22           (.)
23  HYL:    eYe::h, .hhh En he ma:de such a big dea::l
24           a:bout id 'e, s[:pent- .hh
25  NAN:                   [I kno::::::w.=
```

If he's a good guy and of interest to Hyla he would have to be Jewish. The first dimension of this idea seems to be what Nancy challenges when she teases Hyla for having used "Of course", as shown in her unpacking at lines 20–21 – this boy, although Jewish, did not write letters to Hyla after promises that he would.

The next case is taken from a pediatric consultation. Here the mother and son are done with the visit and have exchanged closings with the physician when he asks for confirmation that the boy, having left the room without a sticker, does not in fact want one. The boy here disconfirms this but does so with only "Yeah_".

(18) (eight-year-old boy)
```
1   DOC:    You guys take care, Good tuh see ya, Have uh
2            good holiday.
3   MOM:    You to^o:.
4   DOC:    £Buh bye.(h)£
5            (1.2)
6   DOC:    ^Joshua=Joshua.
7            (0.2)
8   DOC:    Okay. >You ('on't) wanta sticker before you go?<
```

```
9   PAT:          Yeah_
10  DOC:    →     Of c^ourse you do:. (Yes) you can't walk out without uh
11                sticker:?,
12                (0.5)
13  DOC:          Here you go, You can choo:se.
```

In third position the physician receipts the boys disconfirmation with "Of c^ourse you do:.", effectively upgrading the boy's disconfirmation from one that accepts the presupposition that the boy may or may not want a sticker to one that contests this presupposition. The next turn constructional unit (TCU) "you can't walk out without uh sticker:?," shows the physician's orientation to "Of course" as asserting that the alternative is/ was inconceivable (particularly his use of "can't"). This case also offers a glimpse into some of the more explicit ways that adults may socialize children into the use of this interactional practice. Here the physician shows the child that "Of course" is appropriate in situations where an alternative is inconceivable.

In Extract 19 the participant orientation is even more explicit than in Extracts 17–18. Here Dan has been complaining to his wife, Mona, a dental hygienist, that one of his employees must pay for his dental work up front. In line 5 Mona proposes a remedy to the problem: "^We can bill your ins^urance," (on complaints and remedies, see Schegloff [2005]). After 1 second of silence, Dan questions this with the confirmation request "Can ya?" (line 7). This is an environment for "Of course" that we've seen in previous cases – proper dental offices are able to bill insurance companies since insurance companies are meant to pay them, and Mona, as a hygienist, ought to know whether or not that is possible. Additionally, Mona has just stated that they can bill the insurance, so the answer is readily available. Dan's question suggests that it might be the case that Mona's dental office would not be able to bill the insurance (which could insinuate something negative about her office's competence). In confirmation Mona says "'v course we can." (line 8).

```
(19)
1   DAN:          He's probably depressed he's gotta
2                 pay for all this dental work.
3                 (0.5)
4   DAN:          Take all her time to do it.
5   MON:          ^We can bill your ins^urance,
6                 (1.0)
7   DAN:          Can ya?
8   MON:    →     'v course we can.
9                 (.)
10  MON:          Why couldn't we.
```

```
11          (2.5)
12 DAN:     Cuz you're not on thuh: (0.2)
13 MON:     ^Don't you have dental insurance?
14 DAN:     Ye^ah.
15          (2.4)
16 MON:     Do you have to go to their dentist?,
17 DAN:     Ye^ah.
18 MON:     |Oh.
19          (0.5)
20 MON:     Well then maybe not.
```

The analysis here is consistent with other cases: with "Of course" Mona contests the presupposition of Dan's request for confirmation – it is inconceivable that they would be unable to bill the dental insurance for costs if the patient cannot pay on site. Mona's orientation to this as an untenable presupposition is made explicit when, following the "Of course" response, she questions why Dan would have thought that a disconfirmation was possible – why the question was askable (line 10). With this question she brings to the surface what is present in all of the cases of "Of course" answers that we have looked at – in asking Dan to account for posing an unaskable question, she accounts for her use of "Of course" as an answer. In the end, after having taken such a strong position, it is Mona who backs down, realizing that the individual may not have one of the affiliated insurance plans (lines 16–20).

Extract 20 shows a similar situation where a pediatrician, approaching the conclusion of the visit, suggests that the child patient does not need any treatment. At lines 1–2/4 the physician suggests a contingency plan (Mangione-Smith et al. 2001) – if the child continues to complain she can see her regular doctor again (though the expectation is that the problem will resolve). The doctor then goes on to suggest that, if the child is not complaining, the mother need not do anything. In partial overlap with this the mother poses a question (lines 8–9). In this context simply "An' her throat," is hearable as requesting an assessment of the state of the girl's throat. This question presupposes that the physician examined the throat and is in a position to provide an assessment. However, the parent then poses a somewhat different question – one which suggests that the physician might *not* have examined the girl's throat ("Did you look at her throat?").

(20)
```
1 DOC:      And she is old enough tha:t i- if it's still bothering
2           her (0.5) she'll let=you know an' you ju[st let Doctor=
3 MOM:                                              [Yes:.
4 DOC:      =Halfus take uh look at 'er.
```

```
 5  MOM:      Definitely.
 6  DOC:      If she seems like she's better, she's not complaining
 7            any more °then you don't [(need to °)
 8  MOM:                              [An' her throat, Did you
 9            look at [her throat?
10  DOC:  →          [(Oh it's fine.) <Of course I (looked in her)
11            [throat.
12  MOM:      [I didn't notice.
13  MOM:      .hh
14  DOC:      ( Ah [::.)
15  MOM:           [I heard you're very quick.
16            (0.2)
17  DOC:      Huh huh
18  DOC:      Well they don't hold their mouth open for:
19            [per(h)iods of time (        )
20  MOM:      [(you haf:ta be ready. qu(h)ick.
21            ((clicking noise))/(0.5)
```

In response to the questions the physician first offers an assessment, aligning with the presupposition of the first question and offering a response
made relevant by the first question. However, in overlap with this answer,
the mother completes her second question at which point the physician
responds immediately. The answer to the first question obviates the need
to answer the second. However, rather than letting the second question go,
the physician holds the turn, addressing the mother's morally problematic
suggestion. We see this first in her effort to hold the turn across a transition
relevance place: she uses an abrupt-join (Local and Walker 2004) which
mitigates against the mother initiating a turn of her own here. Second, "Of
course I looked in her throat." (lines 10–11) is hearably defensive. There is
good reason for this since, as a pediatrician seeing a child patient for upper
respiratory tract infection symptoms, she would indeed be remiss had she
not examined the child's throat. Here, her reliance on "Of course" makes
this visible by claiming that the mother's insinuation that she had failed to
look in the girl's throat is inconceivable; she is not "that kind of doctor."

The mother accounts for her suggestion that the physician had diag-
nosed prior to inspecting her daughter's throat with "I didn't notice." The
mother here suggests that, despite the physician treating it as inconceivable that she had failed to examine the child's throat, asking the question
was actually reasonable given the circumstances. It is further defended with
"I heard you're very quick." which again defends the mother's question
design as defensible.

A final instance is shown in Extract 21. Here Justin, Tex, Nick and Dan
are talking. Tex and Dan have been friends since they were kids and have
been reminiscing about past experiences together for the benefit of Nick

and Justin who are newer friends. Justin comments that Dan's mother is "cool" but that he has not met Dan's father. Tex, the insider here, refers to Dan's dad in the turn "£That's Kramer.=hmh". This turn is of the sort that indicates deep familiarity with someone, not unlike "that's so (like) Sam". In response, Justin requests confirmation ("Your dad's name's Kra:mer?," – line 7). Although it was Tex who made the remark (line 5) and Justin's confirmation request is addressed to Dan (note: "Your dad's" as well as Justin's gaze), Justin nonetheless has epistemic access to the name.

```
(21)
1    JUST:          I never met your dad but (.) >°(we stayed at your [house )°<
2    TEX:                                                            [Humpf
3    TEX:           (£He used=tuh hafta fight: mo:m by uh- trillion folds.=[huh)
4    DAN:                                                                 [Yes
5    TEX:           £That's Kramer.=hmh
6    DAN:           I- hh if you me [et 'im-
7    JUST:                          [Your dad's name's Kra:mer?,
8    JUST:                          [((gaze to Dan))
9    DAN:     →     Yeah of course.
10   JUST:          Huhuhuhuhuh of course?, Huhuhu [huhuhuh
11   DAN:                                          [He's uh legend. HE's UH
12                  FUCKIN' LEGend (   ,)
13   JUST:    ⇒     Wh(h)y i(h)s i(h)t of c [ou(h)(h)rse.
14   DAN:                                   [Je::sus. .hh huh
15                  (.)
16   DAN:           I mean if you knew my dad you'd know he's Kramer. I mean_
17   TEX:           God. (0.5) That man. (.) I tell you. (1.2)
18   TEX:     →     [>Kramer's picked me up numerous times.<
19   NICK:          [(whistling)
20   DAN:           °hh hh°
21   TEX:           and saved my life.
22   JUST:          °Huhuhuh°
```

An issue that is likely relevant here is that at the time of this recording a television program *Seinfeld* was extremely popular and one of the key characters was named Kramer. It is likely that Justin finds it unbelievable that Dan's father just coincidentally shares a name with this popular television character. It is probably this issue that allows Justin's question to be heard as morally problematic: could it possibly be true?

In response to the request for confirmation, Dan confirms with "Yeah of course.", thereby treating it as inconceivable that his father could be named anything other than Kramer.[10] Moreover, it treats Justin as having

---

[10] The turn-initial "Yeah" shows that speakers may use "Of course" either on its own or in combination with an unmarked interjection token as discussed later. See Extract 16 as well.

insinuated that, despite Tex having just indicated that Dan's father's name was Kramer, it might not be. This case, though, is unusual because Justin challenges Dan's use of "Of course". Justin first laughs and then repeats "of course?," with rising intonation, a practice for challenging a speaker and thus requesting that s/he account for something just said (Schegloff *et al.* 1977; Selting 1996). Dan offers as his account that "He's uh l̲e̲gend. HE's UH FUCKIN' L̲E̲Gend (,)". However, as an account it fails to explain why he used "Of course" and instead expands on his father's qualities. At line 13 Justin then explicitly requests an account for Dan's use of "Of course" with "Wh(h)y i(h)s i(h)t of cou(h)(h)rse."

In partial overlap Dan appears to protest Justin's quarreling with "Je::sus." However, it is unclear whether he has already understood the import of Justin's turn or not. In any case, the rest of his turn does address Justin's request for an account. In particular, he claims that "Of course" was defensible because it would be impossible for his father not to be Kramer, appealing to intimate knowledge of his father: "if you kn̲e̲w my dad you'd know he's Kr̲a̲mer."

In most cases of "Of course", the grounds for treating the question as unaskable are rooted in general knowledge (e.g., how much hair can a person have naturally) or in previous interaction (e.g., when the speaker just said she had sushi for Masao). Here, although Tex had just implied that Dan's father's name is "Kramer," what Justin contests is the legitimacy of a claim that someone's name could not have been otherwise. Since names are given prior to any personality characteristics being available, how could Dan possibly claim that his father's name could not be otherwise? Thus, this is precisely Dan's vulnerability and why he is asked to account for his use of "Of course". However, it is also how he is able to account for his usage: his father's character is such that he *is* or *embodies* "Kramer." Tex adopts the same position – that Dan's father's name could not be otherwise (lines 17–18/21) which both affiliates with Dan and shows that his use of "Of course" was understood by Tex in much the same way.

I have offered two forms of evidence that, in response to a polar question, "Of course" contests the presupposition that both a confirmation and a disconfirmation are possible. First, "Of course" is used in contexts where questioners suggest something morally problematic with their question and do so despite having epistemic access to this not being the case either in the immediately prior interaction, in interactional history or through general knowledge. Second, in a subset of cases we can observe clear participant orientations to "Of course" as a practice for contesting this dimension of a question's presuppositions in the form of comments on, or challenges of, the answer. With "Of course", question recipients treat questioners' morally problematic insinuations as inconceivable.

Multiple responses

Yes or *no* type responses to polar questions bring a sequence of action to possible completion and therefore can constitute closure of the sequence initiated by the question (Schegloff 1968, 2007b; Schegloff and Sacks 1973). However, to confirm with *Yeah* or *Uh huh* not only does nothing more than confirm (Heritage and Raymond 2005; Raymond 2003) but also implicitly accepts the question "as is," including not only its terms but also its legitimacy as a social action. Question recipients are not always willing to accept all aspects of an action and design (Heritage 1998; Heritage and Raymond in press; Raymond 2003; Stivers and Hayashi 2010; Stivers and Heritage 2001). Speakers may want to confirm but also to address problems with the presuppositions of the question, the action(s) it implements or the knowledge states it implies for the questioner and/or the recipient. Different response forms have different affordances: the sheer existence of the many different confirmation tokens suggests that. Additionally, the way that different forms of confirmation are deployed simultaneously (e.g., a head nod in overlap with *Yes*) and serially (e.g., "Oh Yeah of course we would") also suggests that each does slightly different interactional work.

Considering different sorts of confirmation, repetitional answers, for instance, are more "agentive" than unmarked interjections (Heritage and Raymond in press). Return to Extract 3 where Jessie requests confirmation. Unmarked interjections in this context would be "yeah", "uh huh" or "mm hm". Mike's use of a partial repetition here allows him to assert independently that he is committed to "E:verything." in his own turn rather than merely *confirming* that he is committed to everything. By resisting the precise terms of the question he is asked, he is able to use his confirmation to add to his claim that he is a committed kind of guy within the only TCU he has rights to expect (Sacks et al. 1974). Similarly, in Extract 6 when Marcia confirms Susan's question about driving up with "Oh yea:h." she is able, within a single TCU, both to confirm that Susan is correct and to indicate that the question is ill fitted to the particulars of the interaction or sequence (Heritage 1998).

Now with "Of course" we have seen a resource that speakers also use to manage multiple functions within a single TCU. "Of course" can, on its own, both confirm the proposition of the question and simultaneously challenge the question's presupposition of askability (Extracts 9–12). However, in some cases "Of course" is delivered in combination with other turn elements. In Extract 22 "Of course" is *oh*-prefaced which affords the turn yet more interactional work within a single TCU. Here Bill is proudly telling how he wrote a complaint letter to a typewriter company and received a new keyboard. At line 14 Ellen asks whether he used the school letterhead.

```
(22)
 1  BILL:     So eh [said I:'m uh .hh As you c'n ima:gine I em=
 2  (BEN):          [(        )
 3  BILL:     =outra:ged at yer uh uh: yih know (0.2) poor engineering,
 4            (.) but I am confident that, [yer prompt attention =
 5  (LOR):                                 [(              )?
 6  BILL:     [dih this matter will .hhh uh:: not force me=
 7  (ELL):    [°°(          )°°
 8  BILL:     =dih take stronger action.
 9  ELL:      Oh^: hu [h ^heh heh^ ^.hihh What didju [(rahda vers'ry)
10  BILL:             [°huh°
11  BEN:                                              [That's ohweez
12            ah: wunnuh know what the hell d'z 'ee mea:n by
13            stronger a:'tion[s.(wuh)]
14  ELL:                      [D i d   ]ju uh use the school letterhead?=
15  BILL:  → [Oh of cou:rse,
16  ELL:     [|Oh-ho that's good.
```

In response, Bill answers "Oh of cou:rse," (line 15). Heritage (1998) shows that an *oh*-prefaced response to inquiry indicates a shift of attention. What has occasioned that shift is commonly the question's inappositeness. Both *oh*-prefaces and "Of course" responses are common in contexts where the answer is already available, and both treat the question as inappropriate, but the exact grounds are somewhat different and they thus do slightly different interactional work. In this case, "Of course" contests the morally problematic suggestion that Bill might not have written his letter of complaint on letterheaded paper – presumably a foolish thing to do in terms of underscoring his professionalism and improving his chances of the company resolving the problem. The *oh*-preface suggests that the question is inapposite. In addition to the problematic suggestion that Bill might have failed to do the obvious and use the school letterhead, the question is asked at a less than ideal juncture in the interaction. Here the telling has reached completion and it is the time for appreciation. This question harks back to the writing of the letter. Questioning such details at this point undermines appreciation of Bill's accomplishment.

"Of course" is also used in combination with repetitional answers (see Extracts 19–20). In Extract 20 the physician responds to the mother's question of whether she looked in the girl's throat with "<Of course I (looked in her) throat." Whereas "Of course" challenges the morally problematic presupposition that she might not have looked at the girl's throat, the repetitional answer quarrels with the question's proposal that the physician accept a position of reduced agency with respect to having checked her patient's throat. In particular, the physician has suggested no prescription treatment for the girl's upper respiratory tract infection. In a context where

the mother has been told simply to wait, only bringing her daughter back for another evaluation if symptoms do not improve, the questioning of a diagnostic finding is a practice for resisting the treatment recommendation (Stivers 2005b, 2007b).

"Of course" is not always turn-initial. In Extracts 16 and 21 the response is "Yeah of course". The delivery in both cases is in one intonation contour, but pragmatically and syntactically the turns are possibly complete at "Yeah"/ "ja". This leaves "Of course" more vulnerable to overlap than if the "Of course" were delivered TCU-initially (Sacks *et al.* 1974). This vulnerability is even more clear in situations where the two responses are delivered in discrete intonation units. For instance, see Extract 23. At line 11 Lesley asks her mother (on the telephone) whether she could work out what she'd written in her response letter – the letter Mum has just indicated she's answered. In line 12 Mum initiates repair with an open class repair initiator (Drew 1997; Schegloff *et al.* 1977). In Drew's analysis of the repair initiation here, he suggests that Lesley's inquiry is sequentially ill fitted because it "fails to take properly into account the implications (as regards 'working it out') of her (i.e., Mum's) prior answer [line 10]" (1997: 85). Lesley does not immediately respond to Mum's repair initiation, and, after a brief silence, Mum continues with "<u>Oh</u> yes. ^Ye:s yes'v course I could." (lines 14–15). The first TCU (line 14) seems to be primarily concerned with claiming recognition of what Lesley is asking about. The second TCU, though, answers our target question "^Could you work it <u>a</u>ll out,":

(23)
```
1   LES:        .t And it's got tuh be re do:ne,
2   MUM:        (        )
3   LES:        .t Right down intuh th'ja:w.
4   MUM:        ^Just at the wrong ti:me uhh!=
5   LES:        =That's ri:ght.h
6               (.)
7   LES:        Yes.
8   LES:        <Didju get my letter,
9               (0.5)
10  MUM:        Uh yes thank you, I've writ- (.) I've answered it.=
11  LES:        =.TCH! Oh yes. ^Wey (.) ^Could you work it all out,
12  MUM:        Pardon?
13              (.)
14  MUM:   →    Oh yes.
15  MUM:   →    ^Ye:s yes'v course I could.
16  LES:        What did you thin:k then.
17  MUM:        Uh well ^wait (.) that(.) ('ll)/(should) be in my letter.
18  LES:        .t.k Okay,
19              ()
20  LES:        Uh huh,
```

Here the sharp pitch reset on the first *yes* of line 15 suggests a shift away from the repair sequence. However, the contour there suggests possible turn completion, whereas the second *yes* revises the first with "y̲e̲s'v course I could" being through produced in one intonation contour. Thus, Mum reanalyzes the question and redoes an answer that is better fitted to it – better fitted precisely because it includes "yes", "Of course" and a partial repetition. All of these are packaged within a single intonation contour which, as mentioned earlier, mitigates against turn incursion by Lesley. In this way there is a division of labor such that *yes* merely confirms whereas "Of course" challenges the morally problematic suggestion that she might not have been able to work it all out, and the repetition challenges the action of questioning her ability to work it out.

The ordering is arguably important precisely because of the turn-taking system constraints (Sacks *et al.* 1974). The floor is treated as a desirable and scarce resource. Although often participants grant one another multiple TCUs, the system is such that a speaker's right to only one TCU can be invoked at any point. Speakers orient to this in many ways. In these cases, the fact that multiple confirmations are packaged within a single intonation contour orients to the increased vulnerability to turn incursion that would come with segmenting the turn into multiple TCUs. Still, the fact that the sequence is pragmatically and syntactically complete after one of these confirmations increases the chances that a co-participant will compete for the floor. Thus, we can see a prioritization in the use of more than one element (Heritage and Raymond 2005: 24), suggesting that the second is more dispensable. In cases with multiple elements, the ordering tends to be quite stable: [Oh] + [Yes] + [Of course] + [Repeat] where each element is optional, except that as a turn preface *oh* cannot stand alone. When "Of course" is delivered without "yes", it prioritizes contesting the question's askability. By contrast, when "Of course" is preceded by "Yes", confirmation or affirmation is arguably prioritized, and the challenge to the question's askability is secondary to that.

Discussion

Although questions significantly constrain recipients' next interactional moves, they do not determine them. Recipients can and do push against the constraints and at times break them. However, even when question recipients operate within a question's constraints, they do not merely provide information, just as questioners do not merely request confirmation or information. In the questions we examined, questioners commonly designed questions that insinuated that something morally problematic might be the case, despite epistemic access to the contrary. Precisely in these environments question recipients consistently pushed against the constraints being imposed on them – by pushing back on these constraints they objected to the moral implications of what the questioners were asking. With their use of "Of course", question recipients consistently asserted that they were (or someone else was) not "the kind of person" the questioner had suggested with their question. Thus, we have a window into one of the ways in which interactants manage their social relationships at a micro-level.

When speakers contest a question's askability, this is not, by definition, disaffiliative. Just as *oh*-prefaced responses to assessments can, at times, indicate stronger agreement precisely because they index epistemic independence (Heritage 2002a), so too can "Of course" at times be affiliative and at other times disaffiliative. Return, for instance, to Extract 11 where brother and sister are discussing the hat that Joyce plans to give their friend for his birthday. When Joyce challenges Stan as to whether he really paid their friend for the hat Stan took, Stan's "Of course" is disaffiliative. This is because her question implies that Stan is the kind of person who might simply take someone's hat without giving anything in return. Understandably, Stan takes issue with this assumption.

Similarly, in Extract 20, the mother challenges the physician's good medical practice when she questions whether or not she has examined the girl's throat. When the physician retorts with "Of course", this is clearly disaffiliative. The physician does not let stand the presupposition that she might be the kind of physician who would fail to check the throat of a child who came to the doctor with upper respiratory tract infection symptoms.

Although "Of course" may lend itself to such disaffiliative situations, it is not inherently disaffiliative. Consider Extract 23 in which Lesley is talking to her mother. Lesley questions whether her mother could make out all of the letter. One potential problem here is that a daughter is questioning her mother's ability to read her writing. "Of course", although challenging, is also affiliative because it conveys that there is no question of Mum not being able to read her daughter's writing. Similarly, recall Extract 13 in which the girl at the doctor's office asks about a lollipop and the mother responds with "Of course". There too the context is affiliative in that, although the mother challenges the child's presupposition, she does so in order to convey that there is no need to question the regular reward. The same is routinely seen in office encounters in which a colleague asks whether the other can spare some time and the response is "Of course". There again the situation is affiliative: the questioner suggests that her colleague might not have time for her whereas her recipient contests the presupposition that this might be the case, asserting that s/he is someone for whom readiness to "spare time" needn't be doubted.

At times questioners who ask these problematic questions may do so in sacrifice to a larger interactional project. Consider Extract 10 in which Geri asks Shirley whether Shirley introduced her boyfriend to Geri's mother. Shirley's "Of course" treats Geri's question as morally problematic – what kind of person would she be to be in such a situation and fail to introduce the two? However, notice too that the telling had gone somewhat off-track relative to its preface of "yer mother met Michael las' night". Geri's question does work to promote talk on that dimension of the telling rather than on the dog's behavior, etc. But to ask this question at this juncture does make Geri vulnerable to precisely this response.

Conclusion

Theories of both human communication and language evolution continue to debate whether language use is primarily concerned with information transfer (Nowak and Krakauer 1999; Shannon and Weaver 1949) or whether it evolved to foster and build social relationships (Dunbar 1996). Question–answer sequences might initially appear to be primarily a site of information transfer. However, as we have seen, they are at least equally places where interactants monitor each other's behavior on moral grounds, whether that is grounded in epistemic access, rights or authority. Interactants have a moral responsibility to design their questions in ways that take into consideration what they have epistemic access to – what has happened in the just-prior interaction, what they know about their interlocutor and what they can infer from general knowledge. Failures on any of these fronts, even if in the service of larger interactional projects, are accountable, and interactants treat it as their responsibility to enforce a moral code of conduct in social interaction.

5   Addressing epistemic incongruence in question–answer sequences through the use of epistemic adverbs

Trine Heinemann, Anna Lindström and Jakob Steensig

Introduction

Scholars working within quite divergent research traditions have argued that conversation requires speakers and recipients to assume that some things are held in common. These assumptions can range from the idea of a shared language and culture to details derived from joint experiences including prior conversation (Clark 1996; Grice 1975; Stalnaker 1978). In the conversation-analytic and ethnomethodological traditions, common ground, or intersubjectivity, figured as a central feature of interaction from early on. As demonstrated, for instance, by Garfinkel's ethnomethodological breaching experiments (Garfinkel 1967), failure to apply background knowledge when interacting with others has moral consequences. Reflecting on these experiments, Heritage concluded that "there is no quicker way, it appears, of provoking moral outrage than by not using background knowledge to make sense of other people's actions" (Heritage 1984b: 182).

The centrality of background knowledge to talk-in-interaction is evident in that languages provide resources dedicated to pointing out that information is shared. This chapter focuses on one such resource, namely the adverbs *jo* (Danish) and *ju* (Swedish). We begin with the observation that *jo/ju*, when used in an answer slot, claims that the questioner failed to take into account shared knowledge, which should have informed the design of the question. The inclusion of *jo/ju* in a slot where an answer is due thus embodies a claim of "epistemic incongruence," in that the basic epistemic configuration of a question (Hayano this volume) – that the answerer knows something the questioner does not know – is challenged.

We would like to thank all the contributors to this book, who have assisted with very useful comments and suggestions. Very thorough comments to written versions of the chapter have been provided by Lorenza Mondada, Birte Asmuß and Tanya Stivers. These comments have improved the chapter, and we are solely – and equally – responsible for any remaining errors or shortcomings.

Focusing on the social consequences of using *jo/ju* in responses to questions, we show that this practice can be affiliative or disaffiliative, depending on whether it renders the questioner morally responsible for failing to apply background knowledge or not. Our notion of affiliation builds on Jefferson's use of the term in her work on how recipient responses relate to speakers' projects (Jefferson 1988, 2002; Jefferson and Lee 1992 [1981]; Jefferson, Sacks and Schegloff 1987), and on Stivers's proposal that affiliation is an observable behavior which "displays support of and endorses" the co-participant's "conveyed stance" (Stivers 2008: 36).

Extract 1 introduces the practice we will be analyzing in the chapter. It is drawn from a conversation on a Swedish television talk-show between the host, Kristian Luuk, and Fredrik Reinfeldt, the leader of a political coalition. Luuk and Reinfeldt are talking about a recent weekend retreat where Reinfeldt met with members of the three other parties in the coalition.

(1) (Swedish, talk show, video)
The 'cd guy' mentioned in line 6 is the leader of the Christian Democratic party. SA is the studio audience.[1]

```
1 LUUK:  *    >Vem   blev  fullast      sen  på  kvällen<,
                >Who  got   most_drunk  then on  evening_the<,
                >Who got most drunk later on in the evening<,

2 SA:         hah-[hah

3 REIN:  →     [Ja::   eh  allså de e  de e  ju    eh två  nära
                [Yea::h uh  PRT  it  is it is  ADV  uh two  near
                Well::uh y'know it is it is JU two almost

4             nog    helnykterister    å   en  halv  höll  ja  på  å
                enough whole_teetotallers and one  half  held  I   on  to
                total teetotallers and a half I was about to

5             säja  s[å  att  eh-
                say  s[o  that uh-
                say so uh-

6 LUUK:        [De e  han kdkillen    som  inte  [dricker nåt
                [It is he  cd_guy_the  who  not   [drinks something
                It is the cd guy who doesn't drink anything

7 REIN:                                    [.rr Nä:e
                                             [.rr No:
                                             .rr No:
```

---

[1] The transcripts use the conventions explained in the list at the beginning of the book. For each data extract we provide information about language (Swedish/Danish), context (news interview / everyday, etc.) and the modality and/or medium (telephone, face-to-face, video, audio). Except for the data from broadcast material, all personal information has been anonymized. Throughout the chapter, the question is marked with * and the part of the response that contains *jo/ju*, or is seen as contrasting with this feature, is indicated with →.

8   *inge   vidare*
           nothing more
           nothing much

Luuk's wh-question in line 1 is designed to elicit the identification of
the person who got the most drunk. Reinfeldt's turn-initial 'yes' in line
3 does not conform with this question format and the prolongation of
the response token *Ja::* indicates that a non-straightforward response is
about to be produced, in a similar way to what has been shown for 'well'-
prefaced responses to wh-questions in American English (Schegloff and
Lerner 2009).[2] Reinfeldt then characterizes the people who were present
(lines 3–4) and addresses their status as (non)drinkers (two and a half of
the people at the meeting were almost total teetotallers, i.e., non-drinkers).
This list thus serves as an account for Reinfeldt not producing an answer to
the question, an account that challenges a presupposition of the question,
namely that everyone at the meeting was drinking alcohol. The content in
the account turns out to be something which the questioner, Luuk, claims
to already know, when he formulates his knowledge about the drinking
habits of one of the meeting participants in line 6.

Our focus is on responses like the one in lines 3–4. They treat assumptions in a question as problematic (in this case, that somebody got drunk)
by providing an account that runs counter to these assumptions. These
accounts contain a modal adverb, the Swedish *ju* (line 3 in Extract 1) or
the corresponding Danish one, *jo* (see extracts below). We will therefore
refer to these accounts as "*jo/ju*-accounts." We argue that *jo/ju* appeals to
the recipient (in this case the questioner) to treat what is said as shared
information. This argument is backed up in Extract 1 by the fact that the
questioner in line 6 displays that (and what) he already knew, that at least
one person didn't drink.

The question–answer sequence in lines 1–4 in Extract 1 resonates with the
nonconforming response described by Raymond (2003). Raymond argued
that nonconforming responses represent "the most overt, sequence-specific
method for managing trouble with, or misalignments between, speakers
regarding, [*sic*] the particular situation of choice posed by [a question]
in its sequential context" (Raymond 2003: 948–949). Looking exclusively
at *yes/no* interrogatives, Raymond (2003) concluded that, whereas "type-
conforming responses accept the terms and presuppositions embodied in a
[question,] ... nonconforming responses treat the design of the [question] –
and the action it delivers – as problematic in some way" (Raymond 2003:

---

[2] In Danish and Swedish, the response particle *ja* has a broad range of functions and can,
among other things, project a non-aligning responsive action (cf. A. Lindström 2009;
Steensig 2005).

949). This argument is applicable to the question–answer sequence in Extract 1, where the response both failed to conform with the design of the question and treated the question as problematic. However, we argue that the inclusion of *ju* does more than just claim a problem with the question. Additionally, and of central importance for the investigation at hand, the speaker claims that this problem was already known to the questioner. We thus argue that when *jo/ju* is used in answer slots it identifies and points to an epistemic incongruence (Hayano this volume). Our analysis will show that the social consequences of this practice depend on the activity that is pursued within the question–answer sequence.

This chapter is organized as follows: first, we briefly introduce the adverbs we analyze in their linguistic context and account for our data corpus. After that, we discuss previously identified practices for dealing with problems of epistemic incongruence. This discussion shows, among other things, that the relationship between epistemics and social affiliation is scalar rather than dichotomous. We then turn to our main analytic section, where we show how *jo/ju*-accounts can be employed in various positions within the answer slot, and how this positioning, in combination with the ongoing activity, shapes the social and moral claims raised within the sequence. The chapter concludes with a discussion about how our findings shed light on the relations between epistemics, affiliation and morality.

Linguistic features and data corpus

In line with sociolinguistic research claiming that the separation of Danish and Swedish into two different languages is a consequence of nation building rather than a reflection of empirical differences according to linguistic criteria (Romaine 2000), we treat the Danish *jo* and the Swedish *ju* as interchangeable items. This is warranted by the fact that they occur in the same syntactic and sequential positions and are employed for the same social practices within these positions.

Etymologically, the adverbs had a temporal meaning, 'ever' (Katlev 2000: 334). In modern Swedish and Danish this temporal aspect has disappeared, and the adverbs are now described as attitudinal or epistemic in meaning (Allan, Holmes and Lundskær-Nielsen 1995: 357; Christensen and Christensen 2005; Teleman, Hellberg and Andersson 1999: 114–115). Syntactically, *jo* and *ju* are clausal adverbs (Allan *et al.* 1995: 357; Hansen and Heltoft 2008: 79), usually placed after the finite verb in a main clause in both languages, and on occasion after a clause, as indicated in the following examples from our data (the finite verbs are *är* in Extract 2 and *ku* in 3):

(2) (Swedish)

> Leijonborg är **ju**   nykterist
> Leijonborg is ADV teetotaller
> Leijonborg is JU a teetotaller

(3) (Danish)

> Det ku' **jo** være arbejdsløshedskassen   **jo**
> it   could ADV be   the_unemployment_office ADV
> It could JO be the unemployment agency JO

There is no comparable adverb in English, so all attempts at translating *jo* and *ju* are but rough approximations. Often 'you know' is used to translate the adverb, but this translation does not do full justice to its actual function.

There has been some prior research into the meaning and function of *jo* and *ju*. It has been argued that Swedish *ju* expresses something as self-evident and true (Aijmer 1977; Teleman et al. 1999: 114), but also that it implements such different speech acts as persuasion, accusation, explanation and protest (Aijmer 1977: 211). Kotsinas noted that *ju* tends to be used in contexts in which the speaker is emotionally involved (Kotsinas 1994: 72), and Eriksson (1988) suggested that *ju* can be used to persuade and give weight to an argument as it has a reminding quality, indexing a reference to shared knowledge. Therkelsen (2004) concluded that Danish *jo* indicates that the opposite view of the one expressed in the *jo*-utterance has been considered and rejected.

In sum, prior research on the Swedish *ju* and Danish *jo* has linked the adverbs to epistemics in the sense that they can have a reminding function, indexing shared and self-evident knowledge. They can apparently also have modal and pragmatic functions, associated with emotional involvement and argumentative contexts. None of the studies have, however, been able to conclusively demonstrate this connection.

The difficulty in pinpointing the function of *jo* and *ju* has to do with the fact that participants rarely display their understanding of these adverbs, but rather orient to the actions carried out by the utterances containing them. Ideally, then, the study of *jo* and *ju* would compare utterances in which these adverbs occur with similar utterances without them. Another problem may be that prior work has attempted to find a set function that holds across a range of sequential contexts. However, as has been shown in research carried out in the conversation analysis (CA) – tradition, the meaning of a lexical item is always inextricably tied to its sequential context (e.g., Heritage 1984a, 1998, 2002a on *oh* in different sequential positions; Sorjonen 2001 on Finnish *yes* tokens and their interactional functions). As eloquently noted by Moerman, "every utterance is nailed into its very place. Participants found its sequential intelligibility there; and there the analyst must discuss it" (1988: 69). Our procedure has therefore been to identify a sequential context, answers to questions, in which *jo/ju* are systematically used and for which comparable sequences *without* the adverbs could be found. We have developed our argument on the basis of instances of *jo/ju* in this sequential context, drawing on a corpus of thirty hours of audio and video recordings of naturally occurring Danish and Swedish interaction. The bulk of our data consists of everyday interaction in private settings but also includes examples from institutional contexts such as the home-help service, broadcast interviews, employment agencies and help-line phone calls.

Preliminary overview of epistemic incongruence and social affiliation in question–answer sequences

In order to show the epistemic incongruence that *jo/ju*-accounts index, we will discuss other practices that are used to propose epistemic incongruence in question–answer sequences. One practice, described by Keevallik (this volume), consists of the question recipient claiming no knowledge ("I don't know"), thus undermining the presupposition implicitly oriented to by the questioner: that the question recipient has access to the knowledge required to answer the question. Another set of practices focuses on the questioner, by claiming that s/he should have known something that should have prevented her/him from asking the question or caused her/him to ask the question differently. These practices include the use of "of course"-type responses (Stivers this volume), which directly challenge the "askability" of the question, as well as practices such as "*oh*-prefacing" in English (Heritage 1998) or responding with multiple response tokens in Danish and German (Golato and Fagyal 2008; Heinemann 2009). Like "of course"-type responses, these latter practices indicate that the questioner should have known, but they do so without challenging the "askability" directly. Whereas practices like the use of "of course" place the onus of (not) knowing on the questioner, practices like using "I don't know" place the onus of knowing on the recipient.

That epistemics is intertwined with social and moral issues is evident in the types of accounts that question recipients do or do not produce when their responses fail to meet the expectations set up by questions (or other first pair part utterances) (Heritage 1984b, 1988; Keevallik this volume; Mondada this volume). These accounts can be designed either to attribute blame for a faulty question to the questioner, or, alternatively, to free the questioner of such responsibility. Thus, as Heritage (1984b, 1988) illustrates, a question recipient may claim full responsibility for any epistemic incongruence within a question–answer pair, by producing a "no fault" account. One aspect of such accounts is that, through them, a speaker can invoke a "'contingency' which might not, could not, or even should not properly be known to the first" (1984b: 272). To emphasize this aspect, we term this particular version of "no fault" accounts, "*my* fault" accounts. The extract below, from a Danish face-to-face interaction, shows one way of doing this. Bodil is asking Ane how much a caller display unit (glossed as a 'telltale' in Danish) costs.

(4) (Danish, everyday, video)
Ane is eating during the sequence; Bodil is looking towards Ane during the whole sequence.

```
1 BODIL:    Nu   ø:h Så'n  en sladrehank °som du        si'r°
            Now  u:h Such a   telltale      °as  youSG say°
            Now  u:h One of these telltales °as you say°
2       *   'a'  ko [st ] er så'n  en, °
            what co [st ]    such one,°
            what does such one cost,°°
3 ANE:  →                [Ja,]  ((while chewing))
                         Yes,
4                    (0.8) ((Ane is still chewing))
5 ANE:  →   Det  ka' jeg ikk' husk'   vi  købt'  den på te'bud.
            That can I   not remember we  bought it  on offer.°
            I can't remember we bought it on sale,
6 BODIL:    .hh Er de:t- en:   i      [(forbinder) (        )]
            .hh Is  i:t-  one: youPL [(connect (          )]
            .hh Is i:t- one: you (connect) (          )
7 ANE:                             [O'  så('n)  en lille ø]:hm
                                   An' such(a)  a   little u:hm
```

The design of the question in lines 1–2 shows that Bodil expects the recipient to know the answer to the question: she refers to the object she is inquiring about with *så'n en* ('one of these') and adds 'as you say', signaling that the recipient has talked about the object before. As is evident from the response delivered in line 5, Ane cannot answer the question. By grounding her inability to answer the question in terms of "remembering," rather than "knowing," she can be heard to accept the expectation that she had the access required to answer. This is further substantiated by the subsequent account, 'we bought it on sale', which can be understood as an account for why Ane cannot remember the price of the telltale. This is presented as new information, without any claim that the questioner should have known. The design of Ane's initial response and her subsequent account thus shows that she alone shoulders the responsibility for not being able to answer the question. In so doing she also

Table 5.1. *Epistemic (in)congruence and moral responsibility in responses to questions*

Knowledge distribution	Affiliative = Recipient responsibility	Disaffiliative = Questioner responsibility
Q−, R+	Congruent response	
Q−, R−	"*My* fault" accounts	No knowledge claims without further action
Q+, R+		*da*-responses
Q+, R+		"of course"-responses

accepts that it is reasonable for Bodil to expect that she would be able to answer.

"*My* fault" accounts, such as the one exemplified in Extract 4, stand in contrast to "no knowledge" accounts. Both Keevallik (this volume) and Mondada (this volume), for instance, show that leaving a "no knowledge" claim as the only response to a question is a strongly disaffiliative move that renders the questioner responsible for having produced a question that cannot be answered. As Heinemann (2009) describes for Danish, this onus on the questioner can be further upgraded. She illustrates how the modal adverb *da* is used in answers that go against the expectation of a question. In a "no knowledge" response, which in itself rejects the knowledge assumptions of the question, "the addition of *da* emphasizes this rejection thus indicating the self-evident nature of [the recipient's] lack of knowledge and implying that [the questioner] should have known better than to ask [the recipient] this question" (p. 176). More generally, "the presence of *da* casts a prior action as morally problematic and serves to rebuke the recipient for her failure to take shared knowledge or values into account" (p. 178).

Both "*my* fault" accounts and the disaffiliative response practices described above address the basic incongruence in knowledge between questioner and question recipient. A congruent question sequence is based on the questioner not knowing (Q−) and the recipient knowing (Q+). Table 5.1 shows the knowledge distribution and moral responsibility for the types of responses to questions we have discussed above. It shows that, in cases of knowledge incongruence, it is the attribution of moral responsibility that is central for whether the response becomes an affiliative or a disaffiliative move.

Bearing this in mind, we will now investigate the relationship between the epistemic incongruence claimed in the *jo/ju*-account on the one hand and issues of social affiliation and morality on the other.

Epistemics and morality in *jo/ju*-accounts

In this section we analyze the three types of *jo/ju*-accounts that we have found to be the most prevalent and analytically distinguishable in our data: (1) accounts that challenge the questioners' implied (or claimed) ignorance of what they ask about; (2) accounts for why the recipient does not know the answer; and (3) accounts that treat the question as a moral transgression.

"As you should know" – jo/ju-*accounts that challenge the questioner's ignorance*

We will start by focusing on sequences where *jo/ju* is part of an account in a slot where an answer is due. These accounts present information that undermines the grounds for asking the question. Through the inclusion of *jo/ju*, this information is marked as something the questioner should already know. We thus gloss these as "as you should know" accounts. That these accounts challenge the questioner's ignorance is evidenced by questioner uptake, which, in our data, involves an acknowledgement of prior knowledge. Extract 5 below is a case in point. Helena and her partner Mårten are trying to figure out what birthday present they should get for Mårten's younger sister Camilla. Our analysis focuses on the question–answer sequence initiated in line 3.

(5) (Swedish, everyday conversation, video)
```
1 HEL:    Mm:,
2         (2.0)
3 HEL: *  Har   hon  nå        kaffekoppar eller servi:s
          Has   she  some/any  coffee_cups  or    a_dinner_set
          Does she have any coffee cups or a dinner set
4         (sådär)?,
          (such there)
          (like that)
5         (1.8)
6 MÅR:→   Hmhh ja(h)a hon fick ju    va    va:'re sextifyra
          Hmhh ye(h)s she got ADV what was't sixtyfour
          Hmhh ye(h)s she got JU what was it sixty-four
7      →  gla:s   av   Katr(h)i(h)n i   sin studentpresent ( )
          gla:sses from Katr(h)i(h)n  in her graduation_gift ( )
          gla:sses from Katr(h)i(h)n for her graduation ( )
8 HEL:    Ju:st  de,
          Ri:ght that
          Oh  that's ri:ght
```

9 MÅR: °Ike:aglas   (0.8) nämen annars   tror   ja inte hon
          Ike:a_glasses (0.8) no_but otherwise think I   not she
          Ike.a glasses (0.8) but otherwise I don't think she

Given the activity context of this sequence, a search for a suitable birthday gift, Helena's question (lines 3–4) prefers a "no".[3] Mårten's confirming
response is thus dispreferred and it is delivered as such by means of a delay
(line 5), a turn-initial hesitation (*hmhh*), and a laugh token. This is followed
by a specification of the kind of "china" that Camilla received at a previous
celebration (lines 6–7), accounting for why the answer is not the expected
"no". We further argue that the inclusion of the adverb *ju* in line 6 marks
the information in the account as something the questioner should know.
The word search marker 'what was it' (line 6), which invites the recipient
to collaborate in the construction of the answer, corroborates this analysis,
as does Helena's uptake in line 8 where she uses an expression that displays a recollection of something previously known (Betz and Golato 2008;
Emmertsen and Heinemann 2010). Mårten's reluctance to shoulder the role
of the knowing participant in this exchange is further underscored by his
hesitant continuation in line 9. He does continue, however, thus showing
that he did not consider Helena's question unaskable (Stivers this volume).

In sum, this sequence reveals epistemic incongruence: the answerer
claims in his *ju*-account that the questioner knew something, whereas the
question implied that she did not know. The questioner ratifies the answerer's claim by acknowledging that she did in fact know, and the activity
engaged in within the sequence proceeds. Although the questioner is held
responsible for the epistemic incongruence, the *ju*-account is produced and
treated as an affiliative reminder rather than as an accusation that the questioner purposefully ignored information.

Another case in which the *ju*-account is used as an affiliative reminder
is shown in Extracts 6a and b. We provided a general analysis of this (as
Extract 1) in the introduction.

(6a) (Swedish, talk show, video)

1 LUUK: *   >*Vem blev fullast   sen på kvällen*<,
             >Who got most_drunk then on evening_the<,
             >Who got most drunk later on in the evening<,

2 SA: hah-[hah

3 REIN: →   [*Ja::   eh allså de e de e ju   eh två nära*
                 [Yea::h uh PRT it is it is ADV uh two near
                 Well:: uh y'know it is it is JU two almost

---

[3] Swedish does not distinguish between 'some' and 'any', but the use of *nå* ('some/any') in a
yes/no-question does tilt the question toward a negative answer (which is why 'any' is used
in the third line translation).

4	*nog*	*helnykterister*	*å*	*en*	*halv höll ja på å*

4 *nog   helnykterister   å   en   halv höll ja på å*
   enough whole_teetotallers and one half held I on to
   total teetotallers and a half I was about to
5 *säja s[å att eh-*
   say s[o that uh-
   say so uh-
6 LUUK: *[De e han kdkillen   som inte [dricker nåt*
               [It is he cd_guy_the who not [drinks something
               It is the cd guy who doesn't drink anything

As we noted in our earlier analysis of this extract, Reinfeldt in lines 3–5
offers an account that runs counter to the question's assumption that all
participants in the political get-together got drunk. The inclusion of *ju*
marks this as shared knowledge. In the next turn (line 6), Luuk provides
a B-event statement (Labov and Fanshel 1977: 100) that displays that he
indeed was aware that at least one of the participants does not drink
alcohol. Luuk's concession initiates a guessing sequence where he lists the
participants one by one until he targets the people who do fit the terms of
the original question (line 16 in Extract 6b).

(6b) (continuation of 6a; ten lines omitted)
16 LUUK: *du   å   Maud [dra mig baklän [ges .hh*
         youSG an' Maud [pull me backwa[rds .hh
         you and Maud you're kidding .hh
17 REIN: *[ja*
                       yes
18 SA: [*hah-hah- hah*
19 REIN: *vi satt där   å   sjöng hm*
         we sat there an' sang hm
         we sat there singing hm

As in Extract 5, the *ju*-account does not halt the progressivity of the
activity in the sequence. Although the interactants have renegotiated the
asymmetrical epistemic relationship embodied in the question to a more
symmetrical one, they are affiliated in terms both of the ongoing story
and of the perspective that drinking is normal and acceptable behavior. By
revealing that Luuk actually shares his awareness of who does not indulge
in alcohol, Reinfeldt builds an alliance with the talk-show host that allows
Reinfeldt to position himself as an outsider vis-à-vis the two non-drinking
participants at the political get-together.[4]

---

[4] An upshot of this sequence is that Reinfeldt got drunk. Reinfeldt's ensuing description of
the innocuous behavior that he and Maud engaged in (line 19) may serve to counter the
potential political damage of the portrayal of Reinfeldt as a drunk.

In the extracts above, *jo/ju*-accounts that are produced in the slot where an answer would be relevant serve as kind reminders that the questioner was aware of / had access to information that could (and should) have informed the design of the question. The answerer accepts this and the activity in play continues in due course. As evidenced throughout this volume and by, for instance, Enfield (2006), Golato and Fagyal (2008), Heinemann (2009), Heritage (1988), Heritage and Raymond (2005), Raymond and Heritage (2006), interactants can and will sanction one another in more or less subtle ways for causing epistemic incongruence. By contrast, our initial examples of *jo/ju*-accounts illustrate the existence of a resource through which interactants can raise the issue of epistemic incongruence without raising issues of disaffiliation or moral responsibility.

"As we both know" – jo/ju-*accounts after first accounts*

The *jo/ju*-accounts in the previous section addressed the epistemic basis of questions by marking the questioner's claim of ignorance as incorrect. We will now examine cases where the *jo/ju*-accounts come *after* a first account in a response to a question. These first accounts are "no knowledge" claims that point to another problem with the epistemic congruency in the question, namely the assumption that the recipient will know the answer. We will argue that the addition of *jo/ju* presents the account as shared.

"No knowledge" claims are in themselves accounts, in that they provide an explanation for why the question recipient does not provide the aligning next action after a question (Beach and Metzger 1997; Heritage 1984b; Keevallik this volume; Mondada this volume). These accounts orient to the trajectory of the sequence – i.e., that an answer is due – and thus reflect the "preference for progressivity" (Stivers and Robinson 2006). At the same time, however, "no knowledge" accounts are explicitly *not* answers and, as such, this type of response fails to align with the ongoing activity that the question initiated. In addition to this disaligning feature, "no knowledge" accounts are also potentially disaffiliative because they invoke an epistemic incongruence in terms of what the question recipient can be expected to know, and hence, when produced in isolation, point to the questioner as being morally responsible for asking a question that is problematic (Keevallik this volume). In this potentially problematic context, accounts that follow "no knowledge" accounts may mitigate their disaffiliative nature, because such accounts provide a reason for why the question recipient was not after all in possession of the knowledge required to answer the question. The inclusion of an appeal to shared knowledge (inherent in the *jo/ju*) in such an account may initially appear to be a disaffiliative move.

However, at least in some cases, the appeal seems to be along the lines of "as we both know", implying that "with this shared knowledge, you will understand why I am unable to answer".

The first extract that exemplifies this is drawn from a Danish face-to-face conversation between an elderly woman, Lena, and her care assistant, Birte. Lena has just been reporting on the latest news from her daughter who lives in the States. The daughter has reported to Lena that they have not had much rain in the area where she lives. In line 1, Birte inquires whether the lack of rain has damaged the crops.

(7) (Danish, home-help, face-to-face)

```
1 BIRTE:  * Jahm'  [a'   det g]å'   u'-   A' det gå'   u'   ove:rehm (.)
            Yes_b't [is   it   g]one out- Is it   gone out ove:ruhm (.)
            Yes but has it hit-   Has it hit uhm (.)
2 LENA:              [(mange) ]
                     (many)
3 BIRTE:  * afgrøder å'   så   no'e'      da?
            crops    and  such something PRT?
            crops and stuff  then?
4 LENA:  → Ja   det ve'  jeg itt' fordi=eh    nu   bor hun jo
            PRT it   know I    not because=uh now  live she ADV
            Well I don't know because=uh now she lives JO
5           inde   i  en (  ) by    der,   .hhh=
            inside in a  (  ) town  there, .hhh=
            in a (  ) town there, .hhh=
6 BIRTE:  =Jerh,=
            =Yeah,=
7 LENA:   =Men hun sa'  a'   de    ha'de al'så manglet vand?,
            =But she said that they had   PRT lacked    water?,
            =But she said that they had y'know lacked water?,
```

Lena's response in lines 4–5 displays that she has trouble answering the question due to lack of knowledge. First, she prefaces her response with the particle *Ja*, which marks that she is dealing with the question without, yet, answering it (see Extract 1). Then she produces a "no knowledge" claim ('I don't know'). At this point, then, Lena has postulated an epistemic incongruence in terms of what she, as a question recipient, can be expected to know, and has rejected the presupposition of knowledge that is embedded in Birte's question. However, rather than leaving the moral responsibility for the faulty question with the questioner, Lena continues with an account for why she does not have access to the knowledge that is required to answer the question. The account is explicitly designed as such, by being initiated with the causal conjunction *fordi* ('because').

Lena's account is that her daughter lives in town, which implies that the daughter does not have direct access to knowledge about crops and hence could not relay such knowledge to Lena. We saw a similar account for not being able to provide an answer in Extract 4 above. In that case, however, the information in the account was presented as something the questioner could not have known, which we saw as a "my fault" account. Here, however, Lena includes the adverb *jo* in her account. By doing so, she marks the information given in her account as shared. Rather than claiming that the recipient should have known, the *jo*-account here claims that this knowledge is something "we can recognize as a good reason for not knowing." Thus, Lena's *jo*-account is designed to appeal to Birte's understanding of the information as a valid account for why Lena cannot answer the question in the terms it was asked.

Birte acknowledges the account, without addressing the knowledge issue at all, and Lena continues her report. So, in this case the questioner accepts the response and there are no observable signs of social disaffiliation. It seems, thus, that a *jo/ju*-account can be used as an affiliative move, to mitigate the potential problematicity of a "no knowledge" account.

The "no knowledge" account and the subsequent *jo/ju*-account of Extract 7 above were produced in an otherwise affiliative context. However, similar "no knowledge" responses and subsequent *jo/ju*-accounts are found in more problematic situations, and it is here that the affiliative nature of the *jo/ju*-accounts comes to the fore.

The following extract illustrates a more problematic setting. Sara's partner Tobias is at a music event with Orvar. Sara is talking to Orvar on the telephone, as Tobias is not available to take her call. She wants Tobias to leave the music event to come home and is trying to persuade Orvar to that effect.[5] As indicated by Orvar's turns in lines 1–5, he is trying to reject the idea that he is responsible for Tobias's whereabouts and instead suggests that Sara talk directly to Tobias. In response to this proposal, Sara produces only a minimal response token (line 2) and Orvar consequently pursues acceptance (Davidson 1984; Pomerantz 1984c) of his proposal by elaborating with more specific suggestions as to how Sara and Tobias could talk (line 3). This elaboration reaches turn-completion after *upp*, but receives no uptake from Sara. In further pursuit of acceptance, Orvar then produces the increment 'if nothing else' in line 5. This provides Sara with another possibility for responding to Orvar's suggestion, but instead she produces the question 'how long do you need Tobias', which is the question – along with the corresponding response – that we are primarily interested in here.

[5] It would be somewhat misleading to describe this sequence merely in terms of Sara persuading Orvar to allow Tobias to return home. Through her insistence and pursuit, Sara is also enacting and demonstrating her social identity as Tobias's partner.

(8) (Swedish, telephone, everyday)

```
1  ORVAR:        ä   du      får   väl   prata  me   honom  helt  enkelt,
                 uh  youSG   must  PRT   talk   with him    quite simply,
                 uh suppose you have to talk to him quite simply
2  SARA:         M:m:?,=
3  ORVAR:        =ringa å:  (0.2) ö::  vi   kan  ringa  upp
                 =call an':  (0.2) u::  we   can  call   up
4  (SARA):       hhhh=
5  ORVAR:        ⇒om  inte  annat<,
                 ⇒if   not   other<,
                 ⇒if nothing else<,
6  SARA:     *   Men du,     hur  länge  behöver'u    Tobias?,
                 But youSG,  how  long   need youSG   Tobias?,
                 But you, how long do you need Tobias?,
7  ORVAR:  →     De  vet    ja  'n(°te°)
                 It  know  I   no(°t°)
                 I don'(°t°) know
8                (0.4)
9  ORVAR:  →     >de  beror    ju    på:<,
                 >it  depends  ADV   on:<,
                 >it depends JU<,
10 SARA:         Ja::   en (ti [mma/timme)?,
                 PRT   an (ho[ur)?,
                 Well an (hour)?,
11 ORVAR:                      [( )
12               (0.2)
13 ORVAR:        #(J)a:a:  >de hade ja nog  tänkt    att   de
                 PRT      >it had I  PRT  thought that  it
                 PRT >I had actually thought it
14               skulle  va  lite    mer<   men,
                 should be a_little more<  but,
15 SARA:         pt  .h hhh  <men Orvar då:>
                 pt .h hhh  <but Orvar then:>
                 ((sighing)) ((mock?-complaining))
```

Sara's question in line 6 is introduced with the phrase *men du* ('but you'), which marks the utterance as disjunctive from preceding talk (Mazeland and Huiskes 2001). With this question, Sara adds further pressure on Orvar to take responsibility for Tobias's whereabouts. First, she uses the formulation 'you need', indicating that Tobias's whereabouts are indeed Orvar's responsibility. Second, by framing the question as a wh-question, she limits the answer options to a specification of a certain amount of time that will pass before Orvar "will return" her partner. Sara's question is thus designed to pin Orvar down on a matter he has resisted taking responsibility for.

As in Extract 7, the question recipient, here Orvar, responds with a "no knowledge" account, displaying epistemic incongruence in terms of what he can be expected to know. Orvar thus directly rejects the presupposition of Sara's question – that he knows and is capable of answering. The response is in line with Orvar's earlier reluctance to take responsibility for Tobias's whereabouts, though he implicitly accepts that he is responsible in that he neither challenges nor rejects the implication of Sara's 'you need'. In contrast to the previous extract, Orvar's "no knowledge" account here seems to be designed as a stand-alone, claiming that Sara somehow has the moral responsibility for asking a faulty question (Keevallik this volume). However, after a short pause (0.4 seconds), during which Sara has not provided any uptake, Orvar produces yet another account, which includes the adverb *ju*. The *ju*-account invokes a general contingency – which, it can be expected, other people share – that you can never quite know (at least in detail) how long things like this might take. As is Extract 7 above, but in contrast to the *jo/ju*-accounts in the last section, this account does not point to specific information that the questioner "should have known," but rather appeals to a shared understanding of the initial "no knowledge" account as reasonable under the circumstances.

In contrast to the prior extract, we here see the questioner rejecting the reasonability that is pursued through the *ju*-account. Thus, in line 10, Sara upgrades her attempt to pin down Orvar, by producing a *yes/no*-question within which she proposes a limited time frame (an hour) for Orvar's need of her partner. Orvar is thus forced into a position where he must either accept or reject the time frame. As lines 12–13 attest, he rejects the time frame and, by using the expression 'a little more', he once again rejects the idea, pursued in Sara's question, that he could give an exact time.

Though the issue of when Tobias will return to Sara is not resolved in this sequence, the participants reach some degree of affiliation. At the beginning of this extract, Sara was attempting to assign responsibility to Orvar, and Orvar was resisting this. At the end of the extract, Orvar takes on some responsibility for when Tobias will return home and agrees to enter into a negotiation about the time frame for this. This realignment between Sara and Orvar is accomplished through him providing an account for why he was incapable of providing an answer to Sara's question – that is, the *ju*-account. With this, Orvar claims that his "no knowledge" account was the best he could do under the circumstances and, as such, it should not be understood as a directly disaffiliative response assigning Sara moral responsibility for having asked a faulty question. The *ju*-account serves as a mitigating factor in an otherwise problematic sequence, in which each contribution runs the risk of being a step-up in an ongoing and escalating conflict.

The *jo/ju*-accounts in this section accounted for a "no knowledge" account. As shown by Keevallik (this volume), "no knowledge" accounts have strong disaffiliative potential when standing alone. They are, consequently, often followed by more accounting. We argued that the inclusion of *jo/ju* in this further accounting contributed to showing that the lack of knowledge was a reasonable thing under the circumstances. Even though the *jo/ju*-accounts contain information that the questioner could have had, or appeal to norms that the questioner should have respected, they are not designed to treat the questioner as morally responsible for asking a faulty question. They are, in this context, used instead to mark the content of the *jo/ju*-account as something that may be a shared understanding and, therefore, also an acceptable reason for not knowing the answer to the question. So, these accounts imply less that "you should have had this information before asking" than that "we share this so you can see what I say now is a reasonable account."

"Your fault" accounts – treating epistemic incongruence as a moral transgression

The analysis so far suggests that, although *jo/ju*-accounts index epistemic incongruence, they do so by promoting a sense of shared understanding between questioner and answerer. These accounts enhance social affiliation between the parties. When *jo/ju* are present in first accounts, it serves as a kind reminder that the questioner knew something that could have been taken into consideration in framing the question, and when *jo/ju* are present in accounts for (no-knowledge) accounts, they serve as an appeal to the questioner to the reasonability of the first (no-knowledge) account. A *jo/ju*-account is thus a resource for dealing with questions that are epistemically ill fitted in a way that preserves the moral integrity of both questioner and answerer. We will now turn to a different set of extracts in which the epistemic incongruence raised by *jo/ju*-accounts is treated as a moral transgression. Consequently, we gloss this type of *jo/ju*-accounts as "*your* fault" accounts.

We begin by looking at a case where *jo* occurs in a first account, as in the "As you should know" section, but where that account is a type of "no knowledge" account, as in the "As we both know" section. Here, then, the two types of epistemic incongruence are intertwined, so that what the questioner "should know" is that the answerer "does not know." In contrast to the extracts shown so far, the *jo*-account seems dedicated to accusing the questioner of asking an epistemically ill-fitted question. The extract is drawn from a Danish telephone conversation. Mie's company has been providing Jens with occasional work. Mie is now trying to arrange a callback with Jens to fix some dates when he can work for Mie's company. In lines 1–2, Mie initiates this arrangement by inquiring whether Jens will be available on the following Monday.

(9a) (Danish, everyday, telephone)

```
1 MIE:     =eJah.  .hh ehh Men a' der:   en chance for vi  ka'
           =eYes.  .hh ehh But  is there: a   chance for  we can
           =eYes.  .hh ehh But is there any chance that we can

2          få   fat  i   dig      mandag?
           get  hold in  youSG Monday?
           get hold of you Monday?

3 JENS:    Jerh,
           Yeah,

4          (0.5)

5 JENS:    M' det'  der   en stor chance for.
           But that's there a   big  chance for.
           There's a big chance of that.
```

Mie's initial inquiry is open-ended ('is there any chance that we can get hold of you on Monday?') and can be heard to invite Jens not merely to confirm but also to give specifics about when and how he can be reached. Jens's initial minimal response merely confirms. That this is an insufficient response is evident from the 0.5 seconds' silence in line 4, where Mie may be holding out for a more forthcoming response. However, when Jens reclaims the turn in line 5 he merely re-enacts the confirmation by recycling part of Mie's question. The sequence continues as follows.

(9b) (Danish, everyday, telephone)

```
6  MIE:  *  Jerh.  Å'  å'  hvor  er det  så   ^hjemme?
           Yeah. And and where  is that then ^home?
           Yeah. And and where is that then, at home?

7  JENS: → .hhh Hhhøh D- a- det ka' jeg jo    ikke si':  hh=
           .hhh Hhhøh D- a- that can I   ADV  not  say: hh=
           .hhh Hhhuh I can JO not say:hh that=

8          =ehm ehm: Mandag formiddag a'  jeg hjemme. Jeg
           =ehm ehm: Monday fore_noon am I    home.   I
           =ehm ehm: Monday morning I'm home. I

9          lukker Boregård op øh klokken halv
           close  Boregård up eh o'clock half
           open up Boregård eh at nine thirty.

10         ti.  .hh Så inden halv ti  a' jeg hjemme.
           ten. .hh So before half ten am I   home.
           .hh So before nine thirty I'm home.
```

Mie's pursuit in line 6 treats Jens's answers as insufficient. Her multi-unit question includes both a wh-question inquiring where Jens will be and a candidate answer to that, that he will be at home. The candidate answer is in itself designed as a question (Pomerantz 1988), as is evident in the B-event formulation (Labov and Fanshel 1977: 100) and the rising intonation. The candidate answer narrows down the possibilities for responding to either a confirmation or a disconfirmation and thus specifies Mie's initial inquiry further. It also presupposes that Jens can answer the question with either 'yes' or 'no', i.e., that he knows where he will be on the Monday. Jens responds (line 7) by claiming that he is unable to answer Mie's question, thus producing a kind of "no knowledge" account. As in other "no knowledge" accounts, this one points to an epistemic incongruence between what the questioner (Mie) expects the question recipient (Jens) to know and what the question recipient claims to know (or not to know).

Though inability is generally considered a smaller breach of morality than unwillingness (Clayman and Heritage 2002; Heinemann 2006; Keevallik this volume), Jens's account appears less forthcoming than similar accounts that supply "no fault" reasons such as not remembering (cf. Extract 4). As is typical with dispreferred actions, the account is delayed by hesitation markers and self-repair (Pomerantz 1984a). Furthermore, the account includes the adverb *jo*. As demonstrated in the "As you should know" section, when *jo/ju* are positioned in first accounts, the question recipient points to things that the questioner "should know" and could thus have taken into account in framing his/her question. In this case, because the first account is also a "no knowledge" claim, what Jens points to as known by Mie, the questioner, is his inability to answer her question. Jens thus implicates Mie in asking a question that she knew he would be unable to answer.[6] That this is done in the context of a pursuit is probably not incidental. Jens's "no knowledge" account not only challenges Mie's pursuit, it also sets up a situation in which the answer he subsequently does provide, in lines 8–10, is hearable as a generous concession to Mie, who is treated as someone who has persisted beyond reasonable limits in her attempt to pin Jens down.

In Extract 9 above, the adverb *jo* was a key component that allowed the prospective answerer to challenge the epistemic terms of the question. In the next extract, by contrast, the challenging quality of the answer does not rest solely on the inclusion of *jo*. Instead *jo* seems to be part and parcel of a larger activity that is inherently accusatory.

[6] This observation is in line with Drew's (1993) study of complaints, in which deliberateness is used as an aggravating and substantiating factor in reports of complainable behavior (p. 315).

The extract is drawn from a Danish face-to-face interaction between Vagn and Regitse, who are husband and wife. The couple are on a day trip to the countryside and have stopped for coffee at a privately run café. Noticing that Vagn was carrying a packet of cigarettes, the proprietress has explicitly told Vagn, in the presence of Regitse, that he is allowed to smoke inside. The extract begins with Vagn in line 1 lighting a cigarette. Our analysis focuses on the question posed by Regitse in line 2, *Måtte du ryge?* ('Were you allowed to smoke?'), and Vagn's response to this question.

```
(10) (Danish, everyday, video)
1               (1.8) ((Vagn lights a cigarette))
2 REG:    *    Måtte     du      ryge?
               May-PST  youSG   smoke?
               Were you allowed to smoke?
3               (0.2)
4 VAGN:   →    Ja   det  var  da   det hun såj' jo.   Det  go'  de
               PRT  that was  ADV  that she said ADV.  That do   they
               Yes that was surely what she said JO.  They do it
5               jo    å'  selv herinde,
               ADV   also self here-in,
               JO themselves in here as well,
6               (1.0)
7 VAGN:   °°Hm hm°°
8 REG:     °Hm,°
9               (2.1)
```

In line with our analysis of previous extracts, Regitse's question in line 2 presupposes that the question recipient, Vagn, is more knowledge-able about the question matter than the questioner (Regitse). However, by initiating the question–answer sequence after her co-participant has engaged in the very behavior that she is questioning, Regitse in addition raises a question of accountability. Such questions are in principle unanswerable, because a confirming answer would be in disagreement with the questioner's position on some matter, whereas a disconfirming answer would contradict information that the answerer previously provided (Heinemann 2008). The challenging character of Regitse's question is further emphasized by the past tense of the verb *måtte* ('were allowed'), which implies that permission for smoking has already been asked for and denied.

In his response, Vagn rejects both the challenge and the epistemic incongruence proposed by Regitse (i.e., that he has information she does not have access to). First, he confirms that he is indeed permitted to smoke. He then adds an account that supports this answer, *det var da det hun såj' jo* 'that's DA what she said JO'. As shown by Heinemann, the epistemic adverb *da* in answer turns "serves to target and reject a position taken (implicitly) by the questioner" (Heinemann 2009: 174). Vagn thus rejects the possibility that there can be any answer to the question posed by Regitse other than 'yes'. Whereas answers that incorporate the adverb *da* are, in themselves, challenging, Vagn in this case ups the ante by also including *jo*. As argued throughout, with this epistemic adverb, Vagn indexes that the information delivered in his turn was known to Regitse. Specifically, his response here claims that Regitse has knowingly asked a question biased toward an answer in opposition to what she knows is the case (i.e., she has implied that Vagn is not allowed to smoke when she in fact knows that he is).

In contrast to the extracts in the "As you should know" section, Vagn's *jo*-account thus does not serve as a kind reminder of knowledge already available to the questioner, but explicitly addresses the moral implications of the epistemic incongruence in Regitse's question. The hostility of Vagn's account is further emphasized by his providing a second account 'They do it JO themselves in here as well'. Though this account is positioned after a first account, it cannot be interpreted as an account for that account, but should rather be understood as yet another account for his 'yes' answer at the beginning of his turn. Thus, he further substantiates this answer by stating that the people who run the café themselves smoke in the room where he and Regitse are sitting. With this, he addresses a potential (but unstated) objection from Regitse, namely that he ought not to smoke just because he has been told he *can* do so (that is, this account shows that the permission to smoke wasn't just a concession, but that the room is *for* smoking). As was the case for the first account, Vagn here includes the epistemic adverb *jo*, thus indexing this account as one that Regitse also had access to prior to asking the question.

In contrast to the more affiliative nature of the *jo/ju*-accounts described in prior sections, the *jo/ju*-accounts in this section work as "your fault" accounts that address the moral implications of the epistemic incongruence of a question, laying the blame for this incongruence squarely at the feet of the questioner. The hostility that is conveyed through these "your fault" accounts can, of course, not be ascribed solely to the presence of *jo/ju* and the fact that these adverbs index information given as "already shared" by the questioner. Rather, the adverbs here serve to *emphasize* the moral transgression of the questioner because they are embedded in accounts that in themselves "blame the questioner" and that are produced as part of a larger disaffiliative activity in which the questioner also plays a role (in Extract 9 Mie persists in trying to pin Jens down when he has resisted this; in Extract 10 Regitse asks an unanswerable question).

Discussion

This study has focused on how people selected as answerers can address epistemic incongruence in question–answer sequences by including Danish *jo* and Swedish *ju*, adverbs that appeal to shared knowledge, in their responses. Our results contribute to a growing literature in conversation analysis that shows that interactants pay close attention to shared knowledge and experience when they engage in social activities. When *jo/ ju* are positioned within a first account for why a question recipient cannot answer a question in the terms it was asked, they serve as an affiliative reminder of knowledge that the questioner had. This is what we glossed as an "as you should know" account. Similarly, when *jo/ju* are positioned in second accounts that serve as accounts for "no knowledge" claims, *jo/ ju*-accounts index an appeal to shared knowledge; these were glossed as "as we both know" accounts. Though this appeal again introduces epistemic incongruence in terms of what the questioner knows, this is done in the service of explaining why the question recipient's "no knowledge" claim was a reasonable one under the circumstances and should not be interpreted as a disaligning and disaffiliative move.

In both first and second accounts, then, *jo/ju* serve to index epistemic incongruence, but they do so in the service of a larger affiliative activity, which is to explicate the question recipient's problem with answering the question. By indexing epistemic incongruence, *jo/ju*-accounts thus provide a platform of shared knowledge from which the participants can progress with the activity that they are already engaged in – by, for instance, jointly working out the best answer to the question (the "As you should know" section) or by the question recipient providing the best possible answer under the circumstances (the "As we both know" section). In these sequences the indexing of epistemic incongruence is done in the service of "finding a way out," for both questioner and question recipient.

The *jo/ju*-accounts that we termed "*your* fault" accounts differ from this in that they treat the questioner as responsible for having, knowingly, made the wrong knowledge attributions. As we saw in the section about these accounts, they are used both in cases where the recipient claims not to know, and the questioner should have known that this is so (Extract 9), and in cases where both recipient and questioner know and the recipient claims that this should have made it unnecessary for the questioner to ask (Extract 10). This type of *jo/ju*-account thus assigns the moral responsibility for asking a faulty question to the questioner, just as in the other response practices that claim that the questioner is responsible for incorrect knowledge attribution, like "of course" responses (Stivers this

Table 5.2. *Epistemic (in)congruence and resources for managing affiliation and moral responsibility in answers to questions*

Knowledge distribution	Affiliative = Recipient responsibility	Affiliative = shared responsibility	Disaffiliative = Questioner responsibility
Q–, R+	Congruent response		
Q–, R–	"*My* fault" accounts		"No knowledge" claims without further action
Q+, R+			*da*-responses
Q+, R+			"of course"-responses
Q+, R+	"As you should know" (kind reminders)		
Q–, R–		"As we both know" (acceptable reason)	
Q–, R– *or* Q+, R+			"*Your* fault" accounts

volume), "multiple response tokens" (Golato and Fagyal 2008; Heinemann 2009) and *da*-responses (Heinemann 2009).

Table 5.2 is an overview of how knowledge and moral responsibility get worked out in the *jo/ju*-accounts described in this chapter, and in the other practices referred to above (and in Table 5.1). At the more affiliative end, we find uses of *jo/ju*-accounts through which the answerer takes upon herself (part of) the responsibility for not answering in a conforming or preferred way. This is done differently, according to whether or not the reason for not providing the expected answer can be a "no knowledge" account. At the disaffiliative end, we find the "*your* fault" accounts that occur within "no knowledge" accounts, claiming (through *jo/ju*) that the questioner should have known that the recipient does not know.

Our finding, that *jo/ju* can be used in the service of affiliation as well as disaffiliation, corroborates previous work that has suggested that practices that are potentially disaligning or disaffiliative may in fact be employed to further social solidarity, when used in sequential positions or activities in which these practices are in fact the least costly remedy (Emmertsen and Heinemann 2010; Pomerantz 1984c; Svennevig 2008), i.e., where they serve to fix, circumvent or minimize an otherwise potentially serious inter-actional trouble by treating that trouble as something other than social discord.

In line with other conversation analytic work on specific lexical items (cf. Sorjonen 2001; Heritage 1984a, 1998, 2002a; Betz and Golato 2008), our findings concerning *jo/ju* and their particular use in accounts clearly support Moerman's observation that the meaning of lexical items is inextricably tied to the sequential context in which they are used. Of course, *jo/ ju*, like other lexical items, can be said to carry a generic meaning or function, something like 'appealing to shared knowledge' (cf. Heritage 1984a on *oh* as generically indexing a change-of-state). But what this implies for the actual use of the adverbs can only be established through paying attention to the various sequential positions in which they are produced. Locating exactly what the inclusion of a lexical item such as *jo/ju* means in a particular sequential context is a task that is magnified by the fact that the adverbs have a non-transparent meaning – as opposed to, for instance, explicit claims of knowledge attribution, like "I don't know" (Keevallik this volume; Mondada this volume) or "you know" (Asmuß this volume). We can see that, among other things, recipients do not retort to a *jo/ju*-account with a 'No, I don't know!' or 'No, this is not shared knowledge!', thus contesting the *jo/ju*-producers' claim of epistemic incongruence. As noted by Jefferson (1986), there are a number of practices in interaction which are so elusive that their implication is difficult, if not impossible, for interactants (and analysts alike) to capture – and hence sanction. The elusive or non-transparent nature of lexical items like *jo/ju* may make them especially fit for the kind of subtle epistemic and social affiliation deployment that we have tried to document here. However, in order to substantiate such a claim, this postulated "subtle" use of *jo/ju*-accounts should be compared with similar practices that use more transparent devices.

6   The epistemics of make-believe

Jack Sidnell

Introduction

Between the ages of three and five or thereabouts, children engage in a form of imaginative play that involves a transformation of ordinary objects and persons into characters in a fictional world. Such "make-believe" or "pretend-play" has long been of interest to scholars of child development, and a number of theories concerning the role it plays in the child's moral and cognitive maturation have been advanced.[1] Considerably less

I would like to thank all the participants in the epistemics workshops in Lyon and in Nijmegen for inspiring and illuminating discussion on the topic of knowledge in interaction. For comments on the presented version of this chapter I thank Nick Enfield, John Heritage, Mardi Kidwell, Anna Lindström and Steve Levinson. For extremely insightful written comments on an earlier version I thank Mardi again, as well as Tanya Stivers and Michael Lambek. Many thanks also go to Tanya for bringing her exceptional ability to organize a mess of observations into a coherent argument to bear on this chapter!

[1] See, for instance, Garvey (1977), Göncü (1987, 1993). The many ways in which this line of research contrasts with the one developed here can be seen especially clearly in an article by Lillard (1993). There, the author attempts to show that young children's pretense does not involve them recognizing "mental representations." Lillard employs a standard technique which involves showing children a scene and then asking them questions about what has happened, such as "Is he pretending he's a kangaroo?" The answers given to these questions are then taken to represent the child's "understanding" of pretense. Lillard (1993: 380) writes:

> The present experiments set out to determine if young children evidence an appreciation of the role of mental representation in pretense, and the results suggest they do not. When presented with simple vignettes about a protagonist who, for example, was hopping around, but either knew nothing about kangaroos, did not know that kangaroos hop, or simply was not thinking about being a kangaroo, 4-year-olds tended to claim that she was nonetheless pretending to be a kangaroo. These findings imply that children's earliest understanding of pretense is as acting-as-if...

The method divorces make-believe from the rich and informative contexts of talk and action of which they are naturally a part. Moreover, the approach seems to conceptualize make-believe as something that happens first and foremost in the "heads" of individuals. Indeed, the author suggests that "pretense can occur in the absence of pretense actions, but not in the absence of mental representations" (1993: 373). The research presented here argues for a completely different appreciation of make-believe as a publicly available system and as a form of social interaction.

attention has been paid to the actual structures and practices associated with the activities of make-believe.[2] This is unfortunate given the obvious importance that these play in the everyday lives of children. In an attempt to redress this situation, in this chapter I treat make-believe as a form of social interaction and attempt to describe some of its basic features. As in any other form of social interaction, participants in make-believe orient to it as a normatively organized set of practices – one practice can make another expectable or "conditionally relevant" (see Schegloff 1968, 2007b), and if that second action is not done it can be found absent by the participants.

I will show that epistemic rights to talk about make-believe characters and events flow from participation in the activity. In activities that are essentially sole ventures, imaginative transformation is accomplished unproblematically by the use of bald assertions (e.g. "It's a Rubik's cube"). At the other end of the scale, a child who talks about a character being animated by another participant typically uses an interrogative format to do this (e.g. "Do they say you can't hide from me?"). Between these two extremes, in joint play, children operate on the assumption of shared rights to talk about the objects and events within the play domain. Where such shared rights are challenged – as happens when, for example, one child categorically asserts that an object within the joint domain "was shot" and as a result "died" – the co-participants may respond with complaints that highlight this as a morally problematic action. We can see then that participants in make-believe orient to knowledge as a structured domain that is imbued with significant moral importance.

Imaginative transformation: an essential feature of make-believe

All make-believe involves an imaginative transformation of one or more aspects of the objectively available environment of the "here" and "now." For instance, plastic blocks become a "Rubik's cube," small pieces of wood a "swimming pool," the space on the table in front of the child becomes a park on a "beautiful summer day" and the plastic figurine she is holding becomes a girl enjoying the sunshine, and so on. Such transformations may be essentially "one-off" moments produced apparently for their own sake or they may be constituent parts of a larger play activity involving the participation of several children.

These transformations may be effected and made publicly available to the other co-participants in two main ways: they may be asserted or they

---

[2] A few notable (and in some cases partial) exceptions here are Goldman (1998), Sawyer (1997), Schwartzman (1978).

may be proposed. Assertions can further be distinguished in terms of the extent to which they constitute the official business of the talk. While those transformations I describe as stipulations are highly explicit, others are done implicitly, *en passant*, in the course of some other activity.

I will show that assertions and proposals are used in different epistemic contexts and thus reveal a moral ordering in the activity of make-believe. In particular, assertions indicate epistemic primacy on the part of the speaker, whereas proposals orient to joint epistemic rights. We will see that, normatively, assertions are used in the context of individual play whereas proposals are used in joint play. We will also see that violations of this order are treated as such by the children. I turn first to describe assertions which are the official business of the talk – "stipulations" – and the sequences of talk of which they are a part.[3]

Exclusive epistemic rights in independent play: "stipulations"

Where children are engaged in individual and independent play, they operate on the assumption of exclusive epistemic rights to the objects within their play domain. As the sole participant in an activity, a child is free to talk about the objects within that activity without conferring with others. In this situation, children routinely employ bald assertions in talking about play objects. A subset of these assertions are instances of the action I term a *stipulation*. A first example of the action I mean to identify by this term is provided in Extract 1. Here, Andy has picked up a cube-shaped collection of small plastic building blocks. These are configured in such a way as to allow for one side to be rotated on the other in a manner similar to a "Rubik's Cube" – a toy invented by Hungarian Erno Rubik in the 1970s which became an international sensation in the 1980s (see Figure 6.1). The dates are relevant to the analysis insofar as the reference is somewhat esoteric today and thus is presumably addressed to the adult in the room.

---

[3] This study is based on recordings of four- and five-year-old children taken from a larger corpus of recordings of children between the ages of four and eight. Children were taken from their classes during regular school hours to a special room in which a camera was already set up. There, they were presented with various play things including blocks for building, plastic toy animals, Duplo and so on. They were told only that they should "play together." No further instruction was given and the children generally played with minimal intervention from the one adult in the room. Sessions lasted between twenty-five minutes and one hour. The corpus for four-year-olds consists of nine sessions amounting to about eight hours of video-recorded interaction. The corpus for five-year-olds is significantly larger and consists of twenty recordings, amounting to approximately eighteen hours of recorded interaction.

Figure 6.1 Rubik's Cube © Stockphoto.com/malerapaso

(1)
```
1 ANDY:   →  Look i- Look it's ih-    ((Andy turns to face adult while
2                manipulating the blocks in his hand)) (0.8)
3                i[h- ]
4 MAR:        [ A][HH:: ] nO::[: :      ]
5 REB:            [(hhn)]       [(hh hn)]
6 ANDY:   →  look it's a Lu::bik's cu:be
7                (0.2)
8 ADULT:  →  it's a R̲ubik's Cube.
```

Here at line 6, while rotating parts of the cube he is holding and turning to face the adult, Andy announces "look it's a Lu::bik's cu:be". The object is not, in fact, a Rubik's Cube (Figure 6.2a and 6.2b). Rather, with this turn Andy is pointing to a similarity between the thing he is holding and the object known as a "Rubik's Cube." However, Andy *does not format this as the noticing of a similarity*. Rather, he identifies this object as something that it is not.

In his fascinating discussion of the roots of art in "Meditations on a hobby horse," Gombrich (1963: 1) argues that the combination of broomstick and "crudely carved head" is not, in the first instance, the "image of a horse" but, rather, the "substitute" for one. Behind the deceptive simplicity of arguments about "images" and the importance of likeness between an image and the thing "signified" there is, Gombrich suggests, at least one unwarranted assumption – "that every image of this kind necessarily refers to something outside itself – be it individual or class."

> But nothing of the kind need be implied when we point to an image and say "this is a man." Strictly speaking that statement may be interpreted to mean

Figure 6.2a 1 Andy: → Look i- Look it's ih

Figure 6.2b 8 Adult: → it's a R̲ubik's Cube.

that the image itself is a member of the class "man". Nor is that interpretation as farfetched as it may sound. In fact our hobby horse would submit to no other interpretation ... If the child calls a stick a horse ... the stick is neither a sign signifying the concept horse nor is it a portrait of an individual horse. By its capacity to serve as a "substitute" the stick becomes a horse in its own right. (Gombrich 1963: 2)

These imaginative acts then, whether realized in art or in the play of children, are acts of "creation" and not "imitation" – "the child 'makes' a train either of a few blocks or with pencil on paper" (Gombrich 1963: 3).[4] The basic form of a stipulation (and of imaginative transformations more generally) can be understood, then, as:

$$X = Y$$

Returning to the example in Extract 1, we can see that Andy designs his talk and embodied conduct as a "showing" of the object he is holding (Kidwell and Zimmerman 2007). Thus, as he says "look" for the first time in line 1, Andy is still facing the box of plastic blocks from which he has recovered the object he is holding. However, as he self-repairs this talk he rotates his body so as to be facing the adult. In swiveling, Andy knocks over another box of toys and this causes a minor disruption at lines 4–5. After the adult picks up the fallen box, Andy produces the turn again, now facing the adult and demonstrating the way in which one side of the object he is holding can turn on the other in a way similar to a Rubik's Cube.

Some stipulations are thus also "showings," as Kidwell and Zimmerman (2007) define them, which both position another as a recipient and invite that person to respond in an activity-relevant way. Consider in this respect the following cases:

(2)
8   SAM: That's why I- (.) I've never known y[ou:?
9   JOS: →   [Oh yeah
10   →   watch this .hhh It's a blue-see racing

(3)
1 NIC: →   Like that. See? (0.5) (.) This is a swimming pool.
2   →   (0.3)
3 ERIN: If I:: sai:d tha:t doesn't look like a bridge
4   .hh it'll be rea:lly mean right?

---

[4] Consider also Gombrich's description of the origin of the hobby horse:
> Let us assume that the owner of the stick on which he proudly rode through the land decided in a playful or magic mood – and who could always distinguish between the two? – to fix "real" reins and that finally he was tempted to "give" it two eyes near the top end. Some grass could have passed for a mane. Thus our inventor "had a horse." He had made one.

What Gombrich describes here is just such an imaginative transformation as is discussed in this chapter. It is interesting that Gombrich selects the example of the hobby horse in so far as its use does not necessarily co-implicate another child. Rather, the hobby horse can be ridden as a solitary "imaginary" pursuit. As such, Gombrich finds here evidence that "substitution may precede portrayal and creation communication" (1963: 5). The way in which, in the data shown here, children design their stipulations for others (with "look" and "watch" and "pretend" and so on) speaks against the ultimately a-social, monologic account that Gombrich develops. Before leaving this, I would call attention to the fact that Gombrich notes just the same parallel between play and magic (i.e., ritual) as I do.

(4)
35 ANDY: → Loo::k. it's- Look it's a whole cloud of bees
36   coming to sting thum ahh. Ahh ahh
37   (1.0)
38 ANDY: dahh ahh ahh ahh ah we're getting sti:::nged.
39   We're getting stinged by a cloud of bee::s.

Here we see a range of ways in which the stipulation that some object is "a blue-see racing" (Extract 2), a "swimming pool" (3) or a "whole cloud of bees" (4) is designed as a "showing" to invite the attention of a recipient. In Extract 2 the stipulation is built with "watch", in 3 with "See?", and 4 with "Loo::k". By prefacing the turn in these ways the speaker appears to be doing two things. First, these prefaces clearly request the gaze and thus the attention of a recipient. Second, these prefaces help to constitute the utterance as a sequence-initiating action – the first pair part of an adjacency pair which makes a second part (a response) relevant next (Schegloff 1968; Schegloff and Sacks 1973).

As first-positioned sequence-initiating utterances, stipulations make particular kinds of responses conditionally relevant. Consider Extract 1 again in this respect. Here the stipulation elicits a repeat of what Andy has just said:

(5)
6 ANDY: → look it's a Lu::bik's cu:be
7   (0.2)
8 ADULT: → it's a Rubik's Cube.

A repeat in this position can be used to accomplish a range of different actions, one of which is confirmation (see Schegloff 1996a; Stivers 2005a). This does not, however, appear to be what the turn is doing. Rather, by virtue of the intonation and sequential position of this utterance, the repeat appears to be a vehicle for appreciation (Jefferson 1972) while at the same time offering an embedded correction of Andy's pronunciation of the word "Rubik's" (Jefferson 1987).

In producing an appreciative response, the adult aligns with the course of action that Andy has initiated (see also Kidwell and Zimmerman 2007). That is, the adult does not challenge the identification of the object as a "Rubik's Cube." Rather, the response produced displays an orientation to Andy's turn as doing something other than "literal" description or identification. Indeed, by appreciating the talk, the adult accepts the imaginative transformation offered – saying "yes I can see it in that way too."

In other instances the stipulation elicits not a verbal response but rather a next action in a larger course of action. For instance, in Extract 2, Jason requests the co-participants' attention with "watch this" and then announces "It's a bl<u>ue</u>-see <u>ra</u>cing". In response, the other participants re-orient and join in the activity as spectators. The response to a stipulation may also be less than fully endorsing. Consider the following instance in which Rhonda stipulates to it "being a beau::tiful summe:r da::y."

(6)
1 RHON: It's a beau::tiful summe:r da::y.
2   (0.6)
3 VIV: Are you sure it's a beautiful summer day?
4 RHON: [Yes.   It] is.
5 DIA: [O:KA::Y]

Notice then that, although Vivian questions the description, in doing so in this way she simultaneously acknowledges Rhonda's *right* to stipulate the features of her own playworld – that is, Vivian does not challenge the stipulation by saying, for instance, "I don't think it is a beautiful summer day." Rather, by asking whether Rhonda is "sure" she indicates doubt but nonetheless acknowledges Rhonda's ultimate authority over her own playworld (see the discussion below in the section titled "Epistemic communities").

Extract 7, below, illustrates another way in which a recipient can withhold full endorsement of a stipulation. Here, Nicholas and Erin are building with pieces of wood called "Kapla." At line 1, Nicholas lays a piece on top of an arrangement and says "See? (0.5) ( ) (.) This is a swimming pool." Erin's response is complex. She first notes that it would be "rea:lly mean" if she said that what Nicholas has built does not look like a "bridge." She goes on to say "I think it <u>doe:s</u> look like a bridge. a rea:l bridge.".[5]

(7)
1   NIC: → Like that. See? (0.5) ( ) (.) This is a swimming pool.
2   (0.3)
3   ERIN: → If I:: sai:d tha:t doesn't look like a bridge
4   .hh it'll be rea:lly mean right?
5   (0.4)
6   But I think it <u>doe:s</u> look like a bridge.
7   a rea:l bridge.
8   (2.8)
9   NIC: Do(hh .hhh) yeah (0.2)
10   That's like a bridge with a

---

[5] Although Nic has indentified the thing he is building as a swimming pool, the piece he sets down just as he says this "bridges" two other pieces. It would appear then that Erin has heard that a stipulation has been produced but has confused what she has heard with what she has seen. Notice that Nic's response incorporates Erin's mention of a bridge while maintaining his original identification of the object as a "swimming pool."

11   swim [ming pool (in it)
12 STEP: [(Look at the box)/(looks like a box)] right?

Here then we see that a recipient can, in responding to a stipulation, evaluate the degree to which the object being talked about actually resembles the thing it is proposed to be.[6]

These stipulations have a "one-sidedness" to them. Thus, although the stipulator is clearly inviting others to acknowledge and accept the stipulation in ways we've seen above, the action itself is in no sense co-authored. This is also evident in their structure: stipulations take the form of bare and bald assertions. They are never modulated by epistemic downgrades such as "I think" or "it looks like" or "I guess" or "maybe," nor are they ever formated as interrogatives. Speakers use such turn-design features to take into account and to accommodate the perspective or knowledge of another participant. For instance, when one child is talking about objects in another child's epistemic domain (such as part of a structure that child is building) they frequently employ "I think" or some other such device which downgrades the presumed certainty that attends a bare assertion. Consider, for instance, the following case in which Jesse is building a structure with a toy called "Marble-run" – this involves fitting together various pieces to create a relatively stable structure that can stand on its own. At the point where the talk begins, Tanya is holding out a piece of track and has positioned it in such a way that Jesse should be able to see it in his peripheral vision. As Jesse struggles to fit his pieces together, Tanya produces the talk at line 3 – a solution to the problem with which he is visibly wrestling.

(8)
                    ((Tanya is holding out a piece))
1 JESSE: Gimme this one now you (rats) ((Jesse takes the piece))
2   (0.8)
3 TAN: → Uhm I think it's upside down,
4 JESSE: Wha oh oh oh aaaah
                    ((Tanya flips over one of the pieces in front of Jesse))

By holding out the piece so as to make it available to Jesse, Tanya shows that she is assisting him in his efforts but not claiming the status of a

---

[6] This type of challenge occurs only in situations such as this where the stipulating child can be understood to have built/constructed a "representation" of the object. Notice here then that the challenge which Erin alludes to (though never actually articulates) involves a criterion of resemblance. Interestingly, in cases where the object transformed was not constructed by the child but rather manufactured (e.g., a plastic octopus) the challenge typically invokes the intent of the maker – that is, that the object is intended as a representation of "an octopus" and not "Squidward" (see below).

collaborator, a co-builder of the structure. On the contrary, by the positioning of their bodies relative to the structure being built, both participants display an understanding of this as Jesse's project. In addition, Jesse's "Gimme this" seems to call into question Tanya's status even as an assistant. In summary, both Jesse and Tanya display in their embodied conduct an understanding that this is Jesse's project. It is in this context that Tanya offers her solution to Jesse's problem, prefacing the utterance with "I think" here to specifically deal with an epistemic asymmetry – this structure and the project of building it are a part of Jesse's epistemic domain.

Another context in which children routinely use "I think" to downgrade their assertions is in talk with adults. Consider, for instance, the following cases, in which talk directed to an adult is prefaced by "I think". In Extract 9, Kara surveys the room before remarking to the adult, "I think (.) I think I've been here before". In 10, Roger turns 90 degrees to look at the adult, saying "I think we're gonna miss library."

(9)
```
11 GRACE:        [uhh:    (.) m- ]
12 KARA:    →    [I think    (.) I th]ink I've been here before
13                    with s[omebody    els] e.
14 ANNA:                    [have you?    ca] n you sit on (the) seat [um Kara?
15 GRACE:                                                            [I have too:
```

(10)
```
13 BEN:        hh hh hnh .hhh hhh hn:h hh (.) hh hh
14                .hh[H
15 ROGER:    →      [I think we're gonna miss library.=
16 CARL:            =and [ she's I:n    f o o -]
17 ADULT:                [no:: ca- Carol's gonn]a take you (.) but we should
18                go back now soon (0.4) is it time to go back?
```

In both these cases we see children directing talk to an adult and talking about matters they can presume that the adult knows about (i.e., whether this child could possibly have been in the room before; whether they will in fact miss library). In this context, "I think..." is deployed as an epistemic downgrade.

So we can now take stock of what these contrasting cases reveal about the stipulations we've so far considered. Specifically, the fact that stipulations are always produced as bald assertions and never incorporate such design features as downgrading "I think" evidences their epistemic "one-sidedness" – the fact that they are located squarely within the speaker's epistemic domain. Second, Extracts 9 and 10 suggest a further contrast. Make-believe is unlike much of what children find themselves talking about in so far as it is not "owned" by adults (Sharrock 1974). Whereas in many aspects of their lives children are novices relative to expert adults, in make-believe this common relationship is suspended.

Shared epistemic rights in joint play: proposals

So far we've considered the way in which children use assertions, in particular stipulating utterances, to imaginatively transform the objects available to them in independent play. These, I've suggested, are typically produced as epistemically unmodulated "showings" of the object and thus make relevant a restricted set of responses in second position. Stipulations of this kind are sequentially organized with the entire trajectory of action devoted to the twin tasks of transforming and presenting the object to others.[7]

In contrast to the examples we've considered so far, many imaginative transformations are produced in the midst of joint play. In this context, children typically do not employ bald assertions to stipulate about objects in the play domain but rather *propose* transformations to their collaborators. As such, where two or more children are actively working together to establish and sustain the pretense, each event or action within the activity is treated as a matter to be negotiated by the participants. This negotiation exhibits a clear patterning, with one child proposing an action or event and others agreeing (or not), to varying degrees, with that proposal.

Consider the examples given as 11 and 12 in which one child proposes something to the others. In 11, the proposing character of the utterance is conveyed by the framing expression "Let's pretend"; in 12 it is conveyed by the tag "okay?"

(11)
6   JEFF: Let's pretend we were all friends
7   and we all had connected houses.
8   BEN: No we were- We <u>were</u>- We were friends
9   but we didn't have connected hou[ses.
10 JEFF: [No but
11   if we had connected houses ...

(12)
1 BEN: And then (0.2) and then he went.
2   ba:ck. There. so quietly but he
3   made a little mistake, and his .hh (.)
4   da::d woke up and then h- he died, okay?

---

[7] Not all such stipulative utterances are showings explicitly addressed to another. Some appear to be produced as self-talk.

```
5 JEFF:    No he got in big (.) trouble.
6 BEN:     [.h ya he got in big trouble.
7 PETE:    [no? no? nuh no: [No. no.
8 BEN:                     [My- My- My guy,
```

These "proposals," whether constructed with "Let's pretend..." or with the "okay?" tag, invite one or more of the co-participants to agree to and thus to ratify the reality that is being proposed. In both cases, the design of the response displays an orientation to shared epistemic rights to implement the imaginative transformation. In 11, in response to the proposal "Let's pretend we were all friends and we all had connected houses.", Ben produces a partial agreement/acceptance – he accepts that "We were friends" but rejects "we all had connected houses.". In 12, in response to Ben's complex proposal (which involves this character going back, making a mistake, waking his dad up and subsequently "dying"), Jeffrey offers "No he got in big (.) trouble.". Notice that this is again partial agreement/ acceptance – Jeffrey is clearly accepting that the character went back, made a mistake and woke up his dad but not the consequence that "he died,", for which "he got in big (.) trouble" is offered as a substitute. In these responses then, we see recipients orienting to the "proposal" character of the first utterance by "pushing back" on it – accepting some but not all of what has been suggested. Notice that in 12, Jeffrey's partial acceptance with modification is accepted by Ben with "ya he got in big trouble." (line 6).

Whereas imaginative transformations formatted as assertions claim epistemic primacy over the transformation, proposals orient to the collaborator as having shared rights and authority over it. This is evidenced both by the distribution of the two practices in two distinct environments and also by the way recipients respond to them.

Given that proposals prefaced by "pretend" invite recipients to accept and hence to ratify what is being proposed, it is not surprising to find that the production of the "pretend" or "let's pretend" preface is often associated with significant effort to secure the gaze and attention of the recipient (see Goodwin 1980). Consider the following instance (13), in which Andy is attempting to establish a landscape upon which the make-believe can take place. As he produces the talk in lines 1 to 4 he is first looking at the Lego structure he has constructed and then (at "this is land,") at the floor beside him. When he is saying "the ground is water", he is fully under the table. He may thus be unaware that none of the other participants are attending his talk. When he begins again at line 6 he has just resurfaced from underneath the table to find Sean looking elsewhere and, as can be seen from the transcript, at line 7 Sean begins talking to the adult. When

Andy restarts the turn at line 8 with markedly raised pitch and volume, Sean swings around to re-orient, now directing his gaze at Andy. Andy then continues the utterance.

```
(13)
1   ANDY:        Prete:nd, this is land, (.)
2                pretend down here is water.
3                pretend the ground is water and right-
4                and on the table is the (line).
5                (2.0)
6                Pretend uhm=
7   SEAN:        =There's no other [(
8   ANDY: →                        [^Pretend the chai::rs,
9                (.) uhm and t(h)ables, uhm are islands and
10               the ground is water.
```

Consider the more elaborate instance (14) below. Here Ben is narrating the make-believe events and seems to have secured Jeffrey as a recipient for this. At line 4, Pete begins a make-believe proposal with "pretend.". His first saying of the word is produced in overlap with Ben and the second and subsequent ones fail to elicit the gaze of the other participants. Four times he attempts to develop the proposal beyond the "pretend" preface but without success.

```
(14)
1   BEN:         and he:- it was in:- and he was slee:ping?
2                an' it was the middle of the night.  (.h)
3                and the b(h)a(h)b[(h)y was los[t.
4   PETE:                          [Pretend.  [pretend,
5                pretend, pretend, di- pretend my:: mom, ( )
6                pretend dis. one. pretend dis one. .uhh
7                (pretend). This is- pretend
8   BEN:         It was ni:ghti:me, all the moms're sleeping.
9   PETE:        Ya right. Right right right.
10  BEN:         Was it nightime Jeffrey?
```

Pete's talk here resembles the engine of a car that turns over and over on the power of the battery but never starts. What prevents him from developing the proposal is the lack of recipient gaze – since, as we've seen, these proposals specifically invite recipients' acknowledgement and alignment, children treat recipient gaze (or some other sign of recipiency) as required for their production. When they fail to secure the gaze of the intended recipient, the turn and action of proposing is routinely abandoned. Notice then that, at line 9, Pete eventually takes up a recipient role in relation to Ben's further elaboration of his make-believe world.

Violating shared epistemic rights in joint play: report-formatted assertions

We can compare Extract 11 and 12 with 15 and 16 below. In these latter cases, one child reports something that (just) happened in the make-believe world using an unmodulated assertion. In both cases this report is addressed to another child, and in both cases the other child to whom the report is addressed is implicated in the action reported.[8] In 15, the horse that is reportedly shot "belongs" (within the current activity) to the recipient Sean. In 16 the transformer that is "blown away" belongs to the recipient Pete.

(15)
10 ANDY: An- and we shoo:t the horse.
11   (.)
12   Ba::ng. He's dead.
13 SEAN: NO:::::,HO:. NO I DON'T WAN-
14   No that not part of the ga::me.

(16)
28 SEAN: tornado was so strong that it blew-
29   it blew your transformer awa [y.
30 PETE: [NO::::::mmmm((Stomping foot))
31   (0.2)
32   I DO:N'T LI::KE THA::T

These "reports" then treat the matter as a *fait accompli*. Not surprisingly, in comparison with the proposals we considered above, these report-formatted transformations routinely elicit strong reactions from the other child who is co-implicated. Specifically, in both cases, the report elicits an aggravated, and in 16 a rather violent, response from the other child. Rather than negotiate the particulars of the event/occurrence as the participants did in 11 and 12, here the response is outright rejection with " NO:::::,HO:. NO I DON'T WAN- No that not part of the ga::me." or "I DO:N'T LI::KE THA::T".

Cases like this are deviant because, in each, an assertion format (i.e., report) is used in a joint play context where epistemic rights are shared and thus there is an expectation that each next transformative action or event will only be proposed and thus be open to negotiation. And in each case we observe the deviant action being treated as a violation of the moral order governing make-believe. Moreover, in each case, this in turn

---

[8] I use the word "report" to describe these instances since, in them, the action is described as past ("tornado was so strong that it blew-it blew your transformer away.") or current ("An- and we shoo:t the horse. Ba::ng. He's dead.").

leads into "remedial action." In the first instance, originally Extract 15 but now reproduced as 17 below to show the subsequent talk, when Sean continues his objection with "You're not suppose to kill animals in the game.", Andy retorts by saying that Sean himself had earlier proposed that some of the characters were "dead.". Andy thereby offers a justification for the imaginary action he has promoted (see Austin 1961; Goffman 1971b).

(17)
```
10  ANDY:   An- and we shoo:t the horse.
11          (.)
12          Ba::ng. He's dead.
13  SEAN:   NO:::::,HO:. NO I DON'T WAN-
14          No that not part of the ga::me.
15          (0.2)
16  ANDY:   bu-
17  SEAN:   You're not suppose to kill anima[ls in the game.
18  ANDY:                                  [uh
19          Wull- well then then why you say, okay pretend
20          that one's dead. Why you doing that?
21  SEAN:   No no I:: didn't say that. No they're only dead
22          when they're in the ra:vi::ne.
```

In the second case, given below as 18, Sean first apologizes (line 34), then remarks that he was "only suggesting that." and, finally, explains that he's "angry too::" because of something that Pete has been proposing (stopping Sean's tornado or putting it on fire).

(18)
```
28  SEAN:   tornado was so strong that it blew-
29          it blew your transformer awa[y.
30  PETE:                              [NO::::::mmmm((Stomping foot))
31          (0.2)
32          I DO:N'T LI::KE THA::T
33          (0.2) ((Banging fist on table))
34  SEAN:   Sorry.
35  PETE:   My transformer can't blow away because
36          it's so stro::ng.
37  SEAN:   Okay, I on- I was I was only suggesting that.
38  PETE:   Mine can't- mine can't blow awa::y.
39          It's too strong and it can't it can't ( )
40  SEAN:   Um, wel- wel- well I:: an' a well I'm angry too::
41          because I don't want the tornado to be stopped or
42          put on fire or my guy freed from it.
43  PETE:   Wait a minute, there's another tornado in there.
```

In these examples we see some of the moral structuring of make-believe. Notice then that in 17, Sean first objects on the basis that one is not "suppose to kill animals in the game.".. That is, Sean responds here by invoking a moral rule assumed to govern participants' conduct within activities of make-believe. And notice that Andy responds to this by citing Sean's own earlier proposal – saying "well then then why you say, okay pretend that one's dead. Why you doing <u>that</u>?" – thereby implying a principle of equivalent rights (if you can do it, then so can I). In 18 a rather different set of moral issues appear to be involved. Here then Pete objects to Sean's report on the basis of his not liking it (line 32). Tracking this a bit further, we can see that Sean in fact orients to the morally problematic status of what he has done by, first, apologizing (line 34), and, second, attempting to excuse himself by saying that in fact he "was only <u>suggesting</u>". What Sean does here indicates that children understand what I have described as "reporting" (which treats make-believe action as a *fait accompli*) as a morally problematic action that violates a generic "seek co-participant's endorsement" rule. Indeed, in his subsequent talk (lines 40–42), Sean casts what he has done as punitive retribution for an earlier attempt by Pete to stop his tornado which resulted in him being angry too.

In this and the preceding section I have described two quite different formats used to effect imaginative transformation in joint play. Each makes relevant a distinct range of responses and, though we have not seen it here, each is occasioned within a distinct sequential environment. The proposal format is clearly much more other-attentive: it specifically invites the other to accept and thus to ratify what is being proposed. The "report" format, in contrast, treats the matters reported as a *fait accompli*. I have suggested that, because joint play involves shared epistemic rights distributed among the co-participants, in this context the report-formatted assertions are "deviant." Participants treat these actions as violating basic rules of make-believe play. Proposals, on the other hand, by inviting co-participant endorsement, attend to the shared epistemic rights that flow from joint participation in the play activity.

Reality disjuncture in make-believe

We've seen that in joint play children operate on the assumption of shared epistemic rights and normatively design their imaginative transformations as proposals that seek endorsement from another child. Moreover, by prefacing these proposals with "pretend," children actively recruit the recipiency of one or more other participants. Where this is not successful, they may recycle the preface or abandon the proposal altogether (the latter treats securing a recipient as a necessary prerequisite to proposing). Where recipiency is secured, an initial proposal or subsequent move in the extended, make-believe episode makes relevant a limited set of responsive next actions. We've seen that responses may be aligning or non-aligning. Aligning responses are those that acknowledge and sustain the make-believe activity and the pretend world constituted by it, whereas non-aligning responses do not. Within the set of aligning responses it is possible to distinguish fully endorsing responses from partially endorsing ones (e.g. Jeffrey's "No he got in big (.) trouble." in Extract 12 above).

Non-aligning responses challenge another child's rights to stipulate features of the pretend world. Consider in this respect the following case (19) in which Sean and Roger are playing, more or less independently, on opposite sides of the table. Occasionally, as in the case here, their pretend worlds merge. This begins with Sean stipulating about a figure he is holding in his hand. Roger perhaps hears this "An ea:gle, it flying over and (finding it feeding after)" as a potential threat to the safety of the characters with which he is playing, and retaliates with "Well: I can get your mouse. right away.". When Sean responds by suggesting that his "mice are magic." and that "They can turn invisible.", Roger continues the attack. At line 10, Sean stipulates to their invisibility.

(19)
```
1   SEAN:     An ea:gle, it flying over and (finding it feeding after)
2             (0.2)
3   ROG:      Well: I can get your mouse. right away.
4             (0.4)
5   SEAN:     No::. My: mice (.) uh- (.) my mice are magic.
6             They can turn invisible.
7             (1.0)
8   ROG:      Well watch this.
9             (0.4)
10  SEAN: →   Ffffuh (0.2) They're invisible.
11  ROG:  →   No they're not. They're under the table.
12  SEAN:     No: I'm d- ju- pretending they're invisible.
13            I can never make something rea::l turn invisible.
14            Invisible ( ) no one can't see them.
15            (1.6)
16            .hh
17            (1.0)
18  SEAN:     Ah?- Does- Do they say you ca:n't hi:de from me.
              ((long pause))
```

Roger's response to this is clearly non-aligning. In saying "No they're not. They're under the table." Roger refuses to accept the pretense, instead asserting the objectively available facts concerning the present location of the mice. When Sean responds by explaining that he is only pretending, Roger withdraws his gaze and returns to his own activity. When Sean attempts to sustain the game, Roger does not respond at all.

Figure 6.3a The cartoon character "Squidward"

Consider now the following rather more complex case (20). Here Carter has decided the plastic figurine he is holding is "Squidward" (a character from the children's television show *Sponge Bob Square Pants*).

(20)
```
1   CART:   → Squi:dward. [Squidward squidward.
2   WILL:                 [(we) live down there.
3   CON:       Here squid [ward,
4   MIKE:   →             [That's a octopus
5   WILL:      (  ) raa raa raa:
6   CART:      Squidward.
7   MIKE:   → That's a octopus
8                  (1.4)
9   WILL:   → m- Mister Octopus?
10  MIKE:   → Yeah it's Mr Oct- ow everyone (.) ow.
11  (  ):      enhh
12  WILL:      Everyone listen up.
```

Where the transcript begins, Carter is apparently addressing the figurine he is holding with the name "Squidward." Mike's unmodulated assertion at line 4 – "That's a octopus" – is thus a correction of Carter's naming/ description of the same object as "Squidward." The object is principally in Carter's epistemic domain insofar as he has been holding and animating it. However, the children are playing with this and all the other objects together. More to the point, there is an ambiguity about the status of the utterance. The figurine is not in fact an intended representation of the character "Squidward" though Carter has nominated it in this way (see

Figure 6.3b The octopus figurine on the table

Figure 6.3a and b). On the contrary, it would appear that it *is* in fact a representation of an octopus. Mike, then, may be treating this as a literal and, as such, an objectively false or inaccurate description, whereas for Carter this utterance is perfectly adequate in so far as it is premised on what he takes to be an already established imaginary transformation of the object.[9]

In the segment shown above, Carter does not counter the challenge, but consider what happens moments later:

```
(21)
 1  CART:      and Squidward hh.
 2  MIKE:      Okay: so (.) you have to go right here.=
 3  WILL:  →   =Mister. Oc[topus.
 4  MIKE:                 [Okay you can go right here.
 5  CART:  →   No  (this  is / Mister) Squidward.
 6                 (0.2)
 7  WILL:  →   That's octopus. That's Mister Octopus.
 8  MIKE:      He:: goes right here.
 9                 (0.4)
10  WILL:      [Listen up.
11  CART:      [(How 'bout) Mister Squidward hh?
12  MIKE:      Go get Mister Squidward ( [)
```

[9] In this case there appear to be two moral orders coming into conflict – if Carter is playing by himself he can just decide/stipulate that the object is "Squidward." If he's playing jointly, then he has to secure agreement to this.

```
13  WILL:                    [Listen up
14                     Listen (up) now
15  MIKE:              Kay?
16  CART:              [Why is he upside down?
17  MIKE:              [(  )
18                     (0.2)
19  (  ):              Bhhh phh phh
20  (  ):              (  )
21  CART:      →       Mr. Squidward has his head down there.
22                     Look at Mr. Squidwardhh.
23                     (0.2)
24  ADULT:             Mm hmmm.
25  CART:              He has his head do::wn.
26  WILL:      →       It's no:t Mr. Squidward.
27  MIKE:              Yeah (.) [It's a octopus.
28  WILL:                       [(You can't do it.)
29  WILL:      →       It's Mister Octopus.
30  MIKE:      →       It's a: o-ctopus.
31                     (.)
32  WILL:      →       Yeah because look at the bottom.
33                     (0.2)
34  WILL:              °It's a Octopus°
35  MIKE:              °Yea::h°
36  (  ):              (Hey look)
37                     (2.0)
38  MIKE:      →       An'- you can pretend it's only a (.)
39             →       octopus a jellyfish an:d Squidward.
40  WILL:              O::r::
41                     (0.2)
42  CART:              Uhm well I'm gonna name it Squi:dward.
43  MIKE:              Okay.
44  WILL:              Or you can pretend it's Doctor Octopus.
45  (  ):              (Dr. Octopuh-)
46  MIKE:              That's a bad guy from the Spiderman (story).
```

Here we find Carter again insisting on the name/description "Squidward" and once again being corrected – now by Will. Here Carter *does* reject the correction saying, at line 5, "No (this is / Mister) Squidward.". The piece of this to which I want to draw our attention is at line 32. After Carter again refuses to accept the correction of Squidward by "octopus," Will invokes "objective" features of the object in question – inviting the others to witness something about it that apparently marks it distinctively as an octopus – "look at the bottom.". This is followed by a hushed exchange between Michael and Will in which they reconfirm to one another its identity as an octopus. Finally, Michael rules on allowable pretenses, saying: "An'-you can pretend it's only a (.) octopus a jellyfish an:d Squidward.".

So here Michael and Will seem to be challenging Carter's right to stipulate the identity of the object. Their insistence that the object is an octopus brings it back to the real world, in which a description may be evaluated in terms of the degree to which it corresponds with that world.

Epistemic communities

There is a sense then in which Andy's stipulation of the object he is holding in Extract 1 cannot be found incorrect (or correct). *As a literal description*, it is clearly incorrect, but to treat it this way would be to miss the point of the utterance. Andy is not offering a literal description but rather performing a momentary baptism. The distinction is equivalent to that which Austin makes between constatives – "the cat is on the mat" – which are properly evaluated on a criterion of truth or falsity, and performatives – "I bet the cat is on the mat" – which are properly evaluated on a criterion of felicity. These assertions then are epistemically "safe-ground" in the sense that they are not assessable on epistemic grounds. Notice then that "I think it's a Rubik's Cube" would have been an altogether different utterance – hearable as a possible literal description of the object rather than an instruction on how to look at it.

Stipulations are "performative" utterances (Austin 1962). Moreover, they bear an obvious resemblance to the "ritual" and "magical" uses of words examined by anthropological followers of Austin such as Tambiah (1985) and Rappaport (2002 [1999]). Centrally, participation in the activity of make-believe implies acknowledgement of and commitment to the "illocutionary force" of the initial stipulation. Rappaport talks about this in terms of "acceptance," noting that to participate in a ritual is to publicly accept its products. Having born witness to the wedding of Jane and John, one may continue to hold reservations about the likelihood the union will last but not about the *fact* of the union. In the examples we have considered, we see this unfold sequentially: in aligning, a second participant ratifies, or "buys into," the pretend world that the first participant has established. By not aligning, the second participant essentially rejects the activity of pretending being proposed. Moreover, by aligning with a make-believe proposal, a recipient tacitly agrees to treat some common-place object as something other than it plainly is. Insofar as they depart from it, make-believe proposals and their aligning responses presuppose a basic and fundamental orientation to the "real world" as anyone can see it. However, they simultaneously bracket and constrain the relevance of this reality to the activity they constitute. We have seen, however, that children do not always fully align with and thereby endorse the make-believe proposals of others. One way that children express disalignment in this context is by reasserting the relevance of what a thing "really is" or by calling attention to objective features of an object that do not fit with the imaginative transformation that has been proposed. This suggests a fundamental and ubiquitous tension between "real" and "make-believe" that pervades all the sequences described, even if it is not always made explicit.

In these explicit stipulations, others are recruited as "spectators" or as "witnesses" to the stipulated facts. Their involvement is necessary and made relevant, but is nevertheless basic. The situation is much more complicated in extended episodes which are built through the joint and collaborative participation of more than one child. We see this in the elaborate attempts to secure recipiency through "pretend" prefaces.

In all these moments of make-believe, the participants attempt to establish an "epistemic community" – a set of participants who recognize and agree to certain basic "facts" about the world in which they are at that moment participating. That community may exist for just a few seconds – as when the participants momentarily acknowledge that the blocks Andy is holding constitute a "Rubik's Cube" – or a few minutes – as when the floor is made into water and the table into land – or longer, as the case may be. All stipulations presuppose some such epistemic community, though some are so entrenched and naturalized that we barely notice that they depend on a community of persons who acknowledge and ratify them. Consider, for example, the stipulation that transforms certain rectangular-shaped pieces of paper into currency.[10]

Stipulations and other practices of (imaginative) transformation resemble then the ritual performatives described by anthropologists such as Tambiah (1985) and Rappaport (2002 [1999]). The latter, invoking Austin (1962, 1971) but also Durkheim (1915) in an attempt to develop the *sociology* of speech acts, made the point that, whereas constatives are evaluated according to the degree to which they correspond to the world, performatives create a world against which future constatives are judged. So, for instance, the performative utterance by which John and Jane are wedded fundamentally alters the worldly conditions against which subsequent utterances, such as "John is a bachelor," "Jane is single," "John and Jane are married," are to be evaluated. Or consider the blessing that transforms ordinary H_2O into holy water. For members of the appropriate epistemic community such an action fundamentally transforms the water in a way that chemical analysis cannot reveal. Perhaps even closer to the imaginative transformations considered here is the Eucharist in

---

[10] Many currencies have the stipulation reproduced on each instance. For example, Canadian bills are inscribed with the words "Ce billet a cours légal/ This note is legal tender."

which wine and wafers are transformed (via transubstantiation) into Christ's blood and flesh respectively (for members of the relevant epistemic community).

The examples from ritual help to highlight the character of the transformation being effected and, ultimately, the character of these "knowables." Specifically, no amount of chemical analysis can distinguish holy water from ordinary H_2O. Similarly, one is not able to determine by X-ray or physical exam whether John is a bachelor. These are, to put it rather grossly, "cultural" facts that can only be known by those competent in the culture. Stipulations and other practices of (imaginative) transformation can thus be seen as tools for establishing such facts – for creating them *de novo*. This is no less true of the children's stipulations than it is of wedding "pronouncements" or priest's blessings. These differ not in *kind* but in their degree of permanence/duration, and this is a function of the degree to which the epistemic community within which they are lodged is institutionalized and enduring. In the case of children's stipulations, that community may exist for only a few seconds, being embodied in the aligning verbal and visible responses of the co-participants. In the extended episodes of make-believe the community within which these imaginative transformations are lodged may endure for ten minutes or longer. In the case of a national currency the community may continue for many years. It is important to see, though, that even the stipulation underlying a currency can lose the epistemic community within which it is recognized and has force. Roman coins for instance no longer have value as currency nor do French francs or Dutch guilders.

Within an epistemic community knowledge about "stipulated" or "make-believe" objects and events is distributed in predictable ways. We find that children orient to territories of knowledge – asymmetrical distributions of rights and responsibilities to know – in make-believe just as they do outside it. Consider again the following extract in which Sean is playing with Roger:

(22)
1 Sean: An ea:gle, it flying over and (finding it feeding after)
2   (0.2)
3 Roger: Well: I can get your <u>m</u>ouse. right away.
4   (0.4)
5 Sean: No::. My: mice (.) uh- (.) my mice are magic.
6   They can turn invisible.
7   (1.0)
8 Roger: Well watch this.
9   (0.4)
10 Sean: Ffffuh (0.2) They're invisible.
11 Roger: No they're not. They're under the table.

```
12  Sean:        No: I'm d- ju- pretending they're invisible.
13               I can never make something rea::l turn invisible.
14               Invisible ( ) no one can't see them.
15               (1.6)
16               .hh
17               (1.0)
18  Sean:    →   Ah?- Does- Do they say you ca:n't hi:de from me.
                 ((long pause))
```

Notice here that in a bid to continue the jointly produced "make-believe" events, Sean asks Roger: "Do they say you ca:n't hi:de from me." Why does Sean format this as a question? Why not simply assert what these characters say? It is, after all, a make-believe world that is being constructed, so what they say cannot have been determined in advance. The answer to this is that the characters about which Sean is speaking here are not "his." Rather they "belong," in the context of this game, to Roger – they fall within his territory of knowledge. Sean's question format here orients then to Roger's greater rights to decide what these characters say and do – indeed, to his ultimate authority on this matter. Consider also the following case in which Jeffrey is building a structure attached to the larger structure that has been jointly constructed by the three boys in the room. At line 1 Jeffrey announces – with a bald stipulative assertion – "This is my sleepover room.". Although he formulates his turn as an agreement by beginning with "yeah", at line 7, Ben introduces a significant modification by characterizing this as "the sleepover room.". Notice though that he does this in such a way as to acknowledge Jeffrey's greater epistemic rights by including the tag "right?", thereby requesting confirmation of what he is saying from Jeffrey. When this does not receive a response, Ben repeats the turn.

```
(23)
1   JEFF:        This is my sleepover room.
2   PETE:        Guess what.
3                (0.2)
4                Guess what.
5                (.)
6                Guess what.
7   BEN:     →   yeah that's the sleepover room.
8            →   right?
9                (1.0)
10           →   That's the sleepover room right?
11  JEFF:        °right°
```

In the following case, the boys are talking about the same part of the structure that Jeffrey has been building. Here Ben suggests "It was a:lso a trap right?", again employing a tag question which attends to Jeffrey's greater epistemic rights by inviting him to confirm.

(24)
1 BEN: It was a:lso a trap right?
2 JEFF: Yes

In these contexts then, we see one participant orienting to the greater epistemic rights of another. In each case the greater epistemic rights appear to flow directly from the role that that participant performs in the larger activity of make-believe – in 22 the characters Sean is talking about have been animated by Roger and indeed one of them is in his hand; in 23 and 24 Ben is talking about a part of the structure that Jeffrey has built.

This brings us back to the one-sidedness of the stipulations with which we began. We can see now that what gives them this character is that the objects being spoken about fall completely within the speaker's domain – within her territory of knowledge. Indeed, by stipulating about these objects the child simultaneously claims some kind of privileged access to them – having seen something not otherwise observable to others, the child produces an announcement in which that "something" is presented: "Look, it's a Rubik's Cube". In contrast, in the extended episodes we've considered here, the children are managing, through the details of their talk, clearly overlapping territories of knowledge. Such overlapping territories imply socially distributed rights and obligations to know, and children's orientations to that distribution can be seen in the range of practices described. In using interrogative formats, in soliciting co-participant attention with "pretend" prefaces, and in proposing – rather than reporting – what happens in the make-believe world, children attend to an asymmetrical arrangement of rights and obligations to knowledge.

Part III

Epistemic resources for managing affiliation
and alignment

7   Territories of knowledge, territories of experience: empathic moments in interaction

John Heritage

> ...if I tell you something that you come to think is so, you are entitled to have it. And you take it that the stock of knowledge that you have is something that you can get wherever you get it, and it is yours to keep. But the stock of experiences is an altogether differently constructed thing. As I say, in order to see that that is so, we can just, for example, differentiate how we deal with a piece of knowledge and how we deal with someone else's experience, and then come to see that experiences then get isolated, rather than that they are themselves as productive as are pieces of knowledge.
>
> (Sacks 1984: 425)

Introduction

The relationship between knowing something and having experienced it is deeply entrenched in interactional practices associated with assessment and evaluation. In the following sequence, for example, both parties have recently attended the same bridge party:

```
(1)
1 NOR:  →  I think evryone enjoyed jus' sitting aroun'
2          ta::lk [ing.]
3 BEA:  →        [ h h] I do too::,
4          (0.3)
5 NOR:     Yihknow e-I think it's too bad we don't do that once'n
6          awhile insteada playing bri:dge er .hh
```

Here Bea agrees with Norma's assertion in a straightforward fashion, uninhibited by the need to manage differential access to the event in question.

In 2, by contrast, Eve has only second-hand knowledge of the movie *Midnight Cowboy* (lines 4–6), whereas Jon and Lyn have been to the movie. When Eve reports an account of the movie as 'depressing,' Jon and Lyn agree, indexing their direct and independent access to the movie with *oh*-prefaced assessments (lines 7 and 8):

I would like to thank Nick Enfield, Alexa Hepburn, Leelo Keevallik, Manny Schegloff, Jakob Steensig and Tanya Stivers for comments and reactions to earlier versions of this chapter.

```
(2)
1  JON:        We saw Midnight Cowboy yesterday -or  [suh- Friday.
2  EVE:                                               [Oh?
3  LYN:        Didju s- you saw that,  [it's really good.
4  EVE:                                 [No I haven't seen it
5              Jo saw it 'n she said she f- depressed her
6  EVE:        ter[ribly
7  JON:  →        [Oh it's [terribly depressing
8  LYN:  →                 [Oh it's depressing.
9  EVE:        Ve[ry
10 LYN:  →       [But it's a fantastic [film.
11 JON:  →                             [It's a beautiful movie.
```

Later, both Jon and Lyn leverage this superior epistemic access into a subsequent evaluation of the movie which departs from a view of it as merely "depressing" (Heritage 1998, 2002a).

Still more problematic are cases in which one party evaluates some state of affairs to which the other has no access at all. In the following sequence, Emma's sister Lottie has returned from an apparently exhilarating trip to visit friends in Palm Springs. Her method of representing the house she stayed at centers on its inaccessibility to her sister:

```
(3)
1  LOT:   h h Jeeziz Chris' you sh'd see that house E(h)mma yih'av
2         |no idea.h[hmhh
3  EMM:             [I bet it's a drea:m.
```

Patently lacking the resources to enter into a direct appreciation of the house by the very terms of Lottie's assessment, Emma aligns with Lottie's evaluation by means of a subjunctive expression of her likely evaluation, thereby achieving a simulacrum of agreement (Heritage and Raymond 2005).

There are, then, events, activities and sensations which a person is entitled to evaluate by virtue of having experienced them, and in which shared evaluation is possible and legitimate by virtue of shared experience. However, there are others to which the experiencer has primary, sole and definitive epistemic access. Because persons conceive experience as 'owned' by a subject-actor, and as owned in a singular way, a 'problem of experience' arises. In particular, when persons report first-hand experiences of any great intensity (involving, for example, pleasure, pain, joy or sorrow), they obligate others to join with them in their evaluation, to affirm the nature of the experience and its meaning, and to affiliate with the stance of the experiencer toward them. These obligations are moral obligations that, if fulfilled, will create moments of empathic communion. As Durkheim (1915) observed, such moments are fundamental to the creation of social relationships, to social solidarity, and to an enduring sociocultural and moral order. However, recipients of reports of first-hand experiences can encounter these empathic moments as a dilemma in which they are required to affiliate with the experiences reported, even as they lack the experiences, epistemic rights, and sometimes even the subjective resources from which emotionally congruent stances can be constructed.

Under these circumstances, the recipient's capacity for empathic response – "an affective response that stems from the apprehension or comprehension of another's emotional state or condition, and that is similar to what the other person is feeling or would be expected to feel" (Eisenberg and Fabes 1990; see also Baron-Cohen 2003 and Rogers 1959) – and the communication of that response may undergo significant challenge. This chapter describes some of the resources that are available to recipients under these circumstances, and considers ways in which tellers can facilitate moments of empathic communion notwithstanding the difficulties involved. It does so by drawing on several large corpora of interactions in British and American English. No attempt is made to develop distributional evidence for the chapter's claims. Rather, the chapter aims at conceptualizing affinities between the affordances of particular methods of describing experience, and the responses those descriptions can invite.

Empathic moments

The most basic way that a teller can facilitate a moment of empathic communion is by projecting its emergence in advance, and by constructing its development step by step. Conversational practices geared to these ends have been well described in accounts of news delivery (Maynard 2003; Terasaki 2004) and story telling (Goodwin 1984; Jefferson 1978; Sacks 1974; Stivers 2008). In particular, pre-announcements and story prefaces project the type of action to come and, most importantly, its valence to the teller. In the following case from Terasaki, A's pre-announcement (lines 1–2) projects two pieces of positive news. Each of these attracts a strongly affiliative response from his interlocutor (lines 7 and 11):

```
(4) (Terasaki 2004: 176)
1   A:    I fergot t'tell y'the two best things that happen'tuh
2         me t'day.
3   B:    Oh super.=What were they
4   A:    I gotta B plus on my math test,
5   B:    On yer final?
6   A:    Un huh?
7   B:  → Oh that's wonderful
8   A:    And I got athletic award.
```

```
 9  B:      REALLY?
10  A:      Uh huh. From Sports Club.
11  B:  →   Oh that's terrific Ronald.
```

By contrast, as Terasaki (2004: 174) also notes, news that has potential for empathic response can be presented in a fashion that subordinates its relevance to some other interactional goal. Thus in 5, as Maynard (2003: 90) points out, information about a death in a family (line 6) known to Lottie is presented as background to the announcement that a golf game can go forward as planned.

(5) (Maynard 2003: 93)
```
1  Emm:      =Bud's gon'play go:lf now up Riverside he's js leavin'
2            (0.2)
3  Lot:      Oh:.
4            (0.5)
5  Emm:      So: Kathern' Harry were s'poze tuh come down las'night
6        →   but there wz a death'n the fam'ly so they couldn'come
7            so Bud's as'd Bill tuh play with the comp'ny deal so I
8            guess he c'n play with im so
9  Lot:  →   Oh:: goo::d.
```

In 5 it is the news about the golf game (and not the death in the family) that is registered with Lottie's "Oh:: goo::d." (line 9). Thus as Maynard (2003: 90) notes, "interactional organization and structure supersede utterance content in achieving and displaying the talk as news."

In some circumstances, competing dimensions of a news announcement may hamper the emergence of an empathic response. In 6 Andi informs her friend Betty that she is pregnant. Since Betty is a sufficiently close friend to know that Andi's partner Bob has had a vasectomy, Andi's announcement will clearly be both surprising (and puzzling) and, eventually, something to affiliate with.

Betty's initial response to the announcement ("Oh my good^ness!" line 8) conveys surprise rather than empathic affiliation. And her continuation ("hhow- (1.0) did you have a reversal-") continues this focus with an attempt to understand how this surprising event came about:

(6) (Maynard 2003: 93/109)
```
1  And:      .hhh well: speaking of bo^ttoms are you sitting down?
2  Bet:      Ye^ah.
3  And:      Well we have some news for you.
4  Bet:      What?
5  And:      .hhh that may come as a bit of a surprise ehhh!
6  Bet:      I see- what are you telling me?
7  And:      hhhh! Bob and I are going to have a baby.
8  Bet:  →   Oh my good^ness! hhow- (1.0) did you have a reversal-
```

```
9                he have a reversal?
10  And:         Yea:h.
11               (1.0)
12  And:         .hhh [::::::::::
13  Bet:              [Whe::^n
14  And:         tch eYup. Last March.
15               (0.4)
16  And:         .mhhh ((sniff))
17  Bet:  →  OH [MY GOO:D^NESS:
18  And:            [And (huh)
19  And:         it was [very successful [very quickly hh::h .hhh
20  Bet:  →           [OH I'M SO    [^HAPPY.
```

It is only after it has become completely clear that Bob is the father of the baby and that the pregnancy is intentional that Betty responds with an enthusiastic and empathic response "OH I'M SO ^HAPPY."

In the absence of prefatory work, empathic moments can slip by unacknowledged. For example, in the following, Edward has called his associate Richard because he has learned that Richard's wife has slipped a disk. After offering Richard assistance with everyday chores, the conversation turns to how the episode occurred. After hearing the trivial cause of the problem ('just' bending over [line 2]), Edward acknowledges the information sympathetically (line 4). Whereupon Richard elaborates by saying that "It hasn't happened fuh ten yea:rs." (line 8):

```
(7)
1   EDW:  W'l what a frightf'l thing How did it happen.
2   RIC:  She jus' bent o:ver as we w'r getting ready tih go out h
3         on Christmas [morning.]
4   EDW:               [O h:  :  ] my God.
5         (0.2)
6   RIC:  .h Yhes i [t hent-]
7   EDW:            [uhh hu:] hh, hu [:h ho:.
8   RIC:                             [It hasn't happened fuh ten yea:rs.=
9   EDW:  =ukhh huukhh ukh >Oh she's had it be|fore.<
10  RIC:  Oh yes=
11  RIC:  =b't not fih te(h)n y(h)ea(h) [a(h)s.]
12  EDW:                               [O h: :]: Lord.
13  RIC:  Yes there we are,
14  EDW:  The:re we are.
15        ((Topic shift into a closing sequence))
```

Here Richard's elaboration juxtaposes the back injury's occurrence on "Christmas morning." with all the attendant alterations in holiday plans, with the infrequency of its onset ('not for ten years'). The import of this juxtaposition is to convey what an unusual and unlucky occurrence it was.

None of this is taken up by Edward (line 9) who, after a noisy throat clear, offers only the pedestrian understanding that Richard's wife has "h̲ad it before." Richard's *oh*-prefaced response treats this understanding as self-evident (Heritage 1998), and continues (line 11) by reintroducing the additional information, now interspersed with troubles resistant laugh particles (Jefferson 1984b) that make light of the situation: "b't n̲ot fih te(h)n y(h̲) ea(h)a(h)s." Here Edward is offered a second opportunity at empathic appreciation of the unluckiness of Edward's wife's (and family's) situation, to which he responds with a perfunctorily intoned and thus pro forma "Oh̲::: Lord." At this point, Richard abandons his pursuit of an empathic response with the summative and closings relevant "Yes t̲here we are,". Edward's reciprocation of this sets the scene for the conversation to enter its closing phase. In this case, Edward simply fails to recognize that what is being presented to him is an occasion for empathic response, even when it is presented twice.

In sum, the construction of empathic moments is subject to the same kinds of constraints that attend most sequences in which large and other-attentive responses are aimed at. In these sequences, there is a telling "that both takes a stance toward what is being reported and makes the taking of a [complementary] stance by the recipient relevant" (Stivers 2008: 32). Pre-announcements and story tellings are the primary vehicles through which stances are enacted and empathic moments are created.

Resources for responding to accounts of personal experiences

In this section, I look at a range of resources that recipients have available to address emerging empathic moments, including resources with which to avoid or decline them. I will begin with the latter.

Ancillary questioning

At the least empathic end of the spectrum are actions that decline affiliative engagement with the experience reported by a teller. The most coercive of these are ancillary questions (Jefferson 1984a) or "refocusings" (Maynard 1980) in which, at the point where an empathic response to the telling would otherwise be due, the recipient raises a somewhat related question about the matter. In addition to declining affiliative engagement with the experience described by the teller, ancillary questions also require that the teller address the agenda raised in the questioner's question. That agenda can involve a considerable departure from the matter on which the teller was previously focused.

For example, in the following piece of narrative (from a conversation between two sisters extensively analyzed in Jefferson *et al.* 1987), Lottie has made previous attempts to introduce a report of nude swimming into the conversation. In the immediate aftermath of Lottie's nude swimming announcement (lines 1–2/4), and in overlap with her enthusiastic assessment of the experience, Emma responds in overlap with a general evaluation of Lottie's swimming partner (line 7), and then with a more disparaging question about her drinking habits (line 8) which could be heard to insinuate a context for the nude swimming itself:

```
(8)
1   LOT:        ...............so I:sabel'n I e-en (h)w(h)e swam in
2               th(h)et p(h)ool until two uh'cl(h)o [ck in the] morning.=
3   EMM:                                           [O h : : ,  ]
4   LOT:        =i(h)i [n the n   ] u:de.
5   EMM:               [#Go::d#]
6   LOT:        .hh u [h o h o : G]od ih wz:] fun.=
7   EMM:  →          [°I:sn't° she]   cu:::te ]
8   EMM:  →    =.hh She still drinkin' er liddle dri:nks?
9               (0.6)
10  LOT:        Ye:ah'n the [: n ]
11  EMM:                    [°Yea]h,°
12  LOT:        we swam (.) ^a:ll day dihday I d-I never: (.) well I got out
13              abaht e'ry (.) five minutes er so e [n then]'n ] take] a ]
14  EMM:  →                                         [°Oh I°]bet]cher ]ta]:nned.
15              (0.2)
16  LOT:        .hh ^YA:H. Kin'a #yea:h.#=
17  EMM:        =Mm hm:,
18  LOT:        .hhh En the:n: (.) ah lef'there e(.)t uh:: (0.7) ts-
19              exa:c'ly et three o'clo:ck.
20  EMM:        .pt.hhhh
21  LOT:        En I didn'git inna any traffic e'all'n then...
```

Here it seems clear that Emma is declining the opportunity of empathic affiliation with her sister's recent experiences, indeed competitively declining it. Subsequently, at line 14, Emma moves away from the account of swimming by topicalizing a likely consequence ("°Oh I° betcher ta:nned.") and thereafter Lottie abandons the topic (though she returns to it later [Jefferson *et al.* 1987]).

Of course, questions can be used to move the conversation toward an ancillary topic without the studied lack of affiliation to be found in 8 (Jefferson 1984b). In 9 Nancy is complaining to her friend Hyla about a visit to the dermatologist. The sequence is opened with Nancy's announcement "My f:face hurts," and culminates first with "It (js) hu:rt so bad Hyla I wz cry:::ing,":

(9)
```
1  NAN:  →  My f:face hurts,=
2  HYL:      =°W't-°
3             (.)
4  HYL:      Oh what'd'e do tih you.
5             (.)
6  NAN:      -GOD'e dis (.) prac'ly killed my dumb fa:ce,=
7  HYL:      =Why: Ho[-ow.       ]
8  NAN:                [(With,)]
9             (.)
10 NAN:      With this ting I don'ee I wzn'even looking I don't kno::w,((8 lines of
             description omitted))
19 NAN:  →  It (js) hu:rt so bad Hyla I wz cry:::ing,=
20 HYL:      =Yhher khhiddi[:ng.   ]
21 NAN:                    [nNo:]::.He really hurt me he goes I'm sorry,
22          .hh wehh .hh I khho th(h)at dznt make i(h)t a(h)n(h)y better
23      →   yihknow he wz jst (0.4) so, e-he didn't mean to be but he wz
24      →   really hurting m[e.
25 HYL:  →                  [.t #w Does it- look all marked u:p?=
26 NAN:      =nNo:, it's awr- it's a'right, jist'nna couple places b't I
27          c'n cover it u:p,=
28 HYL:      =Yea:h,
29 NAN:      But he goes, (.) he:- he goes yih 'av a rilly mild case he goes
```

Prompted to continue with "Yhher khhiddi:ng.", Nancy renews her complaint at lines 23–24 but, rather than empathic affiliation with the pain report, Hyla moves to an ancillary topic, "Does it- look all marked u:p?", which initiates a shift from Nancy's pain experience to the possible consequences of the treatment (lines 29 and beyond). The question is not devoid of self-interest: Hyla and Nancy are scheduled to spend an evening at the theatre later in the day.

And in a third case, sorority member Tara tells her housemates a somewhat self-dramatizing story about an incident the previous evening in which a boy took her home in a taxi. The story is framed with an announcement about 'crying in the cab' (line 1) and explicated with an account of how a boy went out of his way to help her in a 'down' situation. It is concluded with a repeat of the 'crying in the cab' reference (line 46):

(10)
```
1  TAR:   I still can't believe I cried_ in thuh cab.
2             (.)
3  PEN:   You crie::d?, Wh:[::y?
4  ALE:                    [It's [okay.
5  PEN:                          [(Didj-)
6  KEN:   Why'd you cry in the ca:b.
7             (0.2)
```

```
 8  TAR:    Cuz I'm a do:rk_
 9          (0.8)
10  KEN:    Oka:y,
11  ALE:    She's not a do:rk.
12  TAR:    I am a dork.
13  ALE:  → She prob'ly (had)/(got) dust in her eye.=
                                                  ((Story))
39  TAR:    .h an' (so) he's like "Here! let's take uh cab
40          home." an' I'm like "No it's okay. (.)
41          I'm gonna walk." .h and then he's like
42          "No let's take a cab home." and I was like
43          "No I'm gonna walk." an' I was being rea:lly stubborn,
44          .hh Finally he's like there's a cab right there_
45          and he grabs my arm_ .hh We take the cab_ (An')
46          he's like what's wrong. I start crying to him in the ca:b.
47          (.)
48  PEN:  → Mm:::,
49  TAR:    I'm gonna find his phone [number (an') call him.
50  KEN:  →                          [(So were) you drunk or were you
51          sober.
52          (.)
53  ALE:  → You guys have a good day.
```

The story start is unpromising. Kendra (line 10) does not resist Tara's self-deprecating claim to be a "dork" (Pomerantz 1978), and Alex heckles the story's initiation with a quite undramatic explanation (line 13) of Tara's tearful state. At the end of the story, two of Tara's recipients respond in ways that are scarcely aligned to the story's completion, let alone offering affiliation with the experience and sentiments that she reports (lines 48, 50–51 and 53). At line 48, Penny offers a continuer treating the story as incomplete, and Tara adds a further coda to the story (line 49). At line 53 Alex, who had taken a discouraging stance to the story early on (line 13), simply leaves the room without appreciating the story at all. And at lines 50–51, Kendra asks a question which, while registering the story's completion, does not address its emotional import and moves the topic in an ancillary direction. Moreover, in its intimation of intoxication as the underlying cause of the emotions described, the question incipiently undermines the basis on which the story was told.

The motivations for these non-empathic responses are of course various: an account of a risqué event that the recipient does not want to further topicalize (Extract 8), of a visit to the dermatologist that encountered competing relevancies (9), and a self-regarding story (10) that went "too far" (Drew and Walker 2008) and made too great a demand for on-the-spot empathic affiliation from its already reluctant recipients (Jefferson 1984b). Regardless of these motivations, the practice of ancillary questioning is a resource for declining empathic affiliation with the position taken by the teller, while simultaneously enforcing a shift in conversational topic. Both the declination and the escape from further obligation to respond are managed in a single decisive move.

Parallel assessments

With parallel assessments, respondents can focus on focal elements of the experience described by the teller, by describing a similar, but de-particularized, experience or preference. These assessments are "my side" assessments that support or 'second' a first speaker's description but without attempting to enter directly into the experience that is reported. In the following case, described in detail in Goodwin and Goodwin (1987), a brief description of an asparagus pie attracts an immediate, but generic, affiliative response from the interlocutor (line 3):

(11) (Goodwin and Goodwin 1987: 24)
1 Dia: <u>Jeff</u> made en asparagus pie
2   it was s:::<u>so</u> [: <u>goo</u>:d.
3 Cla: →   [I love it. °Yeah I love [tha:t.
4 Dia: [<<u>He</u> pu:t uhm,

Here, as also noted by the Goodwins (1987), the shift in tense in Clacia's response and the repair from "it" to "that:" in her repetition of the assessment, makes it clear that this is a parallel assessment of a type of dish that she also likes, rather than something she directly experienced (Goodwin and Goodwin 1987: 27).

A similar parallel assessment is the following. Considerably later in the call about her trip to Palm Springs, Lottie reintroduces the topic of nude swimming. This time Emma responds with a report of a parallel experience (lines 5–12):

(12)
1 LOT: =So then when Cl<u>au</u>de le(h)f' we(h)e t<u>oo</u>k those s<u>ui</u>ts off(h)
2   en £s:<u>wa</u>:m ar<u>ou</u>n'th[e <u>nu</u>:de eh <u>HUH</u>-u 'n took a s<u>u</u>:nb<u>a</u>:th in=
3 (E):   [(°Awh°)
4 LOT: =the <u>nu</u>:de 'n <u>e</u>'rything.=.<u>hhh</u> [hhh
5 EMM: [W'l <u>you</u> know Abby 'n ^<u>I</u> use'
6   tih do th<u>a</u>t on the ^r<u>i</u>vers if the <u>fe</u>ller'd go down get
7   <u>gas</u>'leen for their b<u>oa</u>:ts,h .hhhh She'd say dih you <u>mi</u>:nd
8   we'd b<u>e</u> inna c<u>o</u>:ve, but <u>we</u>'d take it ou:t (.) <u>u</u>nder the
9   wa(h)ter. Y<u>i</u>hknow bec'z: uh: (.) e we're <u>ou</u>t'n the <u>OPEN</u>. Y<u>i</u>h
10   know. .hh Buh w<u>e</u>'d j's' slip our b<u>a</u>thing sui:t au: en g- en
11   °sw<u>im</u> around in that° r:<u>I</u>Ver that:=uh C<u>o</u>lor<u>a</u>duh R<u>i</u>ver
12   →   til: .hhh Ghh<u>o</u>:d >what=uh< thr#<u>i</u>:ll.#

```
13              (0.2)
14 EMM:  →  I always have liked=tih swim in the °nu:[de°.
15 LOT:                                      [ME: TOO: yih
16          know eh wi- .hh En then .hh ri:ght #eh:
17          theh-# (.) there's two places where thuh ho:t water
18          comes in 'n you c'n git ri:ght up close to'm |'n i'
19          (y) £feels like=yer takin' a dou:che,=£
```

Emma's parallel account culminates in an assessment ("Ghho:d >what=uh<
thr#i:ll.#" line 12) which focuses on her experience of nude swimming in
the Colorado river and does not find an immediate response. However,
her subsequent generalization from this experience (line 14) closely supports the sentiments expressed earlier by her sister across a number of pas-
sages in this extended telephone call, and attracts an immediate affirmative
response together with an escalation (lines 16–19) in the intimacy and granularity of the experiences described (see Jefferson *et al.* 1987: 184–191).

These two cases suggest an emergent dilemma for those who would affiliate with others in empathic moments. On the one hand, the recipient has
not had direct first-hand experience of the event reported, and a parallel
"my side" response risks being heard as flat, pallid or pro forma. On the
other hand, a parallel assessment that is too florid, extended or enriched
in detail – as in (12) – risks being heard as competitive with the very report
that it is designed to affiliate with. Thus it is Emma's retreat to the generic
"I always have liked=tih swim in the °nu:de°.", and not the details of her
activities in the Colorado river, that attracts enthusiastic support from her
sister (line 15), who then proceeds to further details of her own experience.

Subjunctive assessments

Closely related to parallel assessments are their subjunctive counter-
parts. With the term *subjunctive assessments*, I mean to introduce efforts
at empathic affiliation which suggest that if the recipient were to experience the things described they would feel the same way. For example, in an
extension of (11) above, Dianne goes on to describe several special features
of the asparagus pie that Jeff made (lines 4–11):

```
(13)
1  Dia:     Jeff made en asparagus pie
2            it was s:::so [: goo:d.
3  Cla:                   [I love it. °Yeah I love [tha:t.
4  Dia:                                            [<He pu:t uhm,
5            (0.7)
6  Dia:     Tch! put crabmeat on th'bo::dum.
7  Cla:     Oh:[::.
```

```
8   Dia:        [(Y'know)/(Made it) with chee::se,=
9   Cla:        =[°Yeah. Right.
10  Dia:        =[En then jus' (cut up)/(covered it with) the broc-'r the
11              asparagus coming out in spokes.=
12  Dia:   →    =°It wz so good.
13  Cla:        °Right.
14  Cla:   →    °°(Oh: Go:d that'd be fantastic.)
```

In the immediate aftermath of this description, Dianne goes on to evaluate the pie (line 12). Although she does not immediately concur with a second assessment, Clacia responds at line 14 with an upgraded evaluation presented in the conditional (Goodwin and Goodwin 1987: 27). Here Clacia's lack of any direct experiential access to the pie, or a pie like it, mandates a subjunctive second assessment.

Another kind of subjunctive assessment involves epistemic downgrading of access to the assessable. In the following case, Hyla has been to see the movie *Dark at the Top of the Stairs* and has bought herself and Nancy tickets for a stage production of the show. Following a request from Nancy, she recounts the main plot lines:

```
(14)
1   NAN:        Kinyih tell me what it's abou:t?=
                ((27 lines of description deleted))
29  HYL:        =.hh En she's fixed up, (0.4) en she meets this gu:y, .hh a:n'
30              yihknow en he's (.) rilly gorgeous'n eez rilly nice en
31              evrythi [:ng bud li ]ke=
32  NAN:             [Uh h u :h, ]
33  HYL:        =.hh He's ah .hh Hollywood (0.3) s:sta:r's son yihknow who wz
34              a mista:[ke en they [put im in'n [Academy, school,
35  NAN    →           [O o this   [s o u n d s  [so goo:: ::d?
36  HYL:        .hh buh wai:t.='n then, .hhm (0.2) .tch en the: (w)- the
37              mother's .hh sister is a real bigot.
```

Here, as the Goodwins (1987) note in a discussion of a closely related passage, the epistemic downgrade accompanying Nancy's strongly affirmative assessment (line 35) indexes that it is the account of the plot, rather than direct experience of the plot itself, that is the object of the assessment.

The significance of subjunctive assessments is straightforward. Respondents can find themselves in circumstances where affiliation is required but direct or even parallel experience is plainly lacking. Clacia cannot have encountered an asparagus pie of the type that Dianne describes. The very premise of Hyla's account of *Dark at the Top of the Stairs* is that Nancy has not seen it. And Lottie's account of her trip to Palm Springs (Extract 3 above) builds Emma's lack of access into the very evaluation of the house she visited. In cases of this type, subjunctive assessments are a primary resource for affiliative response.

Observer responses

By "observer responses," I mean to indicate responses in which recipients claim imaginary access to the events and experiences described, but position themselves as observers, or would-be observers, to the event. Sometimes such responses can be relatively pro forma, as in the following case, which continues Lottie and Emma's conversation about nude swimming from 12 above:

```
(15)
14 EMM:     I always have liked=tih swim in the °nu: [de°.
15 LOT:                                               [ME: TOO: yih
16          know eh wi- .hh En then .hh ri:ght #eh:
17          theh-# (.) there's two places where thuh ho:t water
18          comes in 'n you c'n git ri:ght up close to'm |'n i'
19          (y) £feels like=yer [ta ]kin']a ]dou]:che,]£=
20 EMM:                          [eh]u h ]uh] u h]a h ]=
21 EMM:     =ahh[ahh a h       ].hhh    ]HUH-HA]HA-AHh ]a h h]ah]agh ]u h]
22 LOT:         [hhhHHU:H]HHUH]HHU:H  ]HA:h ha ]e-u-e ]ah]: ah ]: e ]
            h,=
23 EMM:     =.hhuhhh=
24 LOT:     =E[n we-: ]
25 EMM: →    [#I# C ]'N ^SEE YOU ^TWO KI:D[S ( )          [.hh
26 LOT:                                    [E:N ^SHE wz o[n ONE
27          END,='N=I wz o'uh=other en' with ur legs up,yihknow,'n=
28 EMM:     =[°Oh::::::::-:: G o : : d isn't she cu::te?°          ]
29 LOT:     =[G(h)ee(h)z it f(h)elt (s(h)o) g(h)ood,=hna:h ha:h]hu[uh hu ]
30 EMM:                                                         [°Oh:° ]
31          she's #a cut#ey.=
32 LOT:     =O[h:<]
33 EMM:      [Go ]:d she's uninh:ibitid=eh,
```

Here Emma, having affiliated with the project of nude swimming (line 14) and, through laugher at lines 20–21 (Jefferson et al. 1987), with the more risqué suggestions of lines 16–19, affiliates with Lottie by positioning herself as an imaginary voyeur of the scene. Notably, however, as Lottie escalates her account into a still more granular description of the pool activities, Emma begins to de-escalate her involvement through evaluative assessments of the co-participant of the kind seen in 8 above.

In accounts of agonistic experiences, observers' responses can be enhanced by siding with the teller in the situation, as in the following case in which Nicole, engaged in hairdressing in a salon, is describing an encounter with her ex-boyfriend to a co-worker sitting in the salon:

(16)
```
 1  NIC:    O(h)h: guess who ah seen on uh- (1.3) Thursday?
 2           (0.5) >no.< (0.8) Monday er Tuesday.=I don' know.
 3           (0.5)
 4  SHA:    °Who.°
 5           .hh
 6  NIC:    Mister Mi:les.
 7           (0.7)
 8  NIC:    Thet- the ki:ds wuz at the- (0.9) at the pa:rk, registerin'
 9           fer football; ri:ght,
10           (.)
11  SHA:    Uh huh,
12  NIC:    <I didn e'en really- > D'Shaun didn e'en<- tol' me
13           at the la:st minute_
14  NIC:    .hh (so he's et the plunge), "(Ah)/(Hey) Mom
15           e'rybody's registerin', I need=tuh take Raymond down,"
16           I'm like alright well go 'hea:d, I'll meet=you d^ere.
17           (0.8)
18  NIC:    .h I already knew I wuz gonna run into 'im.
19           (1.7)
20  NIC:    So I: was drivin' Steve's truck.
21           (1.2)
22  NIC:    °'n I Uhm° (0.4) got there, got ou:t,
23           (1.2)
24  NIC:    An' uh: (2.0) y'know I spoke to 'im, he gave me a hu:g,
25           (1.2) So that's i^:t. >I'm like me 'n you really ain't
26           got nuthin t'talk about.<
27           (0.2)
28  SHA:    Mm hm::;_=
29  NIC:    ="Hi:_" ((waving))
30  NIC:    Y'know (we)/(it) was rea:l cordial, (0.8) °thet wuz it.°
31           (1.0)
32  NIC:    So then he says uhm: >somethin' bout when am I gon' let
33           him< te:st dri:ve mah car, I said "I don't see thet-" uh:m
34           "concernin' you," (0.5) "You (no)/(don') test drivi nothin'."
35           (0.9)
36  NIC:    I said an' (uhm)/('en) (.) ^NO I said "I'm not even
37           in my car. Where'd you get ^that fro:m;" (0.3) He w's like
38           "Well who' truck you drivin;" ('n) I said "My boyfriend's,"
39  SHA:  → ((smile)) Eheh! .hh (1.4) God I wish I coulda see' his fa:ce.
```

In the main body of the story, the antagonist is introduced as "Mister Mi:les.", a form of marked recognitional reference designed to establish distance from him (Stivers 2007a). The encounter is portrayed as somewhat fraught ("I already knew I wuz gonna run into 'im." line 18, and ">I'm like me 'n you really ain't got nuthin t'talk about.<" lines 25–26), and its dénouement (line 38) is prepared for at line 20 ("So I: was drivin'

St<u>eve</u>'s truck."). Nicole prepares for the punch-line of the story by raising its granularity (Schegloff 2000a) from general glosses of the casual quality of their interchanges ("rea:l cordial," line 30), into indirect reported speech (lines 32–33), and then into direct reported speech (lines 33–39). This culminates in her report of the ex-boyfriend's question about the ownership of her truck (lines 37–38), and the exquisite put-down with which, by answering his question, she was able to display that she was "over" him. As she delivers "I said 'My b<u>oy</u>friend's,'" (line 38), Nicole turns from her customer and looks directly at Shauna, who responds with a subjunctive "into-the-moment" response: "<u>God</u> I wish I coulda see' his f<u>a</u>:ce.". This response, which places Shauna as a wished-for observer of the scene, unambiguously supports Nicole's position in the interchange. For what Shauna portrays herself as wishing to have observed is the (ideally) disconcerting effect of Nicole's statement on the ex-boyfriend. Moreover, in its (likely) over-estimate of the effect of Nicole's words, it empathizes with, and simultaneously inflates, the extent of her victory.

Observer responses, then, are responses in which recipients place themselves as imaginary witnesses to the scenes of experiences described by tellers. These are, of course, particularly appropriate for vicarious empathic response to scenes of action, and tend to be quite inapposite in the context of reports of feelings or emotions. However, they are intrinsically vicarious and subjunctive in character, offering simulacra of empathic response from a standpoint that is "external" and observational. They are "in the moment" with the teller, yet remain outside of it, close yet detached.

Response cries

With non-lexical response cries – "signs meant to be taken to index directly the state of the transmitter" (Goffman 1981: 116) – recipients more closely approach empathic connection with the reported experiences of their interlocutors. Almost all response cries are amenable to sound stretches which can carry sustained and elaborate prosodic details.[1] While Couper-Kuhlen (in press) has suggested that hopes of one-to-one matches between prosody and semantic aspects of affective or emotional displays are likely

---

[1] As noted by Freese and Maynard (1998: 213):

Recipients' turns in news deliveries tend to employ more dramatic prosody than deliverers'. This difference may be attributed partially to differences in the shapes of the turns; deliverers' turns are constructed as sentential units that evaluate the news as it is reported, while recipients' turns are compact phrases (or even single words) that are more exclusively dedicated to the task of evaluating the news. Because deliverers are producing information-as-news, they have more complex turn-organizational tasks, whereas recipient turns can attend more narrowly to emotive displays.

to be disappointed, she has also pointed to the ways in which sequential context elaborates prosodic detail in ways that invite specific emotional readings. It is in this context that we can consider response cries as vehicles for empathic alignments between speakers and hearers.

For example, in the following case, Jenny's son David took a message asking her to call her friend Vera as soon as possible (see lines 3–4). However, as it turns out, Vera's objective in contacting Jenny – having Jenny spend time with Vera's son and daughter-in-law before they went away – is no longer viable (lines 6–8):

```
(17)
 1  VER:    Hello:,
 2  JEN:    Hello Vera[:?
 3  VER:             [He:llo Jenny ev yih jus got [back
 4  JEN:                                          [I jus got in: en
 5          [David] said thet chu'd called.  ]
 6  VER:    [A h :  ] I thought ah'd a'caught] yuh ah thought you coulda
 7          called up fuh coffee.
 8  JEN:    Oh:::. Have they'av yih visitiz g[one then,  ]
 9  VER:                                     [They'v |go]:ne. Yes,
10  JEN: →  #Oh[:ah.#]
11  VER:       [E ::n ]:- theh'v gun tuh Jea:n's mothuh's no: [w yihkno:w,]
12  JEN:                                                      [Y e : s ::    ]:.
13  JEN:    Mm:?,
14  VER:    Eh:m: ah don't think theh'll get up again ei:thuh.
```

The news conveys a double disappointment – Jenny has missed a social opportunity, but more consequentially Vera's son and daughter-in-law have unexpectedly curtailed their visit (as it transpires, to visit the wife's parents [Raymond and Heritage 2006]). Jenny initially registers the import of Vera's news at line 8 and, on its confirmation, produces a stretched "#Oh:ah.#" with some vocal creak (line 10). The effect is to convey sorrow or disappointment (Couper-Kuhlen in press). While this conveys her own disappointment at a missed opportunity, it also closely affiliates with the tone of Vera's announcement (lines 6–7) conveyed by its "Ah:" preface, and its news that the son and daughter-in-law have left unexpectedly early. Here then Jenny registers a basic level of empathic affiliation while, by not elaborating her response, she does not articulate its precise object, leaving her feelings equivocal between her own (slight) disappointment and empathy at Vera's greater distress (see also Goodwin and Goodwin 1987).

It is a significant feature of empathic response cries that, by not distinguishing between the report of the event and the event itself as the target of response, they can attain a closer degree of empathy with the reported experience than might otherwise be the case. The following is an elaborated instance of this. Pat, whose house burned down the previous night, is recounting what happened:

(18)
```
1  Pat:      =cz ih wz j st like en hou:r one weh- .hhhhhh Oh:: hh!
2            We coulda been, if we were sleepi:ng, (0.2) we would not
3            be here.=
4  Pat:      =or one of us.would probly not be here becuz .hhhh w-our
5            whole bedroom would'v caved in.the whole house is jist
6            three feet of ashes. hh[hhhh
7  Pen:  →                          [Oh:: whho:[w
8  Pat:                                        [It happened within minutes.
9            .hh Within a half hour the house wz go:ne I guess,=
10 Pen:  →   =Ohhh go:(d),
11 Pat:      So it's jist l[i:ke, we wouldn', we just would'na been
12 Pen:                    [.hhh
13           here. hh yihkno:w,
14 Pen:  →   [Ohhh ba:by.
15 Pat:      [There's no way ih wz ih wz jus:, we're jist lucky I guess:,
16 Pen:  →   .hhhh Okay waidaminnit I don'know if yer cryi-in b't I
17       →   hhh(h)a[hhhm uh hu:h] .hhh=
18 Pat:            [(hhhh No.)
19 Pat:      =.hh I wz guh- I- middle a'the night la-ast night I
20           wannhhhidhhhtihh c(h)all (h)y(h)ou .mhhh! I [said   ] oh: I
21 Pen:                                                  [uh hh-]=
22 Pat:      wish I wz at lunch so I c'go talk tuh Penn(h)y
23           hh[hh .hhh
24 Pen:  →     [Yehh(h)ehh .h[hhh
25 Pat:                       [(Cz) that's wd I wz rea:lly, [(But-)
26 Pen:  →                                                 [Oh:::,
27 Pat:      N-I don'know.I really do feel better now. .hh[hhh
28 Pen:                                                   [Yih d-okay.
29 Pat:      =I really really do so don't hh don't be upset for
30           me hhh hnh .hh
```

Across the details of Pat's report, Penny acknowledges successive revelations with a series of breathy response cries (lines 7, 10, 14) that convey a strong sense of empathic affiliation.[2] These culminate with a declaration (lines 16–17) that explicitly claims empathic communion with Pat contemporaneous with its current retelling. Significantly, Pat initially denies the feelings that Penny attributes to her (line 18), but she is prompted to report her feelings of the previous night in a strongly affiliative sequence (lines 19–20, 22–23, 25–26), before concluding with an optimistic projection (Jefferson 1988).

---

[2] On "breathiness" or aspiration as a component of emotional display, see Hepburn (2004) and Whalen and Zimmerman (1998).

Response cries, then, express empathic sentiments primarily through prosody. By responding to reports of events non-propositionally, they advance closer to the lived reality of the feelings the reported events have (or may have) aroused in others. By not discriminating between feelings that the teller associated with the event, and the sentiments the telling is arousing in the respondent, response cries evoke and claim a degree of empathic union and affiliation between teller and recipient. These positive advantages notwithstanding, response cries normally pave the way for more propositional and substantive forms of understanding and affiliation. While building an emotional platform from which this affiliation can be launched, the propositional content of later acts of affiliation will ideally be attentive to, and congruent with, the telling. In 18 above, Penny's act of substantive affiliation (lines 16–17) misfires, and in 20 below we will see similar difficulties in the management of propositional alignment that, as in 18, cause temporary slippage in the empathic affiliation achieved by the parties. In the end, then, response cries frequently issue an emotional IOU that must subsequently be cashed in propositional terms.

The affordances of experience descriptions and their demands

By now we have got far enough to register the considerable diversity of responses to reports of experience, ranging from ancillary questions that, as often as not, fully decline empathic response, through "my side" or parallel assessments that, while affiliative, decline to enter into the experience of the other, to "subjunctive assessments" that enter, as it were, provisionally into the other's experience. Only with the response cries and the "into-the-moment" responses do recipients undertake to engage fully with the experiences reported by the experiencer.

However, we can also note that these reports themselves vary widely in terms of their affordances for empathic response. A report of eating a delicious asparagus pie can be empathically addressed by one who has eaten such a thing (Extract 11), as can a story of nude swimming by one who has done it (Extract 12). Eating asparagus pie with crab meat on the bottom is an altogether more specific experience, however, and one for which, unless she is a chef or a gourmet, a person may have difficulty in managing a convincing display of empathic appreciation. We can thus suggest a certain paradox about empathic moments. Relatively typical experiences are more readily shared, but may not be treated as requiring empathic displays, or at least as requiring less intense displays. More specific experiences, for example a movement-by-movement report of a symphonic concert, or a course-by-course description of a gourmet meal, are less readily shared.

Yet, paradoxically, the more detailed and granular the description, the more obligation may be imposed on a recipient to exhibit empathic union with the describer. These descriptions may obligate empathic responses that require expertise or imagination or both.

It is against this background that we can see the decisive advantages of narrative in general, and of direct reported speech in particular, as a resource for eliciting empathic alignment. For narratives take recipients "into the moment" and supply the resources for empathic response. The enhanced granularity of direct reported speech, which is a frequent climax of narrative accounts (Coulmas 1986; Labov 1972; Polanyi 1982; Tannen 1989), can take a recipient to the very brink of the action and the experiences that it engenders, offering exceptional affordances for empathic alignment (see Extract 16).

In the remainder of this chapter, we will explore these affordances in more detail by reference to a single story.

The sale at the vicarage

In the following story, Lesley tells her friend Joyce about an incident in which she was insulted at a charity sale. The story begins with a preface (lines 2–3) projecting the type of story to come (Jefferson 1978; Sacks 1974). The details of the story are presented with some care. The "sale at the vicarage" is presented as a "known event" to Joyce with the demonstrative "that" (line 5), and the main protagonist is introduced with a marked (and ironical) recognitional reference (Stivers 2007a) as "Your friend 'n mi:ne" (line 10). When this reference is not recognized, Lesley attempts a second marked reference form "mMister: R:," (line 13), this time successfully:

```
(19)
 1  JOY:  °|Ye-:s I'm alright,°
 2  LES:  °Oh:.° hh Yi-m- You |know I-I- I'm boiling about
 3        something hhhheh[heh hhhh
 4  JOY:                  [Wha::t.
 5  LES:  Well that sa|:le. (0.2) at- at (.) the vicarage.
 6        (0.6)
 7  JOY:  Oh |ye[:s,
 8  LES:       [ t
 9        (0.6)
10  LES:  u (.) ihYour friend 'n mi:ne wz the:re
11        (0.2)
12  ( ):  (h[h hh)
13  LES:   [mMister: R:,
14  JOY:  (Oh ye:s hheh)
15        (0.4)
```

```
16 LES:   And em: p ^we (.) ^really didn't have a lot'v cha:nge
17        |that (.) day becuz we'd been to |Bath 'n we'd been:
18        Christmas shoppin:g, (0.5) but we thought we'd better
19        go along t'th'sale 'n do what we could, (0.2) we had^n't
20        got a lot (.) of s:e- ready cash t'^spe:nd.
21        (0.3)
22 LES:   t[hh
23 JOY:   [Mh.=
24 LES:   =In ^any |case we thought th'things were very
25        ex^pen|sive.
26 JOY:   Oh did you.
27        (0.9)
28 LES:   AND uh ^we were looking rou-nd the |sta:lls 'n poking
29        about 'n he came up t'me 'n he said Oh: hhello Lesley,
30        (.) ^still trying to buy something fuh nothing,
```

The sale at the vicarage will predominantly have featured relatively inexpensive items, all of which would be sold for charity. These details are accommodated in Lesley's account of not having a lot of "ready cash to' ^spe:nd" (line 20), after Christmas shopping in Bath (lines 16–18). She is also careful to index the charitable obligations that took her to the sale nonetheless – "but we thought we'd better go along t'th'sale 'n do what we could," (lines 18–19) – and to note that the things were "very ex^pen|sive.". By the time of the reported incident (at lines 28–30), it appears that Lesley has not bought anything at the sale. However, her interlocutor's attack is presented as unprovoked and unjustified. The lack of provocation is portrayed in her account of the circumstances of the remarks, i.e., (i) immediately following their meeting ("he came up t'me 'n he said"), and (ii) as the first action after a greeting ("he said Oh: hhello Lesley, (.) ^still trying to buy something fuh nothing,").[3] The raw injustice of the attack is provided for in Lesley's earlier account of her charitable motivations for attending the sale (lines 18–19).

The reaction sequence is complex and nuanced. It begins with a strongly "into-the-moment" empathic response: Joyce enacts a sharp intake of breath, mirroring the kind of response a recipient would have had as the victim of an unprovoked surprise attack, especially given its evident injustice. After nearly a second, Joyce enacts a second response ("Oo:::: Les ley") which is also compatible with surprise (Wilkinson and Kitzinger 2006), now accompanied by an address term which also expresses empathic affiliation (cf. Clayman 2010). Immediately after the

---

[3] The incorporation of the word "still" into the voicing of this direct reported speech may suggest that, though it is not described in her account, this may not have been Lesley's first meeting with her interlocutor at the sale or, alternatively, that the interlocutor is invoking a previous encounter.

onset of this new response, Lesley mirrors it (Extract 20, line 35) before breaking into troubles-resistant laughter (Jefferson 1984b). At this point Lesley and her friend have precisely matched responses to the reported incident, and Joyce has taken up a strongly empathic position through the use of response cries.

```
(20)
28  LES:  AND uh ^we were looking rou-nd the |sta:lls 'n poking
29        about 'n he came up t'me 'n he said Oh: hhello Lesley,
30        (.) ^still trying to buy something fuh nothing,
31  (  ):  tch!
32  JOY:  .hhhahhhhhh!
33        (0.8)
34  JOY:  Oo[: : :   ]: L e s l e y    ]
35  LES:    [^Oo:.]ehh heh ^heh ]
36        (0.2)
37  JOY:  |I:s[n 't    ]      [[he
38  LES:      [^What]do ^y[ou ^sa[:y.
39        (0.3)
40  JOY:  |Oh isn't he |drea:dful.
41  LES:  °eYe-:-:s:°
42        (0.6)
43  (  ):  tch
44  JOY:  What'n aw::f'l ma::[:::n
45  LES:                     [ehh heh-heh-^heh
46  JOY:  Oh:: honestly, |I cannot stand the man it's just
47        (no[:         )
48  LES:     [I tbought well I'm gon' tell Joyce that, ehh[heh]=
49  JOY:                                                  [( ) ]=
50  LES:  =[heh-heh he-e] uh: ^e[h eh^ hhhhh
51  JOY:  =[O h : : : :.    ] I    [do think he's dreadful
52  LES:  tch Oh: dea-r
53  JOY:  Oh: he r[eally i   ]:s,
54  LES:          [^He dra-]ih-he (.) took the win' out'v my sails
55        c'mpletel(h)y
56        (.)
57  JOY:  I know The awkward thing is you've never got a ready
58        a:n[swer have |you. ]that's r[i:ght,   ]
59  LES:     [No: I thought'v] lots'v ]ready a]nswers
60        a:fterward[s,
61  JOY:            [Yes that's ri::gh[t.
62  LES:                              [Yes
63        (.)
64  JOY:  But you c'n never think of them at the ti:[me
65  LES:                                            [No:,
66  LES:  [No:.
67  JOY:  [A:fterwards I always think (.) °oh I should've said°
```

```
68       [tha̱t. or I]should]'ve said thi̱]s.
69 LES:  [Oh y e s ] e h-    ]r i̱ : g h t.   ]
70       (0.7)
71 JOY:  B[ut I do̱:'nt think a'th'm at the ti:me
72 LES:  [°°Mm̱:.
73 ( ):   ( tc[h) (    [ tch)
74 LES:        [e̱hh hu[h huh
75       (0.8)
76 JOY:  Oẖ:: g-O̱h 'n I thi̱nk Ca̱rol is going, t'the
77       [mee[ting t'n ]i̱ g h t, ]
78 LES:  [ hh [Y E̱ : S ]tha̱t's r]i:ght. i-u̱h
```

After line 35, however, Lesley and Joyce start to take divergent positions about the incident. Perhaps in congruence with Lesley's marked person reference introducing the story, Joyce starts to evaluate the man she knows rather than the behaviors described. She initiates a turn at line 37, abandons it, and then renews it at line 40: "|Oh isn't he |dre̱a:dful." Both the *oh*-prefacing and the negative interrogative aspects of this turn point to its production as a strongly independent position about the man and his character (Heritage 2002a, b). And Joyce sustains this stance further at lines 44 and 46, 51 and 53. At the same time (line 38), Lesley initiates an assessment of the incident in terms of its shock and the difficulty of fabricating a response: "^What do ^you ^sa̱:y.", a stance which she does not pursue, until she renews it at line 54.

Once Joyce has exhausted her initial outrage against the perpetrator (indexed by the recycling of her assessment of him as "dreadful" [lines 51 and 53]), Lesley renews her focus on specifics of the incident and the difficulty of response: "^He̱ dra- ih-he̱ (.) took the wi̱n' out'v my sails c'mple̱tel(h)y" (lines 54–55). This time Joyce affiliates with her in a flurry of "my side" parallel assessments (lines 57–58, 64, 67–68, 71), finally leading to sequence closure and a new topic start (line 76).

Here, then, a sequence that was begun with remarkable empathic affiliation and synchrony slipped into less than full agreement as the parties began to diverge in what they were prepared to treat as the primary assessable aspect of the event. Agreement was restored, though at some twenty lines of distance from the story climax, as both women settled for the difficulties of response to the unexpected insult as the thing to be reviewed. From thence, agreement crystallized into sequence closure.

The sequence is instructive in that, after her initial response to the story climax, Joyce focused on characteristics of the protagonist that she knew *independently of the story* as the basis for empathy, even though that line of response attracted support from Lesley that was lukewarm at best (lines 41, 45, 48, 50, 52). It may be that independently accessible aspects of a scene are often preferred by an empathizer, who wishes empathic affiliation to transcend the particulars of a report, and to escape into independent agreement that is not merely responsive to the report's details alone.

Discussion

The empathic moments discussed in this chapter evidence several knotty dilemmas, both for those who would furnish opportunities for empathic engagement, and for those who are obligated to respond to them. These dilemmas revolve around the moral obligations to respond that arise through tellers' initiatives, and the affordances of the tellings for recipient response.

From a teller's perspective, a key decision concerns the level of granularity with which an experience is to be reported. As previously noted, a relatively generalized account can invite, and legitimately receive, a less committed and more pro forma response. With each increase in detail, a teller increases pressure on the motivation and ability of the recipient to respond empathetically. In this context, the affordances of the telling become ever more critical for, without favorable affordances, the recipient may simply be unable to rise to the challenge. It is perhaps these considerations which motivate the selection of narrative as a primary means with which to express experiences that are both intensely emotional and intensely particular. For the affordances of narrative in general, and the specific value of concluding a narrative with direct reported speech, permit the coincidence of exact detail and the possibility of precisely calibrated emotional response.

For the recipient with the obligation to respond, a first concern is with the affordances for response. Accounts of music that the recipient has never heard, or dishes never tasted, can place stern demands on even the most motivated and dedicated recipient. Yet, paradoxically, even greater difficulties can emerge when recipients have independent access to the persons and places described. For here decisions must be taken as to whether the response is to be made in terms of the account just given, or whether it is to be augmented with the independent personal judgements of the recipient. In the event that the latter choice is made, while there may be a strengthening of the endorsement of the teller's position and emotions, it may be achieved – as in 20 above – at the cost of disattending the specifics of the telling. This can result in a substitution of the recipient's experience for the teller's as the basis for the response, in a process through which the recipient supplants the teller as the "experiencer of record."

Thus, as in other domains of social knowledge, these data suggest a distance–involvement dilemma involved in constructing intimate self–other relations (Raymond and Heritage 2006). In acts of affiliation, Raymond and Heritage (2006: 701) note: "persons must manage the twin risks of appearing disengaged from the affairs of the other, or over-involved and even appropriating of them." It is striking that the management of these risks can become demanding when the parties are close friends or relatives with intimate knowledge of one another's lives and activities, and when the matter to be addressed is emotionally loaded.[4]

Conclusion

Ever since Durkheim's (1915: 415–447) identification of the limits of society with the limits of its collective representations, sociologists and anthropologists have maintained an interest in territories of knowledge and their maintenance, now conceived in contemporary research as socio-cultural extensions of basic referential faculties determined by Tomasello *et al.* (2005) and others as unique to the human species. In recent years, beginning with the work of Alfred Schütz (1962), there has been extensive work on how shared sociocognitive constructs are sustained through practices of interaction (Clark 1992, 1996; Garfinkel 1967; Heritage 1984b; Jefferson 2004; Pollner 1987; Schegloff 1992; Schegloff *et al.* 1977).

At the same time, social scientists have also examined knowledge that is treated as "owned" by virtue of membership in a collectivity (Sharrock 1974). The ownership of knowledge, whether religious, professional, technical or personal, is associated with methods of talking that encode specific rights and responsibilities in the representation of events (Kamio 1997; Kuno 1987). Thus journalists distinguish between first-hand and derivative access to breaking news as relevant for the rights to describe it (Raymond 2000; Roth 2002); callers to emergency services report matters differently depending on whether they are bystanders to an incident or victims (Whalen and Zimmerman 1990); and patients offer medical diagnoses to physicians only under relatively particular circumstances (Gill 1998; Gill and Maynard 2006; Heritage and Robinson 2006). In each of these cases, the distribution of rights and responsibilities regarding what participants can accountably know, how they know it, whether they have rights to describe it and in what terms, is directly implicated in organized practices of speaking. These differential rights extend into the realm of everyday events and their representations, where issues of priority and epistemic territory are the objects of near-relentless interactional calibration (Heritage

---

[4] Issues of a different character emerge when physicians and social workers depart from their customary "neutral" or "service supply" stance (Jefferson 1988; Jefferson and Lee 1992 [1981]) to empathize with patients or clients (Beach and Dixson 2001; Hepburn and Potter 2007; Ruusuvuori 2005), for here professionals depart from a normatively sanctioned stance of "affective neutrality" (Parsons 1951).

and Raymond 2005; Raymond and Heritage 2006; Schegloff 1996a; Stivers 2005a).

In contrast with territories of knowledge, with their teeming range of practices and actions to litigate rights and priorities, territories of experience present a more sequestered aspect. If difficulties with the social organization of knowledge concern the management of ownership and priority in relation to mutually accessible goods, difficulties in the social organization of experience concern the construction of resources by which an interlocutor can reach toward moments of genuine singularity. In empathic moments, two great moral systems grind into one another. The first, concerned with respect for the personal experiential preserves of the individual on which coherent personhood itself ultimately depends, collides with a second that mandates human affiliation within a community of persons and a common social, moral and cultural heritage. Under such circumstances, the practical achievement of an empathic moment concerns, to adapt Garfinkel's (1952: 114) marvelous phrasing, how persons "isolated, yet simultaneously in an odd communion, go about the business of constructing an order together."

8   The terms of not knowing

Leelo Keevallik

Introduction

There is a disparity between expressing what we know and what we don't know in interaction. Participants regularly convey what they know implicitly by stating, telling, assessing, etc. In contrast, what they don't know is typically claimed outright. However, there are sequential environments in conversation where knowledge displays are relevant. For example, the recipient of a question that asks for information is accountable for displaying knowledge. The asker of the question, by virtue of having asked this particular recipient, presupposes that she knows and can answer. Although the recipient has several resources to deal with this, simply saying "I don't know" is a highly sensitive act and has social consequences. Relying on Estonian interaction, this chapter will look at claims of "no knowledge" (*mai tea*, the counterpart of English *I don't know*), showing parallels in Swedish, Russian and English.

   Issues of how speakers manage claims of knowledge across turns have been raised in a number of interactional studies (Beach and Metzger 1997; Goodwin 1979; Heritage 1984a; Heritage and Raymond 2005; Keevallik 2008; Labov and Fanshel 1977; Stivers 2005a). Some of them also specifically deal with lack of, or lesser, knowledge. For example, claiming secondary knowledge about something has been shown to function as a "fishing" device for the recipient to provide primary knowledge about the matter (Pomerantz 1980). Claiming forgetfulness can be a means of encouraging another knowing speaker to participate in the conversation (Goodwin 1987). In these cases, claiming lack of knowledge is used as a strategy to elicit information. In contrast, in courtroom interrogations and therapeutic interviews, claims of "no knowledge" have been analyzed as devices for getting around sensitive issues, potential blame and responsibility (Drew 1992; Hutchby 2002). More generally, "no knowledge" responses to questions have been characterized as non-answers, which display dispreferred

This chapter profited substantially from discussion with Kaoru Hayano, Anna Lindström, Jakob Steensig and Tanya Stivers.

structure and rank lower on the preference scale than informative answers (Clayman 2002; Stivers and Robinson 2006). These studies suggest that displaying knowledge and lack thereof is a significant social issue managed in communicative encounters.

On the other hand, linguists have been interested in the encoding of epistemic modality, which reflects the speaker's judgement of, or degree of confidence in, the knowledge upon which a proposition is based. Languages furthermore encode evidentiality, i.e., whether and how evidence exists for a given statement. Speakers regularly attend to how they have come to know things that they are talking about and mark the propositions as hearsay, based on sensory experiences, or a report (e.g. Chafe and Nichols 1986; Kärkkäinen 2003). Depending on the language, these matters are handled lexically or grammatically. Evidentiality can also be managed sequentially, as when the speaker marks her inference as being based on something a prior speaker just said (Keevallik 2008: 129–140). The current study brings together findings on the systematic linguistic coding of epistemic and evidential matters, and on the sequential nature of human interaction. It explores how a knowledge-based claim is deployed in different sequential positions and analyzes its social implications in the local context. Furthermore, the study moves away from a non-temporal understanding of knowledge coding in linguistics, showing how knowledge states are dynamically shaped, transformed and brought into being at specific moments in interaction.

The chapter focuses on two sequential environments in which "no knowledge" responses are regularly used. In the first environment, a participant is strongly expected to provide information after a question but instead asserts that she lacks the knowledge required to answer. These responses are disaligning in that they do not cooperate with the action sequence set up by the questioner. However, as I will show, this can be mitigated to a greater or lesser extent depending on the turn design. In the second environment, knowledge displays are not relevant but speakers offer assertions of "no knowledge" instead of the expected response to an initiating action.

The main aim of the chapter is to show how individuals in interaction manage the moral responsibility and accountability of not knowing, including how this varies by sequential environment. The social and sequential pressures following a "no knowledge" response will be outlined and discussed in terms of the distribution of responsibility among the participants, and also in regard to different types of knowledge. In comparison to prior conversation analytic studies, this chapter looks more closely into matters of evidentiality that participants orient to when they claim "no knowledge." Finally, the chapter discusses non-epistemic usages of the "no knowledge" response that balance affiliative and disaffiliative actions. The two main functions discussed are thus: (a) to indicate a problem with the question being asked, and (b) to project or convey rejection of a proposal, invitation or offer.

The data for the study include telephone calls and face-to-face events in Estonian. The telephone call corpus consists of 324 calls of two types: telemarketing calls from a daily newspaper and everyday calls between family members, relatives, friends and colleagues. It includes more than ten hours of conversation and about 150 speakers. This is the primary database of the study. In addition, examples have been used from the publicly available Tartu corpus of Spoken Estonian (www.cl.ut.ee/suuline/Korpus – last accessed January 29, 2009), which includes shorter excerpts of talk from a wider variety of audio-recorded situations, including face-to-face events. The corpus is constantly growing and the version for this study included about 900 excerpts and 400 speakers. Instances of *mai tea*[1] ("I don't know") functioning as a response constitute the collection on which this chapter is based. The Swedish and Russian examples come from the databases of two colleagues, Mats Eriksson and Olga Gerassimenko, to whom the author is deeply grateful. The names in the excerpts are pseudonyms.

The majority of the cases of "no knowledge" responses in this study come from non-institutional contexts. This is different from most conversation analytic studies on "no knowledge"-type responses, as they have been based on institutional interaction (Clayman 2001, 2002; Drew 1992; Hutchby 2002). In contrast to institutional settings, in everyday interaction neither knowledge nor the right to extort it is distributed according to participants' roles. Crucially, lack of knowledge is regularly treated as a joint problem and responsibility lies with all participants rather than with the answerer alone. This will be the topic of the first section.

The questioning context

By asking a question, the asker treats the recipient as able to provide an answer and accountable for doing so. Not answering by claiming disability or unwillingness is a disaligning action, because it fails to promote the action sequence initiated by the questioner. A "no knowledge" response

---

[1] The phrase that most straightforwardly disclaims knowledge in Estonian is *ma ei tea* ("I NEG know") 'I don't know.' The negation particle *ei* is regularly latched to pronouns in Estonian, so the phrase is often pronounced as *mai tea*, or even with one word stress as *maitea*. The phrase *mai tea* is an incomplete proposition and an elliptical clause, to use traditional linguistic terminology. In interactional terms, in order for participants to make sense of it, they need to take into consideration the just-prior turn. It is thus an action that is intimately, even grammatically, tied to the interactional sequence in which it occurs. It appears in a number of turn- and utterance-positions in more or less grammaticalized functions (Keevallik 2003: 78–100).

turns out to be a frequent solution in avoiding acceptance of responsibility to answer, as "speakers tend to select accounts that cast themselves as unable rather than unwilling to answer" (Clayman 2002: 242). Claiming "no knowledge" enables the speaker to maintain a more cooperative image than she would if she were "unwilling" to answer and also attends to the conditional relevance of sequence closure (Stivers and Robinson 2006: 375). It formally satisfies the requirement for a response that is made relevant by the question.

However, further accounts for not answering can be designed in different ways. In some cases they suggest the recipient should have been able to answer and thus accepts responsibility for not knowing. In other cases they are designed to suggest the question was ill fitted to the recipient. A "no knowledge" response transforms the knowledge assumptions made in the question and the accompanying ascription of responsibility. The following sub-section examines how participants attend to the interpersonal distribution of responsibility in the question – answer sequence, showing that cooperativeness may be very limited indeed and that the boundary between being unable and being unwilling may be blurred.

"No knowledge" prefaces to answers

As mentioned, an assertion of "no knowledge" in response to a question is a disaligning action. However, sometimes after initially asserting "no knowledge," recipients may continue by providing whatever information they have or a best guess, which results in a more aligning action. In these cases *mai tea* is designed not as *the* response but as a preface. The disruption of contiguity between the question and the answer in these cases is violated (Sacks 1987a: 59). However, by cooperating in ultimately providing an answer, the speaker validates the question's legitimacy and accepts her moral responsibility to answer. Cases like this have also been reported for English (Scheibman 2000; Tsui 1991: 619–620). An example from an Estonian phone call is given in 1, where two people are discussing props for a Christmas play at a church called Varju.

(1)

1 A:	=aga <u>kus</u>	on	sõim.
	but where	be_3SG	crib
	But where is the crib.		

2   (1.1)

3 E: →	**mai**	**tea**	*peaks*	*olema*	<u>*Varjus*</u>	*kuskil.*=
	I-NEG	know	must-COND	be-SPN	NAME-INS	somewhere
	I don't know it should be somewhere at Varju.					

4 A: =*no*   <u>*nii*</u>, .*h sedam- igataes* <u>*meie*</u> *seda*
           NO NII   it-PAR anyway we   it-PAR
           Okay, .h it w- anyway we couldn't
5   *präägu ei   <u>leidnud.</u>*
           now   NEG find-PPT
           find it now.

In this example *mai tea* functions as an epistemic device downgrading the
certainty of the answer. It is prosodically incorporated into the rest of the
turn and heard as an integrated part of it. Although the turn in line 3 consists of two syntactic units, prosodically they form one intonation unit and
thus are delivered as a single turn constructional unit. In this sense, *mai tea*
functions like a sentence adverbial, similarly to *I guess* or *I think* in English
(Aijmer 1996; Kärkkäinen 2003, 2007; Thompson and Mulac 1991). In the
role of an epistemic marker, it can be implemented in different positions
in turns and even clauses (Keevallik 2003: 81–83). Answers with prosodically incorporated *mai tea* typically do display knowledge in what precedes
or follows the *mai tea*, but the knowledge is hedged as the speaker marks
uncertainty. Knowing and not knowing are matters of degree and here
the speaker marks herself to be "partially knowing." Extract 2 in Swedish
shows an identical pattern of best guessing. The question is about cottage
numbers in a children's summer camp.

(2) (Swedish)

1 M: *(Dom   de   gällde)   vicken stuga   e   dom från de=*
           they   this concerned which cottage   are they from they
           Those concerned which cottage were   they from

2 D: → =***Ja vet   inte*** *antagligen tian eller åttnian*
           I   know not probably ten or   eighty-nine
           I don't know probably ten or eighty nine

3 M: *Mmhm*
           Uhuh

"No knowledge" prefaces to answers are perhaps the least disaffiliative of
the uses we will see because, although they initially disalign with the question, they ultimately cooperate. Thus, the *mai tea* is primarily working to
frame the subsequent answer as uncertain.

"No knowledge" as question response

In contrast with *mai tea* prefaced answers such as those in 1–2, a "no
knowledge" response that does not go on to answer is significantly less
cooperative. However, even here the degree of uncooperativeness varies
and there are a number of ways to validate the appropriateness of the

question. In particular, when an assertion of "no knowledge" is further accounted for with an evidential claim, this can mitigate the possible threat to the question's legitimacy. By contrast, a failure to provide such an account implies that some degree of responsibility for the recipient's lack of ability to answer lies with the questioner. For instance, see Extract 3. Here two course-mates are talking about their teacher. L volunteers information and, in line 4, M proffers a possible consequence of that in the form of a confirmation-seeking question.

(3)

```
1  L:     Pohl    tuleb     täna    muus      tagasi.
          NAME come-3SG today by_the_way back
          By the way Pohl is coming back today.

2  M:     täna. h
          Today. h

3  L:     jah?
          Yeah?

4  M:     kas  see  reede   on siis   mingi-
          Q    this Friday  is then   some
          So the coming Friday is there a -

5  L: →   ma ei      tea.
          I  NEG know
          I don't know.

6         (.)

7  L: →   mind    ei    uvita.
          I-PAR   NEG   be_interested_in
          I don't care.

8         (1.2)

9  M:     h ei   no   sees     mõts    et   seminar vä.
          NEG NO this-INS sense-INS that seminar  Q
          No I mean a seminar.

10 L:     võibolla.
          Maybe.
```

The announcement in line 1 is part of an account for why L wants to borrow some course materials from M. M treats the information as news-worthy by excitedly requesting confirmation of the exact day. She then offers for confirmation an upshot (Heritage and Watson 1979: 134–136) of the announcement in line 4, thereby treating L as knowing. With the asser-tion of "no knowledge," L denies having the ascribed knowledge about something taking place on Friday. She thereby shows that the positions of the two participants are epistemically incongruent: while M expected L to also have the information about Friday, L claims not to have it (see

Hayano, this volume, for the notion of *epistemic congruence*). With her subsequent "I don't care.", L declines responsibility for providing an answer. She makes no attempt at any kind of informing as to what might happen on Friday, even though she seems to be clear about where the question was going even before it was actually complete.

This is a disaligning, uncooperative or even hostile way of dealing with a question (Clayman 2001: 422–423). It provides nothing helpful regarding what can be seen in the question about the concerns of the questioner, which is whether the return of the teacher implies any course-related obligations for them as students. In a discussion of a similarly dismissive answer – "I don't know what time it was Jenny, I can't remember really" – Pomerantz (1984b: 610) has pointed out that, even if the recipient was unsure of the exact time, an approximation would have been more helpful, or some starting point to calculate the exact time. Most of the knowledge people have is partial but there are more and less cooperative ways of dealing with it when answering. In contrast to Extracts 1–2 where the answers included a best guess, the response in 3 makes it clear that the question was not adequately designed. In this way, a question can be reflexively treated as unwarranted.

The lack of an account for not knowing implies that the problem with the question lies more with the question and questioner than with the recipient. It shows that the question was illegitimate, improper or inappropriate. This may well work as a strategy in a courtroom setting (Drew 1992) or in an interrogation of a child (Hutchby 2002), but in many other social settings stand-alone "no knowledge" responses are bound to be socially problematic, potentially tainting the reputation of their producer as uncooperative. The following extract (4) comes from a telephone call between colleagues working in the same building.

(4)

1 J: *e ega   ei   oska öelda,*
        EGA NEG can   say-INF
        Can you tell (me),

2   (1.0)

3 J: *kas: ee see: (.) meie   jurist   peab*
        Q   this   our_GEN lawyer have-3SG
        does uhm (.) our lawyer have

4   *seal   üleval   oma pidu   täna   vä.*
        there upstairs own party_PAR today Q
        his/her party upstairs today.

5 E: *ei mina ei   oska seda   küll   öelda.*
        no I   NEG can   this-PAR KÜLL say-INF
        No I cannot tell (you) that.

6   (0.5)

7   J: *aa,   ot   ja   kelle   käest ma küsin.*
           AA OT and who_GEN from I   ask-1SG
           Oh, and who can I ask.

8   E: → *ei   tea,*[2]
           NEG know
           (I) don't know,

9   (0.5)

10   J: *aitäh?*
           Thanks?

11   E: *palun,*
           You're welcome,

The call has started (data not shown) with J's realization that he called the wrong number. Despite this, he asks the question which was obviously planned for somebody else (lines 1–4). It is formulated as a regular polite question to an institution, with the particle *ega* conventionally enhancing the negative expectations of the outcome (Keevallik 2009). Indeed, the recipient claims inability to answer in a full sentence in which the agent 'I' is furthermore emphasized by the particle *küll* (line 5). E underscores that she is the wrong person to ask. Nevertheless, the questioner ventures on with a follow-up question (line 7) which receives a curt "no knowledge" reply (line 8).

The question–answer sequence occurs in a context where epistemic incongruence has already been established: E has declined to belong to the category of people who know about the party. She treats herself as not responsible for having the knowledge. However, a proposal of somebody else with closer relations to the "lawyer" would have been a more cooperative response in line 8. At least in English data, there is a preference for offering whatever little knowledge one possesses over a mere "no knowledge" response (Clayman 2002: 242–243; Stivers and Robinson 2006: 374–375). Along similar lines, in the current Estonian data, no continuation after a "no knowledge" response implies that responsibility for the lack of answer lies more with the questioner than with the recipient. In the case in Extract 4, the answerer neither legitimizes nor furthers the progress of the action sequence, and the call is accordingly terminated.

Extract 5 shows how the questioner explicitly takes responsibility for the question recipient's inability to answer by seeking to redirect the question. This is a cold call, where a telemarketer tries to engage a prospective client and the telephone happens to be picked up by a child.

---

[2] As Estonian is a pro-drop language, the pronoun *ma* ('I') can be dropped.

(5)

1 M: *kas teie   peres   <u>loe</u>takse ka aeg-ajalt*
        Q you_GEN family-INS read-IMS KA sometimes
        Does your family sometimes read

2   *Liivi   <u>Lin</u>nalehte.*
        NAME NAME_PAR
        Liivi Linnaleht.

3 K: → *£m(h)a e(h)i tea,£*
        I   NEG know
        I don't know,

4 M: *ei   <u>tea</u>.*
        NEG know
        (You) don't know.

5   (0.6)

6   *.hhh kas on kellegi   käest <u>kü</u>sida.*
        Q is somebody_GEN from ask-INF
        .hhh Is there somebody to ask.

7   *või [kedagi]   <u>te</u>lefonile kutsuda.*
        or   somebody-PAR phone-ALL invite-INF
        or   somebody to call to the phone.

8 K: [*jaa?*]
         Yeah?

Orientations to questioner responsibility can also be brought to the surface by question recipients. For instance, when challenging the choice of a question recipient, the addressed speaker can explicitly resist the social category that she has been assigned through the question. In Extract 6, from the Russian corpus, the caller asks a medical question of a receptionist at a medical center. The receptionist claims "no knowledge" and accounts for this with a statement about her professional categorization which relieves her of the responsibility to know the answer. She furthermore indicates that this should have been common knowledge with the particle же that functions similarly to the Swedish/Danish *jo/ju* described by Heinemann, Lindström and Steensig (this volume).

(6) (Russian)

1 З: *а как мне   бы:ть, (.) и   с   температурой*
        but how I_DAT be-INF   and with temperature-INST
        But what should I do, (.) with the temperature

2   *и с [( )]*
        and with
        and with [( )]

3 О: →   [*ну:*] *я не   знаю*   *как быть,*
        НУ I NEG know-1SG how be-INF
        Well I don't know what to do,

```
4        (.)
5 O:  →  я же  не  доктор,
         I ЖE no doctor
         I'm not a doctor,
6        (.)
7 O:     пожалуста звоните вот    доктору
         please      call-2PL BOT doctor-DAT
         please call the doctor
```

A "no knowledge" response is thus a recipient's device for negotiating epistemic responsibility in a conversational sequence. It may be implemented in order to show that the current speaker problematizes her responsibility for what has just been assumed to be her area of knowledge: she refuses the social categorization of a knowledgeable person in terms of the seminar on Friday (Extract 3), partying colleagues (4), the family's newspaper habits (5) or medical decisions (6). It rejects the question as irrelevant (Extract 3), or improperly addressed (5 and 6). The recipient of a question furthermore has a choice of aligning by attempting to answer (Extracts 1–2) or disaligning by not doing so (3–6). In the latter case, the questioner can persist (Extract 3) or will have to readdress the question (4–6). By letting the recipient off the hook, the questioner acknowledges that the just-addressed person is not responsible for the answer.

"No knowledge" and evidentiality

Another type of expansion of the turn may also work to mitigate against the implications that the question was poorly designed. It deals with evidentiality. For instance, in Extract 7, which comes from a telephone call about a Christmas fair, following a question about how the porridge was, the recipient first asserts lack of knowledge but then goes on to account for this. In this way the recipient suggests that the question was, in fact, apt, but that it nonetheless cannot be answered. It remediates the potential disaffiliation of the *mai tea* response. The questioner receives the answer with a "third" (*aa*), treating it as news and thus as somewhat counter to expectation, but immediately moves on to the next question.

```
(7)
1 E:     .h aga:: ja  puder  oli        ea    vä.
         but  and porridge be-IMF_3SG good Q
         But and was the porridge good.
2 P:  →  mai   tea,  ma ei::  jõudnud     süüa    seda.=
         I-NEG know I    NEG manage-PPT eat-INF it-PAR
         I don't know, I didn't have time to eat it.
```

3 E: =<u>aa</u>. aga <u>neil</u>   läks   nor<u>maal</u>selt ve.=
        AA but they-ADS go-IMF_3SG all_right   Q
        Oh. But did they do all right.

The above example provides a case when a direct type of sensory evidence is used in the account for why there is "no knowledge." Languages of the world express evidentiality based on more direct sources as well as on more indirect knowledge. Direct sources of information include visual, auditory and other sensory modes of experience (such as tasting), whereas indirect ones consist of reported matters and inferencing/reasoning (Willett 1988: 57). Extract 8 demonstrates how an indirect evidential source is used to explain why the question cannot be answered. P has been telling E about a recording device that had just been installed on her phone. After K's question about the duration of the recordings, P claims "no knowledge" but reports a statement by the researcher about her return date.

(8)
1 K: <u>kauaks</u>   ta: pandi   sulle.
        long-TRA it   put-IMS-IMF you-ALL
        For how long was it installed on your (phone).

2 P: → .hh ööö **ma ei   tea**,   ta üts   et   ta
            I   NEG know she say-IMF_3SG that she
        .hh uhm I don't know, she said that she'll be

3   → tuleb <u>ka</u>heksandal veebruaril   millalgi.
        comes eighth-ADS February-ADS sometime
        back on the eighth of February or something.

4 K: kaheksanda.
        eighth_GEN
        Eighth.

5 P: veebruaril.
        February-ALL
        February.

6 K: aa.
        Oh.

7 P: jah,
        Yeah,

8 K: no   siis umbes <u>kuu</u>   aega   jõuad
        NO then about month time_PAR get-2SG
        So you get to record all your

9   kõik oma £kõned <u>lin</u>distada.£
        all   own calls   record-INF
        calls for about a month.

Here the response expansion is not an account for not knowing. Rather, the question recipient provides the information she has, reporting from a third party. Similar to accounts, though, this type of response expansion mitigates the implication of *mai tea* as indicating that the question was problematic. The answer is worked out collaboratively.

Finally, if the information is not complete, the recipient may give evidence of the source or the basis for the information (Pomerantz 1984b: 611). Pomerantz analyzes a call for an ambulance (reproduced as Extract 9) in which the caller states that he is unaware of why exactly the ambulance is needed, because he himself was only asked to make the call for help.

(9) (Pomerantz 1984b: 611)

```
1 Desk:      What is the problem.
2 Caller: →  I don't know. The desk called me and asked me,
3            would you like to talk to the desk. They
4            called and asked me to call an ambulance. We
5            have one guest here that is ill.
```

"In describing his source of information as second hand, he accountably knows *only* what he was told on the phone and not more, i.e. not the details that an observer of the scene would know" (Pomerantz 1984a: 611). In linguistic terms, he provides an evidential basis for why his knowledge is not first-hand and complete and why he cannot be held responsible for more. Participants in interaction have been demonstrated to work hard to provide answers to questions that are difficult for them to answer, because this promotes progressivity in terms of social actions (Stivers and Robinson 2006: 374–375). This kind of answers are regularly evidentially qualified, as shown in Extracts 7–9.

Evidential claims thus work in at least two ways: either as explanations for not knowing, or to downgrade the directness of knowledge about the matter asked for. Both of these attend to the social implications of claiming "no knowledge" in the sequential position after a question. By explaining the reasons for not knowing, the speaker treats the question as legitimate and thus mitigates the implication, otherwise present in *mai tea* responses, that the question was poorly designed for this recipient.

In sum, a "no knowledge" response can be used for three main functions. First, it can be used as a preface to an answer, marking the answer as less certain. Second, it can be a way to resist answering the question and treating the questioner as responsible for the difficulty. Third, it can be part of a response oriented to the question recipient's own failure to answer when she could be expected to be able to do so but lacks the necessary evidential basis.

Responsibility and types of knowledge

Thus far we have treated all sorts of knowledge as equivalent. However, "no knowledge" responses are implemented and treated differently according to the type of knowledge asked for in the question. The extent to which the answerer can be held accountable for knowing varies. For example, although the course-mate who knows about a teacher's return can be regarded and treated as knowing about the seminar (Extract 3 above), this expectation can also be refuted. Such questions ask for information that the recipient may not necessarily possess. The knowledge assumed in questions can roughly be divided into two types, paraphrasing Pomerantz (1980: 187):

1. Knowables that recipients have rights and obligations to know – for example, one's name, what one is doing and how one is feeling.
2. Knowables to which recipients are assumed to have access by virtue of the knowings being occasioned: things that the recipient may have been told, figured out, seen, and so on.

Pomerantz established this division on the basis of participant orientation in so-called "fishings." In fishing sequences one participant uses type-2 knowables in order to elicit a type-1 knowable from her conversation partner. In information questions discussed in the current study both types of knowables may be addressed and this is consequential in terms of how a "no knowledge" response is treated. When the question is about a type-2 knowable, the "no knowledge" response is less disaligning and more interpretable as an epistemic statement *par excellence*. The recipient need not take full responsibility for answering but may help to figure it out. In contrast, when the question is about a type-1 knowable, such as personal experiences that people "own" (Heritage this volume), feelings and habits, the "no knowledge" claim is immediately treated as displaying problems with the question.[3]

Extract 10 shows a question about a matter in which the recipient is obviously an authority, namely a personal assessment of a Christmas fair at which P performed. P's "no knowledge" response is produced with laughter. The primary stress on the pronoun *mina* ('I')[4] underscores the personal stance P is putting on the claim.

---

[3] In expert interviews, knowledge in the relevant area is also treated as a type-1 knowable: something that the expert is immediately accountable for. An "I don't know" answer to this kind of a question taints the reputation of the recipient as an expert (Clayman 2001: 421).

[4] *Mina* is the long form of the pronoun "I" and it is often used with clausal stress.

(10)

1 E: *oli   ra̱ske   ka   vä.*
        be-IMF_3SG tough too Q
        Was it tough too.

2   (1.2)

3 P: → *no heh **m(h)ina ei   tea,***=
        NO   I   NEG know
        Well I don't know,

4 E: =*oled   l̲ä̲bi   omadega   vä.*
        be-2SG through yourself-COM Q
        Are you worn out.

5 P: öö *hää̲l̲ on küll   läbi   aga m̲u̲u̲ ei   ole.*=
        voice is KÜLL through but rest NEG be
        Uhm (my) voice is worn out but nothing else.

After the "no knowledge" response, E reformulates her initial question, treating P's statement as showing problems with the question. Her reformulation in line 4 displays her understanding that the problem lay not with E's true lack of knowledge but with the design of or import of the question itself. Redesign of the original question is typically done after it becomes clear that the response is disaligning. In Extract 10 the "no knowledge" response is preceded by a long pause, which projects some problem with the question. P's epistemic statement here challenges the question by virtue of the fact that she must in some sense know, as people can be expected to be aware of their personal assessments of the events that they have participated in.

However, the question in line 1 is indeed complex in terms of social selves. By asking whether the performance was tough, the questioner shows compassion but also invites acceptance that the task was hard for the recipient. Accepting this would frame the recipient as a certain kind of person, perhaps incapable. At the same time, denying that it was tough might suggest that what she accomplished was not that significant. Both ways, the answerer would ascribe herself to a category with negative moral dimensions. The question elicits if not a troubles-telling (Jefferson 1988) then at least an evaluation of the degree of experienced hardship, as it comes last in a series of questions about the church event (the 'too' in the question marks that it is a part of a question series). Instead, the answerer resists the question by initiating her answer with a claim of "no knowledge." The dismissive laughter reinforces the hearing that the whole question is rejected as unanswerable, for which the asker bears responsibility. The questioner therefore reformulates it as soon as the disqualifying "no knowledge" statement has been produced. Rather than being a literal claim about knowledge, *m(h)ina ei tea* is here deployed and treated as a display of a problem with the terms of the question. If the question was about a type-2 knowable, there would remain some ambiguity as to whether the question recipient truly knew or not. By contrast, *mai tea* following a question about a type-1 knowable is unambiguously uncooperative and suggests that a redesigned question may elicit an answer. Thus, these questions are more likely to be pursued in the way shown in Extract 10 than questions about type-2 knowables.

When it comes to type-2 knowables, there seems to be more flexibility in contesting the question in terms of what the respondent is accountable for knowing. For example, the recipient may operate on the design of the question in the answer, changing the formulation or the categories used in the question, problematizing the way the question was asked. Extract 11 comes from the same phone call as Extracts 7 and 10, in which a church member asks another about the Christmas fair that the questioner had missed. The relevant question comes in lines 11–12 and initially receives a "no knowledge" response.

(11)

```
1   E:   aga: käis        palju rahvast      vä.
         but  go-IMF_3SG  lot   people-PAR  Q
         But was there a lot of people who came.

2   P:   mitte ühtegi       vaba       hetke        ei    ole.
         NEG  one-PAR-GI  free_PAR  moment_PAR  NEG  be
         There was not a single free moment.

3        (.)

4   P:   mingi  viis minutit         oli        kus    me
         some  five minute-PAR   was_3SG  where  we
         There were some five minutes when we¹

5        saime            teed      juua.       ja   ühe
         can-IMF-1PL  tea-PAR  drink-INF  and  one_GEN
         could drink tea. and

6        piruka           ära   süüa.
         pastry_GEN  ÄRA  eat-INF
         eat a pastry.

7   E:   jube:   mõnus.
         awfully  great
         That's really great.

8        (0.2)

9   E:   te         olete        nii  tublid.
         you-PL  are-2PL  so  able-PL
         You're great.

10  P:   heh
```

11 E: *nii   et   tuli   kuskil nii*
         so   that   come-IMF_3SG   about about
         So there were about

12   *nelikend   inimest   vä.*
         forty   people-PAR   Q
         forty people who came.

13 P: → **mai   tea   kui   palju   käis.**
         I-NEG   know   how   many   go-IMF_3SG
         I don't know how many there were.

14   (.)

15 →   [*ikka   piisavalt.*]
         IKKA   enough
         (there was) enough.

16 E: [*oi   kui   e*] *a.*
         wow   how   good
         Wow that's good.

In the answer to E's initial question about the amount of people (lines 2–6), P has already provided information that the performers had been busy the whole time, which means that they had to give performances in a steady flow (they were giving them on demand). E's guess that this amounts to about forty people is based on some calculation about the time it took to give one performance and the number of people who could attend it at a time. Being an upshot based on P's prior claims, this should be easily confirmable, as E has strong epistemic grounds to arrive at the conclusion. P, however, resists providing the exact number. In her response in line 13, she first denies knowledge about the number of visitors and then rephrases the information in experiential terms in line 15, treating the problem to be one of question design. The complement clause following the "no knowledge" claim makes it clear that a precise number is the reason for her resistance. The subsequent rephrasing is from "forty" in the question to "enough" in the response. This constitutes an answer to the question which guarantees progressivity in terms of action.[5] It can be classified as a transformative answer in which the question recipient retroactively adjusts the question posed to her (Stivers and Hayashi 2010). With the initial claim of "no knowledge" the recipient here resists the question. What we see in the subsequent turn construction unit is that the negotiation hinges on the terms of the question – specifically, the categories to be used for describing the church event and the relevant knowledge in regard to defining the

---

[5] On the other hand, not knowing the exact amount in this context implies that they were not so few people that a count was self-evident. This enables E to provide the positive assessment in overlap with P's answer.

performance as successful. It also deals with the social issues of who has the right to choose the categories, and who has access to the information in a relevant way.

Finally, questions about type-2 knowables regularly raise the issue of whether the answerer belongs to the category of knowing recipients at all. The association of the speaker with the knowable is weaker, and the questioner's attribution of responsibility for knowledge can therefore be lifted more easily, leading to a different sequential treatment of the response. Extract 12 shows a case in which the answerer dissociates herself from some physical arrangement that a third person, the researcher, is responsible for. By now the researcher has left and the two ladies are alone. One of them asks a question that the recipient should, by virtue of doing the recording, know. The recipient, however, claims "no knowledge." Although the question recipient must have some knowledge, by claiming lack of knowledge here she treats this epistemic domain as outside her responsibility. The questioner does not insist on her question, nor does she reformulate the question during the pause in line 3; in line 5 she aligns with B's suggestion that matters of equipment should be left to the researcher. When agreeing, she simultaneously displays that she has adjusted her prior knowledge ascription to B.

(12) (Swedish)

```
1 A:     Men  har  han  inte  glömt        de här  då
         but  has  he   not   forget-PPT   these   then
         But hasn't he forgotten these then

2 B:  →  Ja ja vet    inte(.)  ingen aning
         JA I  know not          no    idea
         I don't know (.) No idea

3        (0.6)

4     →  .h  vi  läter  han  sköta          sitt  själv=
             we  let    him  take_care_INF  own   himself
         .h We'll let him take care of his stuff himself

5 A:     =ja    just    de
         yeah  exactly  it
         Exactly.
```

Disclaiming knowledge of different types is treated differently by participants, which reflects the fact that speakers are treated as more responsible for type-1 knowables than for others.

To summarize, there are several ways of dealing with the moral obligation of answering in the sequential position after a question. The pressure pertains even though problems with the question are indicated with a "no knowledge" response. Questions initiate a sequence with multi-

faceted constraints on what should be done in response. Responses that
resist one or more of these constraints – and are thus uncooperative and
threatening to social solidarity – are treated as accountable and tend to be
explicitly or implicitly justified (Clayman 2002: 246). From more to less
aligning actions, the recipient of a question can either provide her best
guess or evidence for not knowing, reformulate the question in her answer,
or reject it. After a question has received a "no knowledge" as the initial
response, the participants are jointly accountable for working out what
has gone wrong, why the question was asked in the way it was and what
can be done to get a response to it. A "no knowledge" response makes
salient the lack of epistemic congruence between the speakers. The epistemic ecology in an interactional event is thus constantly claimed as well
as reconfigured to the extent that speakers work jointly for it. The "no
knowledge" responses also display resistance to the prior question, to the
way it was asked or addressed, while some of the turn-continuations after
"no knowledge" response validate the legitimacy of the question and the
manner in which it was framed. An epistemic disclaimer can indeed be
used to express low epistemic certainty, as was shown in Extracts 1 and 2,
but it can also challenge accountability and the ascribed responsibility for
knowledge. In each case it indicates some problem with the answerability
of the question.

A second responsive position

So far I have shown that "no knowledge" responses are disaligning and
that, depending on the extent to which they are accounted for, they may
be more or less cooperative. However, we have been focusing on the question–response sequence in which knowledge is presupposed in the question. We now turn to another sequential environment in which knowledge
displays are not due, i.e., in sequences other than questions and answers.
The rationale of these responses is no longer epistemics itself, but the epistemic disclaimer is put into use for other social purposes. Claiming lack
of knowledge can be revealed as "a distinct sort of activity, an equivocal resource for organizing interaction" (Beach and Metzger 1997: 563).
Above, I discussed how the "no knowledge" response could be used not
as a literal epistemic claim but as a means of resisting the question. In this
section, the resistance targets the preferred answer that is made relevant
by the first pair part. The term *preference* refers to a structural relationship (Heritage 1984b: 265–280; Pomerantz 1984a; Schegloff 2007b: 58–63).
After an offering, proposal or invitation, an acceptance is structurally preferred. The "no knowledge" response seems to be a device for escaping
the sequential pressure to provide an answer. It is a means of displaying

resistance to the prior turn, as was also shown after questions. It is typically used in offering, proposing, inviting and assessment sequences.

The following example, Extract 13 comes from a call between a mother and her adult daughter. The daughter has reported that her purse was stolen, and, in line 1, the mother offers to take money to her job where the daughter regularly visits her. In this context, her statement is hearable as an offer of financial support. The daughter receives this with *mai tea* and an argument that she could cope without accepting the offer.

(13)

1 E: *ma võtan   siis töö   [juurde ra]ha   kaasa.*
       I   take-1SG then job_GEN to   money_GEN with
       I'll take some money to my job then.

2 P: [(   )]

3 P: → *no **mina ei   tea,**   täendab noh -*
       NO I   NEG know means   NOH
       Well I don't know, I mean -

4   (0.8)

5 P: → *no ses   mõts   et eee, ma nälga*
       NO this-INS sense-INS that I   hunger_ILL
       I mean uhm, I won't die

6   → *ei   sure, ma saan   järgmine nädal*
       NEG die I get-1SG next   week-ADS
       of hunger, I'll get money

7   → *Mare Balticumist raha   noh.*
       NAME-ELT   money_PAR NOH
       from Mare Balticum next week.

8 E: *ei noh - no sul   on vaja   ju:*
       no NOH NO you-ADS be necessary JU
       No - but you need (some)

9   *jumalukene küll.*
       god   KÜLL
       for god's sake.

The *mai tea* response in line 3 does not accept the mother's offer of financial support. Acceptance would have been the structurally preferred action and anything else in its place is hearable as refusing the offer. However, the "no knowledge" response does so only implicitly, as it can also be heard as remaining in an undecided position. The following account tilts the answer toward the dispreferred response. The mother continues to persuade after it, displaying her understanding of the response as disaffiliative, not adhering to action preference. The "no knowledge" response officially refrains from answering altogether but is treated as disaffiliative.

In a similar way, *mai tea* is used to avoid the projected preferred action in proposal sequences. In Extract 14, E is calling a church where a number of her fellow church members are present. She is talking about a Christmas show that she is directing and one of the actors, her current conversation partner R, has just turned her down. In line 4, R proposes a replacement for herself, Hele, who is also present at the church. The proposal is formulated with a question particle *kas* as well as a proposal marker *äkki*. E receives the proposal with "no knowledge," which, by being less than an acceptance, is heard as not accepting. Her continuation after the pause demonstrates that she indeed does not approve of the proposal and is instead looking for further options.

(14)

```
1 E:    .hh tead      irmus oleks      vaja,     mis- kas seal
                know-2SG very  be-COND necessary that Q    there
                .hh You know  it's really necessary, what- is there

2       on keegi.    äkki   keegi:    võiks     sind     asendada.
        is somebody  ÄKKI somebody can-COND you-PAR replace-INF
        anybody there. Maybe someone could replace you.

3       (0.9)

4 R:    kas Hele      saaks     asendada     äkki.
        Q   NAME  can-COND replace-INF ÄKKI
        Could Hele perhaps replace (me).

5       (1.3)

6 E: →  mai    tea,
        I-NEG know
        I don't know,

7       (1.6)

8 E: →  [kes  seal]  veel on.
        who there else be
        Who else is there.

9 R:    [on ta mui-]
        Is she oth-
```

Again, the response does not accept the proposal, nor does it explicitly turn it down. However, the response is heavily delayed suggesting that a dispreferred answer is coming up. The *mai tea* response is a typical formula for doing a dispreferred answer indirectly. As a parallel example, the English *I don't know* is among the common delay components in a dispreferred response (Schegloff 1988b: 445). Assessments, explicit disagreements, and commitments may be avoided with *I don't know* (Beach and Metzger 1997; Diani 2004; Tsui 1991: 609–617). Similarly to answers to questions, "no knowledge" responses to offers and proposals display that something was problematic with the prior turn and do not align.

Finally, an invitation sequence is shown in 15. The phone call is coming to a close and E who studies at the culture department invites K to come by. Even though an invitation does not make relevant a knowledge display, a "no knowledge" response is used. The counter-argument following the "no knowledge" response contributes to this being heard as a disaffiliative action, not accepting the invitation. Indeed, E receives it with a much more vague expression of hope for a future meeting, displaying her understanding that the invitation was indeed turned down.

(15)

1 E: *nojah, (.) juhul   kui sa   käid ee   sealt e*
       NOJAH case-ADS if   you walk-2SG there-ELT
       Well then, (.) in case you pass by um the

2   *kultuuriteaduskonnast   mööda Laial   tänaval.*
       culture_department-ELT by   NAME-ADS street-ADS
       um culture department on Lai street.

3   *s   astu   sisse.*
       then step_IMP_2SG inside_ILL
       then step inside.

4 K: → *no:h   eks   ma- ph .h no   **ma ei   tea.***
       NOH EKS I   NO I   NEG know
       Well I'll– ph .h well I don't know.

5   → *ma ei   julge tulla   sinna.*
       I   NEG dare   come-INF there_ILL
       I don't dare to come there.

6 E: *no   ma arvan   et   mõne-   mõne::   a:asta*
       NO I   believe-1SG that some_GEN some_GEN year_GEN
       I believe we'll see in a couple- couple

7   *pärast võib-olla nääme   kuskil   vä.*
       after   maybe   see-1PL somewhere-ADS Q
       of years somewhere or.

In responsive positions in which knowledge displays are not relevant, a claim about lack of knowledge is hearably not doing the preferred response while also avoiding the dispreferred one: "Claims of insufficient knowledge delicately delete appropriate or expected 'nexts' by replacing them with a displayed inability to answer" (Beach and Metzger 1997: 579). They constitute a disaffiliative practice of resisting the terms of the first pair part. On the surface, the "no knowledge" response is an account for not doing the projected second pair part. In terms of social action, it resists the trajectory projected by the first pair part. A claim about knowledge is here used as an innocuous statement about a matter that is beyond the speaker's will. It is also incontestable by other participants, as it is only the speaker who knows the state of her knowledge (Heritage 1984b: 272). Furthermore, "no knowledge" responses in positions where knowledge displays were not due are never received with an acknowledgement of new information (a "third"), showing that these responses do something else besides providing information on the speaker's epistemic state. The sequential context constructs the meaning of the phrase as something different from a literal claim of knowledge. Sequentially, the *mai tea* response fills the slot where an answer should go. It also advances the action by implying the dispreferred response although not stating it.

Socially, the practice avoids overt confrontation and the dispreferred response, which paradoxically promotes pro-sociality. The "no knowledge" response constitutes an action that is at the same time more disaffiliative than the preferred response and more affiliative than a straightforward dispreferred response (which rarely occurs). By invoking the state of knowledge as the reason for not doing the expected action, the speaker partially relieves herself from the moral implications of possible alternative accounts, such as unwillingness, disapproval or disagreement. This is an issue well beyond knowledge states of the participants, concerning primarily the social dimension of sequenced actions and the moral demands on participants.

Conclusion

Knowledge is constantly made relevant by participants in interaction, as speakers volunteer information and request it of others. Of equal importance, speakers at times declare "no knowledge." On the one hand, claiming a lack of knowledge may be used as a preface to answering. On the other, it may be an account for not answering. Human knowledge is always partial and fragmentary and may therefore have to be epistemically hedged. The above analysis has shown that claims of "no knowledge," by definition, indicate a problem with answerability of the question. They sometimes reject the question altogether. Other times they indicate the incomplete nature of the knowledge asked for, prefacing best guesses, informings on related matters and reports from third sources. Responses involving a claim of "no knowledge" may express a degree of epistemic certainty but also matters concerned with evidentiality that account for their claimed state of knowledge. Speakers regularly express not only the source of their knowledge, but also what the source could have been.

A look at which practices participants actually engage in when they claim "no knowledge" helps us to see the temporal and sequential nature of epistemics. Epistemic claims are made because of particular sequential contingencies and socially accountable ascriptions of knowledge by other interactants. It is therefore important not to consider epistemics as a mere grammatical phenomenon that can be studied independently from context and social action. Knowledge is not a static information state or a source that is always accessible. It is situated and may be worked out in a conversational sequence across speakers.

Furthermore, participants may negotiate who is responsible for knowing what and when. "No knowledge" is a recipient's device for rejecting knowledge assumptions by the questioner. Knowledge is made relevant in certain sequential environments and wrong assumptions about recipient knowledge can be remediated in later turns. A questioner can reformulate the question to make it answerable, or readdress it. In cases of type-2 knowables, the answerer's lack of responsibility for knowledge may be acknowledged. Particularly when the question recipient does not continue after a "no knowledge" response, the task of figuring out what went wrong and how to repair it lies with the questioner. Simultaneously, the recipient can continue by displaying her understanding of why the question was asked. Knowledge assumptions and responsibility are thus dealt with interactionally; the claim of "no knowledge" transforms the epistemic ecologies in contrast with what has just been assumed in the prior turn. Who knows what and when is a constant concern for interacting parties.

Answering questions is a basic moral obligation for question recipients, and a stand-alone "no knowledge" response is disaligning and uncooperative. Moreover, it retrospectively taints the question as having been inadequately designed or addressed. A "no knowledge" response does not promote the agenda of the question; neither does it cooperate with the proposed activity. It disaligns with the prior action as it does not accept the presuppositions and terms of the question. Nevertheless, it can be developed into an action that is cooperative. The responses that are prefaced with "no knowledge" do not, as a rule, resist the question as completely as the stand-alone ones do, but do so to some degree. The resistance may concern the design, addressing or social implications of the question.

However, besides being used as a problem-indicator after questions, a "no knowledge" response is also employed as a general item of resistance to a number of other first pair parts, such as offers, proposals and invitations. In these cases, claiming "no knowledge" is a practice of hearably not doing the preferred action while also avoiding the dispreferred one, thus minimizing the degree of disaffiliation in the turn. In general, "no knowledge" is a resource for escaping the terms set up by the prior turn while technically providing a response. As such, it crucially manages speaker alignment and social affiliation between the participants. Speakers who are put in the position of responding can resist social categorizations and the status of a "knowing" participant, as well as moral responsibility assigned to these roles.

9   Proposing shared knowledge as a means of pursuing agreement

Birte Asmuß

Introduction

Participants in social interaction rely on different ways of dealing with questions of rights and access to knowledge. For instance, they sometimes deal with questions of rights to know by addressing a person's access to the information as either exclusive or non-exclusive. And they sometimes address questions of rights to know by framing the information as something the co-participants ought to know or ought not to know, thereby making questions of epistemic stance accountable in talk. By dealing with these different aspects of epistemics, co-participants recurrently negotiate rights and access to knowledge as a basis for a common frame of understanding. This means that questions of epistemic stance are inherently related to questions of alignment and affiliation (Heritage and Raymond 2005).

Two of the major studies concerned with epistemics (Heritage and Raymond 2005; Raymond and Heritage 2006) have dealt with the role of epistemics in competing or disaligning actions that are embedded within an otherwise affiliating context. In one study (Heritage and Raymond 2005), the ongoing negotiation of the participants, about who has the primary right to know what, is dealt with as indexing epistemic authority and subordination in the talk. In another study (Raymond and Heritage 2006), epistemic rights are shown to function as a resource for participants to construct and establish identities in interaction.

In contrast to these studies, in the present chapter the focus is placed on the role of epistemics for aligning or affiliating actions in an otherwise disaffiliating context.[1] More precisely, the current study deals with one specific aspect of the negotiation about rights to know, namely when participants appeal to shared knowledge. This can be done by using the expression 'you know' – *du ved* in Danish, on which this study is focused. The study shows

I would like to thank Lorenza Mondada, Tanya Stivers and Jakob Steensig for comments on earlier versions of this chapter.

[1] I would like to thank Kaoru Hayano for drawing my attention to the difference in focus between the studies mentioned before and the current one.

that 'you know' proposes shared knowledge, and thereby pursues agreement in an environment where participants may be approaching disagreement.

The following excerpt gives a first example of the phenomenon that is in focus in this study. Two boys are talking on the phone about a computer game.

(1)[2]

```
1   M:    .h  Jeg har  befriet    Boneyard
          .h  I    have liberated Boneyard
          .h I have liberated Boneyard

2         (0.8)

3   P:    Aha  Fra   hvad,
          uhu  from  what,
          I see from what,

4   M:    .hh Vilgulators=Ka'  du   ikk' huske      når   du   kommer ind
          .hh Vilgulators=Can  you  not  remember   when  you  come    in
          .hh Vilgulators  Don't you remember when you get into

5   M:    i  den der   antidynium som  a' den der   indre by
          in this there antidynium which is this there inner city
          into that antidynium which is the inner city

6   M:    i  Boneyard ikke,
          in Boneyard right,
          in Boneyard right,

7   P:    Jarh
          yeah
          yeah

8   M:    .Hhh Der  vrimler det rundt   me'  så    nogen
          .hhh there are_lots it  around with such  ones
          .hhh there's like crowds of those

9         (0.2)

10  M:    ehh store fyre i  jernrustninger
          ehh big   guys in iron_armor
          ehh big   guys in iron armor

11        (2.4)

12  M: →  .Hh du   ved     sånogen rustninger me'  pigge  p[å]
          .hh you  know that    armor        with spikes o[n]
          .hh you  know that armor with spikes on

13  P:                                                    [J]ah
                                                          [y]es
                                                          [y]es
```

In this excerpt, M reports that he has liberated a place in a computer game. In line 3, the co-participant acknowledges this and initiates a follow-up ques-

---

[2] I would like to thank Trine Heinemann for sharing this data excerpt with me.

tion, 'from what'. M tries to explain in a multi-unit turn from lines 4 to 6 and 8 to 10 who *Vilgulators* are. At a point of turn completion, P does not take over in line 11. Instead, a pause of 2.4 seconds evolves. Then M continues in line 12 with a 'you know'-initial turn and elaborates on the specific types of armor. At the end of this turn, P acknowledges this information in overlap.

What is worth noticing here is the fact that 'you know' is part of an extended sequence. This extended sequence offers opportunities for the co-participant to display affiliation, but these are not taken. Instead the co-participant aligns by responding minimally. In this environment, where a lack of affiliation is displayed, the current speaker produces a turn beginning with 'you know'. In doing so, the speaker appeals to pre-existing shared knowledge, which serves as an invitation to the co-participant to consider what is already in the common ground (Clark 1996). Hence, in an environment lacking affiliation, 'you know' is used to appeal to shared knowledge – thereby creating the opportunity to establish agreement.

The data investigated in this study are in Danish, but 'you know' works as a similar resource in other languages as well, as shown by the following example from an Estonian conversation. Here, the speaker H describes exotic seafood, which he compares to small meat pies, here referred to as 'pastry', that resemble this kind of sea food.

(2) (Estonian)[3]
1 H: [*mingid*] *niuksed,* [*kõva*   ] *koorega* *niuksed,* .*h ee, prrr.*
         [some_PL] such_PL [hard_GEN] shell_COM such_PL, .h ee, prrr.
         They were kind of with a hard shell like
2 U: [.*hhh*   ]   [*ahah*   ]?
         [.hhh   ]   [okay   ]?
         .hhh   okay?
3 H: *tead*   *nigu pirukas. noh eemalt vaatad.*   (.) *a   tegelt*
         know_2SG like pastry. NOH from_afar look_2SG (.) but actually
         you know like a pastry. if you look from afar (.) but actually
4 H: *oli*   [*mingi*] *loom oopis.* (.) *üks kest jäi*   *nigu*
         Was_3SG [some] animal instead. (.) one shell left_3SG like.
         it was an animal (.) a shell was left
5 U: [*ja:h*]
         [yeah]
         [yeah]
6 H: → *järgi. muidu   vaatasid   nigu pirukas, tead   nimodi*
         Over. otherwise looked_2SG like pastry, know_2SG like
         Over. otherwise they looked like a pastry you know with an

---

[3] I would like to thank Leelo Keevallik for sharing this data excerpt with me (Keevallik 2003: 167).

7 H: → *sakilise   servaga   et,   noh   tead   nagu: - noh,*
       indented_GEN edge_COM that, NOH know_2SG like -   NOH.
       indented edge, you know like like

8 H: *nagu piruka   serv on eksju.=*
       like pastry_GEN edge is EKSJU.=
       the edge of a pastry is right.=

9 U: =*oioioioi.*
       =wow.
       =wow.

Here, from lines 1 to 4, H tells about some shellfish he ate which resembled
a small meat pie 'pastry'. There is no relevant uptake after turn completion in line 4, and H continues in lines 6–8 by recycling his prior argument
about the shells resembling pastries. Appealing to shared knowledge, H
inserts 'you know' twice in the ongoing turn. In line 9, U takes over and
affiliates with this by marking the telling as newsworthy: 'wow'.

As indicated by the excerpts above, proposing shared knowledge as is
done by 'you know' serves as a resource to deal with potential disagreement in talk. 'You know' provides an opportunity to pursue agreement in
an environment where agreement is not forthcoming. Before moving on to
investigating in more detail further Danish instances of 'you know', I will
briefly sketch some of the main findings about 'you know' from previous
studies.

Previous studies of 'you know'

The expression 'you know' has attracted major attention during the last
decades from scholars within the field of sociolinguistics. A frequent focus
of these studies has been on relationships between social parameters such
as gender, age and class on the one hand, and the use of 'you know' on the
other (see, e.g., Erman 2001; Fox Tree and Schrock 2002; Macaulay 2002;
Schiffrin 1988: 267–311; Stubbe and Holmes 1995).

Stubbe and Holmes describe *you know* and other "pragmatic devices" as
performing "an indispensable function in oiling the wheels of verbal interaction" (1995: 63). They allocate a range of affective and epistemic meanings to these pragmatic devices. Concerning *you know*, they point out that
it is an "addressee oriented device" (1995: 73) that is predominantly used
in young, working-class, informal speech. Fox Tree and Schrock (2002)
investigate the difference between *you know* and *I mean*, focusing on different aspects of social class. They point to the fact that there is a lower frequency of *you know* in speech of "high-status conversational participants"
(2002: 743). They interpret this as indicating that higher-status addressees

might be less interested than lower-class addressees in inviting inferences by the co-participants.

In line with Stubbe and Holmes (1995) and Fox Tree and Schrock (2002), Erman (2001) focuses on social differences in the use of *you know*. She sees *you know* as a "social monitor" that elicits a response from the addressee, but she does not take the precise placement of *you know* into further account. Instead, she points out that there is a difference in the function of *you know* depending on the age of the speaker. In the adult corpus, *you know* is used to elicit a response from the listener; whereas in the adolescent corpus, *you know* has a "turn-taking and highlighting function" (2001: 1345).

In contrast with these sociolinguistic approaches, Conversation Analysis focuses on the sequential context and interactional achievements of 'you know'. This perspective shows how 'you know' can achieve different actions depending on its sequential placement and context of use. Jefferson (1972) investigates tag-positioned address terms in closing sequences and provides an analysis of 'you know' in this sequential environment. She points out that *you know* in this position can serve as an "utterance lengthener" (1972: 69) that indicates to the co-participant that the turn is possibly complete, and that s/he can take over. Moreover, it marks that the current speaker has not yet come to an end. She concludes that *you know* in TCU (turn constructional unit) final position can serve as a resource to avoid a pause between a prior problematic component and the recipient's response. For the current study this is an interesting observation, as it links the use of *you know* to dealing with problems and potential disagreement in talk.

Keevallik investigates the Estonian version of 'you know' (*tead*) and points out that it indicates that "the interlocutor should know about the matters put forward" (2003: 171). By framing its usage in this way, she opens up aspects of morality embedded in the use of 'you know'. She also points to a continuum from a more informing usage to a more involving one (2003: 172). She differentiates between four different usages of the particle: literal usage, preannouncement, projection of a news delivery, and appeal to the interlocutor's knowledge and involvement. It is the appeal to the interlocutor's knowledge that relates most clearly to the current study. But more than pursuing further the relationship between knowledge and involvement, the current study focuses on the interrelatedness between knowledge and alignment and affiliation, as shown in Extracts 1 and 2, in which 'you know' is used to invoke pre-existing shared knowledge as a means to invite the co-participant to consider what is in the common ground.

Overall, the studies focusing on interactional aspects of 'you know' relate its interactional achievements to questions of agreement/disagreement, morality and knowledge. It is these aspects that will be pursued further in the current study.

The majority of studies about 'you know' have been based on English (New Zealand English: Stubbe and Holmes 1995; British English: Erman 2001; Scottish English: Macaulay 2002; and American English: Jefferson 1972, Fox Tree and Schrock 2002). Only a few studies address 'you know' in other languages, such as Estonian (Keevallik 2003) and Swedish (Lindström and Wide 2005). By focusing on Danish 'you know', the current study contributes to questions of similarities and differences in the use of 'you know' across different languages.

Analysis

The data for this study come from approximately eleven hours of everyday and institutional interactions. The collection consists of twenty-six instances of Danish 'you know' showing the same phenomenon in the same sequential environment. All the face-to-face data have been videotaped to ensure access to the non-verbal aspects of the interaction. The majority of the data consists of two-party conversations. This might be of relevance to the phenomenon in focus here, as its use directly implies speaker selection by addressing a particular co-participant. When there are more than two participants, one participant is selected as the main addressee and potential next speaker.[4]

Format of the turn including 'you know'   In this first section of the analysis, the focus will be on the format of turns that include 'you know'. Here, I will investigate the turn design and the position of 'you know' within the turn.

In the following excerpt (3), the participants are engineers at a building site talking together during their lunch break. They are discussing a problem with a windowsill that is cracked underneath a window. The participants are seated around a table in a lunch room, placed from left to right: A, B and C. Just prior to the excerpt, B starts to present the problem and C takes over, thereby claiming co-tellership of the problem. After having taken over, C establishes eye contact with A, the main story recipient, who acknowledges without showing any deeper understanding of the problem presented. After a 0.5 second pause, C, in line 13, continues to present the problem:

---

[4] I will not go into further detail about this aspect in the analysis, but would like to point out that it might be interesting to pursue this by comparing more systematically the use of 'you know' in two-party conversations and multi-party conversations, respectively. And it might be particularly interesting to pursue questions of conversational schisming (Egbert 1997) and speaker selection (Lerner 2003; Mondada 2007).

(3)
```
13  C:     Uffe han  siger det  blæser  ind,
           Uffe he   says it    blows in,
           Uffe he says it's draughty,

14         (0.4)

15  C:  →  .pt >du ved<     der   ligger jo    ikke en fuge;
           .pt >you know<   there lies   PRT   not  a joint;
           .pt you know there is actually no filler there;

16         (0.2)

17  C:     Der  har   vi  jo   bare    kørt      bundstykket  ind,
           there have we  PRT  simply  driven    basepiece_the in,
           we've simply inserted the base at that point,

18         (0.6)

19  A:     M' der    er pudset     op under,
           b'  there is polished   up under,
           but it's been plastered underneath,

20         (0.2)

21  C:     m:,
           m,
           m,

22         (0.2)

23  A:     M' er det  slået    ^fra?
           b'  is it   coming  ^off?
           b' is it coming off?
```

After a second version of the problem has been presented in line 13, there is no uptake by the main recipient A. The lack of uptake can indicate problems such as a difficulty in understanding or an upcoming disagreement. Thereafter C continues in line 15 by further elaborating on the problem, producing a turn that includes 'you know'. The information provided in the 'you know' turn gives background information about the prior potentially problematic item, namely the fact that it is draughty. In contrast to the turn in line 13, the information given here is provided as information that is well known to the co-participant. Hence, the 'you know' turn is not designed as something you do *not* know or something you *should* know. On the contrary, it is designed as something that the co-participant already knows. Thus, 'you know' claims that agreement is possible, because the interlocutors have joint access to this claim. Moreover, 'you know' indicates that the interlocutors not only can, but should, agree. In that way, there is a moral obligation to display agreement built into the proposal of shared knowledge.

The way 'you know' is produced in Extract 3 is characteristic of the instances that form the basis of this collection: 'you know' is produced fast and without emphasis. It is directly addressed to the co-participant, and it is often placed TCU-initially (as it is here), even though it is sometimes preceded by various kinds of connectors, such as 'so' and 'and'.[5]

Below, there are four examples to support the analysis of the features of turns that include 'you know'.

(4)
```
6   K:  →  alts' >du   ved  <  (a')   hun var  ligesom flyver ik'   o'?
          PRT >you know< (that) she was PRT      flyer  PRT_PRT?
          so you know she was like a flyer right?
```

(5)
```
13  A:  →  =o'   (.) du   ved   [så'n lidt small talk,=
           =and (.) you know [a    bit small talk,=
           =and (.) you know a bit of small talk,=
```
```
14  B:  →                       [°ja°
                                [yes
                                yes
```
```
15  A:  →  = ikk' oss'   [.hh øh  ]
           = PRT_PRT [.hh leh ]
           = night      .hh leh
```

(6)
```
19  K:     [o'   hva'  er] det   så?   .hh er det så     sådan
           [and what is] there then? .hh is it   then like_this
           and what does that mean? .hh Does that mean that .h that
```
```
20  K:  →  at-  .h at   o:h du   ve'   vi  lægger jo   de   her  små
           that .h that uh  you know we place  PRT these here small
           uh you know we place these small
```
```
21  K:     æ:h .hh æ::h (.) sedler     i  hvor   (.) vi stempler
           uh  .hh uh  (.) paper_slips in where (.) we stamp
           uh .hh uh (.) slips of paper in where (.) we stamp
```
```
22  K:     me'  nummer over på etteren' ik'   o'
           with number over at etteren  PRT_PRT'
           with a number at etteren right
```

(7)
```
8   A:  →  altså e-  (0.2) >du   ved   jeg o' <
           PRT uh (0.2) >you know I    PRT<
           so uh (0.2) you know I right
```

9   A: *jeg plejer   jo   o' gøre meget ud af det der   me' at*
           I   usually PRT to do   a_lot out of this there with that
           I   usually make a lot out of that

10 A: °*at*°   *(.) vi   ligesom er   <internt>   (.) stemt   af*
           °that°   (.) we PRT   are   <internally> (.) aligned at
           that (.) we like internally are (.) aligned

In all four examples, 'you know' is produced in a similar way: it is prosodically unmarked and sometimes produced quickly (Extracts 4, 7).
Moreover, it is worth noticing that, apart from 'you know', there are other
features in the turn indicating that the information provided is shared by
the co-participants. As in Extract 3 line 15, in two of the excerpts (6 and
7) the particle *jo* occurs right after the verb has been produced. This is in
contrast to Extracts 4 and 5, where there is no *jo*. Looking more closely at
what information is actually delivered in the 'you know' turn, one possible
reason for this difference might become apparent. In the cases without
jo, the information given is not specific but more generic. In Extract 4,
the general professional term of a person in this position is used ('flyer'),
and in Extract 5 a generic term, namely 'small talk', is introduced. In the
context of a job appraisal interview, which is the setting for both excerpts,
references to 'small talk' and to a known professional position within the
organization must be regarded as general terms, which are unproblematic
for members of the organization concerned. In the cases in which the 'you
know' turn also includes the particle *jo*, the information given in the 'you
know' turn is more specific, revealing something about specific work procedures (Extracts 6 and 7) or events occurring in a very specific situation
(Extract 3). In Danish, *jo* is a particle (see also Heinemann, Lindström and
Steensig in this volume) that marks the information given as not new. In
this sense, *jo* and 'you know' taken together might help to mark the information given as already known to the co-participant, thereby strengthening the appeal to shared knowledge. It is important to note, though,
that whereas *jo* does not select a specific addressee to whom the information should not be new, 'you know' clearly selects an addressee, who
therefore can be made accountable for his/her state of knowledge. In this
way, the moral aspects of knowing come more clearly into play by using
'you know'.

There is another feature in the 'you know' turn that is used recurrently
and which helps to mark the information given as not new. This is the
particle *ik' o'* or *ikk' oss'* (Extracts 4 and 5), also in co-occurrence with *jo*
(Extract 6, lines 19–21). *Ik' o'* or *ikk' oss'* (literally 'not also') is a Danish
particle, which can be translated as the tag 'right' in English. Due to its

⁶ "Etteren" is the name of a specific department (which has been anonymized).

TCU-final placement, the tag can be one more resource to invite the co-participant to display agreement.

In the vast majority of cases in this collection, 'you know' is accompanied by either *jo* or different versions of the tag *ikk oss*. This indicates that, regardless of their different positions in the turn, 'you know' together with both *jo* and *ikk oss* are likely to contribute to the overall function of the turn in focus here: to appeal to shared knowledge rather than merely informing the co-participants about a specific incident or state of affairs.

In order to understand fully what 'you know' actually seeks agreement with, it is important to understand the scope of 'you know'. Depending on its placement within the turn, the scope can be the directly following element in an ongoing TCU, but it can also be the entire following TCU or even the prior turn.

The scope of 'you know' is the entire following TCU or prior turn in cases when 'you know' is placed TCU-initially or close to it, or is placed in TCU-final position (for turn-initial position, see Extracts 3, 4, 5, 7; for turn-final position, see the following Extract 8). In Extract 8, during a job appraisal interview, A, the boss, is in the course of telling his employee, B, about specific work-related competences in which B could improve.

(8)
```
42 A:   =det- det var ikk' fordi    jeg ville    komme me'  nogen
        =it    it  was not because I   wanted come   with some
        =it it was not because I wanted to mention any

43 A:   konkrete situa[tioner hvor  ]   (.) øhm her  der
        concrete situa[tions  where]   (.) uhm here there_is
        concrete situations where (.) uhm there is
                      [((B nods))   ]

44      (0.5)

45 A: → et   eller andet        > d [u ved<.   ].hm:
        one or    something_else > yo[u know< .].hm
        something you know. .hm:
                                   [((B nods))]

46 A:   men mere for: vi  husker    det. (.)  °ikk'°.=
        but more for  we  remember  it.  (.)  °PRT°.=
        but more so that we remember it   (.) right.
```

In this excerpt, the scope of 'you know' is the prior turn (lines 42–45), in which A gives an account. Here, the turn-final placement retrospectively claims that agreement is possible and has not been given. In contrast to that, the turn-initial placement serves as a projection for the display of agreement. The participants' orientation to these different positions supports this argument. Whereas in the TCU-initial position the display of alignment or affiliation recurrently comes after the completion of the

TCU, the display of alignment or affiliation in cases where 'you know' is placed TCU-finally, comes during or directly after the completion of 'you know' (e.g., see Extract 8). Hence the difference between turn-initial and turn-final position relates to the speaker's orientation. Whereas a turn-initial placement enables the speaker prospectively to pursue agreement (Extracts 3, 4, 5, 7), in turn-final position this is done retrospectively.

In contrast to the broader scope in turn-initial and turn-final position, a position in mid-turn has a more local scope, where the participants orient to the element directly following 'you know'. In that way, it prospectively and locally invites a display of agreement. This is the case in Extract 9.

Here, M (boss) and K (employee) are having a job appraisal interview. M starts by telling a story about K's colleague Lasse indicating that Lasse does not always live up to the demands he makes on his team colleagues. K takes over and accounts for Lasse's behavior by telling a story where Lasse (according to K) acted exceptionally well.

(9)

35 K: *En   ting   der   var   (.)   knaldhamrende   godt   han*
        one thing that was (.) exceptionally   good he
        one thing that was (.) exceptionally good he

36 K: *gjorde (.) her   ti' sidst (.)   vi   har   haft   så*
        did   (.) here til last (.) we have had so
        did (.) here lately (.) we have had so

37 K: → *meget me'   (.)   æ:h .hh æh °du   ve'°=*
        much with (.) uh .hh uh °you know°=
        much about (.) uh .hh uh you know=

38 K: → *=Ansvarsføle[lse   over   for]=*
        =responsibil[ity_feeling about for]=
        =feeling of responsibility about=

39 M: [((M nods))   ]=

40 K: *=[produktet   o'   hvA']   er det lige   vi   ska'   [Hvor meget]=*
        =[product_the and what] is is   PRT we shall [How much]=
        =the product and what it actually is we are supposed to How much=

41 M: =[((M nods   ))]   [((M nods))]=

42 K: *=er det*
        =is it
        =is it

Here, 'you know' is placed in mid position within an ongoing TCU between two items linked together ('about. uh .hh uh you know feeling of responsibility'). The scope of 'you know' is a local one, highlighting the item directly following it. As the excerpt shows, the participants orient to the local, prospective scope of 'you know' in mid-TCU position, as the co-participant displays alignment at the first possible point of recognition in line 39.

The excerpts indicate that the placement of 'you know' within the ongoing turn can vary (turn-initial, mid-turn, TCU-final). The placement has an impact on the scope of the proposal for shared knowledge, which is made relevant by 'you know'. The scope can vary from very local in the case of a mid-TCU position to a broader scope stretching over the whole following TCU or prior turn. Consequently, the precise placement of 'you know' serves as a resource for the participants to show each other what precisely the basis for the proposed shared knowledge is, and hence where it is relevant to display agreement. Moreover, there seems to be a relation between the positioning of 'you know' and the obligation for the co-participants to respond to the invitation to display agreement. Whereas, in cases of mid-turn and turn-final placement of 'you know' co-participants recurrently display alignment by either nodding or by using acknowledgement tokens (Extracts 8, 9), in many cases of TCU-initial positioning of 'you know', co-participants do not display alignment in the next turn. This might indicate that the obligation to display agreement differs depending on the positioning of 'you know'.

Moreover, the prospective and retrospective orientation of 'you know' contributes in different ways to the moral obligation to display agreement. Whereas a turn-initial position serves as a resource prospectively to invite agreement, the mid-turn and turn-final positions retrospectively claim that agreement was expected in the previous turn, but has not come yet. Here, 'you know' opens an extra opportunity to display agreement. Consequently, the precise positioning of 'you know' in an ongoing turn serves as a resource for co-participants to produce a stronger or less strong appeal to the co-participant for agreement. Hence, the moral obligation to align and affiliate differs depending on the positioning of 'you know' in the ongoing turn.

Focus on disagreement prior to 'you know'   Having focused on the actual turn including 'you know', I now turn to the activities prior to the 'you know' turn. I do so in order to isolate specific characteristics of the sequence, which indicate that the participants have established a disaffiliative or a disaligning context.

'You know' is used in a context in which affiliation has been invited, but what is produced by the co-participant is only minimal alignment. In this environment of possible upcoming disagreement due to a lack of affiliation, 'you know' proposes shared knowledge. In this way, the use of 'you know' can be seen as an affiliating move in an emerging disaffiliating environment.

Stivers (2008; and see also Stivers *et al.* this volume) introduces a distinction between structural alignment on the one hand and social affiliation on the other. Here, Stivers refers to alignment as a structural phenomenon, producing for instance a type-conforming action (an answer to a question, a continuer to the progression of a story). On the other hand, affiliation is seen as a social phenomenon, in which the participant relates to the stance taken by the prior utterance. This can be done by, for example, elaborating on a question in the form of an answer that is more than just a type-conforming action. In the current study, I show that participants orient differently to alignment and affiliation. As a consequence, the lack of affiliative moves is seen as a possible indication of an upcoming disagreement, whereas the presence of affiliative moves is seen as an indication of agreement.

In Extract 10, shown before as Extract 3, we can see the sequential structure of the upcoming disagreement prior to 'you know'.

(10) (= Extract 3 in full)
```
1   B:    Men  det    sådan,
          but  it_is  such,
          but it's like this,

2         (0.2) ((B shows a line with right hand))

3   B:    (eng-)  Det  sprækker  nu,
          (eng-)  it   cracks    now,
          (eng-) a    crack has started to appear,

4         (2.8) ((C raises his eyebrows))

5   C:    Nå,
          PRT,
          really,

6         (2.2)

7   B:    Men  de:r       da   ikke  andet  end  bare    lægge  en  fuge  ud
          but  there_is  PRT  not   other  than simply  put    a   joint out
          but the only thing to do is apply a bit of filler

8   B:    °mellem    stenpladerne°,=
          °between   stones_the°,=
          between the stones,=

9   C:    =imellem    vores  stenplader   og   så:   vinduesgulvstykket,
          =in_between our    stone_plates and  then  windowbasepiece_the,
          =between our stones and the window base,

10        (0.2) ((C establishes eye contact with A))

11  A:    Ja,
          yes,
          yes,

12        (0.5)
```

13 C: *Uffe han siger det blæser ind,*
          Uffe he   says it blows in,
          Uffe he says it's draughty,

14   (0.4)

15 C: → *.pt >du   ved<   der   ligger jo   ikke en fuge;*
          .pt >you know< there lies   PRT not a joint;
          pt you know there is actually no filler there;

16   (0.2)

17 C: *Der har vi jo   bare   kørt   bundstykket ind,*
          there have we PRT simply driven basepiece_the in,
          we've simply inserted the basepiece at that point,

From lines 1 to 3 and 7 to 8, B presents a problem, namely that something underneath a window sill is cracked and, in the course of this telling, C establishes himself as a co-teller of the problem. In line 10, C establishes eye contact with A, who, at line 11, acknowledges the problem solution. After a short pause in line 12, C continues with a stronger version of the story: he changes B's version from 'a crack has started to appear' in line 3 to 'it's draughty' in line 13. This can be seen as an upgraded version of B's earlier problem by highlighting the negative consequences more than the factual problem of something that has cracked. The potential disagreement taking place in this sequence lies in the lack of involvement of speaker A during the presentation of the problem. Neither when C, in line 9, expands on the problem description given by B, nor when C upgrades the problem description, does A come in and address the nature of the problem. Hence, the turn initiated with 'you know' proposes shared knowledge at a place in the interaction where agreement has not been established. 'You know' here prospectively invites the co-participant to affiliate. Consequently, an opportunity is established for the co-participant to display agreement in a context where disagreement was possibly forthcoming.

In the following excerpt (11), a similar lack of involvement of one participant in the course of the interaction is treated as a possible indication of impending disagreement. As a consequence of this, the co-participant initiates a 'you know' turn appealing to shared knowledge and thereby working to avert possible upcoming disagreement.

The fragment is again taken from a job appraisal interview. A is the boss, and B is the employee. A is getting to a new point in the agenda for the job appraisal interview, which deals with areas for improvement. A starts out by saying that marketing is an area that B might improve upon; then he continues extensively on this, pointing out that they agreed to talk about this issue at the last job appraisal interview a year before. Throughout the entire sequence, B displays a significant lack of involvement. This lack of involvement becomes evident as B produces aligning but no affiliating moves during the interaction.

(11) (= Extract 8 in full)

```
1  A:    O'  s-  o'  så    har   jeg  skrevet  marketing  oss'
         and th- and then have  I     written  marketing  also
         and th- and then I have written down marketing too

2        (0.2)

3  A:    O':  o'  det  har  egentlig  ikk'  noget       o'  gøre
         and and this has  PRT       not   something  to  do
         and this has not really anything to do

4  A:    me'  (.)  at   øh:
         with (.)  that uh
         with (.) that uh

5        (0.7)

6  A:    .pt at    du   ikk'  ha:r  >man ka' sige<
         .pt that  you  not   have  >one can say<
         .pt the fact that you haven't done, some people might say,

7  A:    slået  ti'   inden  fo- for det  område  .hh
         hit    well  with   in  in  the  area     .hh
         so well in this area .hh
```

((13 lines omitted where A elaborates on B's experience in marketing))

```
21 A:    .hmpth men øh: men allerede sidste år
         .hmpt but uh but already last    year
         .hmpt but uh already last year

22 A:    snakkede vi jo   oss'  om     at    (.)
         talked    we PRT also  about that  (.)
         we talked also about that (.)

23 A:    at   når  nu  space det var afsluttet,
         that when now  space it  was finished,
         that once space⁷ was finished,

24       (0.4) ((B nods))

25 A:    så    var  det måske  en idé  o'
         then was  it  perhaps an idea to
         then it might be an idea to

26       (0.2)

27 A:    >° man ka' sige°< prøve o'
         >° one can say°<  try   to
         so to say try and

28       (0.4)
```

---

⁷ "Space" is the name of a project (anonymized).

29 A: *o' rotere dig på en eller anden måde.*
        to rotate you in one or   other way.
        rotate you in some way.

30 A: [*af*] *HÆNgig af hvordan det nu   vil   passe ind   i*
        [de]pending on how   this now will fit   into in
        de pending on how this will now fit into

31 B: [*Ja*]
        [yes]
        yes

32 A: *planer i   øvrigt   ikk' oss'.=*
        plans in otherwise PRT_PRT.=
        the other plans right.=

33 B: =*Jo*
        =yes
        =yes

34   (0.2)

35 A: *Ti'   o' komme lidt   mere over   i den*
        PREP to come   little more further in this
        to move a bit further in that

36 A: *retning   [der   i]kk'=*
        direction [there P]RT=
        direction right=

37 B: [*.pt ja   *]
                         [.pt yeah]
                         [.pt yeah]

38 A: =°*men altså >man ka' sige<° få- (.) få   mere viden*
        =°but PRT >one can say<° get (.) get more knowledge
        =but well one can say to get (.) get more knowledge

39 A: *på området ikk'*
        on area_the PRT
        in this area right

40 B: *Ja*
        yes
        yes

41 A: *.hh o' det jo egentlig derfor   a' jeg har skrevet det.=*
        .hh and it_is PRT actually therefore that I   have written this.=
        .hh and it is actually therefore that I have written this.=

42 A: =*det- det var ikk' fordi   jeg ville   komme me' nogen*
        =it   it was not because I   wanted come   with some
        =it it was not because I wanted to mention any

```
43  A:      konkrete situa[tioner hvor  ] (.) øhm her  der
            Concrete situa[tions  where] (.) uhm here there_is
            Concrete situations where (.) uhm there is
                        [((B nods  ))]
44          (0.5)
45  A: →    et   eller andet          >   d[u ved<.   ] .hm:
            one  or   something_else  >   yo[u know< .] .hm
            something you know. .hm:
                                          [((B nods))]
46  A:      men mere for: vi  husker    det. (.) °ikk'°=
            but more  for  we remember  it.  (.) °PRT°=
            but more so that we remember it (.) right=
47  B:      =.ptkh (0.4) jA, vi  ska'  huske     det.
            =.ptkh (0.4) yes we  shall remember  it.
            =.ptkh (0.4) yeah we should remember this.
48          (.)
49  B:      Det s[ka' ]  vi  nemlig.
            this s[hall]  we  actually.
            this we should really do.
50  A:            [Ja  ]
                  [yes ]
                  yes
```

In the course of A's long account for taking up the topic, there are several places for B to come in and express affiliation. This is the case after lines 21 to 23, where A initiates the positive account for the agenda item, namely that they agreed upon this item at the last job appraisal interview ('last year'). B nods in line 24 to acknowledge A's account, but this nod cannot be seen as an initiative for stronger involvement, as the nod is placed within an ongoing turn by A. Moreover, the nod, similar to verbal acknowledgement tokens, does not show but merely claims understanding (Schegloff 1982). Another place for affiliation is after line 29, where A finishes his account with a clear transitional relevance place. B acknowledges the account in line 31 ('yes') minimally in overlap with A's post-completion in lines 30 and 32. Again there are no clear markers of affiliation by B. A finishes the post-completion with a tag question (*ikk' oss'*), which results in B acknowledging with a type-conforming *jo* in line 33. Still B continues producing aligning, but no affiliating, responses, which leads A to continue his account. In lines 38–39, A reformulates the motivation for change once again by completing the turn with a tag (*ikk'*), thereby appealing once more to his co-participant's involvement. But again B acknowledges minimally (line 40), thereby declining the opportunity to affiliate with A.

In this environment characterized by a lack of involvement by B, A retrospectively appeals, in line 45, to shared knowledge by inserting *du ved* in post-TCU position. After this retrospective invitation to affiliate, B indeed shows affiliation. He does so by directly acknowledging A's account in lines 47 and 49: 'yeah we should remember this'; 'this we should really do'.

In this excerpt, the lack of involvement of one participant is oriented to by the other participant as noticeably absent. The lack of involvement becomes apparent in B's aligning but not affiliating responses. In this way, the appeal to shared knowledge is a resource to establish agreement in an environment in which the absence of affiliating moves can indicate emerging disagreement.

In order to provide an even clearer space for agreement, in an environment where disagreement is on its way, participants in interaction can place 'you know' at the beginning of a parenthetical sequence (Mazeland 2007). This enables them to establish agreement locally on a potentially uncontroversial item, while at the same time being able to return to the ongoing, disagreement-implicative TCU. In his paper on parenthetical sequences, Mazeland (2007) focuses on ongoing TCUs in which a parenthetical is included before completion. The parenthetical is designed in a way that the recipient can respond to it, before the ongoing TCU is taken up again. It is this sequential structure that resembles some of the instances of 'you know' in this collection (for a Dutch example of a parenthetical initiated with 'you know', see also Mazeland 2007: 1824).

In the following excerpt from a job appraisal interview, M is the boss and K is the employee. K complains about her team leader, Peter, who has written a note to employees saying that if they do not follow specific rules and do not deliver products without errors, they might get fired. M shows very little involvement throughout the entire sequence, which may indicate an underlying disagreement.

(12) (= Extract 6 in full)

```
1 K:    Men- [men æh jeg synes (.) jeg synes   måske  (godt)
        but  [but uh I    believe (.) I    believe perhaps (good)
        but but uh I believe (.) I believe perhaps (good)

2 M:         [ja
             [yes
             yes

3 K:    de:t godt nok.    hh altså: (0.8) de:t jo    nok   mere hans (.)
        it_is good enough .hh PRT   (0.8) it_is PRT PRT   more his   (.)
        it is fine .hh PRT (0.8) it is PRT probably more his (.)

4 K:    hans afslutning jeg ikk' (.) ku'   lide fordi   .hh altså
        his closing    I   not  (.) could like because .hh PRT
        his way of closing I didn't like because .hh PRT
```

5 K: *den der,*
          this there
          this one

6   (1.2)

7 K: *jeg opfattet   den som en- en trussel, o'   jeg [men- (.) jeg*
          I   understood it   as   a   a threat, and I   [beli- (.) I
          I understood it as a a threat, and I beli- (.) I can

8 M: [*ja*
                                                         [yes
                                                          yes

9 K: *ka' heller ik' opfatte   den anderledes n[år teksten*
          can either not understand it   otherwise i[f   text_the
          not understand it differently either when the text

10 M: [*(°nej°)*
                                                        [(°no°)
                                                         no

11 K: *den lyder såd[an   vel?*
          it   sounds like[_this PRT?
          it sounds like this right?

12 M: [*nej*
                          [no
                          [no

13 M: *.hnej*
          .hno
          .hno

14   (0.8)

15 M: *nej.*
          no.
          no.

16   (.)

17 M: °*okay*°.
          °okay°.
          okay.

18 M: [(   )]
19 K: [*o'   hva' er] det   så?   .hh er det så   sådan*
          [and what is] there then? .hh is it   then like_this
          and what does that mean? .hh Does that mean that .h that

20 K: → *at- .h at   ø:h du ve'   vi lægger jo   de   her små*
          that .h that   uh you know we place PRT these here small
          uh you know we place these small

21 K: *æ:h .hh æ::h (.) sedler   i   hvor   (.) vi stempler*
          uh .hh uh (.) paper_slips in where (.) we stamp
          uh .hh uh (.) slips of paper in where (.) we stamp

22 K: *me' nummer ovre på etteren ik' o'*
           with number over at etteren PRT_PRT'
           with a number at etteren right

23   (.)

24 K: *.hh er det så   sådan   at   .hh at   o:h når   der*
           .hh is it   then like_this that .hh that u:h when there
           .hh does that mean that when we get back

25 K: *så kommer .hh femten tilbage me'   det nummer,*
           so come   .hh fifteen back   with this number,
           fifteen with this number on,

26 K: *jamen så   ryger   du ud.*
           PRT   then kicked_are you out.
           well then you are fired.

In lines 1 to 11, K establishes a negative stance toward her colleague Peter,
by presenting him as someone who is threatening his co-workers. In line
8, M aligns in overlap with K's ongoing turn by minimally acknowledging
without addressing the stance taken by K, namely that Peter is behaving
in an unacceptable way. M continues in 10, 12 and 13 by locally aligning with K's turn in 9 and 11. After a pause of 0.8 seconds in line 14, M
repeats his prior acknowledgement token. In line 17 he moves into closing
by saying *okay* (Schegloff and Sacks 1973). This repetition of minimal
acknowledgement tokens in an environment that clearly invites affiliation
due to the stance-taking character of the prior utterance indicates that M
is not willing to affiliate with K. In that sense, we can see here an instance
of aligning actions (constructing type-conforming minimal acknowledgement tokens) that are disaffiliating (Stivers 2008) in that they do not clearly
adopt the stance taken by the co-participant. As a result, M's move into
closing after his minimal engagement relative to the clear stance that K has
taken marks disaffiliation, and can be treated as indicating disagreement.
In line 19, K opens up the topic again ('and') and formulates a rhetorical
question ('and what does that mean'), which serves as a preface to her
extended turn. She continues in line 19 by giving a candidate answer to
the question she asked herself ('Does that mean that'). She cuts off after
she has initiated a new TCU with 'that' in line 20, which clearly projects
continuation. At this point, she starts a parenthetical (line 20, 'you know
we place these ...'). In the parenthetical she appeals to shared knowledge
between herself and the boss concerning some work routines. She completes the parenthetical with a tag (*ikk o'*), which M does not acknowledge.
After a micro pause, where the co-participant might respond, K recycles
(line 24) what she said before in line 19.

In this excerpt, it becomes clear that the lack of involvement manifested
by producing minimal aligning actions without performing more substan-

tial affiliating actions leads to an appeal to shared knowledge. The appeal to shared knowledge is done as a parenthetical. This enables the speaker to appeal locally for agreement in a context in which disagreement is emerging. By inserting a parenthetical the speaker creates a place in the interaction to deal with the contingencies established in the prior turn. Moreover, it gives the speaker an opportunity to secure his/her ongoing turn, as turn continuation has been projected. Hence, after having established agreement locally in the parenthetical sequence, the speaker can return to the potentially disagreement-implicative prior turn. In that way, the parenthetical opens up the opportunity to propose agreement locally, when global agreement is not possible or not directly forthcoming.

Another example of 'you know' initiating a sequence that has parenthetical features can be seen in the following excerpt. Here, the parenthetical does not live up to Mazeland's sequential structure of a parenthetical sequence because the initiation of the parenthetical does not take place within an ongoing TCU. Still, I will argue that the parenthetical character of the sequence strengthens the obligation for the co-participants to respond. In this excerpt, two elderly female friends, E and F, are talking about E's problems: she has recently moved into a new flat, where she lacks space. She used to have a table in her dining room, but this is no longer possible in her new flat due to this shortage of space.

(13)

1 E: *Der   ka' være meget i.* [=*Men det' da   ås'   li'ssă*
       there can be   lots   in. [=But it_is PRT also just_as
       there can be lots in it. =But it is also just as

2 F: [*Mm.*
                                   [mm.
                                    mm.

3 E: *meget et spørgsmål om å' finde ud a'   at   no'en*
       much a question of to find out tha- that some
       much a question of finding out that that some

4 E: *a' tingene   ka' du   li'ssă   godt putte ned   i kælderen*
       of things_the can you just_as well put   down in cellar_the
       of the things you can just as well put down in the cellar

5 E: *ikk' al'să .hh der   har   jeg să *eh-**
       not well .hh there have   I   so *uh-*
       right .hh there I have uh

6 E: *(.) efterhănden ăs:' al'să nu   hvor jeg să har   fået   et*
       (.) eventually   also well now where I   so have gotten a
       (.) eventually well now that I have got a

7 E: *spisebord hvor   jeg ka' stille mine stole ve' să har   jeg*
       table   where I   can place my   chairs at so have I
       table which I can put my chairs around I have

8   E: *hevet fire stole op a'   kælderen i[kk',   å'*
          taken four chairs up from cellar_the P[RT, and
          brought four chairs up from the cellar right and

9   F: [*Ja=jah.*
                                                 [yes=yes.
                                                 yes=yes.

10 E: *.hh å'   så'n al'så; Sten han sagde Nåhm' hva' me' dit*
          .hh and then PRT; Sten he   said PRT   what with your
          .hh and then right; Sten he said well what about your

11 E: → *spisebord, du   ved   det ville jeg jo   ikk'- det ku'*
          table,   you know this want I   PRT not- this could
          table,you know this I did not want this I could

12 E: *jeg ikk' ha' her vel,*
          I   not have here PRT,
          not have here right,

13 F: *Nej.=*
          no.=
          no.=

14 E: *=.hh så det '   skilt ad   å'   Lone sagde*
          =.hh so it_has_been taken apart and Lone said
          =.hh so it has been taken apart and Lone said

15 E: *Jeg har fundet så'n en .hh så   fin plads nede=*
          I   have found such a .hh such fine room down=
          I have found such a.hh such a perfect room down=

16 E: *=i   mit- Hun har et lillebitte   kælderrum*
          =in my- She has a tinysmall cellarroom
          =in my She has a tiny cellar

In this excerpt, E talks about her decision to get a new table for the dining room (lines 1–11), even though one of her friends, Sten, has indicated that she should use her old table. At this point in the conversation, the co-participant F has only responded with minimal acknowledgement tokens (lines 2, 9). In lines 10 and 11, E continues by referring to what her friend Sten has said. She inserts a parenthetical in line 11 initiated by 'you know', where she prospectively refers to a shared knowledge about the table being too big for her apartment. This leads in line 13 to F marking alignment ('no') and E going back to her original line of argumentation in line 14 initiated with 'so'.

In this excerpt, the parenthetical initiated by 'you know' appeals to shared knowledge between the participants about the lack of space in her new flat. The initiation of the parenthetical leads here to a parenthetical sequence until the co-participant acknowledges the information given in the parenthetical directly in the next turn.

In both excerpts, the initiation of the parenthetical goes hand in hand with the turn-final use of a particle that invites agreement (excerpt 12, line

22 *ik' o'*; excerpt 13, line 12 *vel*). This seems to be a stronger way to solicit a response and hence it strengthens the obligation of the co-participant to agree with the proposal of shared knowledge. Compared with 'you know'-initiated turns that have a less clear parenthetical character, we can now see a relation in terms of obligation to display agreement: when 'you know' initiates a parenthetical, there seem to be stronger obligations for the participants to display agreement immediately after. Moreover, marking the place for agreement as detached from the place of potential disagreement, as is done by a parenthetical, might be a way to stress retrospectively the potential emerging prior disagreement.

The excerpts analyzed in this section have shown that 'you know' commonly follows a sequence of more or less direct disagreement. The disagreeing quality becomes apparent through aligning moves and the lack of affiliating ones displayed by the co-participants. The information presented in the 'you know' turn is designed not as something the co-participant does not know or should know, but instead as something that the co-participant already knows. In cases where 'you know' initiates a parenthetical, the obligation for the co-participants to display agreement is stronger than in cases where 'you know' is simply part of a multi-unit turn. In this way we can see that the moral obligation for the co-participant to align and/or affiliate with the invitation to shared knowledge differs not just in terms of placement of 'you know' within an ongoing turn (see the prior section), but also in terms of whether it is used to initiate a sequence or not.

Sequence organization after 'you know'

I will now have a closer look at the turn organization after the 'you know' turn. In the data, we have seen several indications that the information given in the 'you know' turn is not designed to be questioned or challenged by the co-participants. Instead, it is frequently acknowledged. The acknowledgement is primarily done in an aligning way through acknowledgement tokens or other minimal tokens of alignment such as nods. The display of alignment seems to lead the speaker to reformulate his main point, which thereafter receives affiliation. In that way the 'you know' turn can be seen as a first step toward agreement in an environment where agreement was not forthcoming. Looking back at excerpt 13, we can see an example of this sequential structure.

(14) (= Extract 13, short version)
11 E: → *du   ved   det ville jeg jo   ikk'- det   ku'*
          you know this want   I   PRT not- This could
          you know this I did not want this I could

12 E: *jeg ikk' ha'   her   vel,*
          I   not have here PRT,
          not have here right,

13 F: *Nej.=*
          no.=
          no.=

14 E: *=.hh så det'   skilt   ad   å'   Lone sagde*
          =.hh so it_has_been taken apart and Lone said
          =.hh so it has been taken apart and Lone said

15 E: *Jeg har   fundet så'n en .hh så   fin   plads nede=*
          I   have found such a .hh such fine room down=
          I have found such a.hh such a perfect room down=

16 E: *=i   mit- Hun har et lillebitte   kælderrum*
          =in my- She has a tinysmall cellarroom
          =in my She has a tiny cellar

After F minimally acknowledges the proposal of shared knowledge, E
goes on, in line 14, to the main storyline, namely that the table which was
much too big for her apartment has been placed in the cellar. This suggests that the turn including 'you know' is designed to get aligning and not
affiliating responses. This can be seen in that the participants orient to the
display of alignment with the 'you know' turn as an indication of agreement to pursue the main line of argumentation.

A display of alignment is not always oriented to as the preferred response
by the co-participant. In the following example, which is a continuation
of Extract 1, we can see that, after the display of alignment, the speaker
pursues affiliation before going on with the prior topic.

(15) (= continuation of Extract 1)

12 M: *.Hh du   ved   sånogen rustninger me'   pigge p[å]*
         .hh you know that   armor   with spikes o[n]
         .hh you know that armor with spikes on

13 P: [J]ah
                                                           [y]es
                                                           yes

14   (0.7)

15 M: *I[kke,]*
         r[ight,]
         right,

16 P: [*Joh*] *Jah*
        [yes] Yeah
          yes Yeah

17 M: *.hh Sånogen. vrimler det jo   rundt   med*
         .hh those.   are=lots it PRT around with
         .hh those. Are there you know crowds of

18 P: *Jerh,*
        yeah,
        yeah,

19 M: *De   hedder   Vilgulators*
        they are_called Vilgulators
        they are called Vilgulators

In terminal overlap with the 'you know' turn, P produces an aligning action in form of an acknowledgement token in line 13. After a 0.7 pause in line 14, M pursues affiliation in 15, which is displayed in 16 by P. This display of agreement enables M to get back to his main point from the start of the excerpt, namely that these creatures are called Vilgulators.

In Extract 14, the speaker gets an aligning response and does not pursue the display of affiliation any further, whereas in Extract 15 the speaker does not accept the display of alignment as sufficient and pursues affiliation instead. This indicates that 'you know' makes relevant alignment, but in some cases affiliation is preferred. After the proposal of shared knowledge has been acknowledged in an aligning and sometimes affiliating way, the prior speaker continues pursuing the topic that was raised prior to the 'you know'.

In a few cases, the 'you know' turn, and thereby the appeal to shared knowledge, is not acknowledged but instead is challenged by the co-participant. This is shown in the next excerpt, where it becomes obvious that it takes extra interactional work to take over the turn at this point and challenge the appeal to shared knowledge. This example comes from a job appraisal interview. A, the boss, explains to B, the employee, that, on the basis of different job satisfaction surveys, he has started to walk around in the mornings and engage in small talk with the employees. A is well aware that not all the employees are equally satisfied with this. B opposes this idea by indicating that this attitude does not apply to him.

(16) (= Extract 5 in full)
1 A: *Altså je- jeg har   gjort det me:'*
       PRT I   I   have done this with
       right I I have done this to

2 A: *me' nogen af de   andre (.) at,*
       with some of the others (.) that,
       to some of the others that

3 A: *det har egentlig været me' udgangspunkt i:*
       this has actually been my starting_point in
       this has actually been my starting point in

4 A: *i   medarbejdertilfredshedsundersøgels[en (he] r)*
       in employeesatisfactionstudy_the   (he] re)
       the job satisfaction study here

5 B: [*J:a,*]
                                                       [y:es,]
                                                       yes,

6 A: *s̲i̲dste:*
          last
          last

7   (.)

8 B: *J̲a̲,*
          yes,
          yes,

9 A: *>j̲a̲nuar   ikk' oss'   < .HH at=at   de:t m̲e̲get <I̲ndivi>duelt*
          >january   PRT_PRT<   .HH that=that it_is very   <indivi>dual
          January right .HH that that it is very individual

10 A: *det̲   der   me' o' k̲o̲mme r̲u̲ndt;*
          this there with to come   around;
          this walking around;

11   (.)

12 A: *o'   spørge (0.2) .hh vo- >h̲a̲r   du   h̲a̲ft en g̲o̲d   w̲e̲ekend.<=*
          and asking (0.2) .hh vo- >have you   had a   good weekend.<=
          and asking (0.2) .hh vo have you had a good weekend.=

13 A: →   *=o'   (.) du   ved   [sä'n lidt sm̲a̲ll t̲a̲lk,=*
          =and (.) you know [a   bit small talk,=
          =and (.) youknow a bit of small talk,=

14 B: →   [°*ja*°
                                [yes
                                yes

15 A: →   *=ikk' o̲ss'   [.hh øh   ]*
          =PRT_PRT [.hh uh   ]
          =right   .hh uh

16 B: →   [*J̲o̲   o'   de̲::t i̲kk'*]
                        [PRT and this_is not]
                        yes and this is not

17 B: *de̲:t   ikk' v̲i̲gtigt   for m̲i̲g.*
          this_is not   important for me.
          this_is not important for me.

In lines 1–2 A initiates a report ('I have done this to to some of the others that'). 'This' here refers to the boss engaging in small talk with some of the employees. He cuts off after 'that' and restarts in line 3, giving a reason for his behavior, namely that he has learned from former job satisfaction studies that some employees, but not all, like their boss to engage in small talk with them. During the course of this report, the co-participant B offers only minimal feedback in lines 5 and 8. At the possible completion point in line 10, B does not take over. He shows no signs of engagement, either verbal or non-verbal. A designs his utterance in line 12 as a continuation of the prior ('and'), and gives a specific example of what he meant before by saying 'this walking around;', namely to ask 'have you had a good weekend'. He thus pursues response from B (Pomerantz 1984c). In line 13, A designs his utterance as a continuation of the prior utterance again by using 'and' directly followed by *du ved*. The 'you know' turn is one more reformulation of his prior explanation 'this walking around;'. This time he reframes it, shifting from the specific example in line 12 to a generic statement 'a bit of small talk'. Right after the 'you know' B minimally acknowledges with 'yes' in a low voice. Precisely at possible completion of the 'you know' turn after the tag ('right'), B comes in and rejects the implication of the prior turns, namely that this attitude could be relevant for him too. He does so in line 16 by first acknowledging in a type-conforming way (*jo*) followed by a connector 'and', which minimizes the underlying disagreement. First thereafter, he formulates the direct rejection ('this is not important for me'). The appeal to shared knowledge is here presented in a generic way ('a bit of small talk'), which is difficult to reject as such. It is the underlying assumption that such behavior should be relevant for B that B opposes.

What becomes apparent in this excerpt is the fact that an appeal to shared knowledge cannot simply be rejected: it would not work just to say 'no'. Instead it takes extra interactional work for the co-participant to deal with the underlying assumption of the appeal to shared knowledge, which is that the co-participant can and will approve of this behavior. The extra interactional work becomes apparent here where the speaker first acknowledges the appeal to shared knowledge as such, and thereafter formulates his rejection of the proposal of shared knowledge. By using the connector 'and' between the acknowledgement and the following rejection, the speaker shows an orientation to the proposal for agreement, which would be challenged to a higher degree if another connector like, for example, 'but' had been used (see line 16). So this excerpt indicates that co-participants orient to 'you know' as being used to establish agreement between the interlocutors. As it is interactionally complex to challenge this appeal for agreement, the 'you know' turn can enable the speaker to pursue his line of argumentation without having to ensure agreement with the co-participant.

Discussion

The analysis indicates that an appeal to shared knowledge in an environment of emerging disagreement can be seen as a move to locally establish agreement. In this regard the instances analyzed here differ from Heritage and Raymond's studies (Heritage and Raymond 2005; Raymond and Heritage 2006) in that, in my collection, questions of knowledge play a crucial role for the establishment of agreement in a disaffiliating context, whereas in their cases disaligning actions are embedded in an affiliating context. So questions of epistemics, and specifically questions of rights to know, are not limited to competing environments, but also play an important role in the negotiation of agreement in talk.

As seen in this analysis, the appeal to shared knowledge comes at a point in the interaction at which the co-participant has repeatedly indicated a lack of involvement by refraining from affiliating and/or aligning actions. This lack of involvement can be seen as an indication of potential disagreement. The appeal to shared knowledge can therefore be seen as an attempt by the interlocutors to avert overt disagreement. Hence, 'you know' is a resource in interaction to deal locally with emerging disagreements, and it is a device which can be used both prospectively and retrospectively to pursue agreement locally.

In this way, 'you know' can be seen as dealing primarily with questions of alignment and affiliation. Questions of knowledge arise secondarily in the way the display of alignment and affiliation is made accountable in the talk. By proposing shared knowledge, the current speaker invites the co-participant to display agreement by aligning or affiliating in an environment in which agreement was not directly forthcoming. Hence, the reference to shared epistemic access implies a display of alignment and/or affiliation by the co-participants.

The appeal to shared knowledge relates to questions of morality, as proposing shared knowledge prospectively implies that the co-participant can agree, and retrospectively implies that s/he probably should have displayed agreement before. In that way, 'you know' creates a moral obligation for the co-participant to display agreement as the appeal to shared knowledge implies that alignment and/or affiliation is possible. This is so because proposing shared knowledge presupposes that the co-participant has sufficient access to the background knowledge. Hence, this study indicates that issues of morality are closely related to questions of epistemic access. Who knows what is not just a question about a co-participant's information state. A proposal of shared knowledge can become an inherently moral issue and can be used as a member's resource to achieve agreement in talk-in-interaction.

10 Ways of agreeing with negative stance taking

Auli Hakulinen and Marja-Leena Sorjonen

Introduction

In this chapter, we investigate the ways in which a claim of epistemic access can be modified by speakers. The analytic phenomena we focus on are modifications in the design of agreeing responses in Finnish. When agreeing with a stance by the co-participant, the speaker, in one way or another, displays knowledge of the referent or state of affairs that forms the object of stance taking. Through the details of her agreeing response, the speaker then expresses the kind of epistemic access she has and her take on the ongoing activity. (See, for example, Goodwin and Goodwin 1992; Heritage 2002a; Heritage and Raymond 2005; Pomerantz 1975, 1984a).

Consider the following exchange from the end of a story telling; old men are jointly reminiscing about times of war ("those times", "times like that"). The turn in line 1 is an evaluation of the story, which winds it up. The recipient agrees with the evaluation and he does so by repeating the verb of negation in the prior speaker's turn (*ei*) twice.

(1)
```
1 SAULI:   Ei       niitä  aikoi tarviis tul   [la.
           NEG.3SG  those  times need  come
           Those times should never return.
2 MAUNO:                                        [E:::i.     e:::i.
                                                [NEG.3SG NEG.3SG
```

By selecting a response type – here a repetition of the negative verb – that agrees with the polarity of the preceding utterance, the recipient positions himself as having access to knowledge equal to that of his/her co-participant and asserts unconditional agreement with her or him (cf. Heinemann 2003: 58–69, 2005; Mazeland 1990). The fact that the element

We would like to thank Trine Heinemann, Anna Lindström, Lorenza Mondada and Jakob Steensig for comments on earlier versions of this chapter. We are especially grateful to Tanya Stivers for acute comments and for helping us to shape up the final version.

repeated is the finite verb (negative auxiliary) in the co-participant's prior utterance makes a strong tie between the response and the utterance responded to. In this chapter, we analyze responses, such as the one in Extract 1, that respond to a grammatically negative statement by the co-participant. We will show that, when responding, the recipients do more than orient to the display of epistemic access and agreement. They also respond to the sequential position of the negative statement and the type of action it performed. Thus, epistemic stance and agreement are unavoidably intertwined with the action characteristics of the prior negative statement.

By responding with a mere repetition of the negative auxiliary, the recipient in Extract 1 leaves the co-participant's utterance intact. What the co-participant said is fully accepted (through ellipsis), and the response contains no elements that modify what the prior speaker said. However, a mere repetition does not exhaust the response types that assert equal access to the object of stance taking. In addition, we will discuss two other types of response that are congruent with the polarity of the prior utterance in that they also contain a repetition of the negative verb. In one of them, the repetition is followed by the adverb *niin* in the same prosodic unit (*ei niin*), and in the other one the recipient responds with a more elaborate repetition, repeating both the negative auxiliary and the non-finite main verb. Through analyzing the usages of these different response types we will show that the recipient, while asserting equal epistemic access and agreeing in the same terms as the other speaker, further contextualizes her agreement through selecting one of the alternatives.

In dealing with the interpretation of interrogative utterances and turns in different kinds of sequential position in conversation, Schegloff (1984) showed that an interrogative can be taken, for example, as an invitation or a complaint and not "just" a question. In a similar vein, the use of a negative statement may involve more than "just" rejecting or denying some state of affairs. For example, one might be doing a negative noticing to show that one knows better, to justify a particular future action. Alternatively, the speaker can bring forth her particular life situation and feelings, for example by saying "a three-shift job doesn't agree with me". The negative statement can also be used as an appeal to the recipient and test shared knowledge and values, inviting agreement and affiliation from the co-participant. Consequently, the response speaker, in addition to agreeing, unavoidably expresses her or his stance with respect to the motivation and relevance of the preceding negative utterance.

In what follows we will show that the assertion of equal epistemic access can be modified in different ways, so that in some cases it is the epistemic character of the response that is modified, whereas in others it is rather its aligning character. We will start with those which work as "baseline" responses in the sense that their design encodes equal epistemic access and unconditional agreement. These are the responses that contain only a repetition of the negative auxiliary (*ei*). We will discuss typical sequential and activity contexts of this type of response. We then turn to a response type which, as compared to a mere repetition of the negative verb, specifies the character of the equal epistemic access expressed. These are responses that contain the adverb *niin* (*ei niin*) which implies that the response speaker had independently arrived at the stance that the co-participant just expressed. We will show that this response type can be used to imply or hint at disalignment with the implications of the co-participant's prior turn. After that, we take up a response type that, while displaying equal epistemic access and agreement, implies disagreement with the action implications of the prior turn. This response type contains not only the negative auxiliary but also the non-finite verb form repeated from the prior turn (*ei oo*). As a contrast case, we will discuss the use of the positive response token *niin* as a response to negative statements. We will show how it can be used for displaying a non-committal stance in situations where asserting equal epistemic access might be a delicate issue, or where the recipient is not otherwise in a position to display that kind of access.

The data for the analyses come from a larger corpus of responses to grammatically negative statements. The data are drawn from various types of interactions: face-to-face and telephone conversations; dyadic and multi-party conversations; institutional interactions and conversations among friends and family members. The database for this study consists of agreeing responses that contain a repetition of the negative verb or are formed with the positive response particle *niin* and are of the type described above.[1]

Equivalent epistemic access and unconditional agreement

A core context of the simple *ei* responses is in sequences where the participants have already developed shared understanding on some state of affairs. A good case is reminiscing about joint experiences (cf. the assessment activity, Goodwin and Goodwin 1992: 155–156). In this kind of context, the negative utterance occurs toward the end of the activity, and it is a generalizing one, bringing stance taking to a peak. (See also Extract 1 above.) This is what happens in the following interaction.

---

[1] The database also contains response types that consist of a repetition of the negative verb followed by an element that, for example, implies secondary epistemic access to what is being talked about (e.g. *ei varmaan* "I guess no") or upgrades the agreement with an implication of primary rights to know (e.g. *ei todellakaan* "definitely no," "no way").

The participants, two smokers, are constructing their shared stance to health instructions. They have found out that each of them is still a smoker, after which they have noted that smoking is one of the joys one has in the summer, the time of the recording. In lines 1–5, they collaboratively state that it is one of the rare joys left in the fall as well. This is followed by a generalizing statement by H (line 6), which gets an unconditional agreement through *ei* from C. They then set smoking in a more general health discourse, the morality of which is viewed in an ironic light. The exchange on the pleasures of smoking comes to an end at line 14. However, the generalization is subsequently turned into carnivalizing the dangers of smoking by H with a negative statement from line 19 on.

(2) (Hair salon)

```
1   C:   £kyllä sitä  ai:na (0.2) keksii   kaikkia.
         sure  PRT  always       invents everything
         £one sure comes up with (0.2) all sorts of.

2        et >aattele  et  ku< syksyllä  on taas   niim p(h)imeetä
         so think-IMP that when fall-ADE is again so    dark
         so >just think while< in the fall it is so d(h)ark

3        ja  ras>kasta£ et<  kyllä se [siihenkik  ]   ku[uluu?]
         and heavy        that sure  it [it-ILL-CLI]   be[longs]
         and heavy£ that it definitely belongs there as well

4   H:                                 [sillonk\  ]      [jo  ]o:\
                                        [then-CLI  ]      [PRT
                                        then as well\     ye ah:\

5   C:   [.joo:,

6   H: → [sillon (.) ei    olem muuta nautin[toa] en:nään.
         [then      NEG is     other enjoyment anymore
         [Then (.) one doesn't have other enjoyment anymore.

7   C: ⇒                                  [ei.]

8   C:   kyllä.
         right

9        (1.2)

10  C:   |joo [kyllä se on\]
         PRT [sure it is ]
         |yeah it sure is\

11  H:        [.hhh joo:] kyl^lä sitä:  tuota\
              [  PRT  ] sure  PRT PRT
              .hhh yeah: sure one: uhm\

12       (0.8)

13  C:   °mm-^m\°
```

14 H: *^kuoleehan   sitä   kuitenki [j̠ohon°ki°.*   ]
             die-3SG-CLI PRT anyway [something-ILL-CLI]
             in any case one will die of some°thing°.

15 C: [*näihän*   *se*   ]*o.*
                        [like.this-CLI it   ] is
                               s̠o it is.

16   (0.4)

17 C: *näin*   *se* *o̠.*
          like.this it is
          s̠o it i̠s.

18   (0.6)

19 H: → *ja   eihän   nyt saa   ennää   r̠anskalaisia pottuja*
        and NEG-3SG-CLI now may anymore french   fries
        and one is not allowed to eat fr̠ench fries

20   → *sy[̠yä eikä]   r̠uisl̠eipää [eikä]*
        eat   not-and rye.bread [not-and
        anymore nor ry̠e bread nor in fact anything at all

21 C: ⇒   [*e:̠:i̠*   ]   [*e:i̯*]

22 H: → *ei   oikeastaam m̠it[tään.*
        NEG   in.fact   anything

23 C: ⇒   [*.ei_*

24 C: ⇒ *e-e̠[i̯*

25 H: [*niin sehän on aivan sama: sitte*
        [so it-CLI is quite same then
        so it is after all just the same then\

26 C: *mm-m?*

27   (0.4)

28 H: *oliko   se*
          was-Q it
          if it was\

29   (0.8)

30 H: *m̠inkälainen n̠autintoaine   mihi   kuolee?*
          what.kind   enjoyment.stuff which-ILL dies
          whatever kind of stimulant of which one dies?

31   (5.6)

32 C: *mää olisinki   p̠y̠y̠tänyt tota mun s̠iskooni tännem*
          I   would.have-CLI asked   that my   sister   here
          I would have asked that s̠ister of mine

33   *m̠ukaan se   on ---*
          along   she has
          along she has ---

H begins to mock the dangers of smoking in line 19 with a parody of health instructions. He does this with a negative statement that presents a three-part list of generalizations about things that one is not allowed to eat (French fries, rye bread, anything at all). The last element of the list is what Jefferson (1990: 66) calls a "generalized list completer." The utterance is treated as shared knowledge and thus as something readily agreeable through the clitic -*hän* suffixed to the negative verb (*eihän* line 19; cf. Hakulinen 2001[1976]).[2] C picks up each of the three items in the list (lines 21 and 23), as well as the entire utterance (line 24) and agrees with them by repeating the negative word from the preceding turn. With these minimal responses she shows, in addition to agreeing, that she has nothing more to add to the topic (for a similar case in Dutch, see Mazeland 1990: 263). In overlap with the last response, H continues with a conclusion from the presentation of the prohibitions; in so doing he treats the *ei* response as sufficient to his negative statement (see Heinemann [2003: 243–266] on the Danish *nej* being an insufficient response to agreement- and affiliation-relevant negative statements).

There is some variation in the production of the responses. The third response in line 23 is inhaled (indicated by a dot at the beginning of the response, .*ei*), adding to the implication that the stance is shared (Hakulinen and Steensig in preparation).[3] The fourth item at line 24 is a two-syllable variant of the negative word. Our intuition is that, through its two-syllable structure, it takes in its scope the whole list indexing a meaning "none of these sorts" and implying an ironic stance. In this position, as well as in line 7, the mere *ei* response offers unproblematic and unconditional agreement. The speakers have shared access to the (generic) state of affairs, and, as smokers, they share the same perspective on the issues of enjoyment and health risk. In that sense, speaker C is affiliating with her co-participant (cf. Heinemann 2003: 79–84, 2005; Jefferson 2002; Stivers 2008).

The negative utterance to which *ei* responds need not be part of a larger activity of stance taking as in Extracts 1 and 2. The mere *ei* may be locally sufficient in other types of sequential and activity contexts also, as in the following example that is part of a troubles-telling (cf. Jefferson 1988). Saara's old aunt has died. She didn't leave much to inherit but there are nine relatives who would, in principle, be the inheritors. However, the aunt left behind a letter with a wish that Saara and her husband inherit everything. Saara has consulted a legal expert, who advised her to show the

---

[2] We have not attempted to translate the clitic in lines 14 and 19 but in line 25 we used *after all* as an approximate translation.

[3] The first two responses (line 21) have lengthenings of different types. We have not studied the role of lengthening of the response.

letter to all the relatives. Saara is now seeking advice and support for her position from Ella, the vicar's wife.

(3)
```
1  SAARA:    [että  ] [.hh [silloh [sil^lo̲  |se sitte:] (.)
             [so    ] [    [ then [then  it  then ]
             so     .hh    then   then it     (.)
2             jaetaan   yheksälle   ja   jokainen   saa
              is.divided nine-ALL  and  everybody gets
              will be divided to nine and each one gets
3             (.) >kahvipaketi<..hh
              coffee.packet
              (.) >a packet of coffee<..hh
4  ELLA:   → >nii. [.hhh sehän   o]n< ju̲st se että: eihän
             PRT [     that-CLI is    just it that NEG-CLI
             >nii. .hhh that's ju̲st it that there isn't y'know
5  SAARA:       [eh   heh    ]
6  ELLA:   → tämmöseltä #v v# va̲nhukselta   [nyt<   ]
             this.kind-ABL    old.person-ABL [now    ]
             from this kind of #o o# o̲ld person now<
7  SAARA:  ⇒                                 [(°°ei.°°)]
8  ELLA:   → >siltähän     ei<   jää    paljo  mittään  ni (.)
             she-ABL-CLI  NEG  is.left much  anything PRT
             >there is hardly anything left from her (.)
9          → ni   yhdeksälle ni   [.hhhh
             PRT  nine-ALL   PRT
             for ni̲ne so .hhhh
10 SAARA:  ⇒                       [e:i    ja   si̲tte tarvii aatella
                                    [NEG  and then needs think
                                    e:i and then we also have to think
11           myös se̲   että siin  on  sit   ha̲udanhoidot ja
             also that  that there is then grave.care   and
             about tha̲t that there's then the question of
12           mu̲ut   tulee si̲t   kysymykseej jos_
             others come  then question-ILL if
             taking care of the grave and other stuff if_
```

The negative utterance here (lines 4, 6 and 8–9) is a generalization ("this kind of o̲ld person") with which the troubles recipient agrees with Saara's imagined caricature of the division of the inheritance that amounts to almost nothing. The sharedness of the generalization is strengthened by the clitic particle *-hän* (line 4 *sehän* "that", *eihän* "not y'know"; line 8 *siltähän* "from her"). The main speaker and troubles-teller, Saara, agrees with this by uttering the negative verb *ei* only (line 10).

As in the previous example, the *ei* speaker offers her response as sufficient to her co-participant's turn. In this case she shows that by moving on, without a prosodic break, to a continuation (*ja sitte* "and then") that adds another aspect to back up her position as an inheritor, and displays that talk about the overall topic has not yet been exhausted (cf. Jefferson 2002: 1355–1356 on a similar type of example in American English conversation).

With Extracts 1–3 we have shown some of the core contexts for the response built with a repetition of the negative auxiliary alone. This response, which expresses equal epistemic access and agreement, finds its home as a response to a negative utterance that conveys a stance, often a generalizing one. At a point at which that utterance is voiced, the participants have already established shared understanding and agreement on a point of view in the overall matter at hand. The *ei* response displays unconditional agreement with the prior turn and affiliation with the co-participant in the sense of feeling the same way.

Equivalent but separate epistemic access – agreeing with the facts but not necessarily with the action implications of the prior utterance

In some cases, the recipient may wish to modify the claim of equivalent epistemic access that the response expresses. One way of modifying the response is to imply that she had separate access to the state of affairs talked about and that she has separately formed the same understanding as the one the co-participant just expressed (cf. Heritage 2002a). This kind of modification is implied when the recipient uses a response type in which *ei* is followed by the adverb *niin* in the same prosodic unit (*ei nii(n)*). The implication is due to *niin*: it is an anaphoric adverb, meaning in some of its usages "in that way; so"; it is also used, for example, as a basic confirming response to a B-event statement.[4] B-event statements express information to which the recipient has privileged access. They stand in contrast to statements about A-events that contain information that the speaker of the utterance herself has privileged access to. (See Labov 1972: 301; Labov and Fanshel 1977: 100–101.)

In Extract 4, what follows is informative of the kind of claims recipients make with the *ei nii(n)* response. Here, the recipient moves, within the same turn, to explicate the basis for her agreement. The participants are

---

[4] The adverb *niin* is a derivative of the pronoun *se* ("it"): it is its plural form in the instrumental (instructive) case. It occurs also as part of the grammatically larger positive response type *nii(n) on* (lit. "so is") to assessments and stance taking (see Sorjonen and Hakulinen 2009). In its use as a response particle, the anaphoric meaning is still discernible (Sorjonen 2001: 281–282, 287).

moralizing about the recently held Eurovision song contest, and one part of the complaint is the participation of non-European countries in it. In the segment, H is establishing facts in favor of the complaint by listing countries that are not European but have participated in the contest. In line 17, C responds with *ei niin* and proceeds then into a continuation.

(4) (Hair salon)

```
1  H:     kyllä minun (.)  minun tuota: #ääö# (0.8) aikana
          PRT my        my    PRT              time-ESS
          sure in my (.) in my erm: #ee# (0.8) time

2         (1.0) <Venäjä>  (0.6) laskettiin   |Aasiaan\
                 Russia          counted-PAS Asia-ILL
          (1.0) <Russia> (0.6) was counted to |Asia\

3  C:     mm:.

4  H:     ei    se Euroopan valtio [ole et]tä silti se
          NEG it Europe's state  [is  PRT  yet  it
          it isn't a European state and yet it

5  C:                              [mm-m?]

6  H:     euroviisuihin    otta[a  |os]aa.
          eurovision-ILL  take[s     part
          takes part in Eurovision ((contest))

7  C:                         [ni(e)i.]
                              [no.   ]

8         (0.6)

9  H:     >ja    samoten niinko< Turkki?
          >and   similarly like<   Turkey?

10 C:     nii-i\
11        (0.4)

12 H:     ja   joskus    on  ollu ^Marokko\ (0.2)
          and  sometimes has been Morocco
          and sometimes there was Morocco (0.2)

13        joka  on  sitten taas\
          which is  then   again
          which is then again\

14        (0.2)

15 C:     joo-o;

16 H: →   ja   eihä       Israelika[a  oo.
          and  NEG-CLI    Israel-CLI   be
          neither is Israel.

17 C: ⇒                  [nii  ei   nii.  mää [aattelij
                         [PRT  NEG  ADV   I    [thought
                         nii ei nii. I was just

18 H:                                   [^mm:.
```

19 C: ⇒ ***just koko aja   et   eihä   ʃs [raelikaan oo.   ]***
            just all   time that NEG-CLI Israel-CLI   be   ]
            thinking all the time that Israel isn't either.

20 H: [*että   mi̱llä*]
                                     [so   what-ADE]
                                     so on what

21   *perust* [*eell*] *a nämä: sitte_ eihän   ne̱   oikei*
            ground-ADE these   then   NEG-CLI they quite
            grounds will these then_ so it isn't really

22 C: [*mm*]

23 H: *niinko* [*euroviisukisat   [ole*]*kkaan.*
        like   [Eurovision games [is-CLI
        kind of Eurovision contest after all.

24 C: [*.ei,*   [*ei.*]

25   (9.00) ((H doing C's hair; after that H changes the topic))

In the continuation, C expresses that what H said was something she
herself had been thinking about during the prior listing of the countries.
That is, she asserts that she was aware of the fact irrespective of the co-
participant having said it. However, as the elaboration refers to her cognitive processes (thinking) during the listing, the recipient can also be heard
as accounting for why she did not produce more elaborate responses earlier
(lines 11, 14). In overlap with C's elaboration, H proceeds (from line 20 on)
to explicate his stance with a turn that ends with a negative statement. The
recipient acknowledges the turn with two simple negative responses (line
24),[5] displaying unconditional agreement with the explication of the stance
to which the listing of the countries has led. These responses are treated as
sufficient by the participants who move to a new topic (line 25).

The separate basis for the agreement can in some cases be traced back
to the preceding talk, to the way in which the response and the preceding turns are connected to each other. This is what happens in Extract 5.
Here a group of youngsters are commenting on the physical appearance of
a female celebrity in a TV program they are watching. The *ei nii* response
in line 10 asserts agreement with the characterization in line 9 that the
celebrity is not slender (the core description is made with hand gestures).

(5)
1   PAVE: *(se o   kyl) aika   i̱so täti_*
                 she is PRT quite big aunt
                 (she sure is) quite a bi̱g lady_

---

[5] The first of them is produced in overlap just as the key element is due next. It is inhaled,
implying shared perspective (Hakulinen and Steensig in preparation). The second one is
said right after the key element.

2 MAKS: *nii   o_*
           PRT is

3 PAVE: *tosi pitkä   ja_*
           real tall   and_

4 AKU: *aika   niinku [tälleeki   iso_*
           quite   like   [this.way-also big_   ((spreads arms))

5 KEA: [*no   kyl   se   on   aika_*
                           [well surely she is   quite_

6   [<*rehevä,*> (#*sillee*#).
                    [<ample,> (like.that).

7 PAVE: [*painaaki   aika   paljo_*
           [weighs-CLI quite   much
           weighs a lot too_

8   (.)

9 AKU: → *nii   on ei   se >mikää   tälläne<_=* **Agreeing**
           PRT is   NEG she any   this.kind   **response to 5–6**
           so ((she))is **she is not >of this kind<=**
           ((depicts slender with his hands))

10 KEA: ⇒ =*ei nii_*   **Agreeing**
                                                response to 9

11 MAKS: *o^ho, (0.5) nyt   joutuu juomaa kaljaa_*
           oh,   (0.5) now one is bound   to drink beer_

The characterization in line 9 to which *ei nii* responds, however, is itself
a demonstration of an agreement with a characterization that the *ei niin*
speaker presented in lines 5 and 6 (*rehevä*, "ample"). *Ei nii*, specifically the
presence of *nii* in the response, subtly underscores the ties between these
turns. What is going on here is a competition over the appropriateness of the
descriptions and rights to characterize. While Aku alternates within the scale
of big and slender (lines 4 and 9), Kea's description is "ample" ("curvy").

In the examples discussed above, the recipient agreed with the co-
participant with a response type that expressed equal epistemic access and
equivalent stance to what was talked about, but simultaneously implied
the separateness of the stance. In both cases discussed, the response aligned
with the activity in progress (cf. Stivers 2008).

That is not always the case, however. The larger ongoing activity may
be such that the negative statement to be responded to by the recipient
allows different types of turns as its response. In these cases, the recipient
may use *ei niin* merely to display equivalent access to the state of affairs
referred to by the co-participant, without aligning with the action implications of the negative utterance.

This happens in Extract 6 in which the recipient responds with *ei niin* to
a factual statement by his co-participant. Four men are solving a problem

they were given in a socio-metric task. Ville Vainio (line 7) is a foreman in a factory where some drinking problems have been found. He has put up a note saying that whoever is found drunk at work will be dismissed immediately. He then finds Kivinen, his close workmate, drunk (cf. line 22). The participants have to decide what Ville Vainio should do. The *ei nii* response occurs in line 17.

(6)

```
1 UM:     juu    ni    se on (.) se on mestarille hh
          PRT  PRT   it is      it is  master-ALL
          yeah so it is (.) it is such a thing

2         semmone juttu että jos se  heittää siitä    nyt
          such       thing that if  he throws it-ELA now
          to the master that if he mentions

3         tätä juttua hh (.) noin        ohimennen vaan
          this story         like.that in.passing   only
          this thing about it hh (.) just in passing

4         ettei            sen enempää  välitä ni (.) .hh
          so.that-NEG  it   any.more cares   so
          without any further attention then (.) .hh

5         se on paha asia. =itte      ku se löi sen lapun
          it is  bad   thing himself as he hit the  scrap
          it is a bad thing.=it was he who put the note

6         sinne ja  itte     se laitto oman nimesä    alle
          there and himself he put    own  name-POS under
          there and he himself signed (it) with his name

7         että (.)  Ville Vainio työjohtaja.
          PRT    Name        foreman
          (.) Ville Vainio foreman.

8         (0.8)

9 NM:     nii:   ja  [se_
          PRT  and  [he_

10 UM:              [erottaa    heti.=
                    [dismisses at.once
                    will dismiss immediately.=

11 NM:    <erottaa  [nii>.
          dismisses [PRT
          <will dismiss yes>.

12 UM:              [mm (.) mut ei       siinä  kyllä
                    [PRT    but NEG there surely
                    mm. (.) but it definitely

13        lue   .hh mitää     että ir-
          read       anything that denounce
          doesn't say .hh anything like de-
```

14   *erotetaan ilman varotusta.*
            dismiss-PAS without warning.
            dismissed without warning.

15   (0.6)

16 UM: → **siinä lapussa   ei lukenu.**=
            the   scrap-INE NEG read
            in the note it did not say (('so')).=

17 NM: ⇒ *=ei_niihhh.hh*

18   (0.3)

19 NM: *mutta: (.) se on taas (.) > tietyst<*
            but   it is again   of.course
            but (.) it is on the other hand (.) >of course<

20   *että se on >tietysti jos< (.) jos tää ehh.hh*
            that it is of.course if   if   this
            that it is >of course if< (.) if this ehh .hh

21   *Kivinen mikä oli se ryyppäs jos (.) jos se o*
            Name   what was he drank   if   if   he is
            Kivinen who it was he boozed if (.) if he has been

22   *helveti hyvä ^työmies ollu nimittäi*
            hell's good worker   been PRT
            a hell of a ^worker see

23   *samallail että (.) siinä että:. mh*
            same.way that   there that
            in the same way so (.) there so:. mh

24   (0.3)

25 UM: *nii et   kuinka niitte töitten* [käy.
            PRT that how   those works [go
            so what will happen to the   assignments.

26 NM: [ja   jos se
                                                 [and if   he

27   *jos se tota: ah (.) jos se on ollu*
            if he PRT   if he has been
            if he erm: ah (.) if he has been

28   *siin   nokkamiehenä ---*
            there foreman-ESS
            there as a foreman ---

Just before the segment, UM has gone through what was stated in the note that the foreman put up and its implications for solving the problem. He ends up by stating the wording "will dismiss immediately" (line 10). He then moves to discuss the note from the point of view of what was *not* stated in it, thereby implying that the dismissing might not be his solution to the task (line 12). The *ei niin* in line 17 is given as a response to a pursuit of a response from the co-participants. What the negative statements (lines 13–17) make relevant is a response that either confirms or disconfirms the proposition (i.e. that the words "without warning" were not mentioned in the note). Simultaneously, they make relevant a display by the recipients of the implications that the negative utterance has for solving the problem.

The *ei nii* response in line 17 provides an agreement with the facts, that is, it confirms that there was no formulation like "without warning" in the note. That is all it does: it does not take up the implications of the negative statement for the task at hand. The separate and independent basis for the agreement implied by *ei niin* may convey that what UM said is self-evident and thus irrelevant. In this way it serves as a rejection of what the negative statement may have implied for solving the problem. A silence follows. By not taking a turn UM is heard to be orienting to the relevance of a continuation by NM. Instead, after the silence, NM brings up another aspect of the situation described in the task.

The equal epistemic access expressed through repeating the negative auxiliary is thus specified as separate and independent access and as a basis for agreement when the response is *ei niin*. This kind of basis for the stance may be specified by the recipient in the continuation of her turn or it can come up in the structure of the preceding talk and sequence. We have seen that the implication that the recipient had independently held the stance may function as a subtle device for competing over the rights to assess or provide characterizations (Extract 5). It can also be used to agree with the proposition expressed in the preceding negative statement while not aligning with its action implications in a sequential context in which the negative statement makes relevant more than an agreement or disagreement as its response (Extract 6).

Displaying resistance in disagreement-indicative contexts

In the previous section, we saw how the recipient may wish to show that she does not agree with the implications conveyed with the prior turn. Furthermore, a negative statement can perform an action which, for some reason, is problematic for the recipient. For example, in a context in which a negative statement can be heard as giving advice, the recipient may respond to it merely as a statement about the world, that is, taking up its epistemics and not orienting to the action the co-participant performed (on interactional delicacy of advice giving, an asymmetrical situation, see, for example, Heritage and Sefi 1992; Hutchby 1995). For doing that, the response types that contain a repetition of the negative auxiliary verb only or together with the adverb *nii(n)* (*ei* and *ei niin*) turn out not to be used. Instead, a more elaborate negative clause is used in these cases to suggest that the recipient does not go along with the interactional function of the prior turn. Variation in the elaborateness of the response has been shown to be relevant with respect to other types of actions, too. For example, Hakulinen (2001), working on Finnish, argued that a full-sentence answer to a *yes/no* question (repeating both the subject and the predicate of the question) may achieve additional goals: while offering an affirmative answer, it also – more or less discreetly – produces a repair of something in the question by changing some or several of the linguistic details in the description of the state of affairs that were presented in it. Raymond (2000), on the other hand, described clausal responses to *yes/no* questions as non-conforming in English, where a confirming response is provided with the response particle *yes* (or its variants).

A response type for implying disalignment is one in which the negative response contains not only a repetition of the negative auxiliary but also a repetition of the main verb (cf. Raevaara 2001).[6] We call responses of this type "elaborated repetitions." The following extract is from a phone call in which two friends are talking about possible fitness training for Sami. Veka offers him different ways of exercising. Sami has already rejected the idea of going to a fitness center because of its stuffiness, and he now claims that he would prefer walking (line 1). To this, Veka presents his advice 'just take up walking home' (line 3) by using a second person singular declarative, which treats the performance of the action as a future fact and unproblematic (cf. Sorjonen 2001: 108–111).

(7)
```
1  S:   |ky:l  mä mielummin kävelen  tua    ulkona.|
        PRT  I   rather    walk    there  outdoors
        |I really prefer walking outdoors.|
2       (1.2)
3  V:   kävelet    tota töide  jälkee himaan    aina.
        walk-2SG PRT works after  home-ILL always
        you just take up walking home after work every day.
4       (.)
5  V:   he heh [.hh
6  S:          [ju:st joo.
               [right yes.
```

[6] In the examples in this section, the main verb that gets repeated is the copula verb *olla* ("to be"). We have also cases with semantically fuller verbs. Raevaara (2001) studied such negative answers by patients to doctors' *yes/no* questions and compared them to negative answers given through the negative auxiliary only. She suggests that a mere negative auxiliary (*ei*) indexes that the answer is inferable from the prior talk, from the physical context or from the documents concerning the patient. In contrast, an answer that contains the negative auxiliary followed by a repetition of the main verb in the question provides new information.

7   (1.7)

8 V: *oot   sää kertaakaa kävelly sitä (.) matkaa_*
        have ou once-CLI walked that   distance
        have you walked that distance at all_

9 → *eihän   se nyt, (.) järjettömän   pitkä oo_*
       NEG-CLI it PRT   unreasonably long is
       it is not so, (.) awfully long_

10 S: ⇒ *e::i   oo, se on, (0.5) alta   kakstoist kilometrii.*
       NEG is it is   under twelve   kilometres
       e::i oo, it is, (0.5) less than twelve kilometres.

11 V: *°joo_°*

12 S: *.hhh to:ta se ov vaa se: että   ku sattuu*
               PRT it   is just that PRT as happen
        .hhh well it is just that

13   *noi   mun tyäajat   just sillee että*
        those my working.hours just so   that
        my working hours are such that

14   *ku mun   pitäs aina   kotii   tuada*
        as I-GEN should always home-ILL bring
        as I should always bring home

15   *joskus   ja välillä   jotai ruakaaki nii_ (1.2)*
        sometime and in.between some food-CLI so
        some food also sometimes and at times so_ (1.2)

16   *sen kantaminen on nii huanoo sitte ku*
        its carrying   is so bad   then when
        carrying it is so bad then when

17   *täytyy sielä päivällä   käydä töissä*
        must   there day-ADE go   job-INE
        ((one)) must go at daytime to job

18   *ettei   niinku: [iltasella   kerkee*
        that-NEG like   [evening-ADE have.time
        so that there is no time to do

19 V: [*nii:.*

20   *käymää kaupassa_*
        go   shop-INE
        shopping in the evening_

In lines 8–9 Veka pursues his line, at first posing a challenging question about whether Sami has even once tried walking home from work. He then motivates his question with a negative assessment by pointing out that the distance is "not so, (.) awfully long_". With this assessment, Sami does agree, but neither by offering the alternative *ei* that would express unconditional agreement, nor by the response *ei nii*, which would implicate that he had independently been thinking of the distance from the point of view of walking. Instead, he performs the agreement by repeating both the negative auxiliary and the main verb, *ei oo* ("(it) is not").

Instead of now taking up the challenge in the question, and seeing the turn as part of advice giving, in the next turn constructional unit (TCU) Sami moves to back up his agreement by specifying the distance (line 10). In this way, he treats Veka's prior turn as one about the distance between different places rather than part of finding a proper way to take exercise. The turn is responded to by Veka with a softly spoken *joo_* (line 11) which treats the prior turn as understood. By not continuing, he leaves the development of talk up to his co-participant.

In his next turn, Sami displays an orientation to the sequential relevance of and the challenge implied in V's prior turn (lines 12–18, 20). He gives a lengthy account of why he is going to reject the advice. The turn-initial phrase *se ov vaa se: että* ("it is just that") conveys an implication that he could otherwise think of walking home if there only wasn't the obligation to carry home heavy shopping. The kind of multi-unit response produced by the recipient is similar to a case discussed by Schegloff (1988a: 124–125). In that extract, students in a dormitory are talking when one of them (Carol, C) has just returned from a trip to get an ice cream sandwich; she did not bring it but rather only a drink.

(8) (Schegloff 1988a: 125)
```
155  S:    You didn' get an icecream sandwich,
156  C:    I kno:w, hh I decided that my body didn't need it,
157  S:    Yes but ours di:d=
158  S:    =hh heh heh heh [heh heh heh   [.hhih
159  ?                     [ehh  heh  heh [
```

In responding *I know* to Sherry's (S's) negatively formatted noticing *You didn' get an icecream sandwich*, Carol first orients to the noticing by agreeing with the state of affairs expressed by it. Then, in the next TCU, she orients to the action performed by the turn, a complaint, by giving an account of her own failure to do what was asked of her.

What we have argued in this section is that agreeing through repeating both the negative auxiliary and the main verb seems to be used as a resource for agreeing with the co-participant but simultaneously conveying that its producer does not share the line of action that the co-participant has taken. A more elaborate response type is formally more independent from the prior turn and might therefore be heard as a claim by the speaker to recast the action or idea offered by the co-participant (cf. Stivers 2005a).

Non-committal response: the positive response token

So far we have been discussing negative statements from the point of view of negatively formatted agreeing responses. In all the cases, a core element of the response is a repetition of the negative auxiliary in the co-participant's turn and in the response. Moreover, in all cases, the recipient asserts equivalent epistemic access to the state of affairs being talked about. However, the recipient may not be in a position to make that kind of assertion, or an assertion like that might be delicate. In such cases, the recipient may use a positive response – that is, a response type that is incongruent with the polarity of the preceding utterance (cf. Heinemann 2003: 64–69, 83–84, 2005; Jefferson 2002: 1362; Mazeland 1990). One such positive response type is *nii(n)*, which is a central means of claiming agreement with stance taking utterances that are grammatically positive (see Sorjonen 2001: 167–208, also 131–165; Sorjonen and Hakulinen 2009).

The lack of epistemic access may be explicated by the recipient after the *niin* response. This is what happens in Extract 9, in which the participants are discussing a rock festival that H just attended (*Ilosaarirokki* line 7). In line 8, C responds with *niin* to H's utterance that the band they have been discussing (called Ultra Bra) does not fit the type of festival it was. C then proceeds to provide a basis for his response – his lack of knowledge. Subsequently, however, he implies that he actually has a different stance from H.

(9) (Hair salon)

```
1  H:      °heh he°.hh° >siis   ku<°  ne   oli
                        PRT as       they was
           °heh he°.hh° >I'mean they were

2          nii  huvittav(h)i [a. hh heh_
           so  ridiculo(h)ous. hh heh_

3  C:                         [nii.

4  H:      sehän  niillehä         vaam puuattiin  sille     koko (.)
           it-CLI them-ALL-CLI just   boo-PAS the-ALL whole
           it- they were just booed at the whole (.)

5     →    [(orkeste]ri) Ultra Pr-et   ei    se oikeen tommose
           [(orchest]ra) Name    PRT NEG it quite  that.kind-ILL
           (band) Ultra Pr- so it isn't quite right in that kind

6  C:      [mm.  ]

7  H: →    Ilosaarirokkii.
           Name-ILL
           of Ilosaari-rock.

8  C: ⇒    nii.= en          tiiä.
           PRT NEG-1SG know
           nii.=I don't know.
```

9 H: ⇒ *sovi.*
       fit

10   (1.8)

11 C: *em   minäkkää   ymmärtäny Ultra Paata (.) Praata*
         NEG-1SG I-CLI   understand Name
         I too didn't understand Ultra Paa (.) Pra

12   *sillon ku   se oli   iha ạlussa   °mutta°* (0.6)
         then when it was just beginning-INE but
         when it was just in the beginning °but° (0.6)

13   *kỵl^lä |niillä   jọtaki iha   hyviä mẹlodioita*
         PRT   they-ADE some quite good melodies
         they do have some quite good melodies

14   *on että_*
         is PRT
         so_

The negative utterance may be located within a sequential context in which
any kind of negatively formatted response would come out as a delicate
action. The delicacy is due to the fact that all negative responses would, as
we have seen, claim equivalent epistemic access to what the speaker is talking
about. In Extract 10, the recipient responds with *nii* (line 16) to a negative
utterance which implies self-blame. This utterance is part of talk between
mother (Irja) and daughter (Sini). As the mother jokingly says that she can
again do her daughter's dishes, the daughter, after rejecting the plan, moves
to complain about the mess in her home. With the negative utterance, she
presents a general moral stance with respect to how women should live.

(10)

1 IRJA: *joo_=no   ^mä voin ilmestyä sinne sitte*
           PRT PRT I   can appear there then
           yeah_=well ^I show up there then

2   *jọhon [kin aikaan.*
           some   time
           at some point.

3 SINI: *[no ^ilmesty   ihmees[sä ni<*
               [PRT appear-IMP wonder-INE PRT
               do show by all means and<

4 IRJA: [*joo.*
                                      [yeah.

5 SINI: *kẹhitellään jotain [häppeninkiä.*
           develop   some   [happening
           let's put together some happening.

6 IRJA: [*^taas tị:skailen*
                         [again wash.dishes-1SG
                         I'll do the dishes

7   *siellä ja |sellasta.*
             there and such
             there and such things.

8 SINI: *£aijaijai mä vois(h)in k(h)yl t(h)i̲skata*
             PRT   I   could   PRT   wash.dishes
             £oh dear I c(h)ould s(h)urely d(h)o the dishes

9   *täs hö hö hö*
             here höh hö hö

10 IRJA: [he he he]
             [   ]

11 SINI: [*.hhh*   ] *itsekin   m(h)ul [on aika kauhee sotku.*
             [   ] self-CLI I-ADE [is quite awful   mess
             [.hhh   ] myself as well I   have quite an awful mess.

12 IRJA: [*nii.*

13 IRJA: *ai. [.joo_*
             oh. [.yeah_

14 SINI: [*tä   on h-   khy- siis tää o ihan hävytön*
                 [this is   indecent   PRT this is quite indecent
                 this is i- w'l- I'mean this is quite inde̲cent

15   → *niinku et   ei   na̲isihmisen   pitäis asuu tämmö*
                                                         [*ses .hh*
         like   PRT NEG woman.human-GEN should live this.
                                                         kind-INE
         like no woman should live in this kind .hh

16 IRJA: ⇒   [*nii.*

17 SINI: *mt ku mul   on noit le̲htii   niinku >joka puolel<*
              as I-ADE is those newspapers like   every side-ADE
             .mt as I have those ne̲wspapers like >everywhere<

18   *sit no tää nyt on tää< ng .h a̲lkovi on sit   niinku*
             then well this PRT is this   alcove is then like
             then well thi̲s is y'know this< ng .h a̲lcove is then

19   *iha: o(h)ma l(h)uokkan[sa=tänne ei   pidä*
             quite own   class-POS   here NEG must
             kind of whole: class of its own=one shouldn't

20 IRJA: [*nii joo.*

21 SINI: *k(h)atsoakaan ja .mhhh*
             look-CLI   and
             even look in here and .mhhh

Were Irja to respond with *ei*, she would claim equivalent epistemic access to what is being talked about and agree with the stance taken. With an *ei nii* response she would also agree with the stance but as one that she had already formed independently. However, being part of prior talk in which the co-participant has complained about her own situation, the negative utterance is heard to concern her personal situation. With *ei* or *ei nii*, the recipient would claim access to the co-participant's life, and agree with the negative statement. The response could then be heard as amounting to a piece of advice (cf. Jefferson and Lee 1992 [1981]). In this type of A-event activity, an elaborate repetition (*ei pitäs*) could even be heard as a reproach.

Considering that the negative statement expresses self-blame and self-criticism, a preferred response would be to reject the criticism (cf. Pomerantz 1984a). What *nii* does is to stand in between the negative agreeing responses and a rejection of the self-criticism. It accepts the stance expressed as valid – "one can think in that way", "one can have a stance like that". As compared to a clear rejection of the complaint (e.g. "it doesn't matter if there's a mess; every woman has a mess ~ has rights to a mess", etc.), *nii* leaves the implications of this non-rejecting response to be inferred and dealt with by the recipient.

Conclusion

We have analyzed a group of agreeing response types to negative utterances, and pointed out a number of interactionally relevant factors in the selection of the response. We have shown that the recipient, while on one level agreeing in the same terms with the other speaker, further contextualizes her agreement through selecting one of the alternatives. In all the cases in which the response contains a repetition of the negative auxiliary, the recipient asserts access to the knowledge at hand. They are different conventionalized means orienting to the prior negative utterance.

The alternative types of responses can be seen differing from each other in terms of whether the recipient is doing more than just agreeing. Through offering the negative word only as a response the recipient conveys that s/he unreservedly and completely shares the perspective of the co-participant. In that sense, we suggest, the recipient both aligns and affiliates with her co-participant– that is, she goes along with the activity in progress (alignment) and displays that she shares the perspective of the co-participant (affiliation) (cf. Stivers 2008). When the response contains more than the negative auxiliary, aligning with the co-participant becomes a more complex issue.

The baseline with the *ei niin* response is that the recipient agrees with the co-participant. However, that is not all. This response type implies that its speaker had separate epistemic access to the state of affairs and thus an independent basis for the stance expressed. Depending on the sequential context, this type of response functions as a more or less innocuous claim of rights to the assertion. But when the preceding turn makes relevant more than agreement, the use of *ei niin* does not necessarily mean that the recipient would align with her co-participant's turn in terms of its action implications. The elaborated repetition expresses agreement with the co-participant as well. Being formally more independent from the prior turn (both the negative auxiliary and the non-finite main verb are repeated), it is heard as a claim by the speaker to recast the action or the idea offered by the co-participant – it provides a disaligning response. What the comparison of the three response variants that contain the negative auxiliary shows is that epistemic access and alignment are graded phenomena. The gradualness is further shown by cases in which the response to the negative statement is grammatically affirmative.

Responding with any kind of negatively formatted response to a negative statement requires that the recipient has epistemic access to the state of affairs referred to by the co-participant. What we have suggested in looking at the different formats a negative response may take is that, by asserting epistemic access, the recipient does more than "just" that: in addition, she judges the sequential position in which the prior negative statement by her co-participant has placed her and, consequently, how a particular type of indication of epistemic access would contribute to the ongoing interaction. On the other hand, epistemic access seems to play a primary role in constructing responsive actions, evidenced by cases in which the action performed by the preceding negative utterance is other than mere stance taking.

11 Epistemics and embodiment in the interactions of very young children

Mardi Kidwell

Introduction

A most fundamental kind of knowing is that which is based on what someone sees or experiences. Direct perceptual access to an event informs our knowledge and understanding of something that has transpired, and both entitles and obligates us to act and to tell others about it in particular ways. As the chapters in this volume demonstrate, one of the most basic and pervasive features of language use has to do with how participants design and implement their talk by reference to their own entitlements to knowledge, and what they figure others' to be. In this chapter, I examine how children aged 14 to 30 months, who are in the early stages of language use, come to have a practiced grasp of how knowledge matters for the organization of interaction – in particular, for how their own and others' differential access to an event motivates and shapes the lines of action they take.

For very young children, an understanding of the relationship between what someone sees and what they know is considered a developmental milestone, one that indexes a major cognitive shift in the way we understand other persons as intentional agents. A long line of research in developmental and cognitive psychology has been concerned with children's abilities to assess another person's knowledge based on his or her perceptual access to an event. Controversies abound as to the age at which these abilities emerge and what they mean for children's early understandings of "others' minds" (Leslie 2000; Lewis and Osborne 1990; Mitchell and Lacohee 1991). For example, in the classic false belief task by Wimmer and Perner (1983), and in many follow-up studies (for a review, see Wellman, Cross and Wakson 2001), 4-year-olds, but not younger children, can predict that individuals will look for an object in the location where they previously saw someone

I would like to thank Tanya Stivers, Jack Sidnell, Lorenza Mondada and Jakob Steensig for their very helpful comments on earlier drafts of this chapter. I also benefited greatly from discussions I had with Kaoru Hayano and other participants in the "Knowledge, Responsibility, and Affiliation in Social Interaction" workshop held at the Max Planck Institute, The Netherlands, 2009. Thank you, too, to Don Zimmerman fer being available to discuss last-minute ideas.

place it, when in fact (and unbeknownst to them) the object was moved in their absence (i.e., they hold a "false belief"). However, when testing procedures are less language dependent, much younger children show that they have at least an initial grasp of the relationship between someone's seeing an event and their knowledge and understanding of it. For example, 2-year-olds have been found to adjust their requests to an adult for a desirable toy based on whether or not the adult was looking when it was put away on a high shelf (O'Neill 1996). Children aged 13 and 15 months, based on their longer looking times at unexpected events, demonstrate that they expect an agent to search for an object in the location where they last saw it placed – not unlike the older children of the Wimmer and Perner research (Onishi and Baillargeon 2005; Surian, Caldi and Speober 2007). At a still younger age, 12-month-old children have been shown to point more frequently to an interesting event when an adult is looking elsewhere (Liszkowski, Carpenter and Tomasello 2007).

Controversies about age aside, these studies in the psychological paradigm point up that some sort of awareness and appreciation of the relationship between what someone *sees* and what they *know* emerges fairly early in human ontology, a relationship that is usually expressed in terms of an understanding of others' mental states: their intentions, desires, feelings, beliefs, goals and so on. A question to consider, however, is: what does this matter for children in the course of their everyday, naturally occurring interactions with others? In other words, what do children understand not only about what others know, but about what others will *do*, based on their perceptual access to an event? I have shown in prior work, for example, that very young children monitor the attentional focus of their caregivers in subtle and complex ways to discern whether or not caregivers see their acts of misconduct, and may continue, cease or revise their activities in accord with their discernments (Kidwell 2005, 2009a; Kidwell and Zimmerman 2006). In situations of children showing and pointing to objects, which we have identified as early engage techniques, children pursue the gaze of an inattentive caregiver in an effort not only to gain recipiency, but also to get her to look, and therefore act, toward the object or person that is being brought to her attention (Jones and Zimmerman 2003; Kidwell and Zimmerman 2007; Lerner, Zimmerman and Kidwell in press). In these varied ways, children show an orientation to the import of where others are looking and what they see for the subsequent lines of action they will take, as well as a facility with being able to both avoid and draw a caregiver's attention to their activities to thwart or enable her probable next moves. Yet another question to consider is: how do children themselves come to grasp that their own access to events is monitorable by others, and counts significantly for what others will expect and require of them in interaction?

In proceeding, I examine how participants' differential involvements in, and perceptual access to, an event is interactionally occasioned and made relevant to participants – adults and children alike – through a sequentially ordered set of practices for orienting to, and inquiring about, events as emergent, temporally unfolding and accountably ordered phenomena. These events are "problem" events, situations of children's self-injury or harassment by a peer, as when one child bites another or takes away a toy. Caregivers' inquiries about these events expose their own access to what has transpired as partial and evolving, and engage children as agents with the authority to describe and explain them. Because these are children in the early stages of language use, a focus on their embodied actions, as these occur in a particular sequential and epistemic context, is especially relevant: this is related, on the one hand, to how children employ their embodied actions as communicative tools for responding to others, and, on the other, to their emerging orientations to how their bodies, as observable elements in an ongoing scheme of action, constitute a resource for inference and action by others. In what follows, I describe the sequential and epistemic organization of these interactions. I then examine children's embodied, vocal and early verbal joint-attentional actions as resources for responding to caregivers, particularly for how children who are "victims" in these situations are able to draw a caregiver's attention to relevant and actionable aspects of a problem scene. Finally, I discuss some of the ways that children who are "culprits" may attempt to avoid adult attention to their activities, namely by "fleeing the scene" and – when adult attention is unavoidable – by producing embodied and verbal actions that work to shape, or alter, an adult's sense of what previously transpired.

Data

The data for this chapter consist of twenty cases involving children aged 14 to 30 months taken from a larger corpus (500 hours) of naturally occurring video-taped interactions of very young children (aged 12 to 30 months)[1] in three different American daycare centers. The cases were chosen in three ways: (1) by watching a small number of tapes from the data set in natural time and capturing instances of problem inquiries (about 5 hours); (2) by randomly searching tapes for peer conflicts that might involve instances of problem inquiries; and (3) by doing a key word search of problem inquiry terms from the comment field of the database (e.g., "what happened?", "what's the problem?", etc.).

---

[1] Cases that were collected for this study include children starting at 14 months of age. While younger children might certainly be participants in the kinds of interactions examined here, cases involving these younger children have not yet been found.

A problem inquiry sequence

The sort of interactional exchange that is of interest in this chapter may be termed a "problem inquiry" sequence. When children in a daycare center cry, or exhibit some other manner of distress, caregivers typically seek to find out why. They may direct broad inquiries to the child, such as "what happened?", and/or offer candidate answer guesses like "did you get hurt?" or "did he take that from you?". Such actions by the adult are part of the institutionally and morally obligated work that they, as parties officially charged with looking after young children (as members simultaneously of the categories "adult" and "caregiver professional"), carry out to find a remedy for whatever pain, unhappiness or discomfort a child may be experiencing. Problem inquiry sequences certainly occur in everyday interaction, and, indeed, bear a close structural similarity to the troubles-telling sequences in conversation first noted by Jefferson (1988). However, these are particular sorts of interactional objects that might find their more natural home in the routine institutional work of some professionals, certainly teachers (Danby and Baker 1998), but also police (Kidwell 2009b), emergency dispatchers (Whalen and Zimmerman 1990; Zimmerman 1984) and others charged with finding remedies to problems. For example, police, upon arriving at the scene of a crime or accident, will ask "what happened?" as part of determining what sorts of services will be needed, including who will need help and who, possibly, will be apprehended as a "culprit" for some act of wrongdoing (Kidwell 2009b).

Problem inquiry sequences as they unfold in the daycare setting between caregiver and child may be glossed as follows:

1. *Problem Indication (child cries, loud noise, etc.)*
   1. CG inquiry ("what happened?", "did he take that from you?")
   2. Child action/response (continued crying, gestures, verbalizations, vocalizations, etc.)
2. *Remedy*

As a sequential matter, the problem inquiry is one that is responsive to a prior set of events (cf. Schegloff on *retro-sequences*, 2007a: especially p. 219, fn. 2). As an epistemic matter, these are events to which participants have differential access: something has transpired to result in a child's crying (or being upset, etc.), but the caregiver has not seen what, and she treats the child to whom she directs the inquiry as having this information. The inquiry is motivated by the project of finding a solution, a remedy, to a problem, which is undertaken as quite moral work having to do with shared orientations (i.e., by caregivers and children alike) to such normatively organized and enforceable matters as the standards of proper conduct between children in the daycare center (for example, that one should not bite, hit, push or take toys from others), and how infractions should be dealt with.

A central matter is how caregivers make inquiries of children and hold them accountable for *knowing*, and more-or-less being able to disclose, about the events that they see and experience, but that others do not. As Pomerantz (1980) has described, there is a certain range of matters that subject actors "*as subject actors*" have rights and obligations to know about, such as one's name, what one had for breakfast, and so on. "Why one is crying" is, arguably, one of the earliest sorts of circumstances in this domain that children are called upon to account for. But for children who are aged 14 to 30 months, language is not yet their primary mode of communication. So a question to consider is: do they understand what caregivers are asking them? And what sorts of resources, embodied and early verbal, might they draw upon to "answer?" As I demonstrate, "answering," or in these sequences, "informing," is a jointly produced, interactional endeavor, not unlike other sorts of question–answer sequences, but one that is pointed up as such due especially to the limited verbal abilities of children in this age range. But caregivers in these interactions are informed not only by the responsive actions of the children who are the targets of their inquiries. Caregivers are also informed by such accessible features of the scene as the activities of other children; the arrangement and deployment of objects; and, not insignificantly, their own commonsense understandings of how certain events typically motivate and precipitate other events in the daycare setting. Such features configure to enable caregivers to make inferences about what must have gone on before to result in a present trouble. As a second central matter, it is precisely this issue of inferring, and the gap between what caregivers see and what they surmise, that children can exploit. As I also show, children themselves are oriented to how caregivers consult a variety of embodied, vocal and material phenomena in discerning the root of a trouble, and what, as a result, they will undertake as a remedy. In particular, children who are in the close proximity of a crying child demonstrably orient to how they may be judged "culprits," and they may undertake, by "fleeing" and other actions, to preempt, or otherwise evade, a caregiver's sanctions.

Before turning to problem inquiry cases in which participants have differential access to the target event, it is worth examining another sort of case: one in which they have mutual access. This case exemplifies what might be termed a "problem remedy" sequence, within which can be embedded a problem inquiry sequence when the problem event is not fully accessible to the questioner. It is presented to underscore the moral character of finding and applying a remedy. In this case, the caregiver sees unfold before her

Figure 11.1

Figure 11.2

eyes a scenario of rather severe magnitude between two children; seeing the event in its entirety precludes the need for inquiry and the caregiver moves directly, urgently, to remedying. The children themselves anticipate her moves, and the "culprit" tries to flee the scene.

Problem remedy: a moral project

In Case 1, the caregiver is looking at two children, Marcus and Checco (aged 30 months), who are sitting on the back of a sofa. Marcus pushes Checco. The caregiver sees the trajectory of the fall to come, and quickly, urgently, reaches out an arm just before they fall (Figure 11.1).

The children tumble to the floor and the caregiver rushes to them. She picks up Checco, who is crying loudly, and wraps him in her arms in a full-on hug (Figure 11.2). Marcus tries to run away, but the caregiver (roughly) pulls him back toward her and reprimands him sternly (Figure 11.2).

As Figure 11.2 demonstrates, the caregiver's embodied actions partition the children as quite different sorts of moral actors entitled to different treatment: with her left arm hugging Checco to her, she treats him as a "victim," an injured party entitled to comforting; with the right, she treats Marcus as a wrongdoer, a "culprit," requiring sanction. As the caregiver pulls Marcus toward her, thwarting his attempt to flee, she directs her gaze at him and begins a reprimand. Checco cries throughout.

(1)(CASE 1 sofa push)
        ((initial lines deleted))
5   CG: I don't like tha:t. / *gazing at M*
6   (0.8)/ *CG shifts gaze to C*
7   CG: I want you to // look at Checco:, *shifts gaze back to M*
8   M: *nods head "yes"*
9   CG: That <u>hurt</u> (y' him). He [// came off of [here, *pats top of sofa*
10 M: [*M tries to run away*
11 CG: [*CG pulls him back*
        ((5 lines deleted))
17 M: (N') // s'pose to go up here. *pats sofa*
18 CG: You're not supposed to push.
19 M: Not s'pose to go up [here.
20 CG: [nuh– I don't like pushing.

At line 5, the caregiver addresses Marcus with a negative evaluation of the event that has transpired ("I don't like tha:t"), one that personalizes the evaluation and makes of it a disapproval. This is followed by utterances that direct him to inspect the other child (line 7), and to attend to him as a victim, as an injured party, as a result of his actions ("That <u>hurt</u> (y' him)…" line 9). Marcus provides a small head nod at line 8, but then he tries to flee again at line 10. Subsequent talk by Marcus at lines 17 and 19 resists the caregiver's focus on his having pushed Checco by invoking the prohibition about sitting on the back of the sofa ("(N') s'pose to go up here."). This is countered by the caregiver with prohibitions about pushing ("You're not supposed to push." line 18), and another disapproval ("I don't like pushing." line 20). Of note is that the caregiver's actions toward Marcus entail not only a reprimand, but, in attunement with early-childhood pedagogy (e.g. Gartrell 2004; Koza and Smith 2007), practices of intervening in and managing children's conflicts that seek to instruct and to invoke his empathy toward Checco. As part of the caregiver's effort at finding a remedy fitted to the actions of both children, this brings Marcus on board the project of finding a remedy for Checco.

In sum, the remedy is a morally differentiated response to the problem that the caregiver has witnessed unfold, and particularized with respect to the actions that she has seen each child, as "victim" and "culprit," respectively, engage in. Moreover, as discussed above, the caregiver's responses to the children are a matter that the children themselves are oriented to and can respond to in anticipatory ways, evidenced especially by the actions of Marcus who tries (unsuccessfully) to flee and thus evade the reprimand, but also by the actions of Checco, who remains where he is, and, in so doing, makes himself available for the caregiver's comfortings. The caregiver's moral project here is, on the one hand, one that exhibits a normative orientation to justice: wronged or injured parties are entitled to reparations, and wrongdoers should be held accountable for their misdeeds. On the other hand, the caregiver applies institutionally and culturally informed techniques for resolving troubles between children, and for "correcting" and guiding their behavior. In the cases to be examined next, in which the caregiver does not see or otherwise have access to the precipitating events that result in a child's crying, another significant moral project is evident as well, one that is integral to that of remedying: treating children as obligated to both know and inform others about their own behavior, particularly their crying.

Differential access as a moral matter

In Case 2, Reagan (26 months), who has been inadvertently knocked down by another child, has been crying and turning in search of a caregiver to help her. After several seconds (9 s), her actions draw responses from two caregivers who have just arrived on the scene, each carrying trays of food, and who each produce different parts of the problem inquiry sequence. CG 1 produces the initial inquiry, but CG 2 offers the remedy; CG 2 also produces a subsequent utterance that re-invokes the inquiry and treats a response by the child, and thus a proper identification of the trouble, as still due:

(2) (CASE 2 knocked down)

Reagan has been standing in the middle of the yard / play area crying and turning for 9 seconds

```
1 R:      %uhh [hhhhhhhhhhhh huh!–% = (abruptly stops crying)
2 CG1:         [What did we m–
3              (2.5) / =R begins walking toward CGs
4 CG1:    What did we mi : ss Reagan, [did you get hurt?
5 R:                                  [% (n) aehhhhhhhhhhh
6         Ehhhhhhh   ehHH  [HHHhhhhhhhhhh hh! %
7 CG2:                     [Can I give you a hug?
```

((3 lines deleted)) *CG2 pushes boys away who've gathered around*
11   (4.0) / *CG2 hugs R* ((looks like she is speaking to her but inaudible))
12 CG2: £ You wa(h)nna go eat? You sa(h)w the foo(h)d? £
13   (1.5)
14   You can tell me what happened when you (   ) sit down.

As can be seen, CG1's actions at lines 2 and 4 are a response to Reagan's crying (and in this case Reagan has been actively trying to recruit caregiver attention), and they seek to identify a precipitating event, a "cause." Starting with the inquiry term, "What" at line 4 (recycled from line 2), the caregiver begins an open-ended question; with "mi:ss" she narrows the parameters of answering to posing to the child the task of formulating an event that the caregiver herself (formulated as the joint "we") has not seen ("What did we mi:ss"). In this way, the caregiver makes the problem of differential access explicit, and asks the child to fill in those event elements that are available to the child but not the caregiver. The caregiver immediately follows the question with a candidate answer question that proposes as a cause a type of trouble: "did you get hurt?". The candidate reveals the caregiver's own range of knowledge of likely precipitating events, but the *yes/no* question format leaves the task of confirmation to the child (Pomerantz 1988; Sacks 1992).

Reagan's crying fails to provide an answer, but her actions are nonetheless responsive. Of note is that, once CG1 begins to address her, Reagan stops crying and approaches her, ready to be a recipient of the anticipated next actions (lines 1, 3). Approaching near completion of CG1's first question, however, she starts crying again. It is at this point that CG2 steps in to provide a remedy (line 7), one that was, of note, also used in Case 1: a hug. CG2 kneels down and enfolds Reagan in her arms, and Reagan stops crying. The remedy, at least for the child, seems to have been successful, but CG2 re-invokes the matter of cause again: "You can tell me what happened when you (   ) sit down." (line 14).

A cause-and-effect world

CG2's invitation to disclose ("You can tell me what happened..."), like CG1's inquiries, treats the child as having knowledge that the caregiver does not. It makes relevant that knowledge differential at the same time that, significantly, it provides a model of the world, and the child's own activities within it, in which events are accountably ordered: that is, if a child cries, there must be a reason, an event that has previously transpired, and children will not be easily let off the hook without providing what that reason is. Establishing a reason is integral to providing a satisfactory remedy, a remedy fitted to the problem. Indeed, a hug, as Cases 1 and 2 as well as other cases in the data set demonstrate, is a widely employed remedy to situations of children's crying (where it has been determined that a child has been injured, frightened or upset in some other way), but interestingly, although it may indeed treat the problem (i.e., get a child to stop crying), it is not typically given without due consideration and work by the caregiver to figure out what the precipitating event has been that has resulted in crying.[2] This is because as a remedy, a hug closes the inquiry sequence, and, as is being argued here, finding cause is its own moral project tied to an accountably ordered world – with persons who will reliably and consistently be called upon to account for problems and other untoward events – as well as to the project of finding a remedy that fits a particular trouble. Thus, CG2's actions in Case 2, although she has already provided a hug, are aimed at keeping the sequence open, and show the child that she will still be pressed to give an account.[3]

The next instance is presented as another case in point. Before a caregiver will provide a remedy and close the sequence, she goes some way toward finding a cause.

(3) (CASE 3 ball)

CG hears a loud thump and turns and looks in Andrew's direction. Andrew begins crying. ((Andrew is 18 months.))

```
 1  A:      % uh huh huh huh huh Eehhhhhhhhhhhh eh %
 2  CG:     What ^happened,
 3          ( .5 )
 4  A:      # a(h)! h! ba::=ou:::[: # ( ( A is off camera ) ); relevant body
            action can't be seen)
 5  CG:                          [ The ba:ll?
 6          ( .2 )
 7          ^What'd the ball do? = ( ( A comes into camera view ) )
 8  A:   →  = # ae(h) u # % Aehhhh hhhhhhh %
            ((2 lines deleted)) / A is crying
11  A:      % b (h)a:  :h[ll ehh % #
12  CG:                 [Yea:h, the ba::ll,
13  A:   →  % Aehhhh[hhhhhhhhhhhhhhh %
```

---

[2] In research reported on by Danby and Baker (1998) in slightly older children (3 and 4 years of age) in an Australian preschool center, caregivers typically did not pursue a thorough explication of cause. Caregiver inquiries targeted "culprit" children, rather than "victims," and were in this way focused on getting "culprits" to resolve the trouble with the other child. Thus, according to the authors, these interactions were heavily solution focused (p. 174).

[3] Of course, the caregiver, in continuing to keep the matter of cause open, shows concern, and attentiveness to the child's problem. This is a related dimension to these problem inquiry sequences, and goes beyond treating the child as accountable for disclosing the cause to treating the child as someone who has feelings, continuing to talk about which (through continuing to talk about "what happened") can alleviate distress.

```
14 CG:              [Did it knock you over?
15                  ( .2 ) / A shifts gaze to CG
16 A:               # Aehehheh hh # / rubs head, shifts gaze to middle distance
17 CG:              It hit your head,
18 A:               small head nod back, shifts gaze to CG in process
19 A:               # Ae[hh #
20 CG:                  [O::hhh,
21 A:                .u [h! .hh!
22 CG:                     [Are you okay?
23 A:               % aehhhhhhhhhhhh #hhh# =
24 CG: →            =Do you need a hug?
```

One might consider that in Case 3 a good place for a hug would be when Andrew, who has already been crying when the caregiver first begins her questioning at line 2 ("What ^happened,"), resumes crying at the first arrowed turn or the second arrowed turn (lines 8 and 13). However, the caregiver is pursuing a line of questioning, an investigation in fact, that keeps the sequence open until she has gotten Andrew to provide her with a sufficient degree of informing (to be discussed in more detail below) for her to be able to arrive at a conclusion, a cause. It is only then that she begins the work of administering the remedy – again, a hug (the third arrowed turn).

A canonical problem inquiry sequence

Case 3 can also be examined for the canonical structure of problem inquiry sequences, one in which the caregiver is successful in getting an informing from the child, an identification of a trouble, to which she provides a remedy. At line 2, the caregiver begins with the open-ended "What ^happened,", and, receiving an answer from Andrew (a proto word for "ball"), topicalizes the problem and narrows to "^What'd the ball do?" (line 7). Then, following from further actions of the child that again topicalize "ball," she produces a candidate, "Did it knock you over?" (line 14), and, still later, after Andrew's action of rubbing his head, she arrives at a conclusion: "It hit your head," (line 17). It is only after arriving at this conclusion, and subsequent actions by Andrew that she treats as confirming with the news receipt "O::hhh," (line 20 [Heritage 1984a]), that the caregiver offers Andrew a hug and other sorts of soothings (not shown) that effectively close the inquiry sequence (line 24).

To consider is that in Cases 2 and 3, the children were assessed by the caregiver as having been injured in some way (Case 2: "did you get hurt?"; Case 3: "Did it knock you over?"), and the apt remedy, a hug and other soothings, were provided (also in Case 1). Indeed, injury is often the first sort of candidate that the caregiver investigates: injuries may be self-caused (as in Case 3), or result through the actions (intentional or inadvertent) of another child, a "culprit," who bites, hits, pushes and/or takes things from others (as in Case 2, although this was never discovered by the caregiver). As we saw in Case 1, the caregiver's actions directed to a "culprit," a wrongdoer, can entail extensive moral, corrective work. Thus, in problem inquiry sequences, the caregiver, in inquiring about and assessing what the problem is for a crying child must also assess whether another child has been involved and in what capacity.

As the next case shows, assessing the role of a possible "culprit" is tied to moral notions of proper behavior in the daycare setting, which, as has already been discussed, is tied to the moral work of finding an apt remedy and the inquiries undertaken to find cause. Interestingly, caregivers' inquiries typically focus on two main sorts of circumstances as candidates for cause: children's crying because they have been injured (whether by their own doings or by the actions of another child), or because of a contestation over an object. In other words, in an environment in which caregivers only have partial access to a problem event, and one in which their main informant's communicative actions may be ambiguous, caregivers rely on typifications – their commonsense understandings of the sorts of events that are *likely* to precipitate other events in a particular context and setting – to discern cause.

Recurrent candidates for cause: injuries and object disputes

In Case 4, the caregiver is sitting on the floor as three children (aged 18 months) run in a circle around her. She hears a child behind her make a loud growl, and turns to look over her shoulder. She sees Brian with his mouth on Andrew's hand, and a glove between them (Figure 11.3).

Brian gets the glove free and continues running in a circle around the caregiver. The caregiver does not act immediately, and in this way she has not yet targeted or officially formulated the event as a problem; rather she treats it as a situation to be monitored, awaiting further developments. When Andrew begins to vocalize (something between a whine and a nascent cry), the caregiver takes action:

(4) (CASE 4 glove)

The caregiver hears a growl and turns to look; sees Brian's mouth on Andrew's hand and a glove between them.

1 A: ehUH [hhhhhhhhhhhhhhh / *rubbing his hands together, gazing at B*
2 CG: [Did he bite you?
3 A: UHhh– / *pulling back on finger, gazing at B*

Figure 11.3

4			(.9) / *CG is pulling A to her*
5	CG:	Huh? Did he get your finger?
6			(2.0) / *CG and A are now looking at A's hands*
7	CG:	// Or did he just take that from you. *shifts gaze to A's face*
8			(.2) / *A shifts gaze up to CG, then back down to hand*
9	CG:	What ^happened,
10			(1.5)
11	A:	#Aehhhhhhh# / *A takes finger and pulls back on it, shifts gaze to CG, holds for 0.7 s (i.e., for duration of vocalization)*
12			(.3) / *A pulls away from CG to chase after B*
13	CG:	Was it your turn?
			((4 lines deleted)) / *CG tells B to be "gentle" to another child*
18	CG:	As soon as you're done with that Andrew would like a turn.

The caregiver produces candidate answer questions over the course of lines 2, 5, 7, and 13: "Did he bite you?", "Did he get your finger?" and then "Or did he just take that from you."; and following an open-ended inquiry ("What ^happened,") she produces another candidate, "Was it your turn?". The questions, while assigning the task of answering to the child (as confirming or disconfirming), produce candidates that circumscribe the caregiver's understanding of what likely transpired (Pomerantz 1988). The questions are informed by what the caregiver initially saw as a partial rendering of prior events: Brian's mouth on Andrew's hand and a desired object (the glove) between them. The set of questions taken together proffer two main circumstances as culturally organized candidates for cause, injury and object contestation, circumstances that are likely given this setting, these participants, and what the caregiver has already seen. Once the caregiver discerns object contestation as the likely root of the trouble, she undertakes an apt remedy. Addressing Brian she says, "As soon as you're done with that Andrew would like a turn." How the caregiver arrives at this as the proper remedy derives from her readings of Andrew's actions (some designedly responsive, others not) over the course of her inquiries.

A child's responsiveness to the caregiver's inquiries

"Did he bite you?", a first guess at line 2, is produced when Andrew begins to cry and rub his hands together. Andrew does not respond; indeed he is looking at Brian who has conveniently positioned himself behind the caregiver, although he may rest his gaze on her briefly. The caregiver pursues an answer with a next question that narrows the scope of bite locations to "finger," which, in fact, Andrew has pulled back and seems to be focusing the rubbing on (line 3). By this point, the caregiver has pulled Andrew to her and the two are looking down at his hand (line 6). In this way, the two orient to the matter as unresolved – that is, that an answer is still pending. After a moment of looking, the caregiver shifts her gaze back up at Andrew's face and, still in pursuit of an answer (or action that might serve as an answer), offers another candidate, one that with "or" initiates an alternate possibility, and with "just", formulates it as less serious in relation to biting ("Or did he just take that from you." line 7). Andrew is responsive to the caregiver's gaze toward him in conjunction with the new question. He shifts his own gaze to the caregiver, but then back down to his finger (line 8). The caregiver, pursuing the possibility of lost recipiency, produces another question, one that ceases further guess attempts and turns over to the would-be answerer the job of answering with an open-ended question, "What ^happened,". Andrew, looking at his finger, pulls back on it; he makes a vocalization, "#Aehhhhhhh#", and shifts his gaze back to the caregiver, which, as will be discussed in more detail below, produces as an "answer," it seems, a joint attentional moment involving the finger (line 11).

Andrew's next actions, however, persuade the caregiver to stick with the last candidate proposal she has made. As Andrew and the caregiver engage in a moment of mutual gaze as he holds onto his finger, Brian runs past (he has resumed running in a circle around the caregiver, thinking he is being chased by the third child), and Andrew slips loose of the caregiver and chases after him (line 12). The caregiver takes this as further evidence in support of her last candidate guess, and makes a next, related one (i.e., related to object losses): "Was it your turn?" (line 13). That she arrives at this as an adequate solution to the inquiry, at least in so far as she can now go ahead and formulate a remedy, is evidenced in her subsequent action toward Brian: "As soon as you're done with that Andrew would like a turn." (line 18).

Joint attention: pointing and showing as resources for answering

One issue to consider here is, was Andrew really answering? He is certainly producing behaviors that the caregiver treats as informative, but how might he be producing them to conform with the caregiver's actions as seeking information about a prior event? Children by 18 months can typically use past tense expressions (Slobin 1971; Tomasello 2003), and before their second birthday they can produce narratives – the temporal linking of events they have seen or experienced – both as monologues (Nelson 1989) and in interaction with others (Antinucci and Miller 1975; Odregaard 2006). It is difficult to discern in the data for this study, however, whether children who are younger than 30 months are "telling about" past events per se in response to caregivers' problem inquiries.[4] In most of these data, children's problem inquiry responses have a certain here-and-now quality related to children's experiences of being distraught (this is what has brought the attention of the caregiver to them in the first place), and of being injured or wronged parties: for example, in conjunction with their crying, they may rub a hand that hurts because another child has bitten it, or they may point at an object another child has because they want it. These embodied and vocal actions are clearly directed to getting a remedy from the caregiver, and in this sense align not necessarily with her project of inquiring about past events, but certainly with her project of remedying a problem, their problem.

Communicative behaviors that begin to emerge at about 9 months of age, and that are well in place among children in the 14 to 30 months age range, are those having to do with their joint attentional abilities: that is, their abilities to share (initiate and follow into) attention with another toward a "third" object (Brown in press; Jones and Zimmerman 2003; Kidwell and Zimmerman 2007; Tomasello 1999, 2008). In other words, children can and do point, hold up objects for others' view, and look at things that others are looking at – actions that they may combine as well with vocal and early verbal behaviors that are designed to draw another's attention to an object and/or get them to act toward it in some way. Thus, as discussed above in Case 4, Andrew pulls back on his finger and shifts

---

[4] There is evidence that children do this at 30 months, as is demonstrated in Case 8. It is possible that younger children do this too, but no such cases were located in the data set.

(3) (CASE 3 ball)

```
13  A:     % Aehhhhh  [hhhhhhhhhhhhhh %
14  CG:               [Did it knock you over?
```

15	(.2) / *A shifts gaze to CG*
16 A:	# Aehehheh hh # / *rubs head, shifts gaze to middle distance*

Figure 11.4

```
17  CG:  It hit your head,
18  A:   small head nod back, shifts gaze to CG in process
19  A:   # Ae [ hh #
20  CG:       [ O : : hhh,
```

his gaze to the caregiver at the same time that he makes a vocalization. In this way, he produces the embodied action *for* the caregiver, a brief joint attentional moment focused on the finger, in the sequential place where an answer is due, before pulling away to run after Brian.

In other cases as well, children "answer" by bringing to the caregiver's attention an area of their body. Interestingly, they may do so in a way that resists the caregiver's candidate formulation of their trouble and offers their own "correct" version. Consider an excerpt from Case 3 again. In response to the caregiver's query, "Did it knock you over?" (line 14), Andrew shifts his gaze to her (line 15) and reaches up and rubs his head in conjunction with making a vocalization (line 16) (Figure 11.4).

As a receipt of Andrew's response, the caregiver produces a declarative formulation of the circumstance that Andrew has depicted for her with "It hit your head," (line 17). Interestingly, Andrew then makes something that looks rather like an affirmative head nod (which could be an affirmation or the result of his shifting his gaze back to CG), followed by a vocalization (lines 18, 19). The caregiver treats this as a confirmation of her prior formulation, and, with "O::hhh," receipts it as news, displaying a change in her knowledge state (line 20; Heritage 1984a).

Caregivers generally treat children's embodied joint attention actions as "answers" to their inquiries – that is, as versions of their troubles and within children's epistemic authority to depict (i.e., through embodied and vocal displays) and offer up for remedy. Sometimes, however, caregivers miss children's efforts at this, as we see in Case 5 (Figure 11.5).

The caregiver in this case formulates a candidate circumstance as a display of empathy: "I hope you didn't get your hand s- stuck in there again," (line 1), in reference to a gate. In fact, the child has been hit several times on the head with a toy lizard by the other child and poked in the

(5) (CASE 5 lizard)

Natalie (24 months) has hit Jessica (approximately 14 to 18 months)[5] multiple times on the head with a toy lizard.

J has been crying for some time
1 CG :   I hope you didn't get your hand s- stuck in there again,
           ((referring to gate))
2 J :   % Aehhhhhhh [Hahhhhhhhh   hahhhhhhhhhhhhhh %
3 CG :   [Did you see what happened? ((to bystander
                       child, "B")) / *reaches up to touch J's hand*
4 B :   [Hah?

5 J :   [*pulls hand away, with other hand reaches up and touches
           head*

Figure 11.5

6 CG :   (   ) / *continues addressing bystander child*

stomach (discussed below), which is caught in the camera view, but missed by the caregiver. When the caregiver reaches up to touch Jessica's hand (she is addressing a bystander child who is looking on with curiosity: line 3), Jessica pulls it away and with her other hand rubs her head (line 5). Her action is produced as an embodied "not x, but y" correction of the caregiver's candidate, but the caregiver does not see it.

Children can also use showing and pointing when asked to do so directly by the caregiver in the course of her inquiry work, as in Case 6 (Figure 11.6a).

As seen below, in response to the caregiver's "Can you show me?" and shoulder touch (line 3), Andrew looks down at his hand, turns his palm up, and raises it (line 5). Then he withdraws his hand (line 6) (Figure 11.6b).

The caregiver continues her inquiry (line 7), then directs Andrew to show her what the problem is (line 9). In response, Andrew points with his other hand to the right and makes a vocalization. Andrew's actions at lines 5 and 10 are of note in that he seems to be trying to provide the

---

[5] The exact age of this child is unknown.

(6) (CASE 6 shovel)

Sadie has just wrested a toy shovel from Andrew's hands (children are 18 months). He begins to cry loudly.

```
1  CG :  Andrew
2          ( 2.1 ) /    CG is walking toward A
3  CG :  Can you  // show m[e?    CG touches A on shoulder
4  A :              % .hhh  [ Uehhh [hhhhhhhhh %
```

Figure 11.6a

```
5  A :                              [looks down at hand, turns
           palm up and raises it
```

```
6  A :    withdraws hand
7  CG :   What's happened, ((CG is non-native
          speaker))
8         ( . 1 )
9         Can you show me?
10 A :    makes a jabbing point to his right
11        // Di : : h!              retracting his hand
```

Figure 11.6b

caregiver with two different "answers": the first having to do with his hand, and the second with something in the direction in which he is pointing. With regards to his hand, Andrew, as is the situation with the children in the prior cases, is bringing to the caregiver's attention a part of his body that is causing him pain (he has had a toy shovel wrested from his hand); in the cases above, children have (likely) been bitten, hit on the head with an object (whether by another child, or inadvertently through their own actions) and had things aggressively wrested from their hands. While there is a "here and now" quality to children's actions in that parts of their bodies hurt, their showing actions enable caregivers to come to conclusions about what happened before (as in Case 3: "It hit your head,"). With regard to pointing, children frequently point to things that they want, and in Case 6, Andrew wants a shovel that the other child, Sadie, has. Again, there is a "here and now" quality to Andrew's action of pointing; whether or not the caregiver understands that Sadie had previously wrested a desired shovel from him, it enables her to see that Andrew wants something at this moment. After determining that it is a shovel of Sadie's that Andrew is after, she undertakes a protracted effort to find him an alternate shovel, which, after more crying, he finally accepts. Remedies in contestations over objects involve caregivers' and children's orientations to the grounds that warrant object possession and use, as in "who had it first" in this case; or, as in Case 4 ("glove") above, who has had it long enough and might let another child have a turn.

In sum, the resources that children mobilize to respond to caregivers' problem inquiries draw on their basic joint attention abilities: they bring to caregivers' attention areas of their bodies that have been injured, and they point to objects that they desire. Critically, children's actions are produced in sequential environments that have been prepared for answers via caregivers' open-ended (e.g., "what happened?") and *yes/no* candidate answer questions: in other words, the question–answer adjacency pair provides for how caregivers will understand children's actions subsequent to their inquiries in the answer slot that questions set up. Further, children may also offer responses that resist caregivers' proposed versions of their troubles, and caregivers (when they see these versions; i.e., CG missed the child's version in Case 5) accept them, in this way orienting to children's authority to shape their (caregivers') understanding of events that they did not see or experience, but that children did.

Thus far, the analysis has focused on the actions of "victim" children: what they do in response to caregiver attention directed to them in problem inquiry sequences. Indeed, in most of the cases, caregiver action is directed to the child who is crying or otherwise making a fuss. But, as discussed at the outset, these sequences are of import for children who may be judged "culprits" as well. Like "victims," "culprits" anticipate, and act by reference to, caregiver action. Further, just as child "victims" can make a version of events visible to a caregiver through embodied actions involving showing and pointing (i.e., in response to caregiver inquiries), "culprits" can engage in actions to conceal versions from her, and/or produce alternate versions, to help them evade reprimand. These efforts by "victim" and "culprit" children alike require a sensibility to how their actions are available and observable to others, at what point in an unfolding sequence of action this matters, and an ability to both draw and avoid others' attention to selective aspects of their actions. In the next section, how "culprits" may go about trying to evade a sanction – and the embodied resources they employ – is examined.

Fleeing the scene

As Case 1 pointed up, children who have caused injury to other children may run away, "flee the scene," to evade a caregiver's reprimand. Something of note in these data is that children undertake their departures rather differently, contingent on whether or not the caregiver sees them. In cases in which the caregiver does *not* see the injurious act to the other child, but may turn her attention to the situation and launch a problem inquiry, children's actions have a distinctly covert quality: that is, these children do not just leave, but do so in a way that minimizes – works to keep out of sight – the fact that they are fleeing.[6] The event that motivates their acts of departure is the crying of the other child.

Consider Case 7 ("lizard") (presented as Case 5 above; discussed in Kidwell and Zimmerman 2006).

Case 7 lizard

Natalie (24 months) hits Jessica (approximately 14 to 18 months) several times on the head with a toy lizard, and then pokes her in the stomach (Figure 11.7a).

Jessica begins to cry loudly. When this occurs, Natalie abruptly withdraws the object as she looks out in the yard in the direction of the caregiver (in this segment and earlier in the encounter it is evident that N is monitoring the CG's attention toward her). Then, holding the object close to her, and still looking, she walks away from the crying child (Figure 11.7b).

Several feet away, Natalie begins to hit a tree with the toy lizard. Thus, she redeploys the object in a new, innocuous and thereby unincriminating line of activity and, moreover, at some distance from Jessica. In this way, Natalie treats Jessica's actions, her crying, as inevitably drawing the caregiver to the scene (which it does), and her proximity to the crying child, and a particular arrangement of objects (her hand, the toy lizard in it) in relation to the child, as implicating her in the activity that has instigated Jessica's crying. In concealing the object, putting distance between herself and the other child, and then redeploying the object in a new activity, Natalie prepares for a somewhat different contingency from that of the caregiver *actually* seeing her strike the other child: she prepares for the contingency that the caregiver – having not actually witnessed these events – will nonetheless draw a link between her and these various "evidences" (the crying child, Natalie's proximity to her, and the object in her hand) to

---

[6] Unfortunately, frame grabs of children fleeing in these circumstances (i.e., the caregiver has or has not seen their acts of misconduct) do not convey very well the differences in their fleeing. The video version of their activities must be consulted to discern this.

Figure 11.7a

Figure 11.7b

infer something about what has transpired previously, and she manages her actions to thwart this inference. Indeed, a few moments later the caregiver arrives on the scene to attend to Jessica, saying (as we saw above):

CG: I hope you didn't get your hand s- stuck in there again, ((referring to gate))

The caregiver's candidate formulation of the circumstance that has led to Jessica's crying is, as we have already seen, wrong. As discussed earlier, Jessica tries to resist the caregiver's version and offer an alternative version by withdrawing her hand and rubbing her head. However, the caregiver, who is continuing the problem inquiry with another child ("Did you see what happened?"), fails to notice.

As discussed previously, there is a gap between what caregivers perceive and what they surmise in these scenarios, which children can exploit. The caregiver hears Jessica crying, and sees her standing next to a gate. Her use of the word "again" formulates that there has been a prior occasion of Jessica getting her hand stuck in it. But the caregiver did not see the multiple times that the other child, Natalie, hit Jessica on the head and then poked her in the stomach. Thus, Natalie, via her orientations to what the caregiver will make of her standing next to the crying child with object in hand, and especially her ability to manage her embodied conduct to escape this association, evades a sanction.

Fleeing and concealing objects can certainly result in such advantages for a child as evading reprimand and other corrective actions by the caregiver, as in Case 7, while remaining at the scene may prove to be less advantageous: in other words, the caregiver may be able to draw a link between the child and a problem event, as is demonstrated in the following case.

Case 8 ball throw

In this case, Leslie (30 months of age) takes aim and throws a ball forcefully at Brianna (18 months of age) at close range. When the child begins to cry, Leslie moves quickly to kiss her, a move designed not only as a remedy for Brianna, but for the possible scrutiny of the caregiver as well: after each kiss, Leslie looks out in the yard in the direction of the caregiver. Leslie's body posture suggests tension and an effort at covertness in a variety of ways when she moves in for the kisses: she hunches over and pulls her hands up close to her body as if she would like to minimize her appearance to the caregiver. Kissing Brianna does not stop the crying, and Leslie, rather than depart after the second kiss, presses herself against the wall and looks out in the yard in the direction of the caregiver. The caregiver, with this view of Leslie standing next to the crying Brianna, calls out to her:

1 CG: Leslie, <u>wh</u>at'd you do::,

While still gazing at the caregiver, Leslie produces a number of "uneasy" body behaviors:

2   9.5 /L *"fidgets": raises her arms up, then down; touches her mouth; grins; touches her foot; looks down, then looks out toward CG* (Figure 11.8)

The caregiver continues her inquiries:

3 CG: Brianna are you ^okay,
4 B: *crying loudly walks toward CG*
         ((21 seconds later)) / *B walks to CG; L walks to CG* ((CG produces some talk that is unintelligible, perhaps to B and/or other nearby children))

Figure 11.8

5 CG: >Leslie what ^happened,
6 L: I threw the ba=|all.
7 CG: You threw the ball?=
8 L: =Yea:h
9 CG: Did it scare her?
10 L: °(n)yeah°
11 CG: Why is she ^crying,
12 L: She wants to (work/walk) with (Marmet/Momet). ((mumbled))
13 CG: *smiles* ((tries to suppress; seems to be amused at the
account/lie that L offers))
14 CG: O:kay. I want you to be careful? because they're younger than you are?

The caregiver's first inquiry to Leslie ("Leslie, what'd you do::," line 1) targets her as an instigator of a misdeed. The question presupposes a prior action by Leslie, and, as with other sorts of problem inquiry questions (e.g., "what happened?"), it is occasioned by the questioner's access to some later event, in this case – as in others previously discussed – hearing a child's cry. The caregiver looks in the direction of the crying child and sees Leslie standing next to Brianna and, further, looking at her (i.e., the caregiver); she makes an inquiry that connects Leslie to the problem event – indeed, one that implicates her as the cause of the problem. In the sequential place that has been prepared for an answer, Leslie, as described above (line 2 and Figure 11.8), produces a number of embodied behaviors that are best described as "fidgety": she raises her arms up and down; touches her mouth; grins; touches her foot; looks away from the caregiver then back in her direction. Following these "non-answer" but reactive behaviors,[7] the caregiver, after

[7] The term "reactive" is used here to get at the more or less uncontrollable aspect of Leslie's behaviors that, while not "responsive" in the sense that they are produced in some way for uptake and action by the caregiver, are nonetheless occasioned by the caregiver's question to her.

several seconds (that include checking on B, and B and L walking to her; lines 3 and 4), continues her inquiries with another problem inquiry question, the canonical "what ^happened," (line 5).

The question does not specify that Leslie has been an instigator of the problem event, but certainly targets her as having had access to it. Of course, with the capacity to talk, Leslie is able to provide a verbal action as an answer (although she might have provided an embodied action). The answer, "I threw the ba=|all.", while accurate and grammatically fitted to the prior question, fails as an acceptable logic. Specifically, the question fails to connect adequately with the matter that has occasioned the caregiver's question in the first place, the other child's crying. The caregiver pursues this dimension with questions that seek to connect how Leslie's throwing the ball might plausibly relate to that situation. She continues with "Did it scare her?" and "Why is she ^crying," (lines 9 and 11). It is difficult to fully comprehend what Leslie's answer (line 12) to this last question is about, but the "She wants to" part that is intelligible clearly retains the "She", and thus the focus on the other child, that is topicalized in the prior question (i.e., "Why is she ^crying,"), and provides a diversion from further accounting about the matter of the ball. The caregiver's smile, which appears partially suppressed, indicates amusement at the answer, as if it were a clever lie. While the caregiver here appears to have suspicions that something more has transpired than Leslie is letting on about, grounded no doubt in her initial access to Leslie's proximity to Brianna and her uneasy manner, Leslie's presumed fuller access to, and involvement in, prior events authorizes her account, and the caregiver ultimately lets it stand. Thus, Leslie, while given a light reprimand that formulates her behavior as unintentional ("I want you to be careful..." line 14), escapes being held fully accountable for her quite intentional (and mean) actions toward the other child.

As the cases in this section demonstrate, children's success at evading reprimand can involve the ability not only to disassociate themselves physically from a problem scene by fleeing and concealing objects, but also, in situations in which children remain at the scene (or are otherwise unable to accomplish fleeing unnoticed), to produce alternative depictions of a prior event using embodied as well as verbal means in a way that minimizes their culpability (and not altogether unlike practices that suspects who are being questioned by police employ [Kidwell 2009]).

Conclusion

It was discussed at the outset of this chapter that children's understanding of what someone sees and what they know emerges early in human ontology. As very young children go about the course of their everyday activities, one sort of recurrent situation that arguably strengthens their grasp of this fundamental epistemic principle as an interactional matter is caregivers' inquiries into their troubles. These inquiries expose a questioner's own incomplete access to an event (and thus their incomplete knowledge and understanding of it), while making relevant, and accountable, children's access. The moral dimensions of these inquiries can be considered in several ways.

First, children, when queried by their caregivers, are treated as entitled and obligated to know and tell about that domain of matters that all of us are most epistemically responsible for: what, as subject-actors, we have seen and experienced. As has been demonstrated in this chapter, children in the early stages of language use mobilize actions that are answers-of-sorts, and are treated as such by caregivers via the interpretive constraints set up by the question–answer adjacency pair. These actions include instances of showing and pointing, basic joint attentional resources that, in conjunction with vocal and early verbal conduct, serve to bring to the caregiver's attention selective aspects of a scene: for example, injured heads and hands, and objects that children desire (a glove, a toy shovel, etc.).

As a second, related point, driving caregivers' inquiries is an orientation to events as temporally unfolding and accountably ordered phenomena – in other words, as phenomena that have beginning and end points that are differentially available to child and caregiver. In this way, their differential access to an event is specifically time-ordered: caregivers hear children cry (or hear a loud noise), the end point of some series of prior events that children have been involved in that have, presumably, motivated in some way the crying – which, notably, caregivers orient to in distinctly typified ways (i.e., as resulting from injury or object contestations). At issue with respect to these first and second points is an epistemic morality that not only presses participants to account for what they have seen or experienced and that others have not, but also is one based on an orientation to the world and its happenings as coming about through "cause" (Garfinkel 1967). Problem inquiry sequences also provide children experience with a practical logic having to do with an accountably ordered social world – that is, one in which some events motivate and precipitate other events. But how do participants figure out what these events are, particularly when they have not seen or otherwise had access to them?

As a third point, children learn that, in so far as caregiver inquiries are based on incomplete access to an unfolding event scenario, there must be inferential procedures that operate in the absence of complete access. Children show an ability to affect this inferential process, to "fill in": not only "victim" children via the responses they make to caregiver inquiries, but also "culprit" children who may flee the scene, conceal incriminating objects and, in the last case we saw, verbalize evasive, even misleading, answers to thwart a caregiver's sanction. While the inherently and fundamentally inferential nature of communication may, as of yet, be lost on children in this age group, these scenarios certainly provide children with experience with others' ways of reasoning, and with the variety of resources that participants draw upon to formulate hypotheses about past events (Sacks 1985). As such, these scenarios also provide children experience with the occasioned, emergent and sometimes malleable character of knowledge as they find success at drawing a caregiver to intervene, or, alternatively, evading an intervention.

As a fourth and final point, the epistemic order that is at issue here cannot be separated out from the practical tasks that constitute it and give it its particular form: it is one that, as it takes shape via problem inquiry sequences, organizes not only participants' rights and responsibilities to ask and to answer, but a moral order having to do with proper conduct – that is, with "good" and "bad" behavior in the daycare setting. In so far as caregivers' inquiries are directed to the project of finding a remedy for a trouble, they partition children as particular sorts of moral actors who are entitled to and warrant different treatments. Caregivers' inquiries point up their efforts to be "fair" in accord with broad, normative orientations to justice, and also in accord with the specific daycare culture in which they work and the pedagogical practices that inform their professional culture. At the very least, "victims" are entitled to comfortings (hugs) if they are injured, and/ or efforts to get desired (and unjustly withheld) objects for them; "culprits" warrant sanctions and efforts to guide them toward proper conduct toward their peers. The sequential trajectories of caregivers' inquiries, actual or would-be upon hearing a child cry, can be anticipated by children, and they enable children to act in ways to draw or avoid adult attention, and, consequentially, what might be considered their "due." At issue ultimately, then, is an epistemics that is rooted in the observability of action. This is action that is available to others sometimes partially and sometimes fully, and that motivates all of us at times (as children have come to exhibit a fair degree of skill with) either to make our conduct a focus of others' attention, or to revise it and/or keep it from others' view—especially in light of the troubles, and thus problems for us, that such conduct may sometimes pose.

Part IV

Toward a framework

12   Sources of asymmetry in human interaction: enchrony, status, knowledge and agency

N. J. Enfield

As conversation analysis forges new directions, it also faces significant challenges in a world of developing research, and shifting research interests. My purpose in this chapter is to address one of these challenges: to define more explicitly the elements of a framework that will license and constrain the observed structures of social interaction, and in turn their proper analysis. Part of the goal is to offer an account of human interaction that is general enough to address broader, interdisciplinary questions of the study of human behavior.

I aim to explicate a theoretical foundation for understanding the kinds of phenomena dealt with in the above chapters – that is, the negotiation of knowledge, responsibility and affiliation in interaction – building on four related concepts: enchrony, status, knowledge and agency. Each builds from the next, where enchrony entails accountability, status relativizes it, knowledge grounds it, and agency distributes it. Each is a source of asymmetry, and each thereby plays a role in defining a possibility space in the morality of knowledge in communication. The four concepts are well established in existing literature, although they may be known by other names, and may not have been brought together in quite the same way as here.

Enchrony

Our first element is a primal driving force for the ever-forward progression of social interaction, a force from which we derive *sequence* (Schegloff 2007b), from its simplest to its most complex manifestations.

With admiration for true primary authority on the topic at hand, this chapter is dedicated to Paul Drew or John Heritage. Very many thanks to Tanya Stivers for urging me to write this chapter, for extensive discussion of the contents, and for supplying me with data. Any errors of fact or interpretation are entirely due to her. For comments on earlier versions of the text, I thank John Heritage, Kobin Kendrick, Lorenza Mondada, Lila San Roque, Jack Sidnell and Tanya Stivers. I also thank participants at a presentation of these ideas at MPI Nijmegen in Spring 2009 for their feedback. This work was carried out within the Multimodal Interaction Project in the Language and Cognition Group at the Max Planck Institute for Psycholinguistics, and was funded by the Max Planck Society and the European Research Council.

Because human interaction is a form of animal communication, we may start with the simple observation that communicative interaction involves formally ritualized patterns of behavior, which bring about relatively predictable effects on others in the social realm (Krebs and Dawkins 1984). This conception of social interaction entails a dynamic relation between a communicative action and the response it elicits. And, in turn, such a reaction may in itself be a communicative action, engendering, in response, a further communicative action (see below). Moreover, any sequence "communicative action and subsequent response" is a unit, not a conjunct. The sequence cannot be derived from independently established concepts "communicative action" and "response." This is because neither may be defined without the other. The *relation* between communicative action and response is critical to defining them both. We may speak of a communicative action in isolation only if we bracket out the notion of response (and vice versa), because in fact a communicative action can only be known to be a communicative action insofar as it is known to elicit a relatively predictable or motivated response.[1]

"Response" here is not the highly constrained notion captured by "answer" (e.g., to a question). It has a more general sense, i.e., that which follows and is occasioned by, and relevant to, something prior. Consider the B lines in the following service encounters (examples from Merritt [1976: 325, 333 and 331, respectively]):

(1)
A: Do you have coffee to go?
B: Cream and sugar? *starts to pour coffee*

A: What'll ya have girls?
B: What's the soup of the day?

A: Do you sell key chains?
B: What?

The B turns do not directly address the ostensive content of the questions that precede them, though each is a response in the sense intended here. In different ways, each is directly relevant to, and occasioned by, what came just before it.

---

[1] Human communicative actions do not merely cause their responses to occur as heat causes ice to melt. This is because responses are oriented not only to the perceptible signs out of which communicative actions are formed, but also to what those communicative actions *mean* or "stand for" (Kockelman 2005; Peirce 1955). A response to some physical event like an action is what Peirce called an *interpretant*. An interpretant makes sense in terms of the sign's *object*, i.e., what the sign stands for.

Once our concept of communication incorporates this fundamental dynamic semiotic process – sign[2] and response – notice what results when we see that the response is typically also a communicative action itself. Each communicative action simultaneously occupies a backward-looking status as "that which responds to what just happened" and a forward-looking status as "that which elicits a response next." Responses to communicative actions are new communicative actions, and they engender new responses, in turn. I refer to the local relation between a sign and its response as *relevance* (cf. Sperber and Wilson 1995). Because a response may be a sign in itself, which may beget a new response, we can derive a potentially unbounded sequence of such pivoting sign–response relations. I refer to this forward-feeding temporal, causal-conditional trajectory of relevance relations as *enchrony* (Enfield 2009: 10).

Why introduce a new term if we already have adequate analytic concepts and terms such as sequence, adjacency, nextness, contiguity and progressivity (Schegloff 2007b: 14)? A first reason is that each of these existing terms denotes something narrower than what I want to denote by the term "enchrony." Enchrony does not replace those terms or concepts. It refers to a more general force that underlies their emergence. A second reason for the term is to draw attention to this family of notions under a single rubric, and to place the rubric within a broader, interdisciplinary set of alternative perspectives for the analysis of human communication. An enchronic perspective on human communication focuses on sequences of interlocking or interdependent communicative moves that are taken to be co-relevant, and causally-conditionally related. Enchrony is a level of temporal-causal grain (typically, "conversational time") that an analyst of communication can adopt, as distinct from other possible perspectives, fitted to other purposes, that focus on other temporal scales and other kinds of causal-conditional process; these include phylogenetic, diachronic, ontogenetic, epigenetic and synchronic perspectives.

An enchronic perspective is grounded in trajectories of co-relevant actions, a phenomenon observed by scholars of social action from Schütz

---

[2] For convenience, I shall sometimes use the word "sign" to refer to a communicative action, though the terms "sign" and "action" are not synonymous. While all communicative actions are built out of signs, not all signs are communicative actions. Like other students of social interaction, I am interested in how communicative actions can be recognized by those who perceive them, and in turn how these actions should therefore be formulated (by those who produce them) in order to secure this recognition. The only kind of theory that can account for how social actions are recognized is a semiotic theory (e.g., Kockelman 2005, 2006b) – that is, a theory that defines the means by which people can use perceptions of their environment as cues for making inferences to what is not directly observable (e.g., others' apparent motivations and goals).

and Mead to Goffman and Garfinkel, to Sacks, Schegloff and Jefferson, to Heritage, Drew and many others since. A communicative action or move (Goffman 1981) has what Schütz (1970) referred to as "because motives" (what gave rise to the move, what occasioned it) and "in-order-to motives" (the goals of the move, what it hopes to bring about): I'm pouring a drink because I'm thirsty, and in order to drink it. The move is a step in a sequence of events where each such step interlocks relevantly and coherently both with something that just happened (or that otherwise already applied in the context of the move) and with something that happens next. This Peircean conception of meaning as inherently dynamic is distinctly unlike the static Saussurean version (Enfield 2009; Kockelman 2005), and it is the one that is best understood by analysts of tape-recorded sequences of human interaction since the likes of Sacks (e.g., 1992: I, 3–11) and Schegloff (e.g., 1968).

Communicative actions in enchronic sequences are hooked together in a special way. They do not randomly follow one another. As both analysts and participants, we incorrigibly take enchrony to be operative, and we go to great lengths to interpret actions as connected by relevance, even when there is no such relation. As Garfinkel advises, people will always understand your actions, just not always in the way you intended. A vivid demonstration comes from a 1960s experiment conducted in the Department of Psychiatry at UCLA (Garfinkel 1967: ch. 3). Subjects were asked to take part in a new form of therapy where they would pose their problems as a series of questions, to which the counselor's answers could only be "yes" or "no." Unbeknownst to subjects, the series of "yes" and "no" responses that they received from their unseen "counselor" were randomly predetermined. Whether an answer was "yes" or "no" had no relation to the question being posed. Yet all the subjects *perceived* the responses "as answers to their questions" (Garfinkel 1967: 89). I cannot do justice here to Garfinkel's rich discussion of the findings regarding this notion of an incorrigible projection of relevance (see his pp. 89–94), but I simply note here the tremendous strength of an enchronic stance adopted in everyday life. It shows up, for instance, in globally attested practices of divination, in which essentially random events – such as whether a ritual spider walks to the left or to the right when released from its lair – are interpreted as properly responsive to questions posed (Goody 1995; Lévi-Strauss 1966; Zeitlyn 1995).

This glue or hook between adjacent moves can be characterized as a pair of arrows, one pointing forward from A to B, one back from B to A (Figure 12.1). These are the two faces of relevance: effectiveness and appropriateness. The forward-pointing arrow represents the effectiveness of A, that is, the sense in which the sign A gives rise to B as an interpretant or relevant

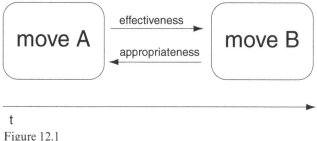

t

Figure 12.1

response. The backward-pointing arrow represents the appropriateness of B, that is, the sense in which B is "fitting" as a next action from A.[3] Now, the following point is critical to the rest of this chapter's argument: *effectiveness and appropriateness are normative notions.* Our attention is only drawn to them when there are violations. The more likely B is to elicit *surprise* or *sanction*,[4] the less appropriate it is to A, and the less effective A has been in eliciting a response.

Here is an example from Schegloff (1992: 1310):

(2)
1 ROG: It's always this uhm image of who I am
2   'n what I want people to think I am.
3   (0.2)
4 DAN: And somehow it's unrelated to what's going on
5   at the moment?
6 ROG: Yeah. But t(h)ell me is everybody like that or
7   am I just out of [it.
8 KEN: [I- Not to change the subject

---

[3] There is a second-order sense in which the arrows can go in the other direction. As John Heritage points out (pers. comm.), a responsive move can have an effect upon the *prior* move by "retrospectively" determining which action the prior move is performing. Note, however, that it does this by exploiting the backward-looking relation of appropriateness: if turn 1 is ambiguous between meanings X and Y (say, an observation versus a complaint e.g., *The trash hasn't been taken out*), then turn 2, by being an appropriate response to Y but not X, is then able to "determine the meaning" of turn 1 (as long as it is allowed to go through, without correction). Paul Drew points out (pers. comm.) that when people make "pre's" to offers or invitations, this is an opportunity for a response to "make" the pre itself into an offer, and, if this is not forthcoming, we can say it never was one. But this is not the same sense of effectiveness as intended here, that is, the sense in which turn 1 is what *causes* or *occasions* or *gives rise to* turn 2 taking place at all.

[4] I am not speaking of surprise or sanction at the content of what is communicated per se, but at the relation of relevance or appropriateness to what is being responded to. And note also that "what is being responded to" can cover not just prior communicative actions such as a question that precedes an answer, but also other types of signs such as (pre-)existing states of affairs, like the physical structure of a grocer's store and the receptive stance of the shopkeeper that "precede" the possibility of a customer stating what he wants to buy.

9   but-
10 ROG: **Well <u>don't</u> change [the subject. <u>An</u>swer me.**
11 KEN: [No I mea- I'm on the subject.
12   I'm on the subject. But- I- I mean "not to
13   interrupt you but-" uh a lotta times I'm sitting
14   in class, I'll start- uh I could be listening. .

In lines 6 and 7 Roger asks, "But tell me is everybody like that or am I just out of it?". This sets up a strong normative expectation that an answer be provided next, and when this is apparently not forthcoming – i.e., when the norm is violated – in lines 8 and 9, Roger is within his rights to sanction Ken and demand his entitlement to be answered, as seen in line 10. Ken's subsequent response shows that he also acknowledges Roger's entitlement.

Of course, surprise and sanction are measurable in degrees. Suppose John asks Paul *Is that a martini you're drinking?* If Paul's response is *No*, this will run against a preference for confirmation (Heritage 1984b), thus departing in one sense from what is preferred or "expected."[5] But at the same time a "No" answer conforms precisely with an "expectation" that the addressee will respond to the question by giving the information that was asked for. A "No" answer may be mildly inapposite, but would not be as readily sanctionable as, say, if the addressee were to ignore the question and remain silent where response had been due; here, *Hey I asked you a question* would be a justified pursuit of the normative target by way of sanction – see the example just above. The possibility space for degrees and kinds of surprise and sanction is a complex one (Schegloff and Sacks 1973). The normative expression of sanction and surprise helps to regiment and qualify the ever-present properties of appropriateness and effectiveness that are inherent in chains of relevance. The inherently normative nature of an enchronic system means that we cannot begin to examine human communication without entering a realm of morally governed social behavior.

To summarize: enchrony is grounded in relevance, from which we ultimately derive not only sequence (in the enriched sense of Schegloff [1968, 2007b]), but also a bedrock of public, norm-governed accountability for each increment in a communicative sequence. The notions of effectiveness and appropriateness, defined as they are by "expectation" and the surprise or sanction that may result from transgression of this expectation, take social interaction and transform it into a morally charged affair. For all social creatures, a poorly formed or poorly chosen move may be

---

[5] By using the term "expected," I do not want to imply that a response must be actively anticipated. It is not so much that one expects a particular response, rather that one does not expect the alternatives.

ineffective, but only among humans can such a mismatch lead to moral sanction. Inappropriate responses draw attention, and are accountable. This accountability is natural given the fundamentally cooperative nature of human social life (Axelrod 1984; Boyd and Richerson 2006). Our instincts for moral policing, including punishment, form an indispensable part of maintaining the viability of a cooperative bias in large social groups (Henrich et al. 2004; Boyd and Richerson 2005). Not surprisingly, these instincts for moral monitoring and sanction are well expressed in communicative practice.

I have described enchrony as a core driving force in the interpretation and production of communicative actions. With it, we derive central structural properties of interaction such as sequence, adjacency, nextness, contiguity and progressivity, well known and described in conversation analysis but barely comprehended in linguistics. We see the lamination of normative reasoning onto this structural trajectory: departures may draw not only surprise at not having been anticipated, but also implicit or explicit sanction for not having been regarded as appropriate. But while enchrony is clearly part of the foundational undercarriage of interaction, it cannot single-handedly account for the phenomena explored in this book. The mechanism of enchrony is a general one. What I have proposed so far does not yet explain how this general mechanism is relativized to different contexts, such that a certain type of response may be appropriate in one situation but not in another. Clearly, what counts as appropriate and effective must be defined relative to elements of the situation, including facts about the people involved in the interaction, as well as the different cultural settings in which interactions take place. To address this, we now build on the idea of enchrony by using it to develop a notion of status.

Status

The second piece of the argument hinges on the concept of *status*. The word "status" is used here in a technical sense, derived from Linton (1936), and fleshed out in recent work by Kockelman (2006b). It will never be used in this chapter to mean prestige or "high status." Status here is akin to the notion of *membership category* used in ethnomethodology and conversation analysis (Sacks 1972a, b, 1992; cf. Schegloff 2007b).[6] A person's status is defined here as a collection of his entitlements (or rights) and responsibilities (or duties) at a given moment, relative to other members of

---

[6] This notion of status does not imply that a social category is immutable or in some other sense not contestable or negotiable.

his social group. We can characterize these entitlements and responsibilities in terms of enchrony and its elements, as introduced in the previous section, without introducing new analytical machinery. The concepts of entitlement and responsibility are defined straightforwardly through the relations of appropriateness and effectiveness that hold for any communicative actions in enchronic sequence. A person's status is functionally no different from a sign that precedes or co-occurs with a piece of their behavior,[7] where the fit between the status and the behavior can be assessed for its relevance. The behavior will have a degree of appropriateness or effectiveness, as measured for instance by the degree of normatively justified surprise or sanction in response.

If John is a university lecturer, we can say that this is a status because it may be characterized as a set of entitlements and responsibilities regarding his social relations with certain other people in certain communicative contexts. While inhabiting or enacting this status, he will have rights and duties in relation to his behavior toward his students. Were he to invite one such student out for cocktails, this might attract surprise and possible sanction, while the same invitation among the same two people would be unremarkable if the lecturer–student relation did not apply. As long as his status as a lecturer is in the common ground of an interaction (and is "activated" in the relevant sense, i.e., that he is relating *as* a lecturer to his interlocutor), the relation of relevance that holds between his status and a piece of his behavior is functionally the same as a relation between two signs or communicative actions in sequence. The appropriateness of his behavior is judged in terms of its fit or relevance given his status. Correspondingly, the effectiveness of his status is measured in terms of its fit to the behavior he produces (see Garfinkel [1967: ch. 4] for a rich exploration of this issue with reference to gender).

As Linton put it, status is *polar* or relational, thus not to be understood in terms of intrinsic properties ascribable to a person as an individual, but defined in terms of how that person behaves *in relation to* others. So, to say that Mary inhabits the status of mother is not to say something about the isolated qualities of Mary. It is to say that she behaves and responds in ways that are appropriate to being in the relation of mother *to* someone (her children). Status is a set of publicly norm-guided expectations as to how a person will or should behave.

---

[7] This is where we need the notion of "sign" as a higher-level category which subsumes communicative actions, among other things. My status is signified in various ways – for example, by the clothes I am wearing – but we do not want to say that by merely putting on these clothes I am performing a communicative action in the normal sense of that term (i.e., a move in a sequence of interaction).

Ryle (1949: 45) described status as an "assemblage of performances," a set of possible actions, or dispositions, that, when filtered through relevance and norms, become entitlements and responsibilities.[8]

> A drunkard at the chessboard makes the one move which upsets his opponent's plan of campaign. The spectators are satisfied that this was not due to cleverness but to luck, if they are satisfied that most of his moves made in this state break the rules of chess, or have no tactical connexion with the position of the game, that he would not be likely to repeat this move if the tactical situation were to recur, that he would not applaud such a move made by another player in a similar situation, that he could not explain why he had done it or even describe the threat under which his King had been. (Ryle 1949: 45)

Our entitlements (what we *may* do) and responsibilities (what we *must* do) are captured under Ryle's general notion of dispositions. I suggest that there is a third category of dispositions that may be termed *enablements*, that is, things one *can* do. If entitlements are what we are allowed to do (e.g., a mother will typically be allowed more immediate access to her child's body than other adults), enablements are what we are capable of doing (e.g., a mother will typically be capable of predicting the preferences and reactions of her own child better than others can). The measure of entitlement is the degree to which surprise or sanction at carrying out the action is normatively justified. The measure of enablement is the degree to which one is capable of carrying it out at all, regardless of how it will be treated by social others.

Through entitlement and enablement we can articulate a fundamental distinction between *claiming* and *demonstrating*. (See Heritage [2007: 255] and his discussion of Sacks 1992: II, 141.) If I want to claim that I am a marksman I can use mere words to do it, or even words supported by a lucky shot. But to *demonstrate* that I am a marksman I have to produce an assemblage of performances that would not be possible were the claim not true. To the extent that inhabiting a status can be determined by isolated definitive facts (e.g., Mary is John's mother because she gave birth to him), it may constitute a mere claim to the total assemblage of performances that may come under the relevant culturally developed notion of the status "mother to." Thus, we might cite Mary's inability to produce this broader range of performances (e.g., failure to accurately predict the behavior of her child, when a nanny has more success in doing so) as evidence that she is a poor example of a mother (in one sense). This would be a case of mismatch between enablements and entitlements. It is a gap between the claim derived from her "official" authority (she gave birth to him so this makes

---

[8] The point was amply elaborated some twenty years later in the work of Sacks (1972a, b) on "membership categorization devices" (Schegloff 2007b).

her his mother) and the demonstration enabled by her "actual" authority. (Below, I will define "official" and "actual" authority as status-based and source-based, respectively.) This is a difference between the two forms of status that Linton called ascribed (mother, brother, etc.) versus achieved (friend, enemy, etc.).

It appears that in the business of maintaining statuses – a desperate pursuit that dominates our social lives – it is not enough merely to possess enablements and entitlements. One must *exercise* these as a way of demonstrating that one has them (and has earned them), both by proving with action that one is capable of carrying them out (not possible in the case of the "bad" mother who cannot reliably predict her child's behavior) and by showing that, having carried them out, no sanction by another is justified (e.g., by disciplining the child for misbehaving, knowing that she cannot rightfully be criticized by others for doing so).

For example, if we are to say that Mary and Jane are close friends, then they have certain entitlements and responsibilities in relation to one another. Their behavior with regard to one another may be judged as more or less effective of, or appropriate to, their status as close friends. Thus, if Jane talks to Mary about her personal troubles, this should cause no surprise and would not be justifiably sanctioned (in contrast, say, to when Jane starts telling her personal troubles to a stranger on the subway). Or if Jane asks Mary for a loan of $100, this is likely to be effective, and would not be inappropriate for close friends. It may, however, be both ineffective and sanctionable in the context of more distant kinds of personal relationship. If Jane and Mary are already (known to be) close friends, then behaviors of the kind just described will be judged as appropriate, and will not justifiably elicit surprise. But, supposing they were not close friends, to behave as if they were could be *effective of* (or constitutive of) that status, i.e., could be a way of creating that status.[9]

Status is a powerful notion because it defines human relations at many levels of grain and in many types of frame. Statuses run from professional relations like doctor to patient or experimenter to experimental subject, to kin relations like older brother to younger brother or grandmother to grandson, to interpersonally achieved relations like best friend to best friend or acquaintance to acquaintance, and finally to context- or experience-defined relations like expert to novice or competitor to competitor. It includes the broadest imaginable range of human types, including ad hoc categories (such as "people you can turn to" [Sacks 1992]).

---

[9] See Pomerantz and Mandelbaum (2005) for a review of practices through which people can "enact incumbency" in types of close social relations.

Of special interest in the rest of this chapter, and in much of this book, is interactants' status relative to each other as complementary participants in roles like speaker (to hearer), or overhearer (to others in a conversation). Recall the example above where we saw that Ken's not answering a question was an accountable failure. That kind of accountability was described in terms of the elements of enchrony: effectiveness and appropriateness. Having introduced the notion of status, we now see that this accountability is relativized. It matters *who* answers the question. If I address you, then it is you who should respond, because it is you who occupies the status of "addressee of the question" (Stivers and Robinson 2006). While another person may well know the answer and be able to respond, possibly on your behalf, this other person does not occupy the same status as recipient of the question. Here we see the relevance relation being relativized to different participants through differences in status. This is illustrated in the following example from Stivers and Rossano (2010):

> Reina asks Tamaryn whether her boyfriend's mother calls to talk to her on the phone [line 1]. Tamaryn fails to answer the question in the course of the following 1.0 second [line 2], but at that point co-present Sandra quips "No that('d) ('ll) be wastin' minutes." (line 3).

(3) (Stivers and Rossano 2010)
```
            [((R gazing in T's direction; T off camera))
1   REI:  → [Does she call you and conversate wit'=ju on your phone?,
2           (1.0)
3   SAN:    No that ('d)/('ll) be wastin' minutes.
4           (0.5)
5   SAN:    [Th-
6   REI:  ⇒ [>Ta- I want Tamaryn tuh answer the damn question.< Don't
7           [answer for (h)  [her
8   SAN:    [O(kay)          [I'm sorry.
9   REI:    ((leaning towards Sandra)) Oh no it's okay.
10  TAM:    She called once to see if my mother had thrown a
11          fit but no: other than that_
```

Although Sandra's response is formally type matched (Schegloff and Sacks 1973) and type-conforming (Raymond 2003) it is nonetheless treated as failing. Reina both indirectly sanctions Tamaryn for not answering (indirect only in that the turn is nominally addressed to Sandra): ">Ta- I want Tamaryn tuh answer the damn question.<" and directly sanctions Sandra for answering on Tamaryn's behalf: "Don't answer for her" (lines 6–7). This sanctioning elicits an apology from Sandra and, ultimately, an answer from Tamaryn (lines 10–11).

Status casts our behavior in the constant light of a measure of appropriateness or fit: knowing this person's current status (that is, the status that is presently activated), how appropriate is her behavior? Or: seeing her current behavior, presuming (as, by default, I will) that it is appropriate behavior, what does this tell me of her status?[10] As Sacks (1992) notes, any instance of "category-bound activity" contributes to our further understanding of, and expectations of, the relevant social statuses.

In this section, I have introduced status as an analytic notion that puts meat on the bones of enchrony. Status provides a mechanism for giving values to the variables of appropriateness and effectiveness, and relativizing these across different types of social relation and cultural setting. Both enchrony and status are sources of asymmetry in communication. From enchrony, there is asymmetry in precedence relations and in the associated one-way notion of response. From status, there is an unequalness of social relations, readily seen in relationships like father–son, shopkeeper–customer or speaker–hearer. There now remains a third source of asymmetry in communication that will account for a further crucial aspect of the problem explored in this book – the distributed nature of responsibility and commitment concerning knowledge and information in communication. We turn now to the issue of knowledge, in relation to the semantic and pragmatic content of propositions. This will require the concept of status, already introduced, and must be fleshed out before we move on to the final piece of the argument, agency.

Propositions and the relativity of knowledge

Human communication, through language, differs from other forms of animal communication in that it can involve the encoding and exchange of propositions. While the informational properties of propositions are not typically a matter of discussion in research on the structures of conversation, they are presupposed. The step into research on matters surrounding knowledge and certainty requires us to have an account of just what it is that propositions encode. We therefore need to address propositional content if we are to have a theory of how asymmetries in knowledge are navigated in social interaction.

In order to pursue our primary interest here – the meanings of social actions in interaction – it is necessary to examine the properties of one of the most common elements of action formulation: the linguistically encoded

[10] We can tell whether two people are friends or strangers from their behavior toward each other; such inferences from social behavior are the basis of Hinde's (1976) account of how the ethnographer ultimately discerns higher-level social structure; see also Dunbar (1988), Enfield (2006). An illustrative case is that of Princess Margaret, who, in a fleeting moment at Queen Elizabeth's coronation in June 1953, revealed the intimacy of her relationship to Group Captain Peter Townsend by leaning over to brush a piece of fluff from his uniform. Through what it showed about the social relation at hand, this little act had big consequences.

proposition (see Lyons 1977). A proposition refers to some entity, and predicates some state of affairs (e.g., a property or event) about that entity. An example is the proposition "She called once", encoded in the utterance produced by Tamaryn in line 10 of the above example. In this proposition, the entity is "she" (referring to the speaker's boyfriend's mother) and the state of affairs is "to have called once." If we know who "she" is and we understand the meaning of the expression "to have called once," then we are in a position to judge the applicability (say, truth or falsity) of the predication to a particular instance. If we understand the meaning of the proposition, then we are able to cite possible reasons the state of affairs holds, and we are able to make inferences from this state of affairs to other propositions. This is, of course, not an account of utterance meaning or action formulation, but it is a necessary part of such an account.

This introduces a triadic relation between a topical entity, a predicated state of affairs, and a person who may judge the applicability of the relation between the first two. We may refer to a person's capacity to make this judgement – measurable by their capacity to attest to the truth of, to give reasons for, and to make inferences from the proposition as understood – as their *knowledge*. We can imagine a gradient of possible states of knowledge between knowing for sure (e.g., I know she called once because I took the call myself) and having no idea. Perhaps I overheard Tamaryn on the phone to somebody who I figured was the boyfriend's mother, but couldn't be sure.

A knowledge state is like a status in that it is causally-conditionally related to its causes and effects, and is measured by the behavior that it makes possible. As argued by ordinary language philosophers like Ryle (1949), it is not so much an issue of my mental state of knowing something to be true. What matters is how I can demonstrate this knowledge through observable action, specifically by giving reasons (my evidence for the truth of the state of affairs, what caused the knowledge, the source of the knowledge) and by making inferences to consequences (what the knowledge enables, what performances are made possible by the state of affairs). I am proposing that knowledge of the truth of a proposition is no different from other status-related dispositions, displayed and demonstrated through an assemblage of performances, like any other kind of status. This is in line with an "inferentialist" view of meaning (Brandom 1994, 2000; Kockelman 2005, 2006a, b), which states that to know the meaning of a proposition is to be able to engage in norm-governed practices of reasoning in relation to that proposition. Such reasoning is simply an assemblage of performances that demonstrates some aspect of one's status – in this case, one's proper understanding of the sentence's meaning, of its veracity and applicability in relation to a particular state of affairs. We have to presuppose that, in the context of Tamaryn's utterance in line 10 of the example above, the participants can and do draw on a capacity to judge the veracity of propositions like "She called once".

What is the relevance of all of this to social interaction? Well, among our most common tools for the formulation of social actions are propositions encoded in language, and it is here that we find ourselves navigating the rocky shoals of asymmetries in knowledge. If I know something, then I can or must commit to the consequences of that knowledge. Consequences include inferences that can or must be made. If I know about something, then I can say things about it.[11] This is how one demonstrates understanding rather than merely claiming it, as shown by line 3 of the following example, constructed by Sacks (1992) and discussed by Heritage (2007):

(4)
1 A: Where are you staying?
2 B: Pacific Palisades
3 A: Oh at the west side of town

Here, Speaker A demonstrates that among his enablements is the ability to correctly deploy a proposition about Pacific Palisades to state that it is found on the west side of the city of Los Angeles. This attests to his knowledge. The key about demonstrating is that it is an honest signal, while mere claiming is not. As Sacks points out, were the speaker to reply in line 3 "Oh, Pacific Palisades", no demonstration of understanding will have been made. One could say it even when one has no idea where Pacific Palisades is. Here is an example in which a speaker merely claims rather than definitively demonstrates their understanding (from Sacks 1992: II, 141):

(5)
1 A: Now you told me you eh-uh-where are you.=Are you at uh:Puh-ih: (·) Palos
        uh:(0.4)
2 B: eh-No in ah:::::uh: (·) t Marina del Rey.
        (0.9)
3 B: Marina del Rey.=
4 A: **=Oh Marina del Re: [y.**
5 B: [Y*a*h.

Cases like this are apparently common, while curiously, as Heritage (2007) notes, real demonstrations of understanding of the kind shown in the made-up Pacific Palisades example are rare (hence the need to fabricate them). Why do people avoid demonstrating their understanding in favor

---

[11] I focus here on the *creative* vector of indexicality (Silverstein 1976), where knowledge of the matter creates the possibility of expounding on it. Conversely, we could focus on a *presupposing* vector, where my expounding on it is a way of indicating (or perhaps merely claiming) my earlier learning experience(s).

of the weaker stance of merely claiming it? There are at least two reasons. First, as John Heritage points out (pers. comm.), a full demonstration of one's understanding goes against a preference for progressivity (Stivers and Robinson 2006), in that it is likely to open up a new sequence, however minimal, thereby risking delaying or completely derailing the trajectory of talk. To avoid this, a recipient might imply understanding with a continuer like "uh-huh", and in this way give the go-ahead without disrupting the speaker's current trajectory. But note how in the Marina del Rey example, the speaker does in fact risk a disruption to progressivity (here eliciting from the speaker a further confirmation "Yah"), yet still without using that opportunity to definitively display recognition. It could still be that Speaker A in the example doesn't recognize the name of the place or doesn't know where it is. This points to a second reason why a mere claim to understanding may be preferable to a full demonstration. To positively demonstrate my understanding by going beyond what was said earlier is at risk of being disaffiliative because it draws attention to the possibility that I didn't in fact know it (i.e., why did I need to demonstrate it?), and through this to the possibility that you might have thought I didn't know it. Showing that I don't feel the need to "prove" that I know something is a sign that I expect to be trusted by the other, or indeed that the other knows what I know (Enfield 2006), and is thereby in itself an expression of trust. Going out of my way to prove that I know it risks drawing attention to these asymmetries, something that can quickly get an interactional trajectory wobbling into turbulence.

While Pacific Palisades examples appear to be rare, they do exist. In the following case from a telephone call (Heritage 2007: 271; transcription simplified here), Marsha has initially not recognized the voice of Ron, an old friend of her daughter. (This occurs prior to the segment supplied below.) When Ron announces his name in line 1, Marsha makes a strong claim to recognition in line 2, but it is no more than a claim, particularly in the context of her initial failure.

(6)
1 RON: This is Ron Mercahno do you remember me?
2 MAR: **Oh for heaven sake Ron Yeah this is Marsha**
3 RON: Marsha right

What comes next is the less frequently observed demonstration of recognition, in line 4:

4 MAR: **You're writing for television**
5 RON: Yeah
6 MAR: The writing for television Ron
7 RON: Yeah

So far we have examined how knowledge is displayed through either claim or demonstration. Now we attend to finer points of distinguishing between (relative) degrees of certainty, and matters of how the knowledge has been obtained. Suppose we both know that Tamaryn got a phone call from her boyfriend's mother, but I was in the room when it happened, while you only heard reports of it later. While we are both equally able to say that she called, there are two reasons why I am better qualified to say it: (1) my knowledge is on firmer ground than yours: because I was present I am more certain than you that it is a fact – that is, I have better evidence than you and so I am more likely to be telling the truth despite the fact that we may both be speaking in good faith; and (2) because I directly witnessed the event I can say more things about it, such as how long the call went on for, how Tamaryn responded and so on. We thus distinguish two components of our knowledge of a proposition: *access*, that is, our source of information and thus our citable reasons for being committed to the truth of it; and *authority*, our capacity to demonstrate the effects of knowing that information, through the dispositions enabled by whatever access we have had. (Access leads *to* the knowledge; authority leads *from* it.)

It is evidently a matter of concern to people that their degree of knowledge, and grounds for knowledge, be made public by means of various kinds of marking, implicit and explicit. If I am less certain of the truth of a proposition (or wish to claim this for some communicative purpose), I may feel the need to hedge, as in "*I think* she called once" or "*Maybe* she called once." I may make explicit reference to my source of evidence, as in "*I heard* that she called once," as is grammatically coded in many languages by systems of evidentiality that obligatorily mark whether I perceived something myself, whether I have it on hearsay alone, etc. (Aikhenvald 2004). Such marking appears to be primarily or literally concerned with first-order absolute knowledge, that is, the relation between the speaker and the content of the proposition.

Based on the preceding discussion, it is useful to introduce a terminological distinction here, between *source-based authority* and *status-based authority*.

Source-based authority concerns actual experience and what it enables. If I was present when Tamaryn took the call from her boyfriend's mother, then I can cite this direct experience in support of my commitment to knowing it. This notion of access is a backward-looking basis for commitment, pointing back to what gave rise to the knowledge. The *authority* in question concerns that which the knowledge makes possible: namely, the range of things I can say or do as a result of that knowledge.

By contrast, status-based authority concerns not what you actually know, but what you *should* know, or are entitled to know, given your status (Drew 1991: 37ff.). Source-based authority and status-based authority are typically in alignment, but sometimes they are not, as in the case of the mother who spends less time with her children than the nanny does (cf. Raymond and Heritage 2006). Concerning the matter of knowledge of the children's personality traits, the nanny has higher source-based authority than the mother, while the mother has higher status-based authority. Were we to measure authority by means of the capacity to cite experience (what gave rise to the relevant knowledge) or the capacity to reason and make predictions about the children's behavior (what is enabled by the relevant knowledge), the nanny would win. But by a different mechanism, as part of the mother's ascribed status as mother, among her normatively defensible entitlements are that she may *claim* maximal epistemic access regarding her children (and therefore higher, or at least not lower, access than anyone else). Note that this is not just so by fiat, but is based on the genuine expectation that she will have maximally broad experience with the children, as a proper result of having fulfilled her responsibility (as also defined by her status as mother) to spend maximal time with the children. The nanny example deals precisely with this mismatch. When the nanny demonstrates better authority of the mother's children than does the mother herself, this reveals that the mother displays diminished (less than maximal) source-based knowledge with regard to her own children. The core of the problem is that this demonstrates that the mother has not fully lived up to her responsibilities as given by her ascribed status as mother. It draws attention to her shortcomings as a mother, and, in effect, draws her status as mother into moral question. It is no wonder such misalignments are fraught.

Heritage and Raymond (2005) explore the difficulties that arise when two speakers pursue a symmetrical goal of agreement on the applicability of a proposition to a known state of affairs, but where these speakers find themselves having to navigate the asymmetries introduced by status and enchrony. Their illustrative case is from a conversation between two friends, Jenny and Vera, who agree that Vera's grandchildren make up a lovely family (2005: 20). Heritage and Raymond introduce a notation for representing knowledge or epistemic commitment. In their shorthand, "K+" with reference to Speaker A is not absolute but relative, meaning "K+ for A and K− for B." This introduces four extreme possibilities (though Heritage and Raymond only specify two) where both A and B may have a value of either K-low or K-high. When both A and B are low, or when both are high, these appear to be symmetrical situations (though I argue in the following section that this can never really be so, due to inherent asymmetries of speech act agency). Possibilities other than the two identified by Heritage and Raymond are conceivable: A's knowledge is more than B's ("K+" in relative terms), but still it's quite low (i.e., approaching "K−" in absolute terms). We can imagine that in some situations it is important to mark one's degree or kind of absolute knowledge, while in other situations it is the relative knowledge that matters. The distinction needs to be made and maintained (see Hayano this volume).

I noted above that knowledge can be explicitly marked. But it is also implicitly marked. Commonly, a proposition coded as a bare assertion (e.g., "She called once") will be taken to convey the strongest possible epistemic commitment, namely "I know for a fact it is true" (Grice 1989). In a bare assertion in English, this maximal epistemic commitment is implied rather than coded. To *code* this one would need to make it explicit, as in *I know that she called once*. This sounds overwrought, and defensive, as if it had been suggested that you *didn't* know whether it was the case. But everyday statements are backed by the everyday assumption that a speaker has adequate evidence for what she is saying (Grice 1989; Pomerantz 1984b). If anything less than full commitment is intended, this should be explicitly marked. As mentioned in Sidnell's chapter on English (in this volume), when we preface a proposition with *I think*, this implies "I don't know it," or – perhaps better – "I don't want to say that I know it."

Note in addition the way that *relative* knowledge is also implied in fundamental ways through the presuppositions that are inherent in speech act types (Searle 1969). Declarative forms – as in *She called once* – imply not just "I know it," but also "You don't." This is one reason that "assessments" (Goodwin and Goodwin 1987; Pomerantz 1984a) – as in *Adeline's such a swell gal* – are problematic in epistemic terms: their packaging is fitted to a strong asymmetry in knowledge (i.e., in declarative format, they are ostensibly "telling" the addressee something), yet their function is often aimed at full symmetry, i.e., securing agreement (Heritage and Raymond 2005).

In this section I have concentrated on a particular mode of status within the domain of epistemic commitment to the content of propositions. As we have seen, the fact that using language includes the encoding of propositions raises a rich set of issues for social interaction. First, there is the matter of access: our source of knowledge, the evidence we have for it, how we acquired it. Second, relatedly, there is the matter of authority: the enablements this access to knowledge brings, such as the capacity to demonstrate our knowledge through reasoning (a capacity of the same kind Ryle offered as evidence for mastery in chess or marksmanship). An individual's knowledge is grounded in access, and is measured by authority. But there is another, parallel basis for a claim to epistemic commitment, namely one's normative rights to certain kinds of knowledge, based on status. If I hold the title of chess champion of South Gelderland, I may have some *claim* to speak with authority about chess, even if I am not all that good a player and was merely lucky to have won (or cheated). And you may even find yourself biting your tongue out of deference to this claim, even when you are certain that what I say about chess is dubious (just as a nanny may find herself doing when a mother is wrong about her own children, or as a student may find herself doing when a lecturer is wrong about his topic). Thus we distinguish between source-based and status-based authority. We then saw that these nearly parallel modes of commitment to knowledge are further relativized across participants in an interaction: one person may always be regarded as higher or lower *than another*, based on source-based authority, or a status-related claim to such authority. It appears that a status-based claim trumps a source-based demonstration when the two are in conflict. This is a paradoxical fact, if true, but perhaps not unexpected given that we are not so much rational as moral animals.

Agency

Our account began by grounding human communicative practice in enchrony – a generic mechanism that yields sequence, relevance and accountability – then relativizing this through the notion of status to culturally determined and locally contextual types of social relation, and finally focusing on the nature of knowledge as a species of status relating to states of affairs and the things we can say about them. The previous section introduced some ways in which speakers and hearers stand in relation to knowledge of propositions and responsibility for the formal expressive (e.g., grammatical) packaging of that knowledge, and how this interacts with respective status beyond speech act participation and into social-cultural categories. We must now introduce a fourth piece of conceptual apparatus in order to fully account for the matters of knowledge, responsibility and affiliation explored in this book. Status alone is not sufficient to account for some of the empirical data that previous work has introduced. We are missing a final source of asymmetry that interacts with enchrony, status and knowledge – namely, agency.

The term "agency" has been so widely applied that it may be wise not to use it at all. Mostly in this chapter I am referring to the elements of "speakerhood" by which a person may have more or less control over various dimensions of an utterance (Goffman 1981). However, I cannot use the term "speakerhood" here because I want to generalize beyond speech. I am trying to capture the type and degree of control and responsibility a person may have with respect to their design of communicative actions and other kinds of signs.

There is no scale by which we may say that a person's agency in communication is simply higher or lower. Instead, agency has multiple distinct components that may be addressed separately. Agency may be distributed across individuals. This introduces an ever-present potential source of asymmetry, logically distinct from the asymmetries inherent to enchrony and status. The compound notion of agency assumed here is akin to Goffman's disassembly of the agent of any speech act into three: animator, author and principal.

Roughly, the three elements of agency can be characterized as follows.[12] First, with respect to any behavior, such as the production of a perceptible sign, somebody will *control* the behavior to a greater or lesser extent. That is, they control the physical execution of the sign such that it can be perceived and attended to by another. Second, somebody will *compose* the behavior, selecting and planning what its form should be so as to bring about the projected effect. Third, somebody will *commit* to the behavior, taking responsibility for its causes and effects, including the appropriateness of its execution in a specific context. In Goffman's terms, who controls the production of the message is its animator; who composes the form of the message is its author; and who is responsible for the effects of the message is its principal (though see Kockelman [2007: 379, fn. 5] for problems with Goffman's "principal").

Goffman made the point that, while the three components of agency in speaking tend to be aligned, they are in fact separable, as shown by examples like the police spokesman who reads a prewritten message (animator, but neither author nor principal), or the head of state who delivers a policy speech scribed by an advisor (animator and principal, but not author). But, normally, each of the three elements of agency in speakerhood is embodied in one and the same person. If a man remarks to his wife, "That dress really suits you," she will know through direct perception that he is the animator of this utterance, and she should normally assume that he composed the specific expression of it, and that he takes responsibility for what it expresses and for the effects it may have. When a listener applies this

---

[12] The present account draws on Kockelman's (2007) account of agency, which is directly grounded in a more general semiotic theory, after Peirce. I leave aside here the complexities of possible finer interpretations of the Goffmanian scheme (Hanks 1996; Irvine 1996; Levinson 1988; Sidnell 2009).

ordinary presumption of alignment of the three dimensions of agency, she is applying an *agent unity heuristic*.[13]

Note the inherent difference in access that we have to the three components of agency. We typically have direct access to animatorship, because we have to be present to perceive the production of an utterance. But we don't typically have direct access to the process of authorship (usually carried out privately, that is, mentally),[14] nor necessarily to the conditions of responsibility and commitment that define a principal (though these are sometimes publicly available through standard signs of status: e.g., accent, clothing, physical features). It is because of the agent unity heuristic that we need special devices to mark when agency is distributed. This heuristic is a powerful one, and if we want a hearer to suspend her standard application of it, formal means are required to signal this. These include signals of quoted speech, contextualization cues, etc.

To illustrate why agency, and in particular the agent unity heuristic, is necessary in the present account, consider the study by Heritage and Raymond (2005:34). The authors present data from conversation in English in support of the argument that "assessing a referent state of affairs in first position implies a claim of primary epistemic and/or moral rights to assess that state." Here is how they summarize their findings.

In sequences of interaction, first position assessments establish a representational field in which second assessments will be found to position themselves in some fashion: through agreement, disagreement, or adjustment (Heritage 2002a; Pomerantz 1984a). In this sense, first position assessments offer a terrain within which agreement will be sought. We propose that these assessments also carry an implied claim that the speaker has primary rights to evaluate the matter assessed. For example, as we demonstrate, persons offering first assessments may work to defeat any implication that they are claiming primary rights to evaluate the matter at hand. Conversely, persons who find themselves producing a responsive assessment may wish to defeat the implication that their rights in the matter are secondary to those of a first speaker. Because assessments are always produced in real time and are unavoidably produced as first and second positioned actions, they bring unavoidable relevance to issues concerning relative epistemic rights to evaluate states of affairs. (Heritage and Raymond 2005: 16)

---

[13] "Heuristic" here refers to an interpretive strategy that applies a simple rule of thumb in order to simplify what might otherwise be a complex decision-making process (Gigerenzer 2007). For example, in selecting which brand of soap powder to buy, I simply buy the same one I've used before, rather than testing out every new brand that comes along to determine whether it's better or worse on some measure.

[14] The psychological process of utterance production can be partially made public through visible indices such as hand gestures (Beattie 2003; McNeill 1985, 2005; cf. Enfield 2009, and references therein).

The account is grounded in the observation that first position implies primary rights. Why might this be so? First, as Heritage and Raymond make clear, enchrony is what underlies the inevitability of actions being taken as "first" (or initiating) versus "second" (or responsive). But why should first position hereby imply primary *rights*? I want to argue that there are three mechanisms, derived from the analytical tools brought together here: (1) being the one to say it; (2) saying it in the form of an assertion; and (3) saying it independently. (Note that these are matters of control, composition, and commitment, respectively.) Let us consider these in turn.

How does an agent unity heuristic contribute to the effects described by Heritage and Raymond? I want to argue the following. When you hear and see me speak, it is directly apparent that I, and only I, am animator of the message. Applying the agent unity heuristic, that is, using the most accessible component of agenthood – control or animatorship – to infer the least accessible – commitment or principalhood – the normal assumption will be that if I and only I am animator of the message, then I am also author and principal of the message. This is an *animator bias*.[15] The issue here is that animating is typically strongly asymmetrical: the tendency is for one person to speak at a time (Sacks, Schegloff and Jefferson 1974; Stivers *et al.* 2009), certain classes of departure notwithstanding (e.g., Lerner 2002). Via the agent unity heuristic this asymmetry is automatically imported to the domain of commitment or principalhood. But in the kinds of interactional contexts in which interlocutors strive to build affiliation through the overt expression of *agreement*, the goal is *symmetry* of commitment.

In terms of the basic social motives for communication discussed by Tomasello (2008), the problem here is that a structure designed for informing is being used for the function of sharing. This may be a kind of exaptation, a panda's thumb of language use. Along lines argued by Marcus (2008; cf. Jackendoff 1997: 20), the system has the klunky quality typical of evolved systems that must constantly come up with ad hoc solutions engineered out of structures which are available but which may have initially evolved for other functions. One of Marcus's examples is the human spine, evolved to maintain a horizontal position from which the body weight hangs down (cf. other mammals), but which now has to hold our weight vertically, something for which it is not well designed at all. There is an ill fit between the source structure and its target function. Similarly, part of the problem documented by Heritage and Raymond is an ill fit between the asymmetry of animatorship in speaking and the intended symmetry of principalhood in agreeing. But there is more.

---

[15] Shooting the messenger is a kind of collateral damage owed to the agent unity heuristic – i.e., where the one who is merely animator pays the consequences of being treated as principal.

As noted already, the speech act of assertion itself carries with it the presupposition of an epistemic gradient in which "I know it, you don't." When we make assessments like "They're a lovely family," we are often saying this not to inform someone: rather we are seeking their agreement (Heritage and Raymond 2005: 20). Languages provide us with devices for explicitly marking that this is what we are doing, such as English tag-type strategies ("*aren't they?*," "*don't you think?*"), or Lao sentence-final particle-type strategies (*nòq1* "agreement-seeking polar question marker" [Enfield 2007: 48–50]). But even with such marking, the speaker who goes first is nevertheless somehow "implying a claim of primary rights to evaluate the matter." And there is yet more.

I have so far proposed that primary rights of the kind described by Heritage and Raymond may be implied by (1) *being the one to say it* (via an agent unity heuristic and an animator bias; if the addressee is "not saying it" then an implication is that they are also not – yet – committed to it); and (2) saying it *in the form of an assertion* (via the presuppositions of that speech act, namely that the addressee is unknowing). Now we want to know why "saying it *first*" also conspires to imply primary rights to what is said. As Heritage and Raymond show, the problem is not solved simply by the addressee saying it too, in second position. Thanks to enchrony, an asymmetry still applies. To see why, we need a distinction between *speech event* and *narrated event*, introduced by Jakobson (1971) for dealing with matters of deixis.

The speech event is the actual situation of speaking, in which the participants find themselves. It is the proximal realm of reference for words like "I," "here" and "now." The narrated event (or, more accurately, the narrated state of affairs, since it is not always an event) is the state of affairs being talked about. So, if Tamaryn says to Reina *She called once*, the narrated event is the phone call, and the speech event is the conversation between Tamaryn and Reina (and Sandra).[16] Note that the speech event is the true realm of enchrony, where relations between communicative actions show effectiveness and appropriateness, regulated by the status of speech act participants. And with regard to knowledge, *absolute* knowledge is calculated with reference to the narrated event (how sure one is that "She called once"), while *relative* knowledge is calculated with reference to the speech event, in addition (how much more sure one is than someone else that "she called once").

---

[16] Sometimes, of course, the speech event *is* the narrated event, or there may be a speech event within the narrated event (in which case words like "I" may have transformed reference, as in *John said "I quit*," where "I" no longer refers to the actual animator of the utterance).

Now, if I make an assertion like *They're a lovely family*, not only do I display a certain epistemic commitment to the proposition in the narrated event ("I know it"), but also I display *a commitment to the appropriateness and effectiveness of expressing this proposition as an utterance that contributes to this speech event here and now*. In this way I may be held accountable for not one thing but two: (1) that I am committed to the content of what I say; and (2) that I am committed to the appropriateness of saying it here and now. Through this, a "first position assessment" implies a unilateral or independent claim of relevance: not only do I know that they're a lovely family and therefore have authority to say it, but *it was my idea to say it in this context* (implying: not yours). This is the key problem with going second. There is a heavy asymmetry in agency in the speech event concerning the "cause" of my saying it now – i.e., what engendered or occasioned my saying it now. In first position, what causes me to say it is that "I wanted to say this, now" (I considered it appropriate), but when I respond by agreeing with what you just said, I am vulnerable to losing all perceived agency in the domain of the speech event: i.e., "I'm only saying this, now, because you just said it."

So there are two problems. One is that, by stating it in first position, I invite an implication of priority through an agent unity heuristic and an animator bias ([a] that I'm animating it implies that I'm committed to it; and [b] that *only* I am animating it implies that only I am committed to it), combined with the inherent pragmatics of formally asserting it ("I know it, you don't"). The second problem is that, by stating it in second position, you risk being perceived to have uttered it only because the other just did. (Or, perhaps better: if you say it in second position, it is possible that you would not have otherwise said it; if you say it in first position, well, you did say it.) The kinds of strategies for upgrading in second position that Heritage and Raymond (2005) describe are precisely designed to defeat these implications (cf. Heritage 2002a).

Consider a situation in which a speaker finds himself saying something that may be interpreted as merely occasioned by what the other has just said. In line 1 of the extract below, Jess asks Mike if he's "boxing right now" – that is, if he's currently training for a fight.

(7)
1 JESS: Are you boxing right now?
2   (0.9)
3 MIKE: I'm gonna start tod^ay.
4   (.)
5 JESS: [Oh:.
6 MIKE: [Tonight actually tuh tell ya thuh tru:th,
7   (0.3)

8   MIKE: Six fiftee:n.
9   (0.7)
10 JESS: At thuh place on Sta:te Street?
11 MIKE: >State Street.<

When Mike responds after nearly a second by saying "I'm gonna start today", it sounds like he might be opportunistically affirming in response to Jess's question. After all, since he's not in training *yet*, a "no" response is equally fitting. Instead he claims that he is going to start today, but he does not give evidence to demonstrate that this was already his intention. No doubt Mike doesn't want it to sound like his announcement in line 3 is only occasioned by her asking, which is consistent with what he does then go on to say: in lines 6–8 he is increasingly more specific about the time of starting (from "today" to "tonight" to "six fifteen"), as an offer of independent evidence that he was already planning to begin today, and not because she just asked.

Conclusion

My objective is a general account of how communicative actions are interpreted, as a function of (1) their context in a sequence of communicative actions, (2) the relative status of the interlocutors involved, including (3) differences in source and authority regarding knowledge about states of affairs being referred to (or otherwise relevant) and (4) the distribution of agency and its features. Taken together these are elements of a framework that is general enough to capture phenomena we already need to capture (e.g., sequence organization, deictic reference, pragmatic implicature), but also able to account for the specific concerns of this book: the complexities of knowledge, responsibility and affiliation. Let me summarize the argument.

I   Enchrony. Communication involves sequences of communicative actions in social interaction, where relevance drives interpretation at every step. This interpretation is normatively guided insofar as communicative actions may be seen as more or less effective of the responses they elicit, and responses may be seen as more or less appropriate to the actions they respond to. Enchrony introduces two critical elements of an account for moral responsibility in the communication of information: (1) sequential asymmetry and the literal primacy of "going first"; (2) the potential for normative regimentation of relevance relations via appropriateness and effectiveness.

II Status. The normative structure of interactional sequence is relativized to categories of human relation, defined by cultural and activity contexts. The notions of appropriateness and effectiveness are thus transformed into normative context- and person-specific entitlements and responsibilities, which may be morally governed. Depending on the status categories a person enacts at a given moment, he will be accountable for his behavior as measured against his associated rights and duties. The relevant categories of status include social roles from mother and brother to police officer and teacher to speaker and hearer: in all cases, there is an "official" sense of what a person should and should not do (or be capable of doing), and an "actual" sense of what they will or will not be capable of doing.

III Knowledge. Because human communication includes the coding of information in the form of propositions, this introduces a range of issues concerning entitlements and responsibilities relating to knowledge encoded in a proposition. A first-order way of analyzing this knowledge concerns an individual's relation to the information. What they know is a direct result of how they know it: that is, their access to the state of affairs. This may be measured by their authority in demonstrating this knowledge. Distinct from this capacity to demonstrate knowledge, based on real access, there is a parallel but distinct claim to authority based on status – e.g., a grandmother *should* know her own grandchildren very well, even if in fact someone else can demonstrate knowledge of them that is as good or better. At a second order there is the matter of relative knowledge – that is, the relation between the type and degree of knowledge of two speech act participants. All things being equal, a grandmother knows her grandchildren better than her friend does, but not as well as her own daughter does – the children's mother. Some ways in which epistemic commitment is formally marked (e.g., in speech) are concerned with absolute knowledge, others concern relative knowledge, yet others are more general.[17] Some marking is explicit, some implicit. Generally speaking, given the statuses and degrees and types of commitment that pertain in a situation, speakers should represent them as accurately as possible, because they are at any point liable to be held accountable – which shouldn't be a problem so long as their strategies of coding are aligned with the facts. Turbulence arises when the many sources of asymmetry fail to align.

IV Agency. A final source of asymmetry in communication concerns the distinctness of the three components of agency. There is an animator

---

[17] Though as Kobin Kendrick stresses (pers. comm.), even those "absolute" markers are used relatively in that they are deployed in ways that orient to the epistemic state of the interlocutor. It may be that the distinction made here between absolute and relative can be more accurately characterized as a cline from the most (explicitly) relative to the least (explicitly) relative.

bias due to animatorship being the most accessible of the three components of agency: thus, if someone is an animator, we assume that
they are also author and principal, unless there is evidence otherwise.
But animating is inherently more strongly asymmetrical than commitment or principalhood. The whole point of building agreement and
affiliation is in a sense to build a "compound principal" consisting of
two or more people in relation to a proposition. The fact that conversation is built around taking turns at unilaterally animating seems to be
in direct conflict with this goal. Three mechanisms are at play. First,
when you are *the one to say it*, the other person is thereby *not* the one
to say it, and, through an agent unity heuristic, they also are at risk of
being implied to be "not committed to it" either. Second, when you say
it *in the form of an assertion*, this implies that the other is unknowing.
Third, when you *say it first*, you say it independently, with the agency
of having spoken unprompted and having seen it as being appropriate in the context, rendering any direct agreement by the other at risk
of being taken as mere following. These asymmetries are grounded in
enchrony and agency and they become problematic when they are not
aligned with the asymmetries of status and knowledge.

Language use is a complex affair, in which propositions with complex
forms of coding are expressed and deployed on an undercarriage that
shares much with other species – that is, a communicative system whose
primary function is to achieve social goals through interaction. Our system
is transformed, however, not only by the complexities of language, but
by something else that is unique to our species: pro-social cooperative
motives and the moral policing that is necessary to keep a cooperative
system going. Facts about human interaction of the kind recorded in the
above chapters show that everyday interaction is beset with the difficulties of reconciling a large set of informational and social-relational asymmetries in communication. Why should we experience these difficulties?
After all, we are well-practiced users of the communicative systems at our
disposal. I suspect that we are doing the best we can with an inherently
imperfect system. Problems of the kind described above, where properties of the system produce these clashes, are a necessary outcome of the
kluge-like nature of the system as an *evolved* system (Jacob 1977; Marcus
2008). A recent account of the evolutionary origins of human communication proposes a path of development of social motives for communication,
going from requesting to helping/informing to sharing (Tomasello 2008).
The core of the problem examined in this book is a conflict between the
unalike gradients inherent in these three communicative functions – for
instance, as discussed above, there is an inherent imbalance in employing

an assertive grammatical format (ostensibly for informing) in utterances whose core goal appears to be sharing. If our communicative system is a truly evolved one, then these are precisely the kind of kluge-like imperfections we would expect to have to work around. Sources of asymmetry in the very fabric of the system give us no time out from the moral dilemmas of social interaction.

References

Aijmer, K. (1977). "Partiklarna ju och väl [The particles *ju* and *väl*]." *Nysvenska Studier* 57: 205–216.

(1996). "*I think* – an English modal particle." In T. Swan and O.J. Westvik (eds.) *Modality in Germanic Languages*. Berlin: Mouton de Gruyter, pp. 1–47.

Aikhenvald, A.Y. (2004). *Evidentiality*. Oxford: Oxford University Press.

Atkinson, J.M. and Heritage, J. (eds.) (1984). *Structures of Social Action: Studies in Conversation Analysis*. Cambridge: Cambridge University Press.

Allan, R., Holmes, P. and Lundskær-Nielsen, T. (1995). *Danish: A Comprehensive Grammar*. London: Routledge.

Antinucci, F. and Miller, R. (1975). "How children talk about what happened." *Journal of Child Language* 3: 167–189.

Auer, P. (1995). "The pragmatics of code-switching: a sequential approach." In L. Milroy and P. Muysken (eds.) *One Speaker, Two Languages: Cross-disciplinary Perspectives on Codeswitching*. Cambridge: Cambridge University Press, pp. 115–135.

Austin, J.L. (1961). "A plea for excuses." In J.O. Urmson and G.J. Warnock (eds.) *Philosophical Papers*. Oxford: Clarendon Press, pp. 123–152.

(1962). *How To Do Things with Words*. Oxford: Oxford University Press.

(1971) [1963]. "Performative-constative." In J.R. Searle (ed.) *The Philosophy of Language*. Oxford: Oxford University Press, pp. 13–22.

Axelrod, R. (1984). *The Evolution of Cooperation*. New York: Basic Books.

Baron-Cohen, S. (2003). *The Essential Difference*. New York: Basic Books.

Barth, F. (2002). "An anthropology of knowledge." *Current Anthropology* 43: 1–18.

Bavelas, J.B., Coates, L. and Johnson, T. (2000). "Listeners as co-narrators." *Journal of Personality and Social Psychology* 79(6): 941–52.

Beach, W. and Dixson, C.N. (2001). "Revealing moments: formulating under-standings of adverse experiences in a health appraisal interview." *Social Science and Medicine* 52: 25–44.

Beach, W. and Metzger, T.R. (1997). "Claiming insufficient knowledge". *Human Communication Research* 23(4): 562–588.

Beattie, G. (2003). *Visible Thought: The New Psychology of Body Language*. London: Routledge.

Berger, P.L. and Luckmann, T. (1966). *The Social Construction of Reality: A Treatise in the Sociology of Knowledge*. Garden City, NY: Anchor Books.

Betz, E. and Golato, A. (2008). "Remembering relevant information and withhold-ing relevant next actions: the German token 'achja.'" *Research on Language and Social Interaction* 41(1): 58–98.

Biber, D., Johansson, S., Leech, G., Conrad, S. and Finegan, E. (1999). *Longman Grammar of Spoken and Written English*. London: Longman.

Bolden, G. B. (2009). "Beyond answering: repeat-prefaced responses in conversa-tion." *Communication Monographs* 76(2): 121–143.

Boyd, R. (2006). "Culture and the evolution of the human social instincts." In N. J. Enfield and S. C. Levinson (eds.) *Roots of Human Sociality: Culture, Cognition, and Interaction*. London: Berg, pp. 453–477.

Boyd, R. and Richerson, P. J. (2005). *The Origin and Evolution of Cultures*. New York: Oxford University Press.

Brandom, R. B. (1994). *Making It Explicit: Reasoning, Representing, and Discursive Commitment*. Cambridge, MA: Harvard University Press.

  (2000). *Articulating Reasons: An Introduction to Inferentialism*. Cambridge, MA: Harvard University Press.

Brown, P. (in press). "The cultural organization of attention." In E. Ochs, A. Duranti and B. Schieffelin (eds.) *Handbook of Language Socialization*. Oxford: Blackwell Publishers.

Brown, P. and Levinson, S. C. (1987). *Politeness: Some Universals in Language Usage*. Cambridge: Cambridge University Press.

Chafe, W. (1976). "Givenness, contrastiveness, definiteness, subjects, topics and point of view." In C. Li (ed.) *Subject and Topic*. New York: Academic Press.

Chafe, W. (1986). "Evidentiality in English conversation and academic writing." In W. Chafe and J. Nichols (eds.) *Studies in Evidentiality*. Amsterdam: John Benjamins, pp. 261–272.

Chafe, W. and Nichols, J. (1986). *Evidentiality: The Linguistic Coding of Epistemology*. Norwood, NJ: Ablex.

Cheng, C. (1987). "Shuujoshi: hanashite to kikite no ninshiki no gyappu o umeru tame no bun-setsuji [Sentence-final particles: sentence clitics for closing the gap between the speaker's and the hearer's recognition]." *Nihongogaku* 6: 93–109.

Chevalier, F. (2008). "Unfinished turns in French conversation: how context matters." *Research on Language and Social Interaction* 41(1): 1–30.

Christensen, R. Z. and Christensen, L. (2005). *Dansk grammatik [Danish Grammar]*. Odense: Syddansk Universitetsforlag.

Clark, H. H. (1992). *Arenas of Language Use*. Chicago, IL: University of Chicago Press.

  (1996). *Using Language*. Cambridge: Cambridge University Press.

Clayman, S. E. (2001). "Answers and evasions." *Language in Society* 30(3): 403–442.

  (2002). "Sequence and solidarity." In E. J. Lawler and S. R. Thye (eds.) *Advances in Group Processes: Group Cohesion, Trust, and Solidarity*. Oxford: Elsevier Science, pp. 229–253.

  (2010). "Address terms in the service of other actions: the case of news interview talk." *Discourse and Communication* 4: 161–183.

Clayman, S. E. and Heritage, J. (2002). "Questioning presidents: journalistic deference and adversarialness in the press conferences of U.S. presidents Eisenhower and Reagan." *Journal of Communication* 52(4): 749–775.

Clift, R. (2006). "Indexing stance: reported speech as an interactional evidential." *Journal of Sociolinguistics* 10(5): 569–595.

Coulmas, F. (ed.) (1986). *Direct and Indirect Speech*. Berlin: Mouton de Gruyter.

Couper-Kuhlen, E. (2009). "A sequential approach to affect: the case of 'disappointment.'" In M. Haakana, M. Laakso and J. Lindstrom (eds.) *Talk in Interaction: Comparative Dimensions*. Helsinki: Suomalaisen Kirjallisuuden Seura (Finnish Literature Society), pp. 94–123.

Curl, T. S. and Drew, P. (2008). "Contingency and action: a comparison of two forms of requesting." *Research on Language and Social Interaction* 41(2): 129–153.

Danby, S. and Baker, C. (1998). "'What's the problem?' Restoring social order in the pre-school classroom." In I. Hutchby and J. Moran-Ellis (eds.) *Children and Social Competence: Arenas of Action*. London: Falmer, pp. 157–186.

Davidson, J. (1984). "Subsequent versions of invitations, offers, requests, and proposals dealing with potential or actual rejection." In J. M. Atkinson and J. Heritage (eds.) *Structures of Social Action: Studies in Conversation Analysis*. Cambridge: Cambridge University Press, pp. 102–128.

de Haan, F. (2008). "Semantic distinctions of evidentiality." In M. Haspelmath, M. S. Dryer, D. Gil and B. Comrie (eds.) *The World Atlas of Language Structures Online*. Munich: Max Planck Digital Library, ch. 77.

de Ruiter, J. P., Mitterer, H. and Enfield, N. J. (2006). "Projecting the end of a speaker's turn: a cognitive cornerstone of conversation." *Language* 82(3): 515–535.

Diani, G. (2004). "The discourse functions of *I don't know* in English conversation." In K. Aijmer and A.-B. Stenström (eds.) *Discourse Patterns in Spoken and Written Corpora*. Amsterdam/Philadelphia: John Benjamins, pp. 157–171.

Drew, P. (1991). "Asymmetries of knowledge in conversational interactions." In I. Marková and K. Foppa (eds.) *Asymmetries in Dialogue*. Hemel Hempstead: Harvester Wheatsheaf, pp. 29–48.

(1992). "Contested evidence in courtroom cross-examination: the case of a trial for rape." In P. Drew and J. Heritage (eds.) *Talk at Work: Interaction in Institutional Settings*. Cambridge: Cambridge University Press, pp. 470–520.

(1993). "Complaints about transgression and misconduct." *Research on Language and Social Interaction* 31: 295–325.

(1997). "'Open' class repair initiators in response to sequential sources of trouble in conversation." *Journal of Pragmatics* 28: 69–101.

Drew, P. and Walker, T. (2008). "Going too far: complaining, escalating and disaffiliation." *Journal of Pragmatics* 41: 2400–2414.

Dunbar, R. I. M. (1988). *Primate Social Systems*. London: Croom Helm.

(1996). *Grooming, Gossip and the Evolution of Language*. London: Faber and Faber.

Durkheim, E. (1915). *The Elementary Forms of Religious Life*. London: George Allen and Unwin.

(1997) [1893]. *The Division of Labor in Society*. New York: The Free Press.

Edwards, D. (1997). *Discourse and Cognition*. London: Sage.

Edwards, D. and Potter, J. (1992). *Discursive Psychology*. London: Sage.

Egbert, M. (1997). "Schisming: the collaborative transformation from a single conversation to multiple conversations." *Research on Language and Social Interaction* 30: 1–51.

Eisenberg, N. and Fabes, R. A. (1990). "Empathy: conceptualization, measurement, and relation to prosocial behavior." *Motivation and Emotion* 14: 131–149.

Emmertsen, S. and Heinemann, T. (2010). "Realization as a device for remedying problems of affiliation in interaction." *Research on Language and Social Interaction* 3(2): 109–132.

Enfield, N.J. (2006). "Social consequences of common ground." In N.J. Enfield and S.C. Levinson (eds.) *Roots of Human Sociality: Culture, Cognition and Interaction.* Oxford: Berg, pp. 399–430.

(2007). *A Grammar of Lao.* Berlin: Mouton de Gruyter.

(2009). *The Anatomy of Meaning: Speech, Gesture, and Composite Utterances.* Cambridge: Cambridge University Press.

Eriksson, M. (1988). "Ju, väl, då, va, alltså: en studie av talaktsadverbial i stockholmskt talspråk [*Ju, väl, då, va, alltså*: a study of speech act adverbials in Stockholm spoken language]." *Studier i stockholmsspråk* 1. (Meddelanden från Institutionen för nordiska språk vid Stockholm universitet 26. Stockholm: Univ. Inst. för nordiska språk.)

Erman, B. (2001). "Pragmatic markers revisited with a focus on *you know* in adult and adolescent talk." *Journal of Pragmatics* 33: 1337–1359.

Fiske, S.T. and Taylor, S.E. (1984). *Social Cognition.* Reading, MA: Addison-Wesley.

Forgas, J.P. (1981). *Social Cognition.* London: Academic Press.

Fox, B. (2001). "Evidentiality: authority, responsibility, and entitlement in English conversation." *Journal of Linguistic Anthropology* 11(2): 167–192.

Fox Tree, J.E. and Schrock, J.C. (2002). "Basic meanings of *you know* and *I mean.*" *Journal of Pragmatics* 34: 727–747.

Franckel, J.J. and Lebaud, D. (1990). *Les Figures du sujet: à propos des verbes de perception, sentiment, connaissance.* Paris-Gap: Ophrys.

Freese, J. and Maynard, D.W. (1998). "Prosodic features of bad news and good news in conversation." *Language in Society* 27: 195–219.

Garvey, C. (1977). *Play.* Cambridge, MA: Harvard University Press.

Garfinkel, H. (1952). "The perception of the other: a study in social order." Unpublished Ph.D. dissertation. Harvard University.

(1967). *Studies in Ethnomethodology.* Englewood Cliffs, NJ: Prentice-Hall.

Garfinkel, H., Lynch, M. and Livingston, E. (1981). "The work of a discovering science construed with materials from the optically discovered pulsar." *Philosophy of the Social Sciences* 11: 131–158.

Garfinkel, H. and Wieder, D.L. (1992). "Two incommensurable, asymmetrically alternate technologies of social analysis." In G. Watson and R.M. Seiler (eds.) *Text in Context: Contributions to Ethnomethodology.* Newbury Park, CA: Sage, pp. 175–206.

Gartrell, D. (2004). *The Power of Guidance: Teaching Social–Emotional Skills in the Early Childhood Classroom.* Clifton Park, NY: Delmar Learning.

Gigerenzer, G. (2007). *Gut Feelings: Short Cuts to Better Decision Making.* London: Penguin.

Gill, V. (1998). "Doing attributions in medical interaction: patients' explanations for illness and doctors' responses." *Social Psychology Quarterly* 61: 342–360.

Gill, V. and Maynard, D.W. (2006). "Explaining illness: patients' proposals and physicians' responses." In J. Heritage and Douglas Maynard (eds.)

Communication in Medical Care: Interactions between Primary Care Physicians and Patients. Cambridge: Cambridge University Press, pp. 115–150.

Givón, T. (1982). "Evidentiality and epistemic space." *Studies in Language* 6: 23–49.

——— (1989). *Mind, Code, and Context: Essays in Pragmatics*. Hillsdale, NJ: Lawrence Erlbaum Associates.

Goffman, E. (1971a). *Relations in Public: Microstudies of the Public Order*. New York: Harper and Row.

——— (1971b). "Remedial interchanges." In E. Goffman, *Relations in Public: Microstudies of the Public Order*. New York: Harper and Row, pp. 95–187.

——— (1981). *Forms of Talk*. Philadelphia: University of Pennsylvania Press.

Golato, A. and Betz, E. (2008). "German *ach* and *achso* in repair uptake: resources to sustain or remove epistemic asymmetry." *Zeitschrift für Sprachwissenschaft* 27: 7–37.

Golato, A. and Fagyal, Z. (2008). "Comparing single and double sayings of the German response token *ja* and the role of prosody: a conversation analytic perspective." *Research on Language and Social Interaction* 41(3): 241–270.

Goldman, L.R. (1998). *Child's Play: Myth, Mimesis and Make-believe*. Oxford New York: Berg.

Gombrich, E. (1963). *Meditations on a Hobby Horse and Other Essays on the Theory of Art*. Chicago, IL: University of Chicago Press.

Göncü, A. (1987). "Toward an interactional model of development changes in social pretend play." In L. Katz (ed.) *Current Topics in Early Childhood Education*. Norwood: Ablex, pp. 108–125.

——— (1993). "Development of intersubjectivity in social pretend play." *Human Development* 36(4): 185–198.

Goodwin, C. (1979). "The interactive construction of a sentence in natural conversation." In G. Psathas (ed.) *Everyday Language: Studies in Ethnomethodology*. New York: Irvington Publishers, pp. 97–121.

——— (1980). "Restarts, pauses, and the achievement of mutual gaze at turn-beginning." *Sociological Inquiry* 50: 272–302.

——— (1981). *Conversational Organization: Interaction between Speakers and Hearers*. New York: Academic Press.

——— (1984). "Notes on story structure and the organization of participation." In J.M. Atkinson and J. Heritage (eds.) *Structures of Social Action: Studies in Conversation Analysis*. Cambridge: Cambridge University Press, pp. 225–246.

——— (1986). "Between and within: alternative treatments of continuers and assessments." *Human Studies* 9: 205–217.

——— (1987). "Forgetfulness as an interactive resource." *Social Psychology Quarterly* 50(2): 115–131.

——— (2000). "Action and embodiment within situated human interaction." *Journal of Pragmatics* 32: 1489–1522.

Goodwin, C. and Goodwin, M.H. (1987). "Concurrent operations on talk: notes on the interactive organization of assessments." *IPrA Papers in Pragmatics* 1(1): 1–52.

——— (1992). "Assessments and the construction of context." In A. Duranti and C. Goodwin (eds.) *Rethinking Context*. Cambridge: Cambridge University Press, pp. 147–189.

(2004). "Participation." In A. Duranti (ed.) *A Companion to Linguistic Anthropology*. Oxford: Blackwell Publishers, pp. 222–244.

Goodwin, M. H. (1980). "Processes of mutual monitoring implicated in the production of description sequences." *Sociological Inquiry* 50: 303–317.

Goody, E. N. (ed.) (1995). *Social Intelligence and Interaction: Expressions and Implications of the Social Bias in Human Intelligence*. Cambridge: Cambridge University Press.

Grice, H. P. (1975). "Logic and conversation." In P. Cole and J. L. Morgan (eds.) *Syntax and semantics: Speech Acts*. New York: Academic Press, pp. 41–58.

(1989). *Studies in the Way of Words*. Cambridge, MA: Harvard University Press.

Haakana, M. (2001). "Laughter as a patient's resource: dealing with delicate aspects of medical interaction." *Text* 21(1/2): 187–219.

Hakulinen, A. (2001a) [1976]. "Liitepartikkelin *-han/-hän* syntaksia ja pragmatiikkaa [On the syntax and pragmatics of the clitic *-han/-hän*]." In L. Laitinen, P. Nuolijärvi, M.-L. Sorjonen and M. Vilkuna (eds.) *Lukemisto*. Helsinki: Suomalaisen Kirjallisunden Seura (Finnish Literature Society), pp. 44–90.

(2001b). "Minimal and non-minimal answers to questions." *Pragmatics* 11: 1–16.

Hakulinen, A. and Steensig, J. (in preparation). "Ingressive speech in interaction." Manuscript, University of Helsinki.

Halliday, M. A. K. (1967). *Intonation and Grammar in British English*. The Hague: Mouton.

Hanks, W. F. (1996). "Exorcism and the description of participant roles." In M. Silverstein and G. Urban (eds.) *Natural Histories of Discourse*. Chicago: Chicago Linguistic Society, pp. 160–220.

Hansen, E. and Heltoft, L. (2008). *Grammatik over det Danske Sprog. Kap. II Ordklassern [Grammar of the Danish Language. Ch. II Word Classes]*. Roskilde: Roskilde University.

Hauser, M. (2006). *Moral Minds: How Nature Designed Our Universal Sense of Right and Wrong*. New York: Ecco.

Haviland, J. (1987). "Fighting words: evidential particles, affect and argument." *Proceedings of the Thirteenth Annual Meeting of the Berkeley Linguistics Society*. Berkeley: Berkeley Linguistics Society.

Hayano, K. (2007a). "*Preference for congruent epistemic stance: Japanese sentence final particles and stance coordination*". Paper presented at the annual meeting of the National Communication Association. Chicago, Illinois.

(2007b). "Repetitional agreement and anaphorical agreement: negotiation of affiliation and disaffiliation in Japanese conversation." Unpublished Master's thesis. Dept. of Applied Linguistics, University of California, Los Angeles.

Heinemann, T. (2003). "Negation in interaction, in Danish conversation." Unpublished Ph.D. dissertation. Department of Sociology, University of York.

(2005). "Where grammar and interaction meet: the preference for matched polarity in responsive turns in Danish." In A. Hakulinen and M. Selting (eds.) *Syntax and Lexis in Conversation*. Amsterdam: John Benjamins, pp. 375–402.

(2006). "'Will you or can't you?': displaying entitlement in interrogative requests." *Journal of Pragmatics* 38: 1081–1104.

(2008). "Questions of accountability; yes-no interrogatives that are unanswerable." *Discourse Studies* 10(1): 55–71.

(2009). "Two answers to inapposite inquiries." In J. Sidnell (ed.) *Conversation Analysis: Comparative Perspectives*. Cambridge: Cambridge University Press, pp. 159–186.

Henrich, J., Boyd, R., Bowles, S., Camerer, C., Fehr, E. and Gintis, H. (eds.) (2004). *Foundations of Human Sociality: Economic Experiments and Ethnographic Evidence from Fifteen Small-Scale Societies*. Oxford: Oxford University Press.

Hepburn, A. (2004). "Crying: notes on description, transcription and interaction." *Research on Language and Social Interaction* 37: 251–290.

Hepburn, A. and Potter, J. (2007). "Crying receipts: time, empathy, and institutional practice." *Research on Language and Social Interaction* 40: 89–116.

Heritage, J. (1984a). "A change-of-state token and aspects of its sequential placement." In J. M. Atkinson and J. Heritage (eds.) *Structures of Social Action: Studies in Conversation Analysis*. Cambridge: Cambridge University Press, pp. 299–345.

(1984b). *Garfinkel and Ethnomethodology*. Cambridge: Polity Press.

(1988). "Explanations as accounts: a conversation analytic perspective." In C. Antaki (ed.) *Analysing Everyday Explanation*. London: Sage, pp. 127–144.

(1998). "Oh-prefaced responses to inquiry." *Language in Society* 27: 291–334.

(2002a). "Oh-prefaced responses to assessments: a method of modifying agreement/disagreement." In C. Ford, B. Fox and S. Thompson (eds.) *The Language of Turn and Sequence*. Oxford: Oxford University Press, pp. 196–224.

(2002b). "The limits of questioning: negative interrogatives and hostile question content." *Journal of Pragmatics* 34: 1427–1446.

(2006). "Revisiting authority in physician–patient interaction." In M. Maxwell, D. Kovarsky and J. Duchan (eds.) *Diagnosis as Cultural Practice*. New York: Mouton de Gruyter, pp. 83–102.

(2007). "Intersubjectivity and progressivity in person (and place) reference." In N. J. Enfield and T. Stivers (eds.) *Person Reference in Interaction: Linguistic, Cultural, and Social Perspectives*. Cambridge: Cambridge University Press, pp. 255–280.

Heritage, J. and Raymond, G. (2005). "The terms of agreement: indexing epistemic authority and subordination in assessment sequences." *Social Psychology Quarterly* 68(1): 15–38.

(in press). "Constructing and navigating epistemic landscapes: progressivity, agency and resistance in 'yes/no' versus 'repetitive' responses." In J. P. de Ruiter (ed.) *Questions: Formal, Functional and Interactional Perspectives*. Cambridge: Cambridge University Press.

Heritage, J. and Robinson, J. (2006). "Accounting for the visit: giving reasons for seeking medical care." In J. Heritage and D. Maynard (eds.) *Communication in Medical Care: Interactions between Primary Care Physicians and Patients*. Cambridge: Cambridge University Press, pp. 48–85.

Heritage, J. and Roth, A. (1995). "Grammar and institution: questions and questioning in the broadcast news interview." *Research on Language and Social Interaction* 28(1): 1–60.

Heritage, J. and Sefi, S. (1992). "Dilemmas of advice: aspects of the delivery and reception of advice in interactions between health visitors and first time mothers." In P. Drew and J.C. Heritage (eds.) *Talk at Work*. Cambridge: Cambridge University Press, pp. 359–419.

Heritage, J. and Stivers, T. (1999). "Online commentary in acute medical visits: a method of shaping patient expectations." *Social Science and Medicine* 49: 1501–1517.

Heritage, J. and Watson, D. R. (1979). "Formulations as conversational objects." In G. Psathas (ed.) *Everyday Language: Studies in Ethnomethodology*. New York: Irvington Publishers, pp. 123–162.

Hill, J. and Irvine, J. (eds.) (1993). *Responsibility and Evidence in Oral Discourse*. New York: Cambridge University Press.

Hinde, R. A. (1976). "Interactions, relationships, and social structure." *Man (New Series)* 11(1): 1–17.

Holzner, B. (1968). *Reality Construction in Society*. Cambridge: Schenkman.

Holzner, B. and Marx, J. H. (1979). *Knowledge Application: The Knowledge System in Society*. Boston: Allyn and Beacon.

Hutchby, I. (1995). "Aspects of recipient design in expert advice-giving on call-in radio." *Discourse Processes* 19(2): 219–238.

(2002). "Resisting the incitement to talk in child counselling: aspects of the utterance 'I don't know.'" *Discourse Studies* 4(2): 147–168.

Hutchins, E. (1995). *Cognition in the Wild*. Cambridge, MA: MIT Press.

Irvine, J.T. (1996). "Shadow conversations: the indeterminacy of participant roles." In M. Silverstein and G. Urban (eds.) *Natural Histories of Discourse*. Chicago, IL: Chicago University Press, pp. 131–159.

Jackendoff, R. (1972). *Semantic Interpretation in Generative Grammar*. Cambridge, MA: MIT Press.

(1997). *The Architecture of the Language Faculty*. Cambridge, MA: MIT Press.

Jacob, F. (1977). "Evolution and tinkering." *Science* 196: 1161–1166.

Jacobs, J. (2001). "The dimensions of topic–comment." *Linguistics* 39: 641–681.

Jakobson, R. (1971). "Shifters, verbals categories, and the Russian verb." In R. Jakobson (ed.) *Selected Writings II: Word and Language*. The Hague and Paris: Mouton, pp. 386–392.

Jefferson, G. (1972). "Side sequences." In D. Sudnow (ed.) *Studies in Social Interaction*. New York: Free Press, pp. 294–338.

(1973). "A case of precision timing in ordinary conversation: overlapped tag-positioned address terms in closing sequences." *Semiotica* 9(1): 47–96.

(1978). "Sequential aspects of storytelling in conversation." In J. Schenkein (ed.) *Studies in the Organization of Conversational Interaction*. New York: Academic Press, pp. 219–248.

(1981). *The Abominable "Ne": A Working Paper Exploring the Phenomenon of Post-Response Pursuit of Response*. Occasional Paper No 6. Manchester: University of Manchester, Department of Sociology.

(1984a). "On stepwise transition from talk about a trouble to inappropriately next-positioned matters." In J. M. Atkinson and J. Heritage (eds.) *Structures of Social Action: Studies in Conversation Analysis*. Cambridge: Cambridge University Press, pp. 191–221.

(1984b). "On the organization of laughter in talk about troubles." In J. M. Atkinson and J. Heritage (eds.) *Structures of Social Action: Studies in Conversation Analysis*. Cambridge: Cambridge University Press, pp. 346–369.

(1986). "Colligation as a device for minimizing repair or disagreement." Paper presented at Talk and Social Structure Workshop, University of California, Santa Barbara.

(1987). "Exposed and embedded corrections." In G. Button and J. R. E. Lee (eds.) *Talk and Social Organisation*. Clevedon, UK: Multilingual Matters Ltd., pp. 86–100.

(1988). "On the sequential organization of troubles-talk in ordinary conversation." *Social Problems* 35(4): 418–441.

(1989). "Preliminary notes on a possible metric which provides for a 'standard maximum' silence of approximately one second in conversation." In D. Roger and P. Bull (eds.) *Conversation: An Interdisciplinary Perspective*. Clevedon, UK: Multilingual Matters Ltd., pp. 166–196.

(1990). "List-construction as a task and resource." In G. Psathas (ed.) *Interaction Competence*. Washington, DC: International Institute for Ethnomethodology and Conversation Analysis and University Press of America, pp. 63–92.

(2002). "Is 'no' an acknowledgement token? Comparing American and British uses of (+)/(-) tokens." *Journal of Pragmatics* 34: 1345–1383.

(2004). "'At first I thought': a normalizing device for extraordinary events." In G. Lerner (ed.) *Conversation Analysis: Studies from the First Generation*. Amsterdam: J. Benjamins, pp. 131–167.

(2007). "Preliminary notes on abdicated other-correction." *Journal of Pragmatics* 39: 445–461.

Jefferson, G., Sacks, H. and Schegloff, E. A. (1987). "Notes on laughter in the pursuit of intimacy." In G. Button and J. R. E. Lee (eds.) *Talk and Social Organisation*. Clevedon, UK: Multilingual Matters Ltd., pp. 152–205.

Jefferson, G. and Lee, J. R. E. (1992) [1981]. "The rejection of advice: managing the problematic convergence of a 'troubles-telling' and a 'service encounter.'" In P. Drew and J. Heritage (eds.) *Talk at Work*. Cambridge: Cambridge University Press, pp. 521–548.

Johanson, L. and Utas, B. (2000). *Evidentials: Turkic, Iranian and Neighboring Languages*. Berlin: Mouton de Gruyter.

Jones, S. and Zimmerman, D. (2003). "A child's point and the achievement of intentionality." *Gesture* 3: 155–185.

Kamio, A. (1990). *Joohoo no Nawabari Riron* [*The Theory of Territory of Information*]. Tokyo: Taishuukan.

(1994). "The theory of territory of information: the case of Japanese." *Journal of Pragmatics* 21: 67–100.

(1995). "Territory of information in English and Japanese, and psychological utterances." *Journal of Pragmatics* 24: 235–264.

(1997). *Territory of Information*. Amsterdam: John Benjamins.

Kanai, K. (2004). "Kaiwa ni okeru ninshikiteki ken'i no koushou: Shuujoshi yo, ne, odoroki hyouji no bunpu to kinou [Negotiation of epistemic authority in conversation: on the use of final particles *yo, ne* and surprise markers]." *Studies in Pragmatics* 6: 17–28.

Kärkkäinen, E. (2003). *Epistemic Stance in English Conversation: A Description of its Interactional Functions, with a Focus on* I think. Amsterdam: John Benjamins.

(2007). "The role of *I guess* in conversational stancetaking." In R. Englebretson (ed.) *Stancetaking in Discourse: Subjectivity, Evaluation, Interaction.* Amsterdam/Philadelphia: John Benjamins, pp. 183–219.

Katagiri, Y. (2007). "Dialogue functions of Japanese sentence-final particles 'yo' and 'ne.'" *Journal of Pragmatics* 39: 1313–1323.

Katlev, J. (2000). *Politikens etymologisk ordbog* [*Etymological Dictionary*]. Copenhagen: Politikens forlag.

Katoh, S. (2001). "Bunmatsujoshi *ne, yo* no danwakooseekinoo [Discourse structuring functions of sentence-final particles *ne* and *yo*]." *Bulletin of the Department of Humanities, Toyama University* 35: 31–48.

Keevallik, L. (2003). *From Interaction to Grammar: Estonian Finite Verb Forms in Conversation.* Uppsala: Uppsala University.

(2008). "Clause combining and sequenced actions: the Estonian complementizer and pragmatic particle *et*." In R. Laury (ed.) *The Pragmatics of Clause Combining.* Amsterdam/Philadelphia: John Benjamins, pp. 125–152.

(2009). "The grammar–interaction interface of negative questions in Estonian." *SKY Journal of Linguistics* 22: 139–173.

Kidwell, M. (2005). "Gaze as social control: how very young children differentiate 'the look' from a 'mere look' by their adult caregivers." *Research on Language and Social Interaction* 38(4): 417–449.

(2009a). "Gaze shift as an interactional resource for very young children." *Discourse Processes* 46(2): 145–160.

(2009b). "'What happened?': an epistemics of before and after in at-the-scene police questioning." *Research on Language and Social Interaction* 42(1): 20–41.

Kidwell, M. and Zimmerman, D. (2006). "'Observability' in the interactions of very young children." *Communication Monographs* 73: 1–28.

(2007). "Joint attention as action." *Journal of Pragmatics* 39: 592–611.

Kinsui, S. (1993). "Shuujoshi *yo, ne* [Final particles *yo, ne*]." *Gengo* 22(4): 118–121.

Kockelman, P. (2005). "The semiotic stance." *Semiotica* 157: 233–304.

(2006a). "Representations of the world: memories, perceptions, beliefs, intentions, and plans." *Semiotica* 162: 73–125.

(2006b). "Residence in the world: affordances, instruments, actions, roles, and identities." *Semiotica* 162: 19–71.

(2007). "Agency: the relation between meaning, power, and knowledge." *Current Anthropology* 48(3): 375–401.

Komter, M. (1995). "The distribution of knowledge in courtroom interaction." *Situated Order: Studies in the Social Organization of Talk and Embodied Activities* . Washington, DC: University Press of America, pp. 107–128.

(1998). *Dilemmas in the Courtroom: A Study of Trials of Violent Crime in The Netherlands.* Hillsdale, NJ: Lawrence Erlbaum Associates.

Kotsinas, U.-B. (1994). *Ungdomsspråk* [*Youth Language*]. Uppsala: Hallgren and Fallgren.

Koyama, T. (1997). "Bunmatsushi to bunmatsu intoneeshon [Sentence-final particles and final intonation]." In Spoken Language Working Group (ed.)

Bunpoo to Onsei [*Speech and Grammar*]. Tokyo: Kuroshio Publisher, pp. 97–119.

Koza, W. and Smith, J. (2007). *Managing an Effective Early Childhood Classroom.* Huntington Beach, CA: Shell Educational Publishing.

Krebs, J.R. and Dawkins, R. (1984). "Animal signals: mind-reading and manipulation." In J.R. Krebs and N.B. Davies (eds.) *Behavioural Ecology: An Evolutionary Approach.* London: Blackwell Publishers, pp. 380–402.

Krifka, M. (2007). "Basic notions of information structure." In C. Fery and M. Krifka (eds.) *Interdisciplinary Studies of Information Structure.* Potsdam: Potsdam University, pp. 13–55.

Kuno, S. (1987). *Functional Syntax: Anaphora, Discourse and Empathy.* Chicago, IL: University of Chicago Press.

Labov, W.1972. "The study of language in its social context." In P.P. Giglioli (ed.) *Language and Social Context.* London: Penguin, pp. 283–307.

Labov, W. and Fanshel, D. (1977). *Therapeutic Discourse: Psychotherapy as Conversation.* New York: Academic Press.

Lambrecht, K. (1994). *Information Structure and Sentence Form: Topic, Focus and the Mental Representations of Dicourse Referents.* Cambridge: Cambridge University Press.

Lave, J. (1988). *Cognition in Practice: Mind Mathematics and Culture in Everyday Life.* Cambridge: Cambridge University Press.

Lee, D.-Y. (2007). "Involvement and the Japanese interactive particles *ne* and *yo.*" *Journal of Pragmatics* 39: 363–388.

Lerner, G. (2002). "Turn-sharing: the choral co-production of talk-in-interaction." In C.E. Ford, B. Fox and S. Thompson (eds.) *The Language of Turn and Sequence.* Oxford: Oxford University Press, pp. 225–256.

(2003). "Selecting next speaker: the context-sensitive operation of a context-free organization." *Language in Society* 32: 177–201.

Lerner, G., Zimmerman, D. and Kidwell, M. (in press). "Formal structures of practical tasks: a resource for action in the social lives of very young children." In C. Goodwin, J. Streeck and C. LeBaron (eds.) *Multimodality and Human Activity: Research on Human Behavior, Action, and Communication.* Cambridge: Cambridge University Press.

Leslie, A. (2000). *"Theory of Mind" as a Mechanism of Selective Attention.* Cambridge, MA: MIT Press.

Levelt, W. (1989). *Speaking: From Intention to Articulation.* Boston, MA: MIT Press.

Lévi-Strauss, C. (1966). *The Savage Mind.* Chicago, IL: University of Chicago Press.

Levinson, S.C. (1983). *Pragmatics.* Cambridge: Cambridge University Press.

(1988). "Putting linguistics on a proper footing: explorations in Goffman's concepts of participation." In P. Drew and A. Wootton (eds.) *Erving Goffman: Exploring the Interaction Order.* Boston, MA: Northeastern University Press, pp. 161–227.

Lewis, C. and Osborne, A. (1990). "Three-year-olds' problems with false belief: conceptual deficit or linguistic artifact?" *Child Development* 61: 1514–1519.

Li, C. and Thompson, S. (1976). "Subject and topic: a new typology of language." In C. Li (ed.) *Subject and Topic.* New York: Academic Press, pp. 457–489.

Lillard, A. (1993). "Young children's conceptualization of pretense: action or mental representational state?" *Child Development* 64: 372–386.

Lindström, A. (2009). "Projecting non-alignment in conversation." In J. Sidnell (ed.) *Conversation Analysis: Comparative Perspectives*. Cambridge: Cambridge University Press, pp. 135–158.

Lindström, J. and Wide, C. (2005). "Tracing the origins of a set of discourse particles: Swedish particles of the type 'you know.'" *Journal of Historical Pragmatics* 6(2): 211–236.

Linell, P. and Luckmann, T. (1991). "Asymmetries in dialogue: some conceptual preliminaries." In I. Markova and K. Foppa (eds.) *Asymmetries in Dialogue*. Hemel Hempstead: Harvester Wheatsheaf, pp. 1–20.

Linton, R. (1936). *The Study of Man: An Introduction*. New York: Appleton-Century-Crofts.

Liszkowski, U., Carpenter, M. and Tomasello, M. (2007). "Pointing out new news, old news, and absent referents at 12 months of age." *Developmental Science* 10(2): F1–F7.

Local, J. and Walker, G. (2004). "Abrupt-joins as a resource for the production of multi-unit, multi-action turns." *Journal of Pragmatics* 36: 1375–1403.

Luff, P., Hindmarsh, J. and Heath, C. (eds.) (2000). *Workplace Studies: Recovering Work Practice and Informing System Design*. Cambridge: Cambridge University Press.

Lynch, M. (1985). *Art and Artefact in Laboratory Science*. London: Routledge and Kegan Paul.

Lynch, M. and Bogen, D. (1996). *The Spectacle of History: Speech, Text, and Memory at the Iran-Contra Hearings*. Durham, NC: Duke University Press.

Lyons, J. (1977). *Semantics*. Cambridge: Cambridge University Press.

Macaulay, R. (2002). "You know, it depends." *Journal of Pragmatics* 34: 749–767.

MacWhinney, B. (2007). "The TalkBank project." In K. P. C. Joan, C. Beal and H. L. Moisl (eds.) *Creating and Digitizing Language Corpora: Synchronic Database*, Vol. I. Houndmills: Palgrave Macmillan.

Mangione-Smith, R., McGlynn, E. A., Elliott, M. N., McDonald, L., Franz, C. E. and Kravitz, R. L. (2001). "Parent expectations for antibiotics, physician-parent communication, and satisfaction." *Archives of Pediatric and Adolescent Medicine* 155: 800–806.

Mangione-Smith, R., Stivers, T., Elliott, M. N., McDonald, L. and Heritage, J. (2003). "The relationship between online commentary use and prevention of inappropriate antibiotic prescribing by pediatricians." *Social Science and Medicine* 56: 313–320.

Mannheim, K. (1936). *Ideology and Utopia*. New York: Harcourt, Brace and World.

Marcus, G. (2008). *Kluge: The Haphazard Construction of the Human Mind*. London: Faber and Faber.

Masuoka, T. (1991). *Modality no bunpoo [Grammar of modality]*. Tokyo: Kuroshio.

Maynard, D. W. (1980). "Placement of topic changes in conversation." *Semiotica* 30: 263–290.

(1991). "The perspective-display series and the delivery and receipt of diagnostic news." In D. Boden and D. H. Zimmerman (eds.) *Talk and Social Structure*. Berkeley, CA: University of California Press, pp. 164–192.

(2003). *Bad News, Good News: Conversational Order in Everyday Talk and Clinical Settings.* Chicago, IL: University of Chicago Press.

Mazeland, H. (1990). "'Yes,' 'no' and 'Mhm': variations in acknowledgement choices." In B. Conein, M. de Fornel and L. Quéré (eds.) *Les Formes de la conversation.* Issy les Moulineaux: Réseaux, pp. 251–282.

(2007). "Parenthetical sequences." *Journal of Pragmatics* 39: 1816–1869.

Mazeland, H. and Huiskes, M. (2001). "Dutch 'but' as a sequential conjunction: its use as a resumption marker." In M. Selting and E. Couper-Kuhlen (eds.) *Studies in Interactional Linguistics.* Amsterdam: Benjamins, pp. 141–169.

McCarthy, E. D. (1996). *Knowledge as Culture.* London: Routledge.

McNeill, D. (1985). "So you think gestures are nonverbal?" *Psychological Review* 92(3): 350–371.

(2005). *Gesture and Thought.* Chicago, IL: Chicago University Press.

Merritt, M. (1976). "On questions following questions in service encounters." *Language in Society* 5(3): 315–357.

Metzger, T. R. and Beach, W. A. (1996). "Preserving alternative versions: interactional techniques for organizing courtroom cross-examinations." *Communication Research* 23: 749–765.

Middleton, D. and Engeström, Y. (eds.) (1996). *Cognition and Communication at Work.* Cambridge: Cambridge University Press.

Mitchell, P. and Lacohee, H. (1991). "Children's early understanding of false belief." *Cognition* 39: 107–127.

Moerman, M. (1988). *Talking Culture: Ethnography and Conversation Analysis.* Philadelphia: University of Pennsylvania Press.

Mondada, L. (2005). *Chercheurs en interaction: comment émergent les savoirs.* Lausanne: Presses Polytechniques et Universitaires Romandes.

(2007). "Multimodal resources for turn-taking: pointing and the emergence of possible next speakers." *Discourse Studies* 9(2): 195–226.

(2008). "Doing video for a sequential and multimodal analysis of social inter-action: videotaping institutional telephone calls." *FQS (Forum : Qualitative Sozialforschung / Forum: Qualitative Social Research)* (www.qualitative-research.net/) 9(3), art. 39.

(2009a). "Emergent focused interactions in public places: a systematic analysis of the multimodal achievement of a common interactional space." *Journal of Pragmatics* 41: 1977–1997.

(2009b). "The embodied and negotiated production of assessments in instructed actions." *Research on Language and Social Interaction* 42(4): 329–361.

Morita, E. (2002). "Stance marking in the collaborative completion of sentences: final particles as epistemic markers in Japanese." In N. Akatsuka and S. Strauss (eds.) *Japanese/Korean Linguistics 10.* Stanford: CSLI, pp. 220–233.

(2005). *Negotiation of Contingent Talk: The Japanese Interactional Particles* ne *and* sa. Amsterdam: John Benjamins.

Moscovici, S. (1981). "On social representations." In J. P. Forgas (ed.) *Social Cognition.* London: Academic Press, pp. 181–209.

(1990). "Social psychology and developmental psychology: extending the con-versation." In G. Duveen and B. Lloyd (eds.) *Social Representations and the Development of Knowledge.* Cambridge: Cambridge University Press, pp. 164–185.

(2000). *Social Representations: Studies in Social Psychology*. Cambridge: Polity Press.

Nelson, K. (1989). *Narratives from the Crib*. Cambridge, MA: Harvard University Press.

Nettle, D. and Dunbar, R. (1997). "Social markers and the evolution of reciprocal exchange." *Current Anthropology* 38(1): 93–99.

Nowak, M.A. and Krakauer, D.C. (1999). "The evolution of language." *Proceedings of the National Academy of Science* 96: 8028–8033.

Ochs, E. (1996). "Linguistic resources for socializing humanity." In J.J. Gumperz and S.C. Levinson (eds.) *Rethinking Linguistic Relativity*. Cambridge: Cambridge University Press, pp. 407–438.

Odregaard, E. (2006). "What's worth talking about? Meaning-making in toddler-initiated co-narratives in pre-school." *Early Years* 26: 79–92.

O'Neill, D.K. (1996). "Two-year-old children's sensitivity to a parent's knowledge state when making requests." *Child Development* 67: 659–677.

Onishi, K. and Baillargeon, R. (2005). "Do 15-month-old infants understand false beliefs?" *Science* 308: 255–258.

Parsons, T. (1937). *The Structure of Social Action*. New York: McGraw-Hill.

(1951). *The Social System*. New York: Free Press.

Peirce, C.S. (1955). *Philosophical Writings of Peirce*. New York: Dover Publications.

Peräkylä, A. (1998). "Authority and accountability: the delivery of diagnosis in primary health care." *Social Psychology Quarterly* 61(4): 301–320.

(2002). "Agency and authority: extended responses to diagnostic statements in primary care encounters." *Research on Language and Social Interaction* 35(2): 219–247.

Picoche, J. (1986). *Structures sémantiques du lexique français*. Paris: Nathan.

Polanyi, L. (1982). *Telling the American Story: A Structural and Cultural Analysis of Conversational Storytelling*. Norwood, NJ: Ablex.

Pollner, M. (1975). "The very coinage of your brain: the anatomy of reality disjunctures." *Philosophy of the Social Sciences* 5: 411–430.

(1987). *Mundane Reason: Reality in Everyday and Sociological Discourse*. Cambridge: Cambridge University Press.

Pomerantz, A. (1975). "Second Assessments: A Study of Some Features of Agreements/Disagreements." Unpublished Ph.D. dissertation. University of California, Irvine.

(1978). "Compliment responses: notes on the co-operation of multiple constraints." In J. Schenkein (ed.) *Studies in the Organization of Conversational Interaction*. New York: Academic Press, pp. 79–112.

(1980). "Telling my side: 'limited access' as a 'fishing' device." *Sociological Inquiry* 50: 186–198.

(1984a). "Agreeing and disagreeing with assessments: some features of preferred/dispreferred turn shapes". In J.M. Atkinson and J. Heritage (eds.) *Structures of Social Action: Studies in Conversation Analysis*. Cambridge: Cambridge University Press, pp. 57–101.

(1984b). "Giving a source or basis: the practice in conversation of telling 'how I know.'" *Journal of Pragmatics* 8: 607–625.

(1984c). "Pursuing a response." In J. M. Atkinson and J. Heritage (eds.) *Structures of Social Action: Studies in Conversation Analysis.* Cambridge: Cambridge University Press, pp. 152–163.

(1988). "Offering a candidate answer: an information-seeking strategy." *Communication Monographs* 55: 360–373.

Pomerantz, A. and Mandelbaum, J. (2005). "Conversation analytic approaches to the relevance and uses of relationship categories in interaction." In K. L. Fitch and R. E. Sanders (eds.) *Handbook of Language and Social Interaction.* Mahwah, NJ: Lawrence Erlbaum, pp. 149–171.

Potter, J. and Wetherell, M. (1987). *Discourse and Social Psychology: Beyond Attitudes and Behaviour.* London: Sage.

Raevaara, L. (2001). "Kysymisestä ja vastaamisesta institutionaalisena toimintana [On asking questions and answering as an institutional activity]." In M. Halonen and S. Routarinne (eds.) *Keskustelunanalyysin näkymiä.* Helsinki: Department of Finnish Language, University of Helsinki, pp. 47–69.

Rappaport, R. (2002). "Enactments of meaning." In M. Lambek (ed.) *A Reader in the Anthropology of Religion.* Malden, MA: Blackwell Publishers (excerpted from Rappaport, *Ritual and Religion in the Making of Humanity,* Cambridge: Cambridge University Press, 1999), pp. 446–467.

Raymond, G. (2000). "The Structure of Responding: Type-Conforming and Nonconforming Responses to Yes/No Type Interrogatives." Unpublished Ph.D. dissertation. Department of Sociology, University of California, Los Angeles.

(2003). "Grammar and social organization: yes/no interrogatives and the structure of responding." *American Sociological Review* 68: 939–967.

Raymond, G. and Heritage, J. (2006). "The epistemics of social relations: owning grandchildren." *Language in Society* 35: 677–705.

Reinhart, T. (1981). "Pragmatics and linguistics: an analysis of sentence topics." *Philosophica* 27: 53–94.

Remi, S. (1986). "Étude comparée du fonctionnement syntaxique et sémantique des verbes savoir et connaître." In S. Rémi-Giraud and M. Le Guern (eds.) *Sur le verbe.* Lyon: PUL, pp. 169–306.

Rogers, C. R. (1959). "A theory of therapy, personality and interpersonal relationships, as developed in the client-centered framework." In S. Koch (ed.) *Psychology: A Study of Science,* Vol. III. New York: McGraw Hill, pp. 184–256.

Romaine, S. (2000). *Language in Society: An Introduction to Sociolinguistics.* Oxford: Oxford University Press.

Rooth, M. (1985). "Association with focus." Unpublished Ph.D. dissertation. University of Massachusetts, Amherst.

Roth, A. L. (2002). "Social epistemology in broadcast interviews." *Language in Society* 31: 355–381.

Roth, M. W. (2005). "Making classifications (at) work: ordering practices in science." *Social Studies of Science* 35(4): 581–621.

Ruusuvuori, J. (2005). "Empathy and sympathy in action: attending to patients' troubles in Finnish homeopathic and GP consultations." *Social Psychology Quarterly* 68: 204–222.

Ryle, G. (1949). *The Concept of Mind.* London: Hutchinson.

Sacks, H. (1972a). "An initial investigation of the usability of conversational data for doing sociology." In D. N. Sudnow (ed.) *Studies in Social Interaction*. New York: The Free Press, pp. 31–74.

(1972b). "On the analyzability of stories by children." In J. J. Gumperz and D. Hymes (eds.) *Directions in Sociolinguistics: The Ethnography of Communication*. New York: Holt, Rinehart and Winston, pp. 325–345.

(1974). "An analysis of the course of a joke's telling in conversation." In R. Bauman and J. Sherzer (eds.) *Explorations in the Ethnography of Speaking*. Cambridge: Cambridge University Press, pp. 337–353.

(1975). "Everyone has to lie." In M. Sanches and B. G. Blount (eds.) *Sociocultural Dimensions of Language Use*. New York: Academic Press, pp. 57–80.

(1978). "Some technical considerations of a dirty joke." In J. Schenkein (ed.) *Studies in the Organization of Conversational Interaction*. New York: Academic Press, pp. 249–269.

(1984). "On doing 'being ordinary.'" In J. M. Atkinson and J. Heritage (eds.) *Structures of Social Action: Studies in Conversation Analysis*. Cambridge: Cambridge University Press, pp. 413–429.

(1985). "The inference-making machine." In T. A. van Dijk (ed.) *Handbook of Discourse Analysis*. London: Academic Press, pp. 2–22.

(1987a). "On the preferences for agreement and contiguity in sequences in conversation." In G. Button and J. R. E. Lee (eds.) *Talk and Social Organisation*. Clevendon, UK: Multilingual Matters Ltd., pp. 54–69.

(1987b). "'You want to find out if anybody really does care.'" In G. Button and J. R. E. Lee (eds.) *Talk and Social Organisation*. Clevedon, UK: Multilingual Matters Ltd., pp. 219–225.

(1992) [1967]. *Lectures on Conversation*. Oxford: Blackwell Publishers.

Sacks, H. and Schegloff, E. A. (2007) [1979]. "Two preferences in the organization of reference to persons and their interaction." In N. J. Enfield and T. Stivers (eds.) *Person Reference in Interaction: Linguistic, Cultural and Social Perspectives*. Cambridge: Cambridge University Press, pp. 23–28.

Sacks, H., Schegloff, E. A. and Jefferson, G. (1974). "A simplest systematics for the organization of turn-taking for conversation." *Language* 50: 696–735.

Saft, S. (2001). "Displays of concession in university faculty meetings: culture and interaction in Japanese." *Pragmatics* 11(3): 3–15.

Sawyer, R. K. (1997). *Pretend Play as Improvisation: Conversation in the Preschool Classroom*. Mahwah, NJ: Lawrence Erlbaum Associates.

Schegloff, E. A. (1968). "Sequencing in conversational openings." *American Anthropologist* 70: 1075–1095.

(1972). "Notes on a conversational practice: formulating place." In D. Sudnow (ed.) *Studies in Social Interaction*. New York: Free Press, pp. 75–119.

(1982). "Discourse as an interactional achievement: some uses of 'uh huh' and other things that come between sentences." In D. Tannen (ed.) *Analyzing Discourse: Text and Talk*. Washington, DC: Georgetown University Press, pp. 71–93.

(1984). "On some questions and ambiguities in conversation." In J. M. Atkinson and J. Heritage (eds.) *Structures of Social Action: Studies in Conversation Analysis*. Cambridge: Cambridge University Press, pp. 28–52.

(1988a). "Goffman and the analysis of conversation." In P. Drew and A. Wootton (eds.) *Erving Goffman: Exploring the Interaction Order*. Cambridge: Polity Press, pp. 89–135.

(1988b). "On an actual virtual servo-mechanism for guessing bad news: a single case conjecture." *Social Problems* 35(4): 442–457.

(1988c). "Presequences and indirection: applying speech act theory to ordinary conversation." *Journal of Pragmatics* 12: 55–62.

(1992). "Repair after next turn: the last structurally provided for place for the defense of intersubjectivity in conversation." *American Journal of Sociology* 95(5): 1295–1345.

(1996a). "Confirming allusions: toward an empirical account of action." *American Journal of Sociology* 102: 161–216.

(1996b). "Some practices for referring to persons in talk-in-interaction: a partial sketch of a systematics." In B. Fox (ed.) *Studies in Anaphora*. Amsterdam: John Benjamins, pp. 437–485.

(1997). "Practices and actions: boundary cases of other-initiated repair." *Discourse Processes* 23: 99–545.

(2000a). "On granularity." *Annual Review of Sociology* 26: 715–720.

(2000b). "When 'others' initiate repair." *Applied Linguistics* 21: 205–243.

(2005). "On complainability." *Social Problems* 52: 449–476.

(2007a). *Sequence Organization in Interaction: A Primer in Conversation Analysis*. Cambridge: Cambridge University Press.

(2007b). "A tutorial on membership categorization." *Journal of Pragmatics* 39: 462–482.

Schegloff, E. A., Jefferson, G. and Sacks, H. (1977). "The preference for self-correction in the organization of repair in conversation." *Language* 53: 361–382.

Schegloff, E. A. and Lerner, G. H. (2009). "Beginning to respond: well-prefaced responses to wh-questions." *Research on Language and Social Interaction* 42(2): 91–115.

Schegloff, E. A. and Sacks, H. (1973). "Opening up closings." *Semiotica* 8: 289–327.

Scheibman, J. (2000). "*I dunno*. . . A usage-based account of the phonological reduction of *don't* in American English conversation." *Journal of Pragmatics* 32(1): 105–124.

Schiffrin, D. (1988). *Discourse Markers*. Cambridge: Cambridge University Press.

Schütz, A. (1962). *Collected Papers*, Vol. I: *The Problem of Social Reality*. The Hague: Martinus Nijhoff.

(1970). *On Phenomenology and Social Relations*. Chicago, IL: University of Chicago Press.

Schwabe, K. and Winkler, S. (2007). "On information structure, meaning and form: generalizations across languages." In K. Schwabe and S. Winkler (eds.) *On Information Structure, Meaning and Form*. Amsterdam: John Benjamins, pp. 1–32.

Schwartzman, H. (1978). *Transformations: The Anthropology of Children's Play*. New York: Plenum.

Schwarzschild, R. (1999). "GIVENness, AvoidF and other constraints on the placement of accent." *Natural Language Semantics* 7: 141–177.

Searle, J. (1969). *Speech Acts: An Essay in the Philosophy of Language.* Cambridge: Cambridge University Press.

Selting, M. (1996). "Prosody as an activity-type distinctive cue in conversation: the case of so-called 'astonished' questions in repair initiation." In E. Couper-Kuhlen and M. Selting (eds.) *Prosody in Conversation.* Cambridge: Cambridge University Press, pp. 231–270.

Shannon, C. E. and Weaver, W. (1949). *A Mathematical Model of Communication.* Urbana, IL: University of Illinois Press.

Sharrock, W. W. (1974). "On owning knowledge." In R. Turner (ed.) *Ethnomethodology.* Harmondsworth: Penguin, pp. 45–53.

Showers, C. and Cantor, N. (1985). "Social cognition: a look at motivated strategies." *Annual Review of Psychology* 36: 275–305.

Sidnell, J. (2005). *Talk and Practical Epistemology.* Amsterdam: John Benjamins.
  (2009). "Participation." In J. Verschueren and O. Östman (eds.) *Handbook of Pragmatics.* Amsterdam: John Benjamins, pp. 125–156.

Silverstein, M. (1976). "Shifters, linguistic categories, and cultural description." In K. Basso and H. Selby (eds.) *Meaning in Anthropology.* Albuquerque: University of New Mexico Press, pp. 11–55.

Slobin, D. (1971). "On the learning of morphological rules: a reply to Palermo and Eberhart." In D. Slobin (ed.) *The Ontogenesis of Grammar.* New York: Academic Press, pp. 215–223.

Sorjonen, M.-L. (2001). *Responding in Conversation: A Study of Response Particles in Finnish.* Amsterdam: John Benjamins.

Sorjonen, M.-L. and Hakulinen, A. (2009). "Alternative responses to assessments." In J. Sidnell (ed.) *Conversation Analysis: Comparative Perspectives.* Cambridge: Cambridge University Press, pp. 281–303.

Sperber, D. and Wilson, D. (1995). *Relevance: Communication and Cognition.* Oxford: Blackwell Publishers.

Stalnaker, R. C. (1978). "Assertion." In P. Cole (ed.) *Syntax and Semantics 9.* New York: Academic Press, pp. 315–332.

Stark, W. (1991) [1958]. *The Sociology of Knowledge: Toward a Deeper Understanding of the History of Ideas.* New Brunswick, NJ: Transaction Publishers.

Steensig, J. (2005). "Hvornår kan ja stå alene efter et ja/nej-spørgsmål' [When can ja ('yes') stand alone after a yes/no question?]." *MOVIN Workingpapers.* www.movinarbejdspapirer.asb.dk.

Stivers, T. (2002). "Participating in decisions about treatment: overt parent pressure for antibiotic medication in pediatric encounters." *Social Science and Medicine* 54(7): 1111–1130.
  (2005a). "Modified repeats: one method for asserting primary rights from second position." *Research on Language and Social Interaction* 38(2): 131–158.
  (2005b). "Parent resistance to physicians' treatment recommendations: one resource for initiating a negotiation of the treatment decision." *Health Communication* 18: 41–74.
  (2007a). "Alternative recognitionals in initial references to persons." In N. J. Enfield and T. Stivers (eds.) *Person Reference in Interaction: Linguistic, Cultural, and Social Perspectives.* Cambridge: Cambridge University Press, pp. 73–96.

(2007b). *Prescribing under Pressure: Parent–Physician Conversations and Antibiotics.* New York: Oxford University Press.

(2008). "Stance, alignment, and affiliation during storytelling: when nodding is a token of affiliation." *Research on Language and Social Interaction* 41(1): 31–57.

(2010). "An overview of the question–response system in American English conversation." *Journal of Pragmatics* 42(10): 2272–2281.

Stivers, T., Enfield, N. J., Brown, P. *et al.* (2009). "Universality and cultural specificity in turn-taking in conversation." *Proceedings of the National Academy of Sciences* 106(26): 10587–10592.

Stivers, T., Enfield, N. J. and Levinson, S. C. (2007). "Person reference in interaction." In N. J. Enfield and T. Stivers (eds.) *Person Reference in Interaction: Linguistic, Cultural and Social Perspectives.* Cambridge: Cambridge University Press, pp. 1–20.

(eds.) (2010). "Question–response sequences in conversation: a comparison across 10 languages." *Special issue of Journal of Pragmatics*: 42(10).

Stivers, T. and Hayashi, M. (2010). "Transformative answers: one way to resist a question's constraints." *Language in Society* 39(1): 1–25.

Stivers, T. and Heritage, J. (2001). "Breaking the sequential mould: answering 'more than the question' during comprehensive history taking." *Text* 21: 151–185.

Stivers, T. and Robinson, J. D. (2006). "A preference for progressivity in interaction." *Language in Society* 35: 367–392.

Stivers, T. and Rossano, F. (2010). "Mobilizing response." *Research on Language and Social Interaction* 43(1): 1–31.

Stubbe, M. and Holmes, J. (1995). " *You know eh* and other *exasperating expressions*: an analysis of social and stylistic variation in the use of pragmatic devices in a sample of New Zealand English." *Language and Communication* 15(1): 63–88.

Surian, L., Caldi, S. and Sperber, D. (2007). "Attribution of beliefs by 13-month-old infants." *Psychological Science* 18: 580–586.

Svennevig, J. (2008). "Trying the easiest solution first in other-initiation of repair." *Journal of Pragmatics* 40: 333–348.

Takubo, Y. and Kinsui, S. (1997). "Discourse management in terms of mental spaces." *Journal of Pragmatics* 28: 741–758.

Tambiah, S. J. (1985). "A performative approach to ritual." In S. J. Tambiah (ed.) *Culture, Thought and Social Action: An Anthropological Perspective.* Cambridge, MA: Harvard University Press, pp. 123–166.

Tanaka, H. (2000). "The particle *ne* as a turn-managing device in Japanese conversation." *Journal of Pragmatics* 35(8): 1135–1176.

Tannen, D. (1989). *Talking Voices: Repetition, Dialogue, and Imagery in Conversational Discourse.* Cambridge: Cambridge University Press.

Teleman, U., Hellberg, S. and Andersson, E. (eds.) (1999). *SAG Svenska Akademiens grammatik IV. Satser och meningar* [*Grammar of the Swedish Academy. Sentences and Clauses*]. Stockholm: Norstedts Akademiska Förlag.

te Molder, H. and Potter, J. (eds.) (2005). *Conversation and Cognition.* Cambridge: Cambridge University Press.

Terasaki, A. K. (2004) [1976]. "Pre-announcement sequences in conversation." In G. Lerner (ed.) *Conversation Analysis: Studies from the First Generation.* Amsterdam: John Benjamins, pp. 171–223.

Therkelsen, R. (2004). "Polyfoni som sproglig begrebsramme og som redskab i tekstanalysen [Polyphony as a linguistic conceptual frame and as a tool in text analysis]." *Sproglig polyfoni. Arbejdspapirer* 1: 79–97.

Thompson, S. A. and Mulac, A. (1991). "A quantitative perspective on the grammaticalization of epistemic parentheticals in English." In E. C. Traugott and B. Heine (eds.) *Approaches to Grammaticalization: Focus on Types of Grammatical Markers*. Amsterdam: John Benjamins, pp. 313–339.

Tomasello, M. (1999). *The Cultural Origins of Human Cognition*. Cambridge, MA: Harvard University Press.

(2003). *Constructing a Language: A Usage-Based Theory of Language Acquisition*. Cambridge, MA: Harvard University Press.

(2008). *Origins of Human Communication*. Cambridge, MA: MIT Press.

Tomasello, M., Carpenter, M., Call, J., Behne, T. and Moll, H. (2005). "Understanding and sharing intentions: the origins of cultural cognition." *Behavioral and Brain Sciences* 28: 675–691.

Tsui, A. B. M. (1991). "The pragmatic functions of *I don't know*." *Text* 11(4): 607–622.

van Dijk, T. A. (ed.) (2006). "Discourse, interaction and cognition." *Special issue of Discourse Studies*: 8.

Vendler, Z. (1967). "Verbs and times." In Z. Vendler (ed.) *Linguistics in Philosophy*. Ithaca, NY: Cornell University Press, pp. 97–121.

Wellman, H., Cross, D. and Watson, J. (2001). "Meta-analysis of theory-of-mind development: the truth about false belief." *Child Development* 72(3): 655–684.

Whalen, J. and Zimmerman, D. H. (1998). "Observations on the display and management of emotions in naturally occurring activities: the case of 'hysteria' in calls to 9–1–1." *Social Psychology Quarterly* 61(2): 141–159.

(1990). "Describing trouble: practical epistemology in citizen calls to the police." *Language in Society* 19: 465–492.

Wilkinson, S. and Kitzinger, C. (2006). "Surprise as an interactional achievement: reaction tokens in conversation." *Social Psychology Quarterly* 69: 150–182.

Willett, T. (1988). "A cross-linguistic survey of the grammaticization of evidentiality." *Studies in Language* 12(1): 51–97.

Wimmer, H. and Perner, J. (1983). "Beliefs about beliefs: representation and constraining function of wrong beliefs in young children's understanding of deception." *Cognition* 13: 103–128.

Wu, R.-J. R. (2004). *Stance in Talk: A Conversation Analysis of Mandarin Final Particles*. Amsterdam: John Benjamins.

Wyer, R. S. and Srull, T. K. (eds.) (1984). *Handbook of Social Cognition*. Hillsdale, NJ: Lawrence Erlbaum.

Zeitlyn, D. (1995). "Divination as dialogue: negotiation of meaning with random responses." In E. N. Goody (ed.) *Social Intelligence and Interaction: Expressions and Implications of the Social Bias in Human Intelligence*. Cambridge: Cambridge University Press, pp. 189–205.

Zimmerman, D. H. (1984). "Talk and its occasion: the case of calling the police: meaning, form and use in context: linguistic applications." In D. Schiffrin (ed.) *Georgetown Roundtable on Languages and Linguistics*. Washington, DC: Georgetown University Press, pp. 210–228.

Index

Lightning Source UK Ltd.
Milton Keynes UK
UKOW06f1630090615

253191UK00002B/111/P